CAMBRIDGE SERIES ON HUMAN–COMPUTER INTERACTION

Designing Interaction

Psychology at the
Human–Computer Interface

Cambridge Series on Human–Computer Interaction

Managing Editor:

Professor J. Long, Ergonomics Unit, University College, London.

Editorial Board

Titles in the Series

1. J. Long and A. Whitefield, *Cognitive Ergonomics and Human–Computer Interaction*
2. M. Harrison and H. Thimbleby, *Formal Methods in Human–Computer Interaction*
3. P. B. Andersen, *The Theory of Computer Semiotics*
4. J. M. Carroll, *Designing Interaction: Psychology at the Human–Computer Interface*

Designing Interaction

Psychology at the
Human–Computer Interface

Edited by John M. Carroll
IBM Thomas J. Watson Research Center

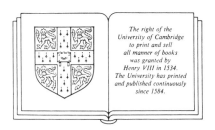

The right of the
University of Cambridge
to print and sell
all manner of books
was granted by
Henry VIII in 1534.
The University has printed
and published continuously
since 1584.

CAMBRIDGE UNIVERSITY PRESS

Cambridge   New York   Port Chester   Melbourne   Sydney

Published by the Press Syndicate of the University of Cambridge
The Pitt Building, Trumpington Street, Cambridge CB2 1RP
40 West 20th Street, New York, NY 10011, USA
10 Stamford Road, Oakleigh, Melbourne 3166, Australia

First published 1991

Printed in Canada

Library of Congress Cataloging-in-Publication Data
Designing interaction : psychology at the human–computer interface /
edited by John M. Carroll.
p. cm. – (Cambridge series on human–computer interaction ;
4)
ISBN 0-521-40056-2. – ISBN 0-521-40921-7 (pbk.)
1. Human–computer interaction – Psychological aspects.   2. User
interfaces (Computer systems) – Psychological aspects.   I. Carroll,
John M. (John Millar), 1950– .   II. Series.
QA76.9.H85D48   1991
005.1 – dc20   90-2419
                                                                            CIP

British Library Cataloguing in Publication Data
Designing interaction : psychology of the human–computer
interface. – (Cambridge series on human–computer
interaction, no. 4).
1. Man. Interactions with computer systems
I. Carroll, John M.
004.019

ISBN 0-521-40056-2 hardback
ISBN 0-521-40921-7 paperback

Contents

Preface   *page* vii

Contributors   viii

1   Introduction: The Kittle House Manifesto, *John M. Carroll*   1

2   Cognitive Artifacts, *Donald A. Norman*   17

3   Some Remarks on the Theory–Practice Gap,
    Zenon W. Pylyshyn   39

4   Comparative Task Analysis: An Alternative Direction for
    Human–Computer Interaction Science, *Ruven Brooks*   50

5   Let's Get Real: A Position Paper on the Role of Cognitive
    Psychology in the Design of Humanly Useful and Usable
    Systems, *Thomas K. Landauer*   60

6   The Task–Artifact Cycle, *John M. Carroll,*
    Wendy A. Kellogg, and Mary Beth Rosson   74

7   Bridging between Basic Theories and the Artifacts of
    Human–Computer Interaction, *Philip Barnard*   103

8   Interface Problems and Interface Resources, *Stephen J. Payne*   128

9   Inner and Outer Theory in Human–Computer Interaction,
    Clayton Lewis   154

10   Local Sciences: Viewing the Design of Human–Computer
    Systems as Cognitive Science, *Andrea A. diSessa*   162

11   The Role of German Work Psychology in the Design of
    Artifacts, *Siegfried Greif*   203

12   Beyond the Interface: Encountering Artifacts in Use,
    Liam J. Bannon and Susanne Bødker   227

13   A Development Perspective on Interface, Design, and
    Theory, *Austin Henderson*   254

14   Working within the Design Process: Supporting Effective and
    Efficient Design, *John Karat and John L. Bennett*   269

15   Discussion: Perspectives on Methodology in HCI Research
    and Practice, *Linda Tetzlaff and Robert L. Mack*   286

Index   315

Preface

On June 19, 1989, we gathered at the Kittle House Inn in Chappaqua, New York, for three days of discussion on the role of psychological science and theory in the design of human–computer interaction (HCI). The workshop was hosted by the User Interface Institute of IBM's Watson Research Center and included ten members of the institute, Rachel Bellamy (visiting from Cambridge University), John Bennett, Robert Campbell, John Karat, Wendy Kellogg, Robert Mack, John Richards, Mary Beth Rosson, Linda Tetzlaff, and myself.

We had also invited a diverse and distinguished set of 11 participants from outside the institute: Liam Bannon, of Aarhus University; Phil Barnard, of the Applied Psychology Unit, Cambridge; Ruven Brooks, of Schlumberger-Doll Research; Andy diSessa, of the University of California, Berkeley; Siegfried Greif, of the University of Osnabruck; Austin Henderson, of FitchRichardsonSmith; Tom Landauer, of Bell Communications Research (Bellcore); Clayton Lewis, of the University of Colorado; Don Norman, of the University of California, San Diego; Steve Payne, of the University of Lancaster; and Zenon Pylyshyn, of the University of Western Ontario.

All of us have traditional research training in basic science, for the most part in psychology and computer science. All of us are committed to discovering a better understanding of how science operates in the complex and rapidly changing design context of human–computer interaction. All had already been working in the context of this concern for several years when we gathered at the Kittle House.

For me, working in this domain has been perhaps most satisfying in allowing me always to feel that I am embarked on a long intellectual journey. I admit that to some extent this is because my starting point was rather naive: I initially assumed that the specific techniques and concepts I had learned in graduate school could be applied directly, that problems could be decomposed into dichotomous contrasts, and that the empirical outcomes of making such contrasts could cumulate into deductive theory. I know now that things are not that simple, but I am still only a step or two down the road. Like many of the other participants, I have come to realize that the issue is not merely how to apply psychology but how to redefine and recreate psychology.

I am developing a bias for workshops. My recollection, which I have cross-validated with several other participants, is that we talked and listened actively for three full days. Somehow the exhaustion did not register until it was all over. The discussions and the myriad important points that were raised persisted all summer and into the next year, goading me to confront fundamental questions even as I engage in what would otherwise be routine science and technology research. Perhaps we *must* adopt such a reflective attitude if HCI is to fulfill its possibilities for psychological science, for computer technology, and for human society.

I thank Wendy Kellogg, John Richards, and Mary Beth Rosson for helping develop the workshop theme, Linda Tetzlaff and Bob Mack for preparing an integrative discussion chapter, Bonnie Zingarelli and Rachel Bellamy for ensuring in many ways that the workshop ran smoothly, the staff of the Kittle House for providing gracious logistic support, and the IBM Corporation for sponsoring the workshop.

Contributors

Liam J. Bannon
University of Oulu
Department of Information System
Science
Linnanmaa SF-90570
Oulu, Finland

Philip Barnard
MRC Applied Psychology Unit
15 Chaucer Road
Cambridge, CB2 2EF
England

John L. Bennett
IBM Almaden Research Center
650 Harry Road, K52/803
San Jose, CA 95120

Susanne Bødker
Datalogisk Afdeling
Ny Munkegade 116
DK-8000 Aarhus C
Denmark

Ruven Brooks
Shlumberger Laboratory
for Computer Science
P.O. Box 200015
Austin, TX 78720-0015

John M. Carroll
User Interface Institute
IBM Thomas J. Watson Research
Center
P.O. Box 704
Yorktown Heights, NY 10598

Andrea A. diSessa
School of Education
University of California
Berkeley, CA 94720

Siegfried Greif
Fachbereich Psychology
Universitat Osnabruck
Postfach 44 69
D-4500, Osnabruck
Germany

Austin Henderson
Xerox Palo Alto Research Center
3333 Coyote Hill Road
Palo Alto, CA 94304

John Karat
User Interface Institute
IBM Thomas J. Watson Research
Center
P.O. Box 704
Yorktown Heights, NY 10598

Wendy A. Kellogg
User Interface Institute
IBM Thomas J. Watson Research
Center
P.O. Box 704
Yorktown Heights, NY 10598

Thomas K. Landauer
Bell Communication Research
435 South Street
Morristown, NJ 07960

Clayton Lewis
Department of Computer Science
Campus Box 430
University of Colorado
Boulder, CO 80309

Robert L. Mack
User Interface Institute
IBM Thomas J. Watson Research
Center
P.O. Box 704
Yorktown Heights, NY 10598

Donald A. Norman
Institute for Cognitive Science
C-015
University of California
La Jolla, CA 92093

Stephen J. Payne
User Interface Institute
IBM Thomas J. Watson Research
Center
P.O. Box 704
Yorktown Heights, NY 10598

Zenon W. Pylyshyn
Rutgers University
Psychology Department
New Brunswick, NJ 08903

Mary Beth Rosson
User Interface Institute
IBM Thomas J. Watson Research
Center
P.O. Box 704
Yorktown Heights, NY 10598

Linda Tetzlaff
User Interface Institute
IBM Thomas J. Watson Research
Center
P.O. Box 704
Yorktown Heights, NY 10598

1
Introduction: The Kittle House Manifesto
John M. Carroll

Human–computer interaction (HCI) is an interdisciplinary area of applied research and design practice. Its key concern is to understand and facilitate the creation of "user interfaces," that is, of computers as experienced and manipulated by human users. In doing this, it seeks to draw on many established areas of science and craft: psychology, computer science, anthropology, management science, industrial design. For example, the applied *psychology* of HCI addresses itself to understanding how human motivation, action, and experience place constraints on the usability of computer equipment and to supporting the development of new computer technology that exploits these constraints.

A fundamental question one can ask about HCI, or for that matter about any applied, interdisciplinary area of endeavor, is what role basic science plays in the application. The chapters in this book focus principally on the relation between contemporary psychology and human–computer interaction. Clearly, the a priori prospects favor a rich and reciprocal interaction. HCI seeks to produce user interfaces that facilitate and enrich human motivation, action, and experience, but to do so deliberately it must also incorporate means of understanding user interfaces in terms of human motivation, action, and experience. This is the conceptual province of psychology. Conversely, the design and use of computing equipment provides psychology with a diverse and challenging empirical field to assess its theories and methodologies.

Nevertheless, while it is clear that psychology has an important role to play in HCI, articulating this role in detail and verifying it in actual practice has proved difficult. The most sustained, focused, and sophisticated attempts to develop explicit extensions of academic psychology for HCI have had no impact on design practice (Card, Moran, & Newell, 1983; Polson & Kieras, 1985). On the other hand, some of the most seminal and momentous user interface design work of the past 25 years made no explicit use of psychology at all (Engelbart & English, 1968; Sutherland, 1963).

How could this be? Such a schismatic relation between science and application, though it may seem anomalous, is not unusual. It has been the general case that basic science provides uncertain and indirect support to applied work (Basalla, 1988; Hindle, 1981; Laudan, 1984; Morrison, 1974). Through history it is perhaps more common to see practical invention entrain scientific explanation than to see the reverse. Bridge building and use of pulleys, for example, were innovated, refined, and rendered routine in use long before basic physics elucidated their underlying principles.

Even if there is substantial precedent for an inverted or haphazard relation between basic science and application, such a status quo ought to be questioned. Clearly, we must *understand* how we do what we do in design, so that we can do it deliberately and repeatedly in diverse and novel situations. Moreover, we must *codify* our understanding of design practice to be able to teach it to others and to work with it directly to improve it. To the extent we can do this at all, we are surely developing and exercising science; to the extent we can do it well, we will integrate and coordinate science and application.

Science in Context

A key to understanding the relation of science and application is context. Application is very much in and of a particular context. One would always like to be general, but essentially an application fails unless it fully accommodates a context. Classical science leans the other way; it values generality, even at the price of fairly narrow boundary conditions. Applied science must seek generality, but it cannot afford the price of narrow boundary conditions. It must meet at least these two requirements:

Specificity: The science must apply specifically to the actual concerns of the target domain; it must be content appropriate.

Significant aspects of a given application domain may be specific to that domain and therefore resist effective analysis by the standard methods, concepts, and theories of the basic science (which have in effect been specialized for the paradigmatic domains of the science).

Applicability: Use of the science must conform to the processes of application in the target domain; it must be process appropriate.

The working context of application may itself be so singular, so complex, and so potent that the standard methods, concepts, and theories cannot be effectively instrumented in practice (that is, even if they meet the requirement of specificity).

Consider first the specificity requirement and the example of bridge building. The Romans built bridges, roads, and aqueducts that have survived for centuries. They did not deduce these feats of engineering from basic physics. They did not have the physics to do this; physics, at that time, failed the specificity requirement. For physics, Roman engineering was a problem to be explained, not an application. Modern physics can meet the specificity requirement; bridge building *can* be an application.

Another example can be found in the history of attempts to apply acoustics to the analysis and design of stringed instruments like the violin. Acoustics had good methods, concepts, and theories for analyzing simple vibrating systems, like strings. It had a more difficult time with relatively complex systems, like vibrating plates of various shapes and thicknesses. It had no chance whatsoever with violins: The plates of a violin are composed of a nonuniform, porous material (wood). The plates are glued together, creating a confined mass of air. The strings are most typically bowed, not plucked. The sound that a violin produces is created by the bowing motion, by the resonances of the wooden body (the top plate, back plate, sound post, bass bar, even the purfling – strips of inlaid wood near the outside of each plate), by the resonances of the air mass confined inside the instrument, and by the interactions of these resonances.

Progress in analyzing the violin as an acoustic system has come from extending acoustics: by understanding the physics of bowed sounds, by developing new scaling theories for analyzing an instrument's sound power across a frequency range (Saunders, 1937, 1946), and by refining new representations for analyzing the vibration of plates as a function of wood stiffness, thickness, arching, even varnish (e.g., Chladni patterns; Hutchins, 1981). The questions at the frontier of this specialized acoustics are at the frontier of acoustics itself – for example, the effects of coupling plates on the separate Chaldni plate eigenmodes and the relation between plate eigenmodes and the main air and wood resonances of an intact instrument.

A third example comes from psychology itself. The psychological analysis of learning developed in the first half of this century was quite unsuitable to educational application. Real human learning is far more complex than animal learning (e.g., maze learning by laboratory rats) or than contrived learninglike exercises (e.g., memorizing lists of nonsense syllables). Some of the most significant aspects of human learning are the learner's prior knowledge and motivation to learn. These aspects cannot be analyzed in a learning theory grounded in simple animal models and nonsense tasks. Accordingly, this psychology of learning was irrelevant to educational application. Where it was applied, it was misleading and perverse (e.g., the promotion of rote discipline).

More recently, the psychology of learning and educational application have developed a more constructive and reciprocal relationship. Psychologists no longer speak of "meaningful learning" as if it were some exotic special case. Educational researchers and designers, while they have found the need for special theories of educational practice, also routinely make use of the psychology of learning (Ausubel, 1960).

Finding that the standard methods, concepts, and theories of the science do not support effective analysis of the significant aspects of an application domain can be a very constructive kind of failure. The examples of learning theory and the acoustics of violins show that the specificity requirement can provide impetus and direction for growing the science itself, for developing new methods, concepts, and theories. However, even if scientific analysis successfully addresses the important aspects of an application domain, it could still fail to do this in a way suited to the actual working context of the domain – that is, it could fail to meet the applicability requirement. (I have adapted the term *applicability* from Barnard's chapter.)

The working context for application can itself be so singular, so complex, and so potent that either the standard techniques cannot be employed at all or it is difficult to see how to modify them. For example, as Brooks mentions in his chapter, civil engineering has its own models of runoff and groundwater. It does not attempt to derive understandings directly from the physics of fluid flow in porous media. Such a derivation might be possible in principle, but even so it would be onerous and not justified in the application. The civil engineering models are in the right form to be useful in the working context of, for example, building bridges.

A suitably detailed acoustic analysis that captured all the important aspects of the violin would still not necessarily make it possible to produce a violin as good as a Stradivarius. The extent to which the acoustic analysis was useful in actually making a violin would depend upon the nature of violin making – the working context for this application. For example, could acoustic science guide the carpentry of planning a violin's front and back plates? Similarly, could even an excellent theory of (meaningful) human learning guide the design of a classroom lesson or the process of curriculum development for ninth-grade biology?

In these examples, it is not enough to merely enhance the science in the sense of scope and richness. Addressing the applicability requirement presupposes a thorough understanding not only of the *concerns* of the target domain, but of the *practice* that has evolved to deal with these concerns. The issue is as much one of form as one of content. A special level or vocabulary of scientific description may be required, couched in a form not reducible to the starting science (Fodor, 1974), or perhaps the best we do is craft (Jones, 1970). The requirements of specificity and applicability provide a framework for understanding the recent history of the applied psychology of HCI. Current work, as represented by the various chapters of this book, is self-consciously addressing these requirements.

Specializing the Science Base

The pioneering developments of the applied psychology of HCI tended to import methods and concepts fairly directly from the academic science. Perhaps reflecting the 50-year struggle to establish psychology as a legitimate laboratory science, a strong early theme was the role of the scientific method in conducting empirical HCI studies (for review, see Shneiderman, 1980). Through the 1970s, psychologists working in HCI (the key research area at that time was the psychology of programming) sought to bring critical phenomena into the laboratory for empirical analysis. They designed factorial experiments with straightforward dependent measures such as error frequencies and performance times.

Unfortunately, little of this work produced much insight into the programming process. It was unable to resolve the large issues of the day surrounding the precise meaning and utility of structured programming techniques in producing less errorful and more maintainable code (e.g., Sheppard, Curtis, Millman, & Love, 1979). Its failure can be understood in terms of the specificity requirement: The scientific method impels dichotomous contrasts, and this works well only if the required controls are possible and appropriate. In HCI these requirements are generally not met. The chaotic and uncontrolled nature of complex activity like programming forced the use of extreme contrasts (structured versus random programs, organized versus random menus) in order to attain statistically significant results. Not surprisingly, such efforts merely confirmed common sense (when they succeeded). In other cases, complex alternatives were contrasted, amounting to a research design of A versus B with both A and B unknown.

The paradigm of direct empirical contrast persists in HCI but its use is more limited: Alternatives are contrasted to determine which of *those two* alternatives are better, not to apply or to extract general principles. In the 1980s, many cognitive psychologists began entering the HCI field, who sought to apply psychological theory (and not merely the scientific method) in order to afford more cumulative progress (Newell, 1973). They drew upon two very successful decades of basic research in the 1960s and 1970s, which had developed information processing descriptions for aspects of language (Fodor, Bever, & Garrett, 1974), memory (Norman, 1970), and problem solving (Newell & Simon, 1972).

This project also foundered on the specificity requirement. The psychology of the 1970s had focused on arenas of skill and experience involving little domain-specific knowledge. Such domains were particularly amenable to information processing description by small production systems. But these theories lacked the scope and richness required for application in HCI. For example, they had little capability for modeling error or error recovery, no serious notion of cognitive development or of expertise, and they modeled human goals and motives as unanalyzed primitives drawn from a checklist. The assumptions these theories required made it difficult to apply them at all predictively (e.g., outside of the friendly confines of list learning, what is a chunk?). Accordingly, the theories could only be applied to modeling fairly limited phenomena, like the nonexistence of negative transfer (an arcane issue directly imported from verbal learning).

A clear theme in the chapters of this book is that the psychology of HCI must be methodologically and conceptually richer, more diverse, and better specialized for application. To some extent this involves better utilizing or directing the basic science that we already have and that we already have been trying to apply in HCI, namely, modern information processing psychology. However, many of the chapters advocate and develop more radical proposals. On the one hand, they argue that we need to apply approaches to psychology beyond information-processing psychology, and perhaps social and behavioral sciences beyond psychology. On the other hand, they argue that information-processing pscyhology *itself* must be fundamentally enriched as a science base.

Better Utilizing Information-processing Psychology

Several chapters are concerned with how extant psychological theory can be more richly utilized. The chapter by Barnard reviews what he calls the first phase of HCI research and criticizes the reliance on simple research designs and measures. He develops a framework for understanding the activity in HCI proceeding from the idea that science provides a *representation* of the real world. To construct and to apply this representation, we must be able to map between it and the world – that is, to interpret it. This mapping involves intermediary, or bridging representations, specialized for the intended domain of endeavor.

In HCI, the real world consists of various artifacts (software, hardware, documentation) embedded in contexts of work and social interaction. In constructing a science of HCI, we make an intermediary representation of this reality, usually involving selection and simplification. Barnard calls this a "discovery" representation. For example, we might select a subset of work contexts, or perhaps contrive a laboratory situation to stand in for a work context; we might select a single artifact for analysis. These situations would represent the real world for the purpose of scientific discovery. Barnard urges that we develop more effective discovery representations. He describes the use of interaction scenarios to assess the extent to which a given theory in the science base makes contact with actual issues in the application domain.

DiSessa shows how an analysis of mental model types can be used to organize design requirements in his Boxer programming language and environment. His analysis of programming tasks suggested several significant types of models: *structural* models, context-invariant descriptions in terms of state space transitions; *functional* models, contextualized descriptions of routine and familiar programming tasks and strategies; and *distributed* models, fragmentary descriptions, often generated spontaneously to address specific concerns of the moment and heavily dependent on prior knowledge.

These models jointly address a substantial range of user tasks and involve trade-offs. Structural models can be difficult to learn but important for debugging and radical invention. They are particularly relevant to experts. Distributed models in contrast are particularly relevant to early learning. The different types of models also jointly suggest design goals. For example, Boxer was designed to make the structural model visible in order to converge the structural and distributed model more rapidly. The mental model types can also be used to "partition" learning problems in terms of their origins in knowledge and skill.

Lewis makes the point that psychological theory might be quite important in HCI design even if it only provided guidance in specialized situations. He distinguishes between "outer" theory – that is, theory that characterizes psychological phenomena without explicating the processes that create these phenomena – and the "inner" theory that describes these processes. He suggests that HCI has focused too much on outer theory and perhaps expected too much of it. Extending consideration to inner theory may have particular benefits in providing non-obvious insights about HCI phenomena, for example, new types of representations to display information.

Broadening the Range of Psychology We Seek to Apply

Other chapters are concerned with broadening the range of psychological theory recruited for application in HCI. For example, Barnard notes that the science base of information processing psychology has not adequately addressed extended sequences of behavior, as opposed to discrete acts; it has not adequately addressed information-rich environments or circumstances in which people have broader task goals.

DiSessa, Greif, and Bannon and Bødker urge the incorporation of concepts and methods from developmental approaches to psychology. They are concerned with qualitative changes in human capabilities and experiences that arise through interactions with the environment. DiSessa criticizes the typical focus on very early stages of skill development in evaluating the usability of software. Skills acquired in a few hours, or even days, may not be representative of the full course of skill development in complex tasks. DiSessa's studies of programming with the Boxer system focus on tasks of design, modification, and use of personal applications by programmers throughout their first year of programming experience with the system.

Greif outlines the "action theory" of German work psychology. This tradition focuses on the conscious self-regulation of concrete activity, often in a workplace context. It emphasizes the importance of designing work activities that are complete, meaningful, and satisfying, that offer ample scope of action for people, and that in the long term facilitate well-being and human growth. He discusses research on learning by exploration in which learners were encouraged to make errors for "stress inoculation" and to learn about error recovery. They were encouraged to decide for themselves how long to train, to adopt individual learning styles in a social context supported by a trainer and co-workers.

Greif contrasts action theory with information-processing theory of the sort embodied in Card et al. (1983). Action theory seeks to model the regulation of activity at a comparable level, but it questions the extremely limited possibility of *self-regulation* inherent in typical information-processing analyses. Greif discusses research that shows how Card et al.'s analysis fails when people are free to choose how to behave, even between two alternative ways of doing a simple task. He concludes that psychological theory can play an important role in design, but as a "tool for thought," not as a deductive foundation.

Bannon and Bødker explore the relevance of "activity theory" to HCI design. Activity theory, like action theory, directs analysis on persons acting in contexts, but at a higher level of description, seeking to understand extended sequences of action in terms of long-term human motives. Bannon and Bødker criticize information-processing psychology for overconcentrating on aspects of people that seem amenable to a computational metaphor. They contend that these aspects cannot be meaningfully detached from real situations of human activity and experience. For example, they argue that not enough information is incorporated in any information-processing task analysis to support design; moreover, in the most relevant sense such task analyses cannot be verified. As Bannon and Bødker put it, the people whose tasks are being described "cannot understand their own work from these descriptions."

Bannon and Bødker press the possibility that *no* simplifying decompositions or descriptions are rich enough to guide design. What is required is a directly experienced, concrete understanding of how a system being designed will actually be used. They call for a cultural–historical perspective to the psychology of HCI.

The chapters by Brooks, Pylyshyn, and Landauer advocate a broad-based "descriptive" psychology of HCI. Brooks suggests that it is premature to develop a formal, idealization-based "technical theory" for HCI. Pylyshyn suggests that the domain may not support what he calls a "deductive science." Landauer concludes that the complexity of HCI situations is just too great for ordinary theoretical analysis. Brooks and Pylyshyn propose that developing taxonomies of user tasks, and canonical notations for describing tasks, would be an effective way to cumu-late what we know about HCI. Pylyshyn draws analogy to de Saussure's program for linguistic description, delineating contrasts between specific tasks to determine which properties of tasks are structural properties. Brooks suggests the same type of analysis could be carried out for user interface techniques. As an illustration, he discusses a notation for menu structures. Landauer and Pylyshyn emphasize small-scale generalizations with paradigmatic empirical demonstrations, tools, and methods for studying natural domains, and sensitivity and craftsmanship in distin-guishing important phenomena from ephemeral ones.

Extending the Scope of Information-processing Psychology

Some of the chapters argue for extending the scope of psychology itself. The chap-ters by Norman, by Payne, and by Carroll, Kellogg, and Rosson develop the point that the structures of the external world – including the structures designed by humans – are critical determinants of activity and experience. As Norman notes, psychology has traditionally divided human tasks into small components, instead of asking directly how people accomplish their tasks. The answer is that people have structured the world to make their tasks simple – for example, arranging objects so that thoughts can be retrieved by finding their referents in the world. The study of artifacts, then, becomes an important area of concern for psychology itself.

Norman describes what he calls "cognitive artifacts," devices that enhance hu-man thought. He shows that our world is teeming with cognitive artifacts: calcula-tors, books, clocks, telephones, radios. Their power resides in their facilitation of our interaction with the world. For example, why use slides in giving a lecture? The answer involves a diversity of specific psychological arguments for the role of such an artifact in the tasks of delivering and understanding a lecture. Norman suggests that an important task for psychology now is to develop a typology of artifacts and an understanding of some of the trade-offs involved in using them. He contrasts a *personal* view of artifacts (as qualitatively changing the experience of a task, the types of errors one makes) with a *system* view (in which they enhance throughput); he contrasts a notion of *passive* artifacts (like books) with a notion of *active* artifacts (like computers), and considers several sources of trade-off (e.g., externalized information is not subject to memory decay but internalized information can be searched faster).

Payne adopts a similar stance, and develops analyses for three aspects of how artifacts restructure tasks for people. He notes that an artifact provides a representa-tion of a task domain through which a user operates on the task domain, an interaction language for mapping domain operators into actions, and a set of re-sponses whose content and timing guide the interpretation of user interactions. Payne stresses that these aspects of artifacts are double-edged, that each poses a distinctive problem for users, particularly for learning, but that each also provides distinctive resources for supporting the user.

Carroll et al. also make the point that the study of artifacts is an important area of concern for psychology in arguing that artifacts in use can be understood as implicitly embodying specific claims about their users, claims about what would have to be the case in order for the artifact to be usable. However, their touchstone is the evolution of technology, and in particular the general tendency for technology to proceed independently of science (or indeed to lead science as it typically has in HCI). They develop a proposal for a science framework naturalized to the existent HCI technology development framework, the task–artifact cycle, and show through an example how a science of HCI might emerge from design practice augmented by tools and techniques for extracting psychological design rationales from artifacts in use.

These diverse approaches to the specificity requirement, to producing a psychological science base that is adequately content appropriate for use in HCI design, are complemented by a set of approaches to the applicability requirement, to producing an applied psychology of HCI that is adequately process appropriate. This is a second major theme in the chapters of this book.

Working within the Design Process

The human-factors evaluation paradigm of the 1970s established a specific and quite limited role for psychology in HCI design work. This role was essentially *reactive:* Designers planned and created a prototype for new computer systems and applications, and *then* psychologists assessed usability. This established what might be called the "evaluation dilemma" for the psychology of HCI: Something already had to have been designed and built in order for psychology to even begin to contribute. But, it turns out, when something is already designed and built, there is great technical and organizational inertia against altering it in any significant way. Hence psychology was always too late to have much impact. Human-factors evaluation came to be seen by designers as a hurdle, not a resource. This organizational context was a formidable obstacle to applicability.

Unfortunately, this difficulty was reinforced by the types of technical contributions psychological evaluation was in a position to make. Task time and error rate are unassailably objective. Even the most truculent designer must acknowledge the scientific facts when task time and error rate can be shown to be too high. But what is too high? Psychologists often conflated statistical significance with practical significance. Moreover, they were not generally able to suggest what to do when task time and error rate were "too high." Evaluation was sometimes able to flag a problem, but it was no help in identifying potential design remedies. It was geared more to methodological credibility than to design relevance.

To make psychology more applicable to design, the results of human-factors evaluation work and assorted inferences from basic psychological theory were gathered together as design guidelines, prescriptions for designers to follow. With the influx of information-processing psychology in the 1980s, guidelines were re-expressed as analytic design models (Moran, 1981; Reisner, 1984). This work, however, also failed to meet the applicability requirement. It rested on a serious underestimate of the complexity of the design process. Simon (1947, 1969, 1973) had introduced the notion of "partial decomposability" to encourage hierarchical simplification of complex problems (Reitman, 1965). This strategy can indeed be powerful, but it can also entrain a distorted view of design, the process of design, as *inherently,* and not merely heuristically, decomposable (Rittel & Webber, 1973).

Actual design is ill-structured in many senses: The possible solutions are not enumerable a priori, decomposing the problem and solving the parts often does not entail progress in solving the overall problem, partial and interim solutions that play no obvious role in the final design may still play an important role in defining the design space of the final design, and the process of solution often includes the discovery of a new goal (Carroll & Rosson, 1985; Carroll, Thomas, & Malhotra, 1979; Guindon, Krasner, & Curtis, 1987). Guidelines and analytic models presume relatively well-behaved problem-solving processes, and hence fail the applicability requirement in HCI design.

The chapters of this book develop a range of ways in which the psychology of HCI can work within the design process. Psychology must describe and understand design as it occurs, it must produce new and useful design representations and other tools, and it must play an active role in the design of computer systems and applications.

Understanding the Design Process

Several chapters describe the process of design. Henderson argues that we must take an extremely broad view of what design is. He describes how the people who install a system contribute to its design by adapting it to a particular customer site. Indeed, he contends that users must also be seen as contributing to design when they "make use" of a system – routinely inventing new practices to "design around" awkward technology. Henderson criticizes recent attempts from information-processing psychology to impact design, on the grounds that they have addressed only use, and no other aspect of the design process. He describes a "design wheel" of activities: use, observation, analysis, creation, and embodiment. All the participants in the design process move around this wheel through time, and this aggregate activity – often not coordinated effectively – defines the design.

Bannon and Bødker develop a similar notion in their point that design is a process of learning. For them, a typical problem is that the designer is a detached observer of "use," and not an active collaborator with the user. Design implicitly and unavoidably creates new conventions for social activity, a new division of labor. But typically these aspects are not themselves designed directly; they merely obtain as side effects. Bannon and Bødker suggest that design be regarded as a meeting place for many arenas of human practice, that it must proceed simultaneously on many levels.

Karat and Bennett and Pylyshyn examine specific aspects of design in more detail. Karat and Bennett studied design-team dynamics and concluded that much of the quality of the final product depends on the quality of interaction in the design group. Focusing on this level of design practice, they describe a program of work directed at encouraging better sharing of information through the design process. Their work shows how the representations used to codify design work can both facilitate and obstruct communication in a design group.

Pylyshyn describes the tendency of designers to design first and then to analyze, posing the question of what kind of response this observation could or should entrain. He distinguishes between a *necessity* analysis of design and a *sufficiency* analysis. The latter focuses on how people in fact accomplish design tasks, the former on the essence of these tasks. In any specific case we cannot know with which we are dealing when we empirically characterize an activity: Is the solution focus of designers a necessary aspect of design activity or is it, for example, an accidental and problematic consequence of specific cognitive demands that we might mitigate by providing various information-management and decision tools? He remarks that frequently this question is simply preempted by a technological innovation that radically reorganizes a task domain.

Supporting Design with Representations and Tools

Other chapters describe design representations and tools grounded in psychological theory and analysis. As Pylyshyn and Grief both note, there is a very uncertain relation historically between scientific value and relevance to practical application. Pylyshyn observes that in the physical sciences recognizing a Platonic distinction between how we see and experience things and their underlying true natures was an important step in the development of physical science. Moreover, he argues that "practical improvements are rarely related to the scientific theories that the innovators hold – and certainly not to the truth of such theories." He suggests that psychology's desire to confront and explain ecologically valid phenomena might even have impaired it as a science.

In Barnard's framework, we apply science through an "application" representation, bridging from science to design, which in HCI typically has meant an engineering model (Card et al., 1983). Barnard acknowledges the limitations of such application representations, and focuses on the problem of providing application representations that better facilitate the designer's work. He discusses programmable user models, which simulate user interaction, and expert systems for user interface design as possible avenues for development.

Brooks also takes up the point that the form of theory must be suitably applicable. He refers to the development of circuit theory as motivated by the fact that the differential equations in Maxwell's Laws do not have closed form solutions. He suggests that task and interface technique taxonomies might provide the kind of design guidance he feels designers want from HCI – guidance specific to the domain and based on systematic study of human behavior: "By indicating what aspects of an artifact are really significant, a good abstraction may lead both to invention of new artifacts that produce these aspects in novel ways or to novel uses for existing artifacts."

Brooks, Payne, and Pylyshyn all make the point that we need to analyze tasks into small and general components, so that, as Brooks suggests, you might contrast manuscript editing with statistical analysis tasks. Payne talks about an example of this in his chapter: the use of his yoked state space analysis to provide specific guidance on how to develop and convey mental models in instruction. Carroll et al.

outline how a set of user interaction scenarios could be used as a design representation grounded in a psychology of user tasks: The design process would consist of the successive detailing of the scenario set, ultimately incorporating device-specific details articulating exactly how particular tasks will be accomplished.

Bannon and Bødker endorse rapid prototyping as a means of letting users find out what a design is about. They question current tool work on design rationale as leaving out too much detail. They also question user-interface, management-system tools, suggesting that one cannot separate user-interface function from application function. They criticize tools based on cognitive architectures, such as the programmable user model described by Barnard, as undermining the necessary direct contact between the designer and the user, replacing the actual user with an idealized computer model.

Of course, rapid prototyping alone could easily degenerate into situated trial and error. Landauer argues that we are already very well equipped to support HCI design, that our tools are powerful, but not deductively theory based. He claims that HCI systems are too complex for theory-based design or analysis. Accordingly, design must recruit the few "homely" engineering principles we have (Fitts's Law, Hick's Law) and a variety of "new but mundane" tools: data-based simulations, qualitative task models, empirical generalizations about user needs and characteristics. He discusses how the invention of the rich indexing technique was a direct and effective response to finding that people do not agree on the right index or name term.

Doing Design as a Psychological Research Method

Some of the chapters show how *doing* design work can be part of the role of psychology in HCI. Building and inventing things is not a traditional activity in psychological research. However, perhaps not surprisingly, one of the best ways to demonstrate the value to design of a psychological concept or method is to use it in design and demonstrate the advantage. Landauer (1987) succinctly captured this in casting "psychology as a mother of invention" in HCI. In his chapter, Landauer discusses several of the Bellcore information applications, in particular, SuperBook. Greif discusses iS (individual system) and the training materials designed for it. Carroll et al. discuss the Training Wheels interface. In these projects, the psychological analysis was developed and tested through the course of the design process.

DiSessa contends that doing what he calls "principled design" is an important research strategy for psychology itself. He suggests that we think of design not as "application" but as playing a more proactive role in the development and testing of scientific principles. Even for its own purposes science needs "to engage in substantial activities, on the scale of the design of an artifact and substantial study of its use." Design projects can also help underwrite science research by producing practical value. Finally, design can serve as an "intuition pump," helping us to articulate more clearly our pretheoretical intuitions about cognitive structures. He illustrates this view with specific work on scoping (assigning names to entities) in his Boxer system.

An interesting parallel can be found in acoustic studies of the violin, mentioned earlier. In that research, it turned out that resolving many of the acoustic issues turned on the production and use of experimental string instruments (Hutchins & Bram, 1973). Indeed, that research has allowed the beginnings of a new musical literature for an acoustically balanced Violin Octet.

A Mutual Opportunity

The difficulty of establishing an applied psychology of HCI is not unique to psychology or to HCI. Historically, most basic science has failed to meet the requirements of specificity and applicability. What may be unique is that a deliberate and sustained effort is being directed at specializing the basic psychological science and at working within the HCI design process. The chapters in this book comprise an interim report on this endeavor. They address the question of how and where we may hope to get leverage from psychology in the practical arena of designing computer equipment and applications.

To identify useful designs, we need to understand the user's domain (specificity); to impact design usefully, we need to understand the designer's domain (applicability). From the standpoint of HCI, these requirements force us to specialize the psychological science base, increasing its scope and richness in many ways. They force us to work more seriously with and within the design process – to understand, support, and participate in design work. This opportunity and challenge for psychology in HCI is also reciprocal. Users and designers are people engaged in the typically complex roles of normal life. A better understanding of and better support for these roles enhances and furthers the objectives of psychology. The development of a better-applied psychology of HCI can offer a case study in developing psychology as a broader science.

Beyond specificity and applicability, a science and its applications must communicate, must be prepared for the possibility of mutual benefit. The relationship between psychology and its application in human–computer interaction design practice has been difficult perhaps *because* the possibilities are so rich, so tantalizing, and the actual accomplishments thus far so limited. In the 1970s psychologists applied the laboratory methods they had cultivated for a half century to the psychology of programming, but with relatively modest success. In the 1980s, they applied information-processing theory, but again with relatively little success. Examining these early efforts suggests specific avenues for cultivating more successful application and, perhaps, for fostering mutual development.

The applied psychology of HCI will be a more specialized psychology. However, the development of a richer psychological characterization of human use of interactive, computational tools may have implications beyond the specificity requirement. In this century, several otherwise unrelated schools of psychology have developed the idea that the environment, including and perhaps particularly the environment created by humans, structures the field of phenomena regarded as "psychological" (Gibson, 1950, 1979; Vygotsky, 1978). Simon (1969, p. 26) considered psychology as a "science of the artificial," by which he meant a science chiefly concerned with how people adapt to environments.

HCI may prove to be the psychological domain in which these ideas can best thrive. The rapid and diverse growth of computer systems and applications creates the most astonishing experiments for us in adaptation, tool use, and technological affordance – whether we like it or not! The development of action theory, activity theory, and a descriptive science of tasks within HCI, along with the developing focus on artifacts as psychologically significant objects, provides us with an unprecedented set of intellectual tools for developing HCI as a flagship science of the artificial.

This project both allows and requires more proactive participation in design itself: design as an object of research, as a method of research, and as a practical activity. And this emphasis may certainly have implications beyond the applicability requirement. Simon (1969, p. 83) characterized human adaptation to environments as a search for good designs, and concluded that "the proper study of mankind is the science of design." From this standpoint, HCI may provide a particularly important area of concern for psychology itself: HCI exists to produce new environments for human behavior and experience. Perhaps for the first time, a systematic understanding of how environments affect people can be used deliberately to create environments to suit human adaptation.

In the 1990s, the tantalizing prospect exists that psychology can become a very proactive "science of the artificial." Many years ago, Simon (1969, pp. 82–83) suggested that the increasing use of computers among intellectual disciplines created increased interdisciplinary communication *because* it created a common ground among the disciplines, the common ground of using computers to design. For HCI, this vision is still daunting and still challenging: We must better understand how to enhance the development of our common ground.

Acknowledgments

I am grateful for comments from John Bennett, Robert Campbell, Wendy Kellogg, Don Norman, Steve Payne, Mary Beth Rosson, and Linda Tetzlaff.

References

Ausubel, D. P. (1960). The use of advance organizers in the learning and retention of meaningful verbal material. *Journal of Educational Psychology, 51,* 267–272.

Basalla, G. (1988). *The evolution of technology.* New York: Cambridge University Press.

Card, S. K., Moran, T. P., & Newell, A. (1983). *The psychology of human–computer interaction.* Hillsdale, NJ: Lawrence Erlbaum Associates.

Carroll, J. M., & Rosson, M. B. (1985). Usability specifications as a tool in iterative development. In H. R. Hartson (Ed.), *Advances in human–computer interaction* (pp. 1–28). Norwood, NJ: Ablex.

Carroll, J. M., Thomas, J. C., & Malhotra, A. (1979). A clinical–experimental analysis of design problem solving. *Design Studies, 1,* 84–92. Reprinted in B. Curtis (Ed.). (1985). *Human factors in software development* (pp. 243–251). Washington, DC: IEEE Computer Society Press.

Engelbart, D., & English, W. (1968). A research center for augmenting human intellect. *Proceedings of Fall Joint Computer Conference, 33*(1), 395–410. Montvale, NJ: AFIPS Press.

Fodor, J. A. (1974). Special sciences, or the disunity of science as a working hypothesis. *Synthese, 28,* 97–115.

Fodor, J. A., Bever, T. G., & Garrett, M. F. (1974). *The psychology of language.* New York: McGraw-Hill.

Gibson, J. J. (1950). *The perception of the visual world.* Boston: Houghton Mifflin.

Gibson, J. J. (1979). *The ecological approach to visual perception.* Boston: Houghton Mifflin.

Guindon, R., Krasner, H., & Curtis, B. (1987). Breakdowns and processes during the early activities of software design by professionals. In G. M. Olson, S. Sheppard, & E. Soloway (Eds.), *Empirical studies of programmers: Second workshop* (pp. 65–82). Norwood, NJ: Ablex.

Hindle, B. (1981). *Emulation and invention.* New York: New York University Press.

Hutchins, C. M. (1981). The acoustics of violin plates. *Scientific American, 245*(4), 170–186.

Hutchins, C. M., & Bram, M. (1973, November). The bowed strings – Yesterday, today and tomorrow. *Music Educators Journal,* 20–25.

Jones, J. C. (1970). *Design methods: Seeds of human futures.* New York: Wiley.

Landauer, T. K. (1987). Psychology as a mother of invention. In J. M. Carroll & P. P. Tanner (Eds.), *Proceedings of CHI + GI '87: Human Factors in Computing Systems and Graphics Interface (Toronto, April 5–9)* (pp. 333–335). New York: ACM.

Laudan, R. (1984). Introduction. In R. Laudan (Ed.), *The nature of technological knowledge: Are models of scientific change relevant?* (pp. 1–26). Dordrecht: Reidel.

Moran, T. P. (1981). The command language grammar. *International Journal of Man–Machine Studies, 15,* 3–50.

Morrison, E. (1974). *From know-how to nowhere.* Oxford: Blackwell.

Newell, A. (1973). You can't play twenty questions with nature and win. In W. Chase (Ed.), *Visual information processing.* New York: Academic Press.

Newell, A., & Simon, H. A. (1972). *Human information processing.* Englewood Cliffs, NJ: Prentice-Hall.

Norman, D. A. (Ed.). (1970). *Models of human memory.* New York: Academic Press.

Polson, P. G., & Kieras, D. E. (1985). A quantitative model of the learning and performance of text editing knowledge. In L. Borman & B. Curtis (Eds.), *Proceedings of CHI '85: Human Factors in Computing Systems,* (pp. 207–212). New York: ACM.

Reisner, P. (1984). Formal grammar as a tool for analyzing ease of use: Some fundamental concepts. In J. C. Thomas & M. Schneider (Eds.), *Human factors in computing systems* (pp. 53–78). Norwood, NJ: Ablex.

Reitman, W. R. (1965). *Cognition and thought.* New York: Wiley.

Rittel, H. W. J., & Webber, M. M. (1973). Dilemmas in a general theory of planning. *Policy Sciences, 4,* 155–169. Reprinted in N. Cross (Ed.). (1984). *Developments in design methodology* (pp. 135–144). New York: Wiley.

Saunders, F. A. (1937). The mechanical action of violins. *Journal of the Acoustic Society of America, 9*(2), 81–98.

Saunders, F. A. (1946). The mechanical action of instruments of the violin family. *Journal of the Acoustic Society of America, 17*(3), 169–186.

Sheppard, S. B., Curtis, B., Millman, P., & Love, T. (1979). Modern coding practices and programmer performance. *IEEE Computer, 12*(12), 41–49.

Shneiderman, B. (1980). *Software psychology: Human factors in computer and information systems.* Cambridge, MA: Winthrop.

Simon, H. A. (1947). *Administrative behavior.* New York: Macmillan.

Simon, H. A. (1969). *The sciences of the artificial.* Cambridge, MA: MIT Press.

Simon, H. A. (1973). The structure of ill-structured problems. *Artificial Intelligence, 4,* 181–201. Reprinted in N. Cross (Ed.). (1984). *Developments in design methodology* (pp. 145–166). New York: Wiley.

Sutherland, I. E. (1963). Sketchpad: A man–machine graphical communication system. *Proceedings of the Spring Joint Computer Conference, 23,* 329–346. Montvale, NJ: AFIPS Press.

Vygotsky, L. S. (1978). *Mind in society: The development of higher mental processes.* (M. Cole, V. John-Steiner, S. Scribner, & E. Souberman, Eds.). Cambridge, MA: Harvard University Press.

2
Cognitive Artifacts
Donald A. Norman

A cognitive artifact is an artificial device designed to maintain, display, or operate upon information in order to serve a representational function.

The distinctive characteristics of human beings as a species are:

1. Their special ability to modify the environment in which they live through the creation of artifacts

and

2. the corresponding ability to transmit the accumulated modifications to subsequent generations through precept and procedure coded in human language. (Cole, 1990, p. 1).

Artifacts pervade our lives, our every activity. The speed, power, and intelligence of human beings are dramatically enhanced by the invention of artificial devices, so much so that tool making and usage constitute one of the defining characteristics of our species. Many artifacts make us stronger or faster, or protect us from the elements or predators, or feed and clothe us. And many artifacts make us smarter, increasing cognitive capabilities and making possible the modern intellectual world.

My interest is in cognitive artifacts, those artificial devices that maintain, display, or operate upon information in order to serve a representational function and that affect human cognitive performance. In this chapter I discuss three aspects of cognitive artifacts:

    I.   Two differing views of artifacts: the system view and the personal view;

    II. Levels of directness and engagement: the relationship between those aspects of artifacts that serve the execution of acts and those that serve the evaluation of environmental states and the resulting feeling of directness of control or engagement;

    III. Representational properties of cognitive artifacts: the relationship between the system state and its representation in the artifact.

Some History

Despite the enormous impact of artifacts upon human cognition, most of our scientific understanding is of the unaided mind: of memory, attention, perception, action, and thought, unaided by external devices. There is little understanding of the information-processing roles played by artifacts and how they interact with the information processing activities of their users.

The power and importance of culture and artifacts to enhance human abilities are ignored within much of contemporary cognitive science despite the heavy prominence given to its importance in the early days of psychological and anthropological investigation. The field has a sound historical basis, starting at least with Wundt (1916), nurtured and developed by the Soviet social-historical school of the 1920s (Leont'ev, 1981; Luria, 1979; Vygotsky, 1978; Wertsch, 1985), and still under study by a hardy band of social scientists, often unified by titles such as "activity theory," "action theory," or "situated action," with much of the research centered in Scandinavia, Germany, and the Soviet Union.

In the early part of the 20th century, American psychology moved from its early interest in mental functioning to the behavioral era, in which studies of representational issues, consciousness, mind, and culture were considered, at best, irrelevant to science. These dark ages ended in the mid-1950s, but by then, the historical continuity with the earlier approaches and with European psychology had been lost. As a result, American cognitive psychology had to recreate itself, borrowing heavily from British influences. The emphasis was on the study of the psychological mechanisms responsible for memory, attention, perception, language, and thought in the single, unaided individual, studied almost entirely within the university laboratory. There was little or no emphasis on group activities, on the overall situation in which people accomplished their normal daily activities, or on naturalistic observations. Given these biases and history, it is no surprise that little thought was given to the role of the environment (whether natural or artificial) in the study of human cognition.

The field has now returned to pay serious attention to the role of the situation, other people, natural and artificial environments, and culture. In part, this change has come about through the dedicated effort of the current researchers, in part because the current interest in the design of computer interfaces has forced consideration of the role of real tasks and environments, and therefore of groups of cooperating individuals, or artifacts, and of culture.

The birth, death, and now apparent rebirth of the interest in culture and artifacts in thought is reflected in a survey paper by Cole, "Cultural psychology: a once and future discipline?" (Cole, 1990). For Cole, cultural psychology builds on the two major assumptions that stand as the opening quotation to this chapter: (1) the human's ability to create artifacts; (2) the corresponding ability to transmit accumulated knowledge to subsequent generations.

In this chapter I emphasize the information-processing role played by physical artifacts upon the cognition of the individual – hence the term *cognitive artifact*. Here, I will not be concerned with how they are invented, acquired, or transmitted across individuals or generations. The goal is to integrate artifacts into the existing theory of human cognition.

The field of human–computer interaction has pioneered in the formal study of the cognitive relationship between a person's activities, the artifact of the computer, and the task, and this chapter is a result of work in that tradition. However, most of the work has been narrowly focused on the details of the "interface" between the person and the machine. But it has become increasingly clear that the nature of the interaction between the people and the task affects the artifact and its use, with the view and use of the artifact varying with both the nature of the task and the level of expertise and skill of the people (e.g., see Bannon & Bødker, this volume, both for a clear description of this philosophy and also for a general review). I agree that we need a broader outlook upon tools and their use, but we also need better scientific understanding of the role played by the artifact itself, and so the main focus is upon the properties of the artifact and how its design affects the person and task.

It is clear that we are entering a new era of technology, one dominated by access to computation, communication, and knowledge, access that moreover can be readily available, inexpensive, powerful, and portable. Much of what will transpire can be called the development of cognitive artifacts, artificial devices that enhance human cognitive capabilities. As we shall see, however, artifacts do not actually change an individual's capabilities. Rather, they change the nature of the task performed by the person. When the informational and processing structure of the artifact is combined with the task and the informational and processing structure of the human, the result is to expand and enhance cognitive capabilities of the total system of human, task, and artifact.

Two Views of Artifacts: The System View and the Personal View

The most obvious analysis of an artifact is that it enhances human ability. According to this analysis an artifact such as a pulley system makes us stronger, a car makes us faster, and paper and pencil make us smarter. By this analysis, artifacts such as written notes, books, and recordings amplify the cognitive power of human memory and artifacts such as mathematics and logic amplify the power of thought. The notions that artifacts enhance or amplify may be natural, but as Cole and Griffin point out in their essay "Cultural amplifiers reconsidered" (1980), they are badly misleading.

Artifacts may enhance performance, but as a rule they do not do so by enhancing or amplifying individual abilities. There are artifacts that really do amplify. A megaphone amplifies voice intensity to allow a person's voice to be heard for a greater distance than otherwise possible. This is amplification: The voice is unchanged in form and content but increased in quantity (intensity). But when written language and mathematics enable different performance than possible without their use, they do not do so by amplification: They change the nature of the task being done by the person and, in this way, enhance the overall performance.

Artifacts appear to play different roles depending upon the point from which they are viewed. When a person uses an artifact to accomplish some task, the outside observer sees the system view, the total structure of person plus artifact (Figure 2.1) in accomplishing that task. The person, however, sees the personal view: how the artifact has affected the task to be performed (Figure 2.2).

Figure 2.1. The system view of a cognitive artifact. Under this view, we see the entire system composed of the person, the task, and the artifact. Seen from this perspective, the artifact enhances cognition, for with the aid of the artifact, a system can accomplish more than without the artifact.

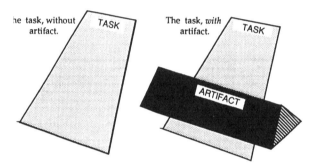

Figure 2.2. The personal view of a cognitive artifact. Under this view, that of the individual person who must use the artifact, the view of the task has changed: thus, the artifact does not enhance cognition – it changes the task. New things have to be learned, and old procedures and information may no longer be required: The person's cognitive abilities are unchanged.

The System View of an Artifact

The two views of artifacts, and an illustration of how cognition is distributed across people and technology, can perhaps most easily be illustrated by example. Consider the everyday memory aid, the reminder or "to-do" list, or in industrial contexts, the checklist for a task (e.g., the checklists used by pilots before each critical phase of flight in a commercial aircraft). From the system point of view, checklists enhance memory and performance; from the personal point of view, they change the task.

At first, the checklist or to-do list may appear to be a memory aid. It can be seen to help us remember what to do during the course of our activities. In fact, there can be no question that checklists change our behavior and prevent some kinds of forgetting: They are so effective in industrial and aviation settings, that their use is often required by regulation. It is tempting to say that a list extends or enhances our memory. After all, with it, we can perform as if we had a perfect memory for the items on the list. Without it, we occasionally forget to take important actions. When we think of the to-do list in terms of what the person-plus-list system can do, we are looking at one view of the artifact. This is the view of the artifact from afar, looking at it in the context of the person and the task to be performed: This is the system view. The system view of the list is as a memory enhancer.

The Personal View of an Artifact

The checklist or to-do list has another view, the view it presents to the task performer: this the personal view. From the point of view of the user of the artifact, using the list is itself a task. Without the list, we must remember or plan all of our actions. With the list, we need to do very little remembering and planning: The planning and "remembering" were done ahead of time, at the time we made up the list. At the time we perform the individual actions we need not repeat the planning and remembering. The use of a list instead of unaided memory introduces three new tasks, the first performed ahead of time, the other two at the time the action is to be done:

1. The construction of the list;
2. Remembering to consult the list;
3. Reading and interpreting the items on the list.

The fact that the preparation of the list is done prior to the action has an important impact upon performance because it allows the cognitive effort to be distributed across time and people. This preparatory task, which Hutchins calls "precomputation" (E. Hutchins, 1989, personal communication), can be done whenever convenient, when there are no time pressures or other stresses, and even by a different person than the individual who performs the actions. In fact, precomputation can take place years before the actual event and one precomputation can serve many applications.

In the aviation setting, flight checklists are prepared by the chief pilot of each airline, approved by the Federal Aviation Authority, and then passed on to the pilots who use them for many years and many thousands of flights without further modification: This is both precomputation and a distribution of the cognitive task of planning across people and time. To the aviation system, the checklist enhances memory and accuracy of action; to the individual pilots, the checklist is a new task inserted into the daily routine, and at times it is apt to be viewed as extraneous to the main goals of the day. As such it is a nuisance and it can lead to new classes of errors: Some of these errors may resemble those that would occur without the use of the checklist, and some may not.

When we compare the activities performed with an without the aid of a reminder list, we see that the conclusion one draws depends on the point of view being taken. To the outside observer (who takes the system view), the same actions are intended to be performed with and without the list, but (usually) they are carried out more accurately and reliably with the list. To the individual user (who takes the personal view), the list is not a memory or planning enhancer; it is a set of new tasks to be performed, with the aspects of the list relevant to memory and planning separated from the aspects of the list relevant to performance.

Every artifact has both a system and a personal view, and they are often very different in appearance. From the system view, the artifact appears to expand some functional capacity of the task performer. From the personal view, the artifact has replaced the original task with a different task, one that may have radically different cognitive requirements and use radically different cognitive capacities than the original task.

This analysis points out that from all points of view, artifacts change the way a task gets done. In particular, artifacts can:

Distribute the actions across time (precomputation);

Distribute the actions across people (distributed cognition);

Change the actions required of the individuals doing the activity.

Levels of Directness and Engagement

When we use an artifact to do a task, of necessity we make use of a representation. Artifacts act as mediators between us and the world, both in execution (between actions and the resulting changes to the world state) and in perception (between changes in the world and our detection and interpretation of the state). The nature of the interaction between the person and the object of the task varies from direct engagement to a very indirect, remote form of interaction. Thus, when we write or draw with a pencil on paper, there is a direct relationship between movement of the pencil and the resulting marks on the paper. When we ask someone else to write or draw for us, the relationship is much less direct. Some interactions are so indirect and remote that feedback and information about the world state are difficult to get and possibly delayed in time, and incomplete or of unknown accuracy. These differences can have a major impact upon task performance and to a large extent are controlled by the design of the task and the artifact. (See the important discussion by Laurel, 1986, which introduces the concept of "direct engagement.")

Bødker (1989) distinguishes among several possible relationships among the person, the artifact, and the objects being operated upon. Thus, the artifact can be used to mediate directly between the person and the object (as in using a hammer or chisel to operate upon nails or wood). Or the artifact can present a virtual object or world upon which operations are performed, eventually to be reflected onto the real object.

In some cases, the virtual world exists only within the computer (as in building a spreadsheet or graphic object that will never exist outside the computer). The object might actually exist outside the computer, but be created or operated upon through the virtual world of the artifact (as in controlling an industrial process through the computer display, or developing the content and format of a publica-

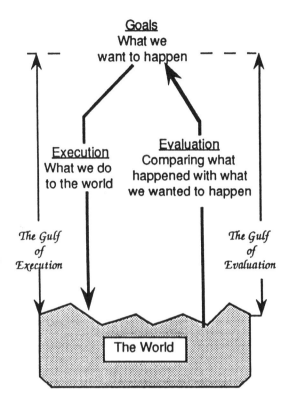

Figure 2.3. The action cycle. Artifacts that support action must support both the execution and evaluation phases of the action cycle, usually through different representations. The gulfs of execution and evaluation refer to the mismatch between our internal goals and expectations and the availability and representation of information about the state of the world and how it might be changed. The gulf of execution refers to the difficulty of acting upon the environment (and how well the artifact supports those actions). The gulf of evaluation refers to the difficulty of assessing the state of the environment (and how well the artifact supports the detection and interpretation of that state).

tion within the computer word processor and publishing system). In these cases, there are several layers of representation: representation$_1$, the represent*ed* world of the real object; representation$_2$, the representing world within the artifact; representation$_3$, the way the artifact displays the virtual world; and representation$_4$, the mental representation of the human.

Actions are performed through a feedback mechanism involving both an execution and evaluation phase (Figure 2.3). Both phases of the action cycle need support from the representational format used by the artifact. The choice of representation and interactions permitted by the artifact affect the interaction of the person with the object, whether real or virtual (Hutchins, Hollan, & Norman, 1986; Norman, 1986, 1988). Different forms of artifacts have different representational implications, which in turn dramatically affect the interactions.

Activity Flow

The gulf of execution refers to the difficulty of acting upon the environment (and how well the artifact supports those actions). The gulf of evaluation refers to the difficulty of assessing the state of the environment (and how well the artifact supports the detection and interpretation of that state). There are two ways of bridging the gulfs. One is by appropriate design of the artifact, the other through mental effort and training. Thus, with increasing skill, a person mentally bridges the gulfs, so that the operations upon the artifact are done subconsciously, without awareness, and the operators view themselves as operating directly upon the final object (Bødker, 1989; Hutchins, 1986; Hutchins et al., 1986).

Bødker introduces the notion of "activity flow" to describe the activity cycle in accomplishing a task. Automatization of effort – and the resulting feeling of direct engagement – can occur where a consistent, cohesive activity flow is supported by the task, artifact, and environment. Interruptions and unexpected results break the activity flow, forcing conscious attention upon the task. For many activities, this "bringing to consciousness" is disruptive of efficient performance.

The problem with disrupting activity flow is that the disruption brings to conscious awareness the disrupting activity, even when this is not the main focus of attention. This is usually undesirable, for it can have negative impact upon the task being performed. In fact, disruptions of this sort can lead to errors when the interrupting activity interferes with the maintenance of working memory for the task. The resulting memory difficulties may mean that the interrupted task is not resumed properly, either by being delayed beyond its proper execution time, by returning to the wrong point in the task, or by being forgotten altogether and never resumed: three classic forms of action errors. But deliberate disruption of the activity flow might be a useful safety device if it forces conscious attention upon critical, safety-related aspects of the task.

Automatic behavior is valuable in many skilled operations, for it permits the attention to be directed to one area of concern even while performing smoothly the operations required for another area – for example, the way in which a skilled typist can enter text automatically while concentrating upon the construction of future sentences. But at times, it might be valuable to force conscious attention to some aspect of performance by deliberately breaking the activity flow.

Thus, "forcing functions" – physical constraints that prevent critical or dangerous actions without conscious attention – could be viewed as serving their function by a deliberate disruption of normal activities. A good example of a deliberate disruption of activity for safety purposes is the use of checklists in industry and, especially, in commercial aviation. In aviation, the checklist is often reviewed by both pilots, one reading aloud the items, the other confirming and saying aloud the setting of each item as it is read. These actions are intended to force a deliberate, conscious disruption of skilled behavior, deliberately breaking the normal activity flow. Safety-related checks and cautions should be disruptive in order to receive conscious attention. Automatic actions are the most susceptible to errors by action slips and to disruption by external events and interruptions. In fact, the checklist can fail in its function: After thousands of usages and years of experience, checklist use can be so routine that it does become automatic, sometimes with serious consequences (Degani & Wiener, 1990; Norman & Hutchins, 1990; NTSB, 1989).

The point is not that one class of interaction or representation is superior to another but that the different forms and modes each have different properties.

Representation and Artifacts

The power of a cognitive artifact comes from its function as a representational device. Indeed, I define a cognitive artifact as an artificial device designed to maintain, display, or operate upon information in order to serve a representational function. It is now time to take a look at some of the representational features of artifacts. This will be brief and incomplete: This work is just beginning and although the work so far is suggestive, a more complete analysis will have to come later.

Representational Systems

A representational system has three essential ingredients (Newell, 1981; Rumelhart & Norman, 1988):

The represented world – that which is to be represented;

The representing world – a set of symbols;

An interpreter (which includes procedures for operating upon the representation).

Surface Representations

Some artifacts are capable only of a surface level representation. Thus, memory aids such as paper, books, and blackboards are useful because they allow for the display and (relatively) permanent maintenance of representations. The slide rule and abacus are examples of computational devices which only contain surface representations of their information. These devices are primarily systems for making possible the display and maintenance of symbols: They implement the "physical" part of the physical symbol system. These are called *surface representations* because the symbols are maintained at the visible "surface" of the device – for example, marks on the surface, as pencil or ink marks on paper, chalk on a board, indentations in sand, clay or wood.

Internal Representations

Artifacts that have internal representations are those in which the symbols are maintained internally within the device (unlike paper and pencil where the symbols are always visible on the "surface"). This poses an immediate requirement on the artifact: There must be an interface that transforms the internal representation into some surface representation that can be interpreted and used by the person. Artifacts that have only surface representations do not have such a requirement, for the surface representation itself serves as the interface.

The Interface between Artifact and Person

Cognitive artifacts need interfaces for several reasons. In the case of artifacts with internal representations, the internal representation is inaccessible to the user, so the interface is essential for any use of the artifact. Moreover, even for artifacts that have only surface representations, the style and format of the interface determine the usability of the device. Here, the standard issues in the field of interface design apply.

We can conceptualize the artifact and its interface in this way. A person is a system with an active, internal representation. For an artifact to be usable, the surface representation must correspond to something that is interpretable by the person, and the operations required to modify the information within the artifact must be performable by the user. The interface serves to transform the properties of the artifact's representational system to those that match the properties of the person.

To the user of an artifact, the representing world is the surface of the artifact – the information structures accessible to the person employing the artifact. One of the basic issues in developing an artifact is the choice of mapping between the representing world and the represented world (or between the surface representation and the task domain being supported by the artifact). In the mapping between the represented world and the representing world of the artifact, the choice of representation determines how faithfully the match is met.

The Object Symbol

One major concern in interfaces is the relationship between control operation and system state. Usually, these two aspects of the interface are separated and handled by different components. The two different aspects are not always present, and even when they are, they may differ considerably from one another in physical location, conception, and form of representation. This independence of control and display was not always true, and it seems to have arisen more by historical accident than by design.

Some controls have the interesting representational property that they serve both as the objects to be operated upon and also as representations of their states (see Figure 2.4). Simple examples occur for any controls operated by physical levers, where the act of moving the lever changes both the system state and also the physical appearance of the device: The position of the lever is both the actual state of the device and also its representation. Norman and Hutchins named the situation where the physical object is both the object operated upon and the symbol of its state the "object symbol" (Norman & Hutchins, 1988).[1]

---

1. The special case in which the same object serves as both a control of its value and a representation of its value was first described by Draper (1986), who argued for the importance of treating input and output to a computer system as a unified activity.

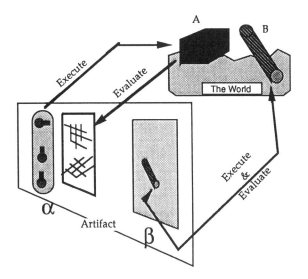

Figure 2.4. The object symbol. When a person manipulates a real or virtual world through an artifact, when the object in the artifact is both the means of control (for execution of actions) and also the representation of the object state (for evaluation), then we have the case of an object symbol. In condition α, the execution and evaluation are done separately. In condition β, the same representation is used for execution and evaluation; β represents the case of the object symbol.

Object symbols used to be the prevailing mode of operation, for they represent the natural and frequently occurring mode of operation with mechanical systems, especially simpler systems. Many mechanical systems have the property that one directly manipulates the parts of interest and that one assesses the state of the device from the position of those same parts. The object symbol situation disappears when controls are physically removed from the site of action.

In the modern world of computer controls, the object symbol is rare. With modern electronic systems, the controls and indicators have almost no physical or spatial relationships to the device itself, which introduces an arbitrary or abstract relationship between the controls, the indicators, and the state of the system. But this state of affairs has come about by accident, not by design. The advantages of separating controls from physical equipment led to a natural separation of object and symbol. Once there was a separation, then the control no longer signaled system state. The result has been separation of the control of state from the indicator of state and, in some systems, a complete neglect of the development of appropriate representational forms for either control or display.

Figure 2.5. Substitutive and additive
dimensions. Each of the ovals represents the representational aspects of
values along the dimension from A to
E. In the substitutive case, the representations replace one another. In the
additive case, each successive representation includes the previous. Examples of additive dimensions are
loudness and brightness. Examples of
substitutive dimensions are pitch and
hue.

A Substitutive Dimension

An Additive Dimension

Additive and Substitutive Dimensions

Many years ago, Stevens identified two forms of psychological representational
dimensions or scales: additive and substitutive (Stevens, 1957). In an additive scale,
the representations could be ordered, with each succeeding one containing the one
before it, plus perhaps new aspects. The psychological percepts of loudness and
brightness (which are the psychological mappings of physical sound and light intensi-
ties) form additive scales. In a substitutive scale, each new item replaces the one
before it, with perhaps some overlap of attributes. The psychological percepts of
pitch and hue (which are the psychological mappings of physical sound frequency
and light wavelength) form substitutive scales.

Restle (1961) showed that these two scale types could be represented in set-
theoretic terms (as shown in Figure 2.5). In an additive scale, "as one moves along
the sequence of sets one picks up new aspects, and one never loses any of the old
ones. Any such sequence of sets is ordered in a strict way, and distances are
additive" (Restle, 1961, p. 49). In a substitutive scale where, for example, one is
moving from state A to state B, "each step of the process involves discarding some
elements from A and adding some new elements from B. Elements from A which
have earlier been discarded are never reused and elements from B which have been
added are never discarded. . . . each move along the scale involves substituting
some elements from B for some of the elements of A" (Restle, 1961, p. 50).

Representational Naturalness

I propose the following hypotheses about the form of representation used in a
cognitive artifact.

> **Hypothesis 1:** *The "naturalness" of a mapping is related to the
> directness of the mapping, where directness can be measured by the
> complexity of the relationship between representation and value,
> measured by the length of the description of that mapping.*

The use of "length of description" as the measure of naturalness is taken from the analogous use in specifying the complexity of a statement in complexity theory. The length of the description is, of course, a function of the terms used for the description. I propose that the terms be psychological, perceptual primitives.

It is important not to confuse the idea of the mapping terms with natural language or conscious awareness. The mapping terms are purely formal and do not imply that the person is aware of them. They are not terms in natural language.

> *Hypothesis 2: Experts derive more efficient mapping terms, thus reducing the complexity of a mapping and increasing its feeling of "naturalness." However, although these derived terms may simplify the mapping relationship, they always extract some penalty in time or computation (and, thereby, in mental workload) for their interpretation.*

Hypothesis 2 accounts for the phenomenon that experts can apparently get used to any representation, without obvious decrease in performance (except for learning time). This hypothesis allows the apparent complexity and naturalness of a representation to change with the development of expert skill. However, because the derived mapping terms are built upon some set of perceptual primitives, these derived terms will need to be interpreted, thereby extracting some information-processing workload. In normal behavior, this will probably not be noticeable, but in times of heavy workload or stress, the extra workload required to use the derived terms should degrade performance.

In other words, although experts can get used to anything and even claim it to be natural and easy to use, less natural representations will suffer first under periods of heavy workload and stress.

Finally, I suggest that the choice of representation for the mapping between the representing world (the surface representation) and the represented world (the task domain being supported by the artifact) follow a guiding principle for appropriateness taken from the work of Mackinlay, Card, and Robertson (1989):

> *Appropriateness principle: The surface representation used by the artifact should allow the person to work with exactly the information acceptable to the task: neither more nor less.*[2]

---

2. This principle is a direct paraphrase of the expressiveness principle for input devices developed by Mackinlay, Card, & Robertson (1989), namely: *"An input device should allow the user to express exactly the information acceptable to the application: neither more nor less"* (emphasis added). Mackinlay et al. were developing a language for describing the mapping between input device and function, which meant they were on a parallel undertaking to the one described here. In principle, their analyses can be translated into the ones needed for the study of the representational properties of artifact.

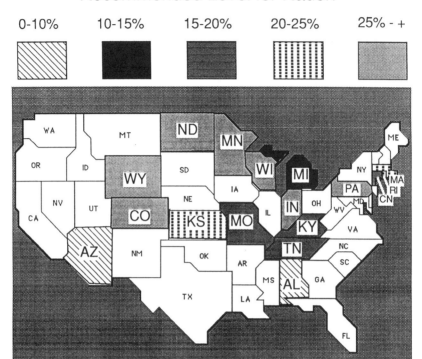

Figure 2.6. An unnatural mapping. Here, percentage (which is an additive dimension) is represented by a substitutive scale – different shadings. And where the shadings can be ordered along an additive scale, the ordering conflicts with the ordering of percentages. (Redrawn from a figure in the *Los Angeles Times,* September 13, 1988, p. 21.)

Using Density to Represent Numerical Value

Example: Contrast the case where an additive scale is used to represent an additive domain with one in which a substitutive scale is used to represent an additive domain. Figure 2.6 illustrates the representation of percentages (an additive scale) by arbitrary shadings. According to Hypothesis 1, the superior representation would be to use an ordered sequence of density (an additive scale) to represent percentages (an additive scale), as shown in Figure 2.7.

Note that there is still a problem with the representation in Figure 2.7, but the problem helps emphasize the point about the importance of matching representational format. The white areas, perceptually, appear to represent the states with the least concentration of radon. This is because white fits on the ordered density scale to the left of (less than) the 0–10% density. In fact, white represents those states for

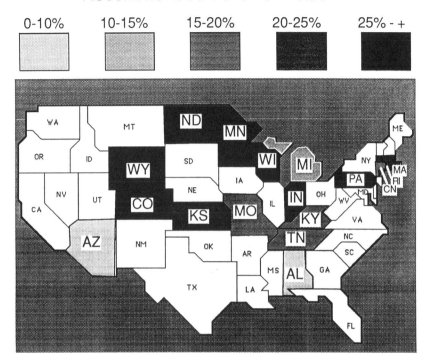

Figure 2.7. A natural mapping. Here, the map of Figure 2.6 has been redrawn so that percentage (which is an additive dimension) is represented by an additive scale – ordered densities of shading. Now, the density ordering matches the percentage ordering. (Redrawn from a figure in the *Los Angeles Times*, September 13, 1988, p. 21.)

which there are no data. One way to represent this situation to avoid the conflict in representational interpretation would be to delete the states for which there is no information from the map. I chose the method shown because the natural misinterpretation helps make the point about the impact of representational scale.

Color hue is frequently used to represent density or quantity, especially in geographic maps, satellite photographs, and medical imagery. But hue is a substitutive scale, and the values of interest are almost always additive scales. Hence, according to Hypothesis 1, hue is inappropriate for this purpose. The use of hue should lead to interpretive difficulties. In fact, people who use these color representations do demonstrate difficulties by their continual need to refer to the legend that gives the mapping between the additive scale of interest and the hues. According to the hypothesis, density or brightness would provide a superior representation. It would probably be even better to use a spatial third dimension for representing this information.

Figure 2.8. Differing representations for numerical quantity. If one simply wishes to compare numerical values, tally marks are superior to Arabic numerals, for the length of the representation is analogous to the numerical value. If one wants to do arithmetic operations, the symbolic (Arabic) representation is better, even though length is not a good indication of value. The Roman numeral representation is a compromise, being somewhat symbolic, but also approximately proportional to the value being represented.

Tally Marks

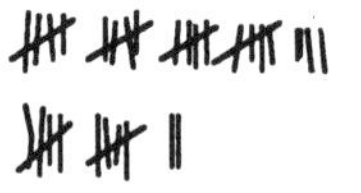

Roman Numerals   XXIII
                  XII

Arabic Numerals   23
                  12

Legends of maps and graphs are usually used to present the mapping rule for the representational code being used. According to my hypotheses, frequent use of legends is a sign of inappropriate representational mapping. With appropriate representations, the mapping code is easily learned and applied: Legends should not be essential to understanding.

Representations for Comparing Numerical Counts

Even such a simple example as counting items in order to compare quantity provides another instance of the use of mapping rules. When one is interested in comparing the values of counts to determine which is greater, according to these hypotheses, the superior form of representation will have the *size* of the representation itself map onto the size of the number. Size comparisons require additive comparisons.

Line length provides an additive representation. The Arabic numeral method for representing number does not. Counting methods that use tally marks to represent the number of objects translate number into length – in this case, the length of the space required to show the tally marks (Figure 2.8). Tally marks, therefore, provide an additive representation in which the size of the representation is related to the value of the number.

Thus, according to Hypothesis 1, Arabic notation is inferior for simple Boolean comparisons because its perceptual representation bears little relationship to its numerical value: There is only a weak perceptual relationship between the physical dimensions of a numerical representation and its numerical value (the physical length of the number – how many digits it contains – is proportional to the logarithm of its value but with a discreteness of resolution good only to within a factor of 10). But Arabic notation is superior to all other common notations when numerical operations need to be performed.

Most people feel uncomfortable with this result because the comparison of Arabic numerals seems natural and straightforward. Here is where Hypothesis 2 comes into play. Most people forget the years of training it has taken to reach this state of naturalness. Moreover, there is psychological evidence that the time to compare two different (Arabic) numbers varies with the size of the difference between the numbers, strongly suggesting that an internal translation has to be made into the more primitive, additive representation, as suggested by Hypothesis 2. Moreover, I would predict that under heavy workload, comparisons of Arabic numbers would suffer.

However, in cases where an exact numerical value is required or where numerical operations need to be performed, Arabic notation is clearly superior – which is why it is the standard notation used today. The form of representation most appropriate for an artifact depends upon the task to be performed, which is one reason that so many different numerical representations do exist (Ifrah, 1987; Nickerson, 1988).

Intrinsic Properties of Representation

Some years ago, Palmer described several properties of representations, including two that he called "intrinsic" and "extrinsic" (Palmer, 1978). The important point of these attributes is that they constrain what one can do with representations. A simple example will suffice.

Consider three objects: A, B, and C. Suppose that we know that object A is taller than both object B and object C, but we don't know which is taller, B or C. We can represent this state of affairs very nicely by symbolic expressions. Let $H(i)$ be the height of object i. Then we know that:

$$H(A) > H(B);$$
$$H(A) > H(C).$$

We do not know the relationship between $H(B)$ and $H(C)$, and this symbolic form of representation does not force us to represent the relationship. That is an important, positive aspect of this form of representation. However, on the negative side, there is nothing to stop us from writing a contradictory statement:

$$H(B) > H(A),$$

or even

$$H(A) > H(A).$$

Suppose we represented the objects by a visual image: In the image, height of the object would be represented by height of the image. A possible representation for the three objects is shown in Figure 2.9.

Note that with an image, it is simply not possible to represent an object without also representing its form and size: In this case, the representation of height is an *intrinsic* property of a visual image. Moreover, it is simply not possible to enter

Figure 2.9. Intrinsic properties of a representation. Using images to represent the objects A, B, and C, we cannot also avoid representing their form and dimensions. Even if we did not know the height of C, we would be forced to select some value under this form of representation.

a contradictory statement in the same way that we could with the other representational format.

The form of representation used by an artifact carries great weight in determining its functionality and utility. The choice of representation is not arbitrary: Each particular representation provides a set of constraints and intrinsic and extrinsic properties. Each representation emphasizes some mappings at the expense of others, makes some explicit and visible, whereas others are neglected, and the physical form suggests and reminds the person of the set of possible operations. Appropriate use of intrinsic properties can constrain behavior in desirable or undesirable ways.

Forcing functions are design properties that use the intrinsic properties of a representation to force a specific behavior upon the person (Norman, 1988). Thus, in normal operation, it is not possible to start a modern automobile without the proper key, for the ignition switch is operated by turning the key: The switch has a built-in forcing function that requires insertion of the key. One of the intrinsic properties of the lock is the lack of affordances for turning. One of the intrinsic properties of a key is the affordance it offers for rotation of the lock (assuming it is the proper key for the particular lock). However, it is possible to leave the automobile without removing the key from the ignition – there is no forcing function.[3]

Any design can be thought of as a representation. The designer has to decide how to represent the features of the device, how to implement the operation, and how to represent the current state. In the choice of design, many factors come into play, including aesthetics, cost, manufacturing efficiency, and usability. The face that the device puts forward to the person is often a compromise among the competing requirements of these different factors, but this face – the interface – is a representation. Forcing functions are simply the manifestations of the intrinsic properties of the design representention.

Representations carry with them many subtle intrinsic properties, often ones not intended by the designer. Line lengths represent quantity, and two lines of different lengths thereby intrinsically present a comparison of the lengths, even if that is not intended by the designer. Many inappropriate uses of graphs can be traced to conflicts with the unintended intrinsic properties of the graphs.

---

3. Bells and alarms that accompany the opening of the door without removing the key are not forcing functions. These are reminders – extrinsic or added-on properties of the system. They can remind the user but they allow the behavior. A forcing function would require the key to open the door, or perhaps make it so that the door would not open with the key still in the ignition. These forcing functions, of course, have undesirable consequences.

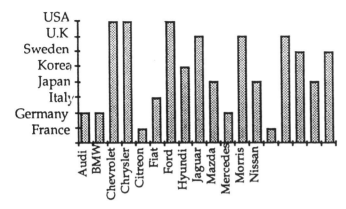

Figure 2.10. Inappropriate use of an additive scale. This example, inspired by Mackinlay (1986), shows that additive scales have the intrinsic property of numerical value and, therefore, they imply numerical comparison. This, of course, is an inappropriate operation for these data. Note that there is no formal problem with the representation save for the erroneous implication.

Additive Scales for Qualitative Information

A marvelous demonstration of how representational format can be misused in graphs is presented by Mackinlay (1986). Suppose we wish to represent the country of origin of various automobiles. Mackinlay points out that the example shown in Figure 2.10 is clearly inappropriate.

Clearly, the choice of a bar graph is inappropriate for this purpose. But why? What is the problem with Figure 2.10? The bar graph does uniquely specify the desired relationship between manufacture and country: There is no formal problem with the presentation. The problem arises from the intrinsic, additive properties of the lengths of bars. Additive scales have the intrinsic property of numerical value and, therefore, they imply numerical comparison. This, of course, is an inappropriate operation for these data. Finally, the bar graph violates the appropriateness principle – that the surface representation used by the artifact should allow the person to work with exactly the information acceptable to the task: neither more nor less. In this case, the bars are capable of carrying more informational structure than the task permits. The excess informational value permitted by the graph is clearly inappropriate: The graph – and any artifact – should use a representation that is nether too rich nor too poor.

Summary

Cognitive artifacts play an important role in human performance. In this chapter I provide the beginning of an analysis of their critical components by focusing upon three aspects of artifacts:

their role in enhancing cognition (the difference between the system and the personal point of view);

the degrees of engagement that one can experience;

the role of representational format.

The study of artifacts can lead to several advances. First, because so many human activities depend upon artifacts, a full understanding of those activities requires an understanding of the human information-processing mechanisms, the internal knowledge of the human, and also the structure, capabilities, and representational status of the artifacts. Second, by understanding the ways in which cognitive artifacts serve human cognition, we may be better able to design new ones and improve old ones.

A major theme of the chapters in this book is the role of artifact, both in support of human activities and also as a tool for the understanding of human cognition. Artifacts play a critical role in almost all human activity. Indeed, as the quotation from Cole with which I opened this chapter suggests, the development of artifacts, their use, and then the propagation of knowledge and skills of the artifacts to subsequent generations of humans are among the distinctive characteristics of human beings as a species. The evolution of artifacts over tens of thousands of years of usage and mutual dependence between human and artifact provides a fertile source of information about both. The study of the artifact informs us about the characteristics of the human. The study of the human informs us of the appropriate characteristics of artifacts. And the study of both the artifact and the human must emphasize the interactions between and the complementarity of the two. The study of the relationship between humans and the artifacts of cognition provides a fertile ground for the development of both theory and application.

Acknowledgments

Much of this chapter reflects joint work and thinking with my research collaborator, Ed Hutchins. I wish to acknowledge my strong debt and gratitude to Ed for his contributions and my thanks for his permission to use them in this way throughout this chapter.

I am grateful to the many people who have commented and aided in this work. In particular, I thank Jack Carroll, Mike Cole, Emmy Goldknopf, and Hank Strub for their comments, intensive critiques, and suggestions. The working group for this conference, of course, was a valuable source of feedback and considerable thanks must go to them and to Jack Carroll for providing the framework for the interaction.

Research support was provided by grant NCC 2-591 to Donald Norman and Edwin Hutchins from the Ames Research Center of the National Aeronautics and Space Agency in the Aviation Safety–Automation Program. Everett Palmer served as technical monitor. Additional support was provided by funds from the Apple Computer Company and the Digital Equipment Corporation to the Affiliates of Cognitive Science at UCSD.

References

Bødker, S. (1989). A human activity approach to user interfaces. *Human–Computer Interaction, 4,* 171–195.

Cole, M. (1990). Cultural psychology: A once and future discipline? Paper presented at the Nebraska Symposium, 1989.

Cole, M., & Griffin, P. (1980). Cultural amplifiers reconsidered. In D. R. Olson (Ed.), *The social foundations of language and thought.* New York: Norton.

Degani, A., & Wiener, E. L. (1990, February). *Human factors of flight-deck checklists: The normal checklist* (Contractor's Report). Moffett Field, CA: National Aeronautics and Space Administration, Ames Research Center.

Draper, S. W. (1986). Display managers as a basis for user–machine interaction. In D. A. Norman & S. W. Draper (Eds.), *User centered system design: New perspectives in human–computer interaction* (pp. 339–352). Hillsdale, NJ: Lawrence Erlbaum Associates.

Hutchins, E. (1986). Mediation and automatization. *Quarterly Newsletter of the Laboratory of Comparative Human Cognition: University of California, San Diego, 8*(2), 47–58.

Hutchins, E., Hollan, J., & Norman, D. A. (1986). Direct manipulation interfaces. In D. A. Norman & S. Draper (Eds.), *User centered system design: New perspectives in human–computer interaction.* Hillsdale, NJ: Lawrence Erlbaum Associates.

Ifrah, G. (1987). *From one to zero: A universal history of numbers* (L. Bair, Trans.). New York: Penguin Books. (Original work published 1981)

Laurel, B. K. (1986). Interface as mimesis. In D. A. Norman & S. W. Draper (Eds.), *User centered system design: New perspectives in human–computer interaction* (pp. 67–85). Hillsdale, NJ: Lawrence Erlbaum Associates.

Leont'ev, A. N. (1981). *Problems of the development of mind.* Moscow: Progress Publishers.

Luria, A. R. (1979). *The making of mind: A personal account of Soviet psychology.* (M. Cole & S. Cole, Eds.). Cambridge, MA: Harvard University Press.

Mackinlay, J. D. (1986). Automating the design of graphical presentations of relational information. *ACM Transactions on Graphics, 5* (2), 110–141.

Mackinlay, J. D., Card, S. K., & Robertson, G. G. (1989). *A semantic analysis and taxonomy of input devices.* Unpublished manuscript, Xerox Palo Alto Research Center.

Newell, A. (1981). The knowledge level. *AI Magazine, 2,* 1–20. Also published in *Artificial Intelligence,* 1982, *18,* 87–127.

Nickerson, R. (1988). Counting, computing, and the representation of numbers. *Human Factors, 30,* 181–199.

Norman, D. A. (1986). Cognitive engineering. In D. A. Norman & S. W. Draper (Eds.), *User centered system design: New perspectives in human–computer interaction.* Hillsdale, NJ: Lawrence Erlbaum Associates.

Norman, D. A. (1988). *The psychology of everyday things.* New York: Basic Books. Also published in paperback as D. A. Norman. (1990). *The design of everyday things.* New York: Doubleday.

Norman, D. A., & Hutchins, E. (1990). *Checklists.* Unpublished manuscript, Department of Cognitive Science, University of California, San Diego.

Norman, D. A., & Hutchins, E. L. (1988). *Computation via direct manipulation* (Final Report: ONR Contract N00014-85-C-0133). La Jolla, CA: University of California, San Diego, Institute for Cognitive Science.

NTSB. (1989). *Aircraft accident report – Delta Air Lines, Inc., Boeing 727–232, N473DA, Dallas-Fort Worth International Airport, Texas, August 31, 1988* (Report No: NTSB/

AAR-88/05, Govt. Accession No: PB 89/04. September 26, 1989). Washington, DC: National Transportation Safety Board.

Palmer, S. (1978). Fundamental aspects of cognitive representation. In E. Rosch & B. B. Lloyd (Eds.), *Cognition and categorization.* Hillsdale, NJ: Lawrence Erlbaum Associates.

Restle, F. (1961). *Psychology of judgment and choice.* New York: Wiley.

Rumelhart, D. E., & Norman, D. A. (1988). Representation in memory. In R. C. Atkinson, R. J. Herrnstein, G. Lindzey, & R. D. Luce (Eds.), *Stevens' handbook of experimental psychology.* New York: Wiley.

Stevens, S. S. (1957). On the psychophysical law. *Psychological Review, 64,* 153–181.

Vygotsky, L. S. (1978). *Mind in society: The development of higher mental processes.* (M. Cole, V. John-Steiner, S. Scribner, & E. Souberman, Eds.). Cambridge, MA: Harvard University Press.

Wertsch, J. V. (1985). *Vygotsky and the social formation of mind.* Cambridge, MA: Harvard University Press.

Wundt, W. M. (1916). *Elements of folk psychology: Outlines of a psychological history of the development of mankind* (Edward Leroy Schaub, Trans.). London: Allen & Unwin.

3
Some Remarks on the Theory–Practice Gap

Zenon W. Pylyshyn

Since there is precedent for beginning on a personal note, I provide mine. Confession, it is said, is good for the soul. My first confession is that I have wanted to contribute to a practical enterprise within cognitive science for many years. Time and again I have set out to investigate why some computer systems are better than others, some languages more perspicuous than others, some layouts more informative than others. But each time I left the problem unsolved because sooner or later I was faced with the choice of either abandoning the original problem of interest and instead doing something that seemed to me both trivial and atheoretical, or else doing something that was relevant to some theoretical issue but had little to do with the practical problem at hand. The difficulty was with the idea of understanding *Why*-questions in general, because that kind of understanding implies being able to relate the phenomenon of interest to some theoretical framework, or at least to some general set of principles.

My second confession is that despite repeatedly abandoning direct research on applied problems in general, and HCI problems in particular, my grant applications continue to mention that the work that I do – on spatial vision and visual attention – is somehow relevant to the design of better computer interfaces ("user-friendly" is, I believe, the term of art). So part of me continues, it seems, to maintain the belief that basic research and theory construction in cognitive science will eventuate in principles that can be used to design displays that are maximally informative, and in general to contibute to a better distribution of labor between machines and their users. That puts me in an uncomfortable position – one from which I hope I can extricate myself. That is why I agreed to come to this workshop and to participate in a discussion of this perplexing dilemma.

Of course, there remains the possibility that there is no dilemma and I should be seeing a therapist rather than attending a workshop, but I will leave that option open for now.

Background: Can There Be a Theory of Practice?

I am torn between two views of the relation between theory and practice. First, there is the side of me that applies for grants and contracts, promotes the support of research, and advocates the investment of time and effort into projects on the promise that it will help mankind – at least in the medium-to-long term. I truly believe what I say to industrialists and governments about the long-term importance of research upon the well-being of citizens. I know, for example, that countries that spend a larger percent of their gross national product on research tend to have better economic conditions, and that countries that have better economic conditions tend to have better health and better standards of living (in fact health is more closely tied to economic well-being than to expenditures on medical care). So I never waver in my commitment to the premise that research and increased knowledge lead to a better life.

The other side of me looks around at the areas where research is being done, especially in the social sciences, and notices that practical improvements are rarely related to the scientific theories that the innovators hold – and certainly not to the truth of any such theories. Rather, practical progress appears to be related to general wisdom, to the occurrence of the occasional good idea, and to the invention of new gadgets, new techniques, and new methods of bringing products to market (i.e., to new manufacturing methods or new ways of organizing the efforts of many – such as in the space program, which involved almost no new science but much innovation on the organization, production, and quality-confrol fronts).

Consider important areas such as education, welfare, economics, and, yes, the design of human–computer interfaces. I very much doubt that any improvements in these practical arts have ever been proposed because of their relation to validated scientific theories. That may be because one cannot have a theory of how things are in practice, in their ecologically natural setting, or what some people refer to as the "real world."

Let me try to defend this view, which I do not take to be pessimistic but merely realistic. The reason I do not take this position as an indictment of social science research is the same as the reason that I do not take the failure of the arts to create wealth (except in the perverse sense of accruing wealth to the art investors) as a sign of their irrelevance or unimportance.

The purpose of basic research is to provide an understanding of the essential nature of the universe, including the human side of the universe, and such understanding is not inherently useful in the project of building worlds. It is, rather, essential to the project of understanding who we are and what the underlying invisible structure of our world is.

Leibniz may have been the first to point out that there cannot be a theory of *practice*. Rationalists since Plato understood that theories in science are not about how things appear, but about how things are *essentially*. That is why the great age of progress in the physical sciences (the late 17th and the 18th centuries) was accompanied by a healthy disregard for what we might now call ecologically valid data. Galileo is an especially vivid example of a scientist whose disregard for the unexpurgated evidence of his senses allowed him to uncover deeper principles governing the physical world. Indeed, the one time when he seemed to depart from this essentially Platonist approach to theory and took observations seriously was in developing his theory of the tides, and that also happened to be the one area where his science went most seriously astray.

The social sciences are in a much worse position with respect to explanatory power than are the physical sciences. For one thing, the social sciences have typically taken one of their central tasks to be accounting for naturally occurring variance, and hence in predicting events as they occur in their natural settings. It is worth considering the possibility that so long as *being relevant to real life* is taken as one of the central goals of psychology, it may not be possible to succeed by applying the style of scientific theorizing that has been so successful in the physical sciences – namely, the discovery of a small set of basic principles from which a large and unexpected set of predictions can be derived. Rather, explanations of everyday naturally occurring events may have a character not unlike that of folk psychology. Phenomena will be explained by reference to massive interaction effects among knowledge, goals, perceptions, and resource-constrained mechanisms that instantiate the relevant processes, and these phenomena themselves may change in response to factors quite outside the domain of the theory – such as the number of hours the subjects have slept, how successful their sex life has been, the condition of their liver, and the acidity of their stomach. If that is true, then the chances of there being a single theory, or even of a set of theories, that will explain behavior as it is found in nature is more than we can hope for. What makes the situation even worse is that in order for a social science theory to be useful it must meet a very stringent criterion: It must do better than the proverbial man in the street (or Granny). Indeed, it must do better than people with field experience in the relevant topic.

Even physicists are powerless compared with practicing experts in explaining, predicting, or controlling most natural physical events, which is why the business of selling expert systems is doing as well as it is, and why expert systems continue to get along without having deep theories built into them (certainly without social science theories). No physicist can predict from basic principles even the most rudimentary of everyday physical occurrences, such as what shape your car will take if it runs off the road, or where leaves will land when they fall off a tree. Such ecologically natural events are not even considered to be within the purview of the basic theory because it is taken for granted that they are the result not only of the unfolding of basic physical principles, but also of a large number of secondary and theoretically uninteresting factors, like the precise shape and strength of each individual square millimeter of the car body and all the resultant forces that get applied, or the wind or something else equally irrelevant to the inherent and essential causal structure of the universe, which alone is the concern of the science of physics.

Similarly, it would be absurd to ask of psychology that it predict, or even postdict from basic principles, who will believe the things I am now claiming or which marriages will last and which will fail. Yet we do ask this of people who are part of the community of psychologists, just as we ask related things of people who are part of the community of physical scientists – namely the clinical psychologists on the one hand, and the practicing engineers on the other. But how is it possible for these practitioners to operate successfully under such conditions? The answer is invariably that they do it not by virtue of their access to explicit underlying causal theories, either physical or psychological, but by virtue of their access to a body of experience, sometimes codified in terms of observations of recurring regularities (i.e, handbooks and published correlations), as well as their general common sense and wisdom.

Engineers do design electrical circuits, machinery, and bridges with little recourse to basic physical principles, let alone quantum mechanics. Of course they do have theories of sorts (e.g., they have Kirchoff's Law), but these are primarily sets of principles specifically developed to summarize regularities at a level appropriate for the design task – not at a level where the most general causal principles need to be stated for purposes of understanding the natural world. Similarly, psychologists do contribute to personnel selection and advertising design, where theory is virtually nonexistent, although correlations and other practical generalizations abound. Moreover, they contribute to counseling and psychotherapy with, in my view, important benefits even while in the grips of obviously false theories – such as operant conditioning, in the case of behavior modification, or psychoanalysis, transactional analysis, neurolinguistic programming, or even primal therapy or any of countless silly fads. Although the efficacy of the therapies is often questioned, I no longer doubt the essential benefits along some dimension or other of many practicing therapists. The reason they are of value is, in my view, that the therapists are often wise and sensitive and caring people.

The same is true of social scientists who have had an influence on practical affairs. For example, the "theories" of people like Gregory Bateson are not so much fundamental laws of psychology as they are insightful ways of conceptualizing some area of human concern, on a par with the analysis of Lévi-Strauss, Freud, Jung, or Darwin. There is no denying that some people have important and valuable insights, both into human nature and into the design of technologies. But we should not confuse wisdom and insightfulness with having a scientific theory. After all, it did not require knowledge of any psychological theory, or even training in psychological research, to make the sorts of insightful psychological observations of practical foibles that are contained in Don Norman's *Psychology of Everyday Things!*

The Relevance of Scientific Research to Practice

But I have been unfair to science. After all, as anyone who has been involved in scientific research knows, science is only asymptotically concerned with deep and general theories. On the way, especially in the social sciences, it is concerned with many other things. Some of these are listed here.

Scientific research is concerned with collecting objective observations and establishing taxonomies. In this respect all sciences, but especially social sciences like anthropology, share something with descriptive and taxonomic disciplines like botany or anatomy. They are more like "natural history" collectors than builders of axiomatic causal theories.

Scientific research is concerned with collecting small-scale generalizations, minimodels, and sets of related principles of limited scope.

Scientific research is concerned with collecting paradigm cases to go with each of its generalizations. This includes paradigm empirical demonstrations, paradigm experimental methods, even paradigm apparatus for doing the experiments.

Scientific research is concerned with developing tools and methodologies for empirically exploring some natural domain of events and properties. After all, most of a scientist's training goes into learning how to solve problems using the techniques of the field and into learning how to carry out experiments to answer particular questions which arise out of theories or out of mere curiosity.

Scientific research involves developing a sensitivity to what matters in a certain field. There is a considerable component of art and craftsmanship, or perhaps intuitive skill, that one picks up while studying in a scientific field. The *practice* of a particular science, as opposed to the theoretical content of that science, is something that has to be learned by apprenticeship, as in any profession. And what one learns includes the ability to ask the right questions, and in the process to distinguish important phenomena from ephemeral ones, essential variables from secondary ones, and "real" effects from artifacts of the method of observation.

All these skills are transferable, to some extent, to practical applications of a scientific domain. That is why training in relevant sciences is important to a practitioner: *not* because general theories in the basic science will tell you what to do in practice. When "theories" do tell you what to do – especially in the social sciences – you can be sure that it is for reasons other than their fundamental truth; for example, it may be because the "theory" serves as a mnemonic device to help recall some generalizations, or it may even be for ideological reasons. The latter is the case, for example, in the appeal to operant conditioning as the basis for the clinical practice of behavior modification. The fact is that when behavior modification works it is because the practitioner recognizes things that the theoretical ideology specifically denies; for example, that in order to apply reinforcements the practitioner must elicit the patient's trust and must get the patient's interpersonal attention (for example, eye contact is essential), that only acts that patients themselves find reassuring or comforting can serve as a reinforcers, and that patients are always trying to figure out what is going on in the therapy so that ultimately it is their interpretations and beliefs, rather than just their behavior, that has to change.

Scientific Research versus Scientific Theory Applied to Practice

If we drop the idea that the discovery of *why* people do things (in the scientific sense of why, in which an explanation is sought in terms of basic principles) is what will enable us to be better practitioners, then we can ask whether the body of science has anything to contribute to, say, the design of practical devices or educational programs or even the process of design itself. I have already indicated that training in research is relevant to the study of practical problems. Is there anything else that can be learned from scientific research that can be of more direct relevance to applied problems of design and HCI?

Clearly there is a lot that can be learned about HCI from research directed at evaluating and exploring the benefits of different design options. But what about more general morals? Is there anything in the research literature that might serve as guideposts or general hints as to what directions we might usefully take? Without pretending to have surveyed a range of literatures that might bear on this question, I can perhaps offer a few general questions from a highly personal perspective.

Lessons from Other Descriptive Sciences

Descriptive sciences in various areas have had considerable success in providing insights on how things are structured and even how they work, at a certain level of abstraction – not so much in terms of basic causal principles, but in terms of recurring patterns that are related to their function.

Take, for example, one of the best-known descriptive sciences, anatomy. I once had a discussion with an anatomist concerning the problems of discovering the structure of an organism by using purely anatomical methods, such as staining techniques. It soon became clear, however, that anatomists do not confine their methods to such techniques except in cases where there is independent reason to think that these techniques lead to distinguishing functionally distinct units (which they often do). Rather, their taxonomic methodology takes into account – often implicitly – what they know about the *function* of different types of tissues or different organs. After all, the purpose is not to distinguish things that look different on the surface, but things that will turn out to have different functions as well.

This illustrates a general point, first articulated with particular cogency by the Swiss linguist Ferdinand de Saussure. He pointed out that structures always occur in pairs. Whenever one finds an internal structure within each object in a set of objects, then there is a structure among distinct objects and vice versa (whenever there is a set of structural relations holding among objects in a set of objects, then there is a structure within each object that is related to this interobject structure): For every *syntagmatic* structure there is *paradigmatic* structure. In linguistics, the way to discover the phonological structure of a sound stream or the syntactic structure of a sentence is by looking at the differences and similarities that exist among sound streams or among sentences. Between-item structure induces within-item structure. That is the principle that linguistics uses, and it is also the principle that anatomy and botany use implicitly. You must know what differences among individuals you want to explain before you know what internal properties count as structural properties.

The same will be true of a descriptive study of artifacts and tasks and other things that we need to study descriptively in applied settings. As we compare tasks to determine the most relevant dimensions of similarity and difference we will at the same time be discovering the structure of these tasks. Thus I agree completely with Ruven Brooks, that task comparison is a central area of study that needs to be pursued if we are to understand how and where computers can usefully be applied and interfaced with work that needs to be done. I also agree that one of the products of such research should be a canonical language for describing tasks. We do not know in advance just how broad a range of tasks can be handled by a canonical language. I suspect that there will be the usual power–generality trade-off, so that the breadth of coverage will depend on what we need to accomplish with our task description. If we want to be able to predict which of two word processors will be fastest to use at asymptote, then we will doubtlessly need to decompose the task to a level similar to that of GOMS. But if we want to decide whether an icon-based or a command-based selection mode is best for some application, we may well be satisfied with a much coarser task taxonomy.

Inner versus Outer Taxonomies

There is an additional complication that arises in the case of tasks and artifacts as they apply to humans. What matters for the human user is not so much the objective structure of the task or artifact, but rather how it is perceived, understood, or *represented* by the person. Here again there is a similarity to many descriptive social sciences, including linguistics and anthropology. Pike (1967) distinguishes between *emic* and *etic* properties. The former are properties as represented by humans and are internal to the cognitive system. The latter are objective properties that are independent of any observer; they are external properties. What matters to what a person decides to do are emic properties. It is not how the world *is* that determines your actions, but how you take the world to be. That is the issue of intentionality of mental life and is one of the features that most sharply distinguishes psychology from other natural sciences. In practical terms, it suggests that if you want to do task analysis and description, you should try to view it from the point of view of the "natives" or the people who will be performing the tasks, rather than from the point of view of the objective outside observer. You should become an expert in the task first. That certainly is one of the messages one finds in studies of human problem solving such as Newell and Simon's (1972).

I should add in passing that although cognitive science has, quite reasonably, been concerned almost exclusively with emic or represented properties, it turns out that etic or physical properties are also important for certain purposes. This is being recognized more often now as visuomotor control becomes a more prominent area of study. When you face the problem of coordinating vision and movements, what is important is not only that you construct a certain internal description of the stimulus (or task) and then make decisions from this representation, which are then converted to motor commands. In addition, you have to link *particular places in the world* with the internal description and with arguments to motor commands. Otherwise your model of the organism leaves it detached from environmental particulars and hence incapable of acting upon places in its visual field. When you think "I must pick up the cup" and then make an appropriate movement, the concept "the cup" must be linked in some way to a particular place in the world. This must apply even when you do not have a unique description for the thing you want to pick up. For example, you may wish to pick up one particular marble from among a set of identical marbles. The description will not enable you select which one and to what location to address your motor movement. That has to be done through some mechanism that, in effect, makes what in language corresponds to an indexical reference; you have to entertain the thought that you want to pick up *that* thing. Such indexicals have been the Achilles' heel of traditional mentalistic models, and have led to some pretty unconventional ideas concerning so-called situated seman-tics. Although this semantical theory may be suspect, the idea that we need to "situate" our cognitive theories, or to ground them to physical properties, is impor-tant and highlights the need to have both emic (represented) and etic (physical) properties in our description of tasks and artifacts. This is especially clear when physical movements are required, since you obviously cannot give an adequate description of a task requiring movements without taking into account such physical properties as distance, mass, and stiffness (for example, of actuators). I mention this issue partly because the idea of cognitive indexicals has been the focus of my own research in the past few years and a statement of our theoretical position has just been published (Pylyshyn, 1989).

Studies of What Users Do

Another message that I think one can learn from recent research concerns the transformative nature of artifacts on tasks, and the pitfalls of studying *what people actually do* as a way of characterizing tasks. The example I want to discuss is the study of the process of design, because that is a problem that I have had an opportunity to look at, at least in a cursory way, in connection with trying to develop a program of research.

Task Demands versus What Experts Do: The Example of Psychological Studies of Design

In studying the design process it has been common to study architects, as represent-ing the prototypical designers. There has been a tradition in architecture to teach students about the stages that one must go through in designing a building. In particular there has been a strong emphasis on distinguishing the *analysis* stage from the *synthesis* stage.

Observations of professional architects, however, revealed that they did not work this way. For example, based on interviews with architects, Jane Darke (1979) confirmed that architects did not start off with a great deal of open-ended analysis, but rather focused quite early on some aspect of the design requirements that seemed important and used that to come up with some possible design ideas very early. Studies comparing problem-solving styles of architects and scientists (Lawson, 1979) also confirmed this general picture of how architectural design proceeds. Lawson gave both groups (as well as inexperienced architecture and science students) a complex blocks-design puzzle to do. The puzzle involved maxi-mizing the amount of a particular color showing while putting the blocks together according to certain geometrical constraints, as well as unstated requirements imposed by the experimenter, who provided feedback as to the legality of each arrangement of blocks. Although both groups performed the blocks puzzle equally well, the scientists made moves in order to try to discover the structure of the problem (in particular, the nature of the experimenter's rules), whereas the architects began by generating solutions until one was found to be acceptable. It appeared that the scientists used a *problem-focusing* strategy, whereas the architects used a *solution-focused* strategy.

In a somewhat different set of studies, Thomas and Carroll (1979) examined software designers. Their findings are also in agreement with the suggestions that designers are solution-focused. Experts, it seems, produce designs first and analyze the problem second or, as Thomas and Carroll put it, their results "suggest perhaps an overfocussing in software design on *quickly* getting *any* program that 'works' (runs) at the expense of other important but less quantifiable goals that would further constraint the solution." The generality of the conclusion about how designers approach their job was also confirmed by others using protocol analysis of architects, systems programmers, and engineers.

This apparently suboptimal way of approaching design tasks has been confirmed even more dramatically in a study of British architects, which suggests that architects, and perhaps many other professional designers, may not provide the best models of how design *should* be done.

A study by the U.K. Building Research Establishment (Pratt, 1984) concluded:

1. Designers seldom work up alternative concepts. They tend to stick with their initial idea, modifying it only as constraints demand.
2. Designers do not follow – and are unlikely to find acceptable – any rigid or inviolate sequence of design decisions.
3. Designers seem to make little attempt to record or even to get feedback from their completed buildings. They therefore tend not to complete the "learning loop" in their design experience. . . .
4. Designers prefer calling up their own or others' past experience in similar jobs to using published information. But they do not keep records, graphic or otherwise, of decisions taken as design progresses.

What are we to make of such findings? Do they suggest that design cannot be automated, or that we should not study designers? The fact that certain ill-structured problems, such as design, are approached in a certain way by experts may not tell us anything about how they *could,* or *should* be approached given certain computational aids. After all, even an optimal problem solver has to optimize a set of variables that include the computing costs of the method. So, for example, it may be very costly (in time or effort) to get all the relevant information, or it may be difficult to keep track of many options. In that case, an early focusing (or solution-focused) strategy may be optimal. But with different intellectual aids, such as appropriate artifacts, it may not be. What is clearly needed in such cases is a way of characterizing the task demands in a way that is as independent as possible of the way that the tasks are currently being carried out within existing extrinsic constraints: what might be called a *necessity analysis* in contrast with the *sufficiency analysis* more common in cognitive science.

Such an objective task analysis is a tall order indeed, because in the end understanding the task requires understanding all elements of the puzzle: the logical requirements that have to be met, the way in which the requirements and constraints are represented by the user, the resource constraints under which the user must operate (in terms of memory and attentional loads, channel capacity, visual and motor acuity and temporal latencies, and so on), and also the way in which the task requirements themselves could be altered if the economies of the process are changed. A natural approach to such a task-analysis problem is a pragmatic one: Try to specify what humanly doable subfunctions you think would *have to* be carried out in order for the task to be possible, leaving aside for the time being the question of which of these tasks might be offloaded to the computer.

Although that is a reasonable enough way to approach the problem, it does neglect an important property of technology; often technology does not enter the picture in the form of techniques or artifacts for carrying out one of the "logically required" subtasks, but as a way to bypass the need for the entire task. That is what is meant when people say that technologies are *transformative*.

This can happen in two ways. One is that the economies (including the cost of human effort) are such that it may turn out to be faster and cheaper to do a slightly different task from the one we were initially studying. In that case we might be satisfied with that even though it was not part of the original task description. This has happened frequently in office automation. The other is that technologies have a way of transforming not only how we do things, but what we do; they do not simply allow us to automate or improve what we set out to do, but often change what we think we want to do.

One of the examples I have sometimes cited to illustrate this point is the task of ironing clothes. One could have spent a lot of time working on a good human–machine interface for efficient ironing, but that could have been rendered irrelevant by the advent of no-iron fabrics. I say it *could have been*. Although this used to be one of my favorite examples of a transformative technology, it now turns out to have been a bad example. Despite no-iron fabrics, the current fashion dictates the use of natural-fiber fabrics, which require even more ironing than the ones that people were concerned with some years ago. Once again we find that the most rational analysis can be rendered irrelevant in the real practical world, which is messy enough to be governed not only by human reasoning, but also by the vagaries of fashion.

So we are back to my theme with which I started: You cannot have a theory of practice, and what practical fields need are perceptive people with some sensitivity to the tasks at hand, the potential for new technologies to help or bypass them, an ability to ask the right questions, and some training on how to answer such questions empirically in particular cases. In other words, there is no substitute for wisdom in dealing with real life.

References

Darke, J. (1979). The primary generator and the design process. *Design Studies, 1,* 36–44.

Lawson, B. R. (1979). Cognitive strategies in architectural design. *Ergonomics, 22,* 59–68.

Newell, A., & Simon, H. A. (1972). *Human problem solving.* Englewood Cliffs, NJ: Prentice-Hall.

Norman, D. A. (1988). *The psychology of everyday things.* New York: Basic Books.

Pike, K. L. (1967). *Language in relation to a unified theory of the structure of human behavior.* The Hague: Mouton.

Pratt, H. (1984). Case studies in design decision making. In R. Langdon & P. A. Purcell (Eds.), *Design theory and practice.* London: The Design Council.

Pylyshyn, Z. (1989). The role of location indexes in spatial perception: A sketch of the FINST spatial-index model. *Cognition, 31,* 65–97.

Thomas, J. C., & Carroll, J. M. (1979). The psychological study of design. *Design Studies, 1,* 5–11.

4

Comparative Task Analysis: An Alternative Direction for Human–Computer Interaction Science
Ruven Brooks

What Would Designers Like from Human–Computer Interaction Science?

Consider the following situation. A human–computer interaction specialist is approached by the head of a software design project with the following request:

We have some people who perform problem-solving task F. They are highly skilled at this task and have spent a long time learning to do F well. Since F is so important to our organization, our management is willing to devote considerable resources to developing new, more interactive tools for doing F. We'd like you to analyze the behavior of these people and tell us what kinds of tools we should build.

If I am the HCI specialist and if I have options as to how to respond to the request, I might begin by wondering what kind of response the project manager would find most useful. If the manager does, in fact, have the task of designing the tools completely, as versus providing a new interface to existing tools, then the following example of analysis might fulfill the manager's expectations:

When F is described using the N notation, problem solving in F seems to occur in two distinct phases. The first phase consists of two activities, and there is a great deal of alternation between them. Both activities 1 and 2 seem to be class C_{27} tasks that are characterized by high memory loads. As the task is now structured, workers must remember information retrieved in activity 1 throughout the processing of an M in activity 2. Since activity 2 is also a high-memory-load task, they have difficulty in remembering the activity 1 information, and they frequently need to return to activity 1 to retrieve the same information. Based on what has proved useful in other applications such as A_{27} and A_{59} with similar structure, what is needed is an external memory tool, in the form of a P, S, or Q display that shows the following six types of information for each M: . . .

The second phase of F is basically a C_{18} task but with aspect α_κ reduced to only a brief notation. The focus of activity shifts to performing the K analysis on each M that has been processed. Experience with other C_{18} tasks suggests that it is useful to look at the information generated in the K analysis to see whether it can be broken apart into independent categories. In fact, the information produced by K analysis can be divided into four types, which the current K analysis tool generates all in one pass and which requires a large number of input parameters, all of which must be correct for the program to succeed. According to the K-analysis specialist, the four types of information are calculated independently, but some of the inputs overlap. Based on the experience with the A_{52} application, which is also a C_{18} task, reorganizing the K analysis into four separate programs is likely to reduce errors despite the redundant entry of parameters.

This sort of response has three properties that are likely to be particularly valuable to the manager in designing the system. First, the response is based on the use

50

of systematically recorded knowledge about human behavior. Although there are clearly insightful individuals in every profession or occupation who are able to observe human behavior objectively, most specialists in domains other than psychology are unlikely to have the skill or knowledge to relate their observations to observations made in other domains. The contribution of the HCI specialist is distinct and, therefore, valuable.

Second, the response is presented in a framework and at a level of analysis that is useful for evaluating the impact of the major design decisions on user behavior. Dividing user activities into phases based on the kinds of problems being solved or on the kinds of information being used for decision making provides a useful basis for both partitioning functionality across different software tools and for predicting possible impacts of new tools on the problem-solving process. An analysis, such as traditional task analysis, that focused only on the individual steps in performing F would not be as useful for partitioning functionality.

Third, the response is highly specific to activity F. It suggests an actual design for the programs and interfaces that should be built for doing F, rather than suggesting principles or guidelines to be used in the design of such tools or metrics for evaluating how good the tools are.

HCI as Descriptive, Engineering Science

As useful as this form of response might be to the designer, most HCI specialists, particularly those trained as psychologists, would feel uncomfortable with producing it. There would probably be two primary bases for their discomfort. First, the advice being given was not based on a model of problem-solving behavior, at least not in the "technical theory" sense used by Newell and Card (1985). Instead, the basis of the analysis is classification of the new task in some kind of task taxonomy and the instantiation of schemata from that taxonomy. There is no reduction of the task to a combination of fundamental, idealized behavioral mechanisms or modeling elements, nor is there any claim that the taxonomy can be derived from a more general model of human behavior.

A second major problem is that the recommendations take the HCI specialist out of the ancillary role of providing tools or methodologies for interface design and into the primary role of the creation of the design itself. To fill this role, the computer-interaction specialist must have two kinds of knowledge:

Knowledge about F, perhaps as much as someone whose main occupation is F, and must be able to represent and describe F explicitly at a very detailed level;

Knowledge about the specifics of other kinds of tasks and about the interface designs that have been used for them (it may even be necessary for the specialist to understand the limitations and capabilities of existing tools for implementing the interface).

Granting for the moment the usefulness of the kind of response given to the software designer, what kind of discipline could produce it? That is, what sorts of models and methodologies should the field of HCI develop if it wants to produce this kind of analysis and advice from a sound scientific or engineering basis, so that the HCI specialists will be competent to provide it?

Adequate Description as Prerequisite to Technical Theory

Newell and Card (1985) argue that what HCI science ought to focus on developing is "technical" theories of HCI. By a technical theory, they mean one that is formal, manipulation-oriented, idealization-based, and cumulative. They argue that such theories provide a sound basis for design because they can provide both abstractions that encourage consideration of a broader or different range of design possibilities and design aids, such as tools for quantitatively evaluating alternatives. As examples, they cite organic chemistry, solid-state physics, molecular genetics, and mechanical engineering.

The previous view of HCI as relying heavily on description and taxonomy seems to contrast strongly with this position. In fact, an examination of some aspects of the earlier position suggests such a descriptive and taxonomic discipline is a natural and probably necessary part of evolution to such theoretical science. A starting point concerns the question of how technical theories for a design discipline are generated. Do they arise from reduction and specialization of some broader, more basic science or are they derived independently? One model of the relationship is that the natural science, physics, uncovers or proposes great laws or equations that describe enduring properties of the physical world. It does this by making hypotheses and collecting data to test the hypotheses. The resultant theories, however, may contain unknowns that are unmeasurable or forms that are insoluble. For example, Maxwell's Laws describe the fundamental electromagnetic interactions, but the differential equations involved do not have general closed-form solutions. To convert these general laws into practical engineering analysis or design tools, engineering makes appropriate simplifying assumptions that allow available numerical techniques to be applied. Assumptions about boundary conditions allow Maxwell's Laws to be simplified so that finite element analysis can be applied.

In general, though, the initial derivation of engineering science from basic science is an extremely rare event. Instead, what typically happens is that engineering analyses are invented independently of basic science. For example, circuit theory describes a set of phenomena that could be equally well described with Maxwell's equations, but which were invented independently because, until recently, Maxwell's equations could not be applied directly. In many engineering disciplines, such as civil engineering, most of the useful models never have been related back to physics or chemistry. Models in civil engineering for runoff and groundwater levels, for example, are not directly relatable to models of fluid flow in porous media.

Even if it is conceptually possible to relate an independently derived engineering theory back to a basic science, there may be no engineering motivation for doing so. In civil engineering, for example, much of the problem with existing models is in obtaining sufficient, meaningful measurements to apply them. Relating them to a more general formulation with even more unknowns is not a particularly attractive activity.

How then do engineering theories arise? A necessary kernel is the development of an appropriate abstraction that discards irrelevant details while isolating and emphasizing those properties of artifacts and situations that are most significant for design. Indeed, this property of abstraction may be more important than the extent to which the abstraction gives rise to manipulatable formalisms or prediction; by indicating what properties of an artifact really are significant, a good abstraction may lead both to invention of new artifacts that produce these aspects in novel ways and to novel uses for existing artifacts.

Given this characteristic, how do useful abstractions arise? Rarely will they be imported, isolated from the rest of their theoretical structure, from some more basic science; instead, it is far more likely that they will be derived from first-order descriptions or taxonomies for the artifacts and phenomena of the design discipline. The most probable reason why structural engineering views arbitrary structures in terms of frames and trusses is because this is the way actual structural components were described at the time the analyses were being developed; in a world in which all architecture consisted of domes, structural engineering would probably have different analysis primitives.

Newell and Card see the role of description as primarily that of identifying the phenomena of interest in a field: "Purely descriptive studies . . . can make important contributions to HCI, if they describe something novel or describe a previously unnoticed aspect of user behavior or serve as a major confirmation of other descriptive studies." In contrast, from the perspective taken here, developing good descriptions, particularly good taxonomy that adequately differentiates artifacts, is important in its own right because it is a useful, possibly necessary, precursor to appropriate formalism and, in turn, to technical theory.

Description as a Means of Communicating Design Experience

In addition to the role that artifact and phenomena description plays in giving rise to abstraction and theory formalization, it continues to play a central role in recording and communicating design experience, even in the mature stages of a design science when more formal analyses are available. The reason that this is frequently the case is that formal models or technical theories try to describe artifacts in as explicit detail as possible; indeed, much of their power depends on having such detailed information available. To make use of circuit theory, one must specify the interconnections and values of each individual component in the circuit. For all but the simplest circuits, though, it will be very difficult for an engineer to decide on the basis of the circuit diagram or, even, the diagram plus input and output signals, what the circuit does and whether it might be useful in some future design.

In contrast, describing a circuit as a "delta modulator analog to digital converter" enables the electrical engineer to recognize the circuit design as one that can be used in other contexts, although it may be little direct help in determining the electrical properties. (It is worth noting that there are many cases in which the mapping does go in both directions; describing a circuit as a "4th order Butterworth filter" both enables an engineer to recognize what the circuit does and provides a starting point for signal analysis.)

Good descriptive languages or systems must be able to express both the requirements or situations that gave rise to particular designs and the structure and properties of the designs themselves. In some engineering disciplines, such as electrical engineering or mechanical engineering, design requirements frequently grow out of the characteristics of other engineered artifacts whose properties are known; in these disciplines, the descriptive language focuses only on the artifacts that are being created, with the requirements being incorporated into the description of the artifacts. Referring to a device as a "delta modulator analog to digital converter" both describes the structure of the device as using delta modulation and gives its function, analog to digital conversion.

In other disciplines, where design requirements are derived from naturally occurring situations, accurate determination and description of the requirements become problems in their own right. In these disciplines, descriptive systems arise to characterize both different classes of design problems and different types of solutions. For example, in civil engineering, a standard textbook on earth-dam design (Sherard, Woodward, Gizienski, & Clevenger, 1963) has chapters both on the environment in which the dam will be built, such as foundation-soil type, earthquake hazard, and wave severity, and on dam designs and construction techniques, such as the use of thin-core versus homogeneous construction.

Making these distinctions serves a purpose roughly analogous to the diagnosis–treatment separation in medicine. Although the mapping from requirements to design may be one to one and "pathognomonic" (distinctly characteristic of a particular disease), keeping them separate at the descriptive level helps to ensure that the requirements are adequately characterized before design takes place. In the case where multiple designs are viable for a given set of requirements, it provides a framework in which the consideration of alternatives is encouraged.

The Current Status of Description in HCI Science

The preceding section argues for the importance of good descriptive systems in engineering or design sciences, both as a prerequisite to developing technical scientific theories and as a necessary prerequisite to accumulating design experience. As a relatively new design science, it is important, for both of these reasons, that HCI have powerful descriptive capabilities available. HCI most closely resembles the class of engineering disciplines, such as civil engineering and petroleum engineering, in which most of the requirements for designs arise out of naturally occurring entities or environments whose properties require considerable investigation before design can begin. In the case of HCI, the naturally occurring entities or environments are those of human behavior, both in isolated cognition and in social interaction.

Following the model for description used in these areas, the necessary descriptive capabilities for HCI should probably be of two distinct types. Languages or notations for describing tasks should permit describing the tasks for which computer applications and computer interfaces are being developed in such a way that commonalities and differences among the tasks are revealed. Similarly, languages or notations for describing computer systems from the standpoint of their appearance to their users should make it possible to identify broad classes of application and interface designs while, at the same time, permitting comparison of similar designs.

Describing Tasks

The description of tasks is an area in which the basic, cognitive science aspects of HCI potentially have the most to contribute. Certainly, HCI science and its broader predecessor, human-factors engineering, do not lack for descriptive and analytic notations; the question is as to whether they are at the right level and have the right sort of architecture to support matching to candidate designs.

One obvious candidate is the technique called *task analysis* from human-factors engineering (Drury, Paramore, Van Cott, Grey, & Corlett, 1987). This technique involves breaking down tasks into components and specifying the flow between components. In order to insure that all of the behavior is captured, it is important that all of the components be specified at as atomic a level as possible.

As the starting point for an HCI task-analysis language, human-factors task analysis has major drawbacks. First, the nature of the components is currently open and ad hoc; a typical example of an atomic task for a nuclear-power-plant monitoring system is "start recirculation pumps." Although there has been some effort to restrict the components by the use of "vocabulary control" for describing them, there is no widely accepted primitive set. This makes cross-task comparison difficult. Does "start recirculation pumps" involve just flipping a switch or does it require adjusting a control until a meter reaches a certain level?

Even if such a set of primitives became widely accepted, though, the very low level of the primitives and the lack of any formalism for summarization makes it difficult to use human-factors task analysis as the basis for task description in HCI. Suppose that such a task analysis were carried out for controlling a nuclear power plant and for piloting an aircraft. Each analysis might have thousands of instances of the task-analysis primitives. How could the similarities and differences between the tasks be determined?

Most of the more recent descriptive efforts in HCI science have focused on developing user models that can be used to analyze, predict, or explain the performance of users with different interface and system designs. Do user modeling systems provide the necessary descriptive capabilities?

The GOMS model (Card, Moran, & Newell, 1983) with its production system representation (Polson & Kieras, 1985) is probably the best established HCI user model, at least in terms of the body of supporting research, and is illustrative of what can be done with user models. Because the intent of the GOMS model is to capture differences in user behavior for specific tasks, its constructs – goals, operators, methods, and selection – are not primitives in the sense of a ground alphabet of symbols out of which higher level constructs are assembled; there is no exhaustive list of, say, goal primitives out of which all goals for all users can be constructed.

Rather, they specify classes that need to be filled in order to construct user models for the specific behaviors and activities. For example, to construct a GOMS model of the manuscript-editing task, one supplies task-specific goals such as EDIT-MANUSCRIPT or LOCATE-LINE.

Constructing a GOMS model does involve task analysis to identify the operations and basic objects of the task that will be manipulated by the methods, but, again, the constructs used for this purpose are ad hoc. In the manuscript-editing task, the constructs include WORD, TEXT-SEGMENT, and PLACE-IN-MANUSCRIPT. An entirely different set of constructs would presumably be needed for, say, task analysis for statistical data analysis.

Although models such as GOMS are of value in comparing interface or application designs within tasks, they have the same problems as human-factors task analysis for deciding what the similarities or differences are between tasks. Consider the problem of deciding whether a hydrocarbon well log data interpretation system should have the same user interface as a statistical data analysis system. Even if a complete GOMS unit-task analysis were available for the statistical analysis system interface, there is no way to decide how to compare the unit tasks for statistical analysis with those for hydrocarbon well log interpretation. (In fairness to the authors of the GOMS model, it must be pointed out that they do not advocate GOMS analysis for task description and note the lack of cognitive skills taxonomy. In its absence, they do provide an informal chart listing some possible skill dimensions and comparing a number of tasks on them, but they do not consider this to be even the beginnings of a powerful system.)

Are there other candidates? Developmental psychology and psychometrics may have something to offer, but the best current bets may come from outside of HCI science or psychological science, from the discipline of "knowledge engineering" for the construction of expert systems. Initially, work in this area attempted to use a single universal set of methods and techniques for all applications. More recently, though, attention has focused on developing problem-solving methods and systems that are specialized for particular classes of problems (Marcus, 1988), and Mc-Dermott (1988) has proposed a taxonomy of these methods. An example of a method within that taxonomy is *propose-and-revise,* which can be used to solve design problems that involve selecting a configuration of components from a fixed catalog.

Although not made explicit, this method taxonomy is presumably equivalent to a taxonomy of tasks that could be attacked by these methods. How to go about classifying a new task is also unaddressed, but using a taxonomy based on the methods required to solve problems seems to hold promise that once a task has been analyzed using this taxonomy, it will be relatively easy both to compare it to other tasks and to map from the task onto computer application and interface designs.

Describing User Interfaces

Strangely enough, given the central role of notation in computer science, a similar description deficiency exists on the interface side. There is, of course, a large and rapidly growing set of formalisms used to describe user interfaces that range from tool kits of components for actual interface construction to various kinds of state diagrams for specifying flow of control to algebraic specification of the semantics of interface components. There are two problems with these notations. The first is that most of these specifications are quite detailed and low-leveled. In some of them, such as the X Window tool kits, the position at which a menu pops up is specified in terms of screen pixel coordinates. Comparing two different interfaces to say how they are alike or different can be done only at the level of line-by-line comparison of specification code, and there are no ways to characterize more generally the differences that are found other than by listing them exhaustively. This makes it impossible to characterize an interface style or "look and feel" except, perhaps, by vague comparison to some existing, well-known interface. Were someone to publish a catalog of interface designs based on this level of description, it is hard to conceive of what the table of contents or the index would look like.

The second problem with using software specification languages as interface description languages for HCI is that the linkage to the task is often obscure. At best, those pieces of software built using facilities structured on a user-interface management system model (as versus a tool kit model) clearly separate the specification of the interface from the calls to the underlying application routines, but it does not make clear the application structure. The notation might make clear that, when "CompleteScoring" is selected from a menu, appl-comp-scr will be invoked, but it provides no help in understanding what the "appl-comp-scr" routine does.

At least the first of these problems is currently under attack from within the user-interface design and development community. There is considerable work underway directed toward higher-level description of interface designs and characteristics. For example, Apperley and Spence (1989) present a notation for menu structures that can specify behavioral characteristics of menus such as whether they are multichoice or single choice and whether they invoke submenus. A description of the entire menu structure of an application of moderate complexity could fit on a single page when shown in a diagrammatic form. An equivalent text string notation has potential as a basis for comparison of applications.

Another example of work in this area, task-action grammars (Payne & Green, 1989), is still basically intended to map between user-interface actions and implementation software routines but even offers some possibilities for addressing the second problem. The "Task Features" and "Co-Occurrence Restrictions" constructs in the grammar can be used to express information about the task beyond the routines of the software implementation. While comparison of simple interfaces by comparing their task-action grammars has been demonstrated, the extension to more realistic interfaces remains an open question.

Directions for Description in HCI

Work on comparative description of interfaces is, in part, driven by the needs of software construction and is therefore likely to progress, although perhaps not in the directions most serviceable to HCI. Work on comparative description of tasks is also likely to go forward, driven by the knowledge-engineering community. What kinds of description system development are still a worthwhile focus for HCI activity?

As the work on problem-solving methods for expert systems illustrates, there may be a large variety of bases for defining task taxonomies, and the taxonomies can vary widely in the range of tasks they cover. The focus of the knowledge-engineering community is likely to be on taxonomies for those aspects of tasks for which automated problem-solving methods are available, and taxonomy refinement and differentiation is likely to be driven more by the appearance of new problem-solving methods than by desires for more detailed or more accurate task description. Furthermore, they are unlikely to provide much for tasks for which they see the problem-solving methods as uninteresting; a taxonomy of data entry tasks is unlikely to emerge from work on inference techniques. Although the knowledge-engineering community is likely to be a source of some types of task taxonomies, they are unlikely to provide the full range of description that would be useful to designers, and further work on description and taxonomy of tasks from an HCI perspective is still worthwhile.

This work ought to have three properties. First, description systems should be hierarchical in the sense that a given description should start with major descriptive categories or labels and then provide further detail within each of these categories. For example, a general class of "qualitative model-fitting tasks" might be defined in which the computing system was being used as an aid to fit a model to empirical data. This might be further broken down into tasks for which the primary problem was to select the mathematical form of the model versus those in which the form of the model is known, but in which parameters must be manually selected and adjusted for an optimal fit. Descriptions that have this structure lend themselves to differential comparison more readily than formalisms, such as those used for task analysis, that are essentially flat with only one level of detail.

Second, descriptive distinctions should have associated operational tests or procedures that can be used to perform classification on new tasks. At this stage, informal but operational distinctions should be preferred over theoretically rigorous but nonoperational ones. For example, suppose that a category of "generate simulation from a theoretical model" were proposed to complement the "qualitative model-fitting" classification given above. Both categories involve working with sets of numerical data, but an associated, operational distinction that could be used to separate tasks was whether an initial set of empirical data was available. Following the argument already given for description as a precondition for technical theory, starting with operational categories is likely to produce analyses and theory that are directly applicable to the actual artifacts and constructs available to designers.

Finally, and most important, the task descriptions should capture the commonalities and differences among the tasks in regard to their interface requirements. For example, social science data analysis, some kinds of economic forecasting, and hydrocarbon well log interpretation might all be described as "iterative parameter fitting of qualitative models to a set of empirical data." Describing all of these tasks as "iterative parameter fitting" suggests that all of them may require interface facilities for keeping track of the multiple versions of the set of parameter values. In contrast, if they were all "model selection" tasks, the interface would have to support tracking the different forms of model that had been tried, instead of the values of the parameters.

Readers of professional publications from a range of engineering disciplines are familiar with the calls for making these disciplines more scientific and rigorous by providing models and analytical tools with more formal structure and derivations from underlying scientific bases. Certainly, there is a similar need in HCI, and, as HCI evolves, more such models and theories ought to appear. In the interim, further work on description along these lines will be directly usable in design and may even be a necessary precondition to the emergence of theories.

Acknowledgments

The comments of other participants in the work were extremely valuable; in particular, Mary Beth Rosson's comments forced me to make explicit distinctions about types of description, which were vague in the original draft.

References

Apperly, M. D., & Spence, R. (1989). Lean cuisine: A low-fat notation for menus. *Interacting with Computers, 1*(1), 43–68.

Card, S. K., Moran, T. P., & Newell, A. (1983). *The psychology of human–computer interaction.* Hillsdale, NJ: Lawrence Erlbaum Associates.

Drury, C. G., Paramore, B., Van Cott, H. P., Grey, S. M., & Corlett, E. N. (1987). Task analysis. In G. Salvendy (Ed.), *Handbook of human factors* (pp. 370–401). New York: Wiley.

Marcus, S. (1988). *Automating knowledge acquisition for expert systems.* Boston: Kluwer Academic Publishers.

McDermott, J. (1988). Preliminary steps toward a taxonomy of problem-solving methods. In S. Marcus (Ed.), *Automating knowledge acquisition for expert systems* (pp. 225–256). Boston: Kluwer Academic Publishers.

Newell, A., & Card, S. K. (1985). The prospects for psychological science in human–computer interaction. *Human–Computer Interaction, 1*(3), 209–242.

Payne, S. J., & Green, T. R. G. (1989). The structure of command languages: An experiment on task–action grammar. *International Journal of Man–Machine Studies, 30*(2), 194–213.

Polson, P. G., & Kieras, D. E. (1985). A quantitative model of the learning and performance of text editing knowledge. In L. Borman & B. Curtis (Eds.), *Proceedings of CHI '85: Human Factors in Computing Systems* (pp. 207–212). New York: ACM.

Sherard, J. L., Woodward, R. J., Gizienski, S. F., & Clevenger, W. A. (1963). *Earth and earth-rock dams.* New York: Wiley.

5

Let's Get Real: A Position Paper on the Role of Cognitive Psychology in the Design of Humanly Useful and Usable Systems

Thomas K. Landauer

For the most part, useful theory is impossible, because the behavior of human–computer systems is chaotic or worse, highly complex, dependent on many unpredictable variables, or just too hard to understand. Where it is possible, the use of theory will be constrained and modest, because theories will be imprecise, will cover only limited aspects of behavior, will be applicable only to some parts of some systems, and will not necessarily generalize; as a result, they will yield little advantage over empirical methods.

Some useful theory will be of familiar homely kinds and have minor impact; examples include Fitts's Law, Hick's Law, the "Power" Law of practice, and laws of visual and auditory perception. More useful "theories" will be of new but mundane kinds. Example here include data-based simulations; qualitative understanding of task performance factors; rules of thumb for the use of color or optimal soft-key shapes; and empirical generalizations about user needs and characteristics.

But direct empirical models, rules of thumb, and formative evaluation together are a more-than-adequate base for important inventions and advances.

To explain and support somewhat this skeleton of dismal assertions and discordantly hopeful moral, I will add a little argument and some case examples.

Mostly, Useful Theory Is Impossible

I claimed that theory is impossible because the behavior of HC systems is chaotic or worse, highly complex, or dependent on many unpredictable variables. Let me be a little clearer about what I mean by "theory" here. In the first place, I mean a theory that is good enough to dictate system design characteristics that support much better human–computer interactive performance than are now produced by art and emulation alone. The problems of such design now involve primarily cognitive issues – how the mind of the user functions in interaction with the information processing and display dynamics of the computer.

A theory to guide such design would have to be both very broad in its coverage of human and machine information-processing phenomena and very accurate in capturing the effects of all the details that can have important effects. I do not mean to imply that theory will be of no help at all; I plan later to give examples of how even presently available theory can sometimes help to improve certain aspects of a given design. But the general theme of this collection of papers suggests to me that people somewhere are expecting much more: broad, detailed, and accurate theories that will replace empirical cut-and-try as the foundation of design. My contention is

60

simply that the theory of human cognition is now and may forever be too weak to be the main engine driving HCI. Nor will it even serve an infrequent (see Carroll, this volume) but crucial role as it has in some other technologies – for example, nuclear energy and semiconductors.

This said, let me continue the case against theory. Human cognition and behavior are manifestly highly complex and exceedingly difficult to model to any useful degree. They are based on a physical processing system with $O\ (10^{11})$ heterogeneous nonsimple elements operating largely in parallel-cooperative statistical fashions, using a huge amount of genetic (10^{10} bits?), remembered (10^9 bits?), and currently received (10^9 bits/sec ?) data that are only partially the same for any two people and manifest behaviors that are well beyond current understanding or simulation – speech, language, and vision, to mention just a few. There has been a great deal of hopeful talk about the possibility that human behavior will be discovered to manifest important regularities at some "emergent level" of organization at which useful broad theories can be built. However, even though the imminent arrival of such theories has been frequently announced from the beginnings of modern psychology almost 100 years ago up to the present (Newell, 1989), nothing remotely resembling what one would hope for as a basis for HCI, nothing with substantial generality, power, and detail at the required level of cognition has ever materialized.

The excuse that the field is young will no longer do; many other sciences have made dozens of stunning advances in the time that psychology has existed. Nor will small numbers or lack of talent explain away the failure. From the mid-sixties to the early eighties scientific psychology was immensely popular at universities, and well-funded graduate programs attracted students with higher average aptitude scores than any other field. This talented group has now had time and grant support enough to test well the opportunities for theoretical advance.

But perhaps we should not expect progress in cognitive science from psychology, but instead from computer science, where the smart money has been going for the last decade. But even the most optimistic protagonists of artificial intelligence talk of 200 person-years of work to encode an adequate approximation to the consensually available part of the conscious portion of the minimum amount of linguistically expressible knowledge required as a base for the acquisition by reading and experience of the rest of the knowledge needed for ordinary human cognition (Lenat & Guha, 1989). Modeling by computer simulation the phenomena of "low-level" perceptual processes (like speech-sound comprehension or visual pattern recognition) seems at least as complex, and the influence of emotional and physiological factors add still more complication, as do social processes.

Now consider that present computer programs and systems have sufficient complexity that most programs cannot be proved, and that irreducible bugs are the norm, and it is apparent that the other side of the interface is also severely limited in its theoretical tractability. When we then put humans and computers together into a jointly functioning interactive whole, we are almost certain to have a situation in which all of the prediction-defying pathologies of highly complex nonlinear dynamical systems will abound. True, it is conceivable that simply understood "emergent properties" may yet appear from the interaction of these two very complex systems. But for the time being, it seems foolish to pin our hopes on such an expectation. It will, I think, be much more realistic, and fruitful as well, to expect that the phenomena of HCI will (a) sometimes manifest extreme sensitivity to starting variable value differences, as happens in weather systems for example, and may occur in HCI as a function of context, memory content, or individual performance trajectories; (b) simply be too computationally complex to calculate in real time to sufficient accuracy, as is the case for fluid flow over surfaces for example, and may occur in HCI as a function of the unlimited content-addressability of human memory, the flood of current contextual influences on individual and group behavior, or the mere combinatorial complexity of the joint states available to two Turing machines; and (c) be subject to too many important variables that are impossible to know in advance in any practical way (which users at company X will have looked up the syntax for rare query type Y?); or (d) be subject to extreme random variation (who will make a typographical error that invokes a rare program bug that causes a crash that takes the administrator three days to fix because backups are done only by a rival department?).

Where Possible, the Use of Theory Will Be Constrained and Modest

I proposed that theories will be imprecise, will cover only limited aspects of behavior, will be applicable only to some parts of some systems, and will not necessarily generalize, and thus will yield little advantage over empirical methods.

As a first example here, let us take the "keystroke model" of Card, Moran, and Newell (1983). It is certainly among the most successful attempts to provide theory for HCI, yet (a) at best its time predictions are good within only about 20–50%; (b) it does not predict or model the consequences of errors, which probably account for the majority of time, individual differences, and dissatisfactions in most computerized tasks; (c) it applies only to the skilled psychomotor performance aspects of tasks, not to visual pattern recognition, knowledge-based activities, or complex decision processes, and it is mute on motivational, learning, and social issues. If a different task were the target, let us say drawing or doing financial analysis, instead of the typing-centered tasks for which it was developed, it does not seem likely that the keystroke model would describe much of the interesting action at all. My guess is that these sorts of limitations are inherent and unavoidable, that the keystroke model is *not* an early poor example, soon to be superseded by grand general theories of cognition (it certainly hasn't happened yet). Rather, the keystroke model is a particularly successful example – because it deals with aspects of behavior that are relatively simple and well understood (because most understandable). Nonetheless, I would guess that the descriptive precision, and certainly the amount of insight into process, offered by the keystroke model could be easily exceeded in any real design problem by the empirical evidence of a crude prototype test with a handful of users or examination by a small panel of experts (Nielsen 1989; Nielsen & Molich, 1990). For a second example, to which I will refer several more times, take the Bellcore group's work on keyword query and hierarchical information display methods. Quite successful modeling of the benefits of full-text indexing has

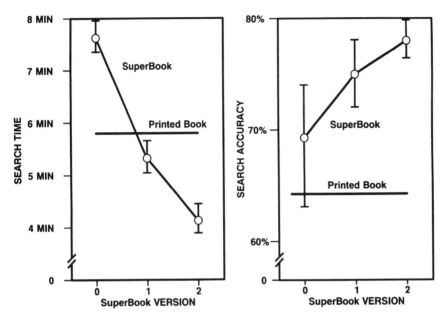

Figure 5.1. Information retrieval performance with successive versions of Super-Book. Version 0 was based on several previously formulated principles and incorporated successfully demonstrated features. Data are from an experiment in which students found answers to a variety of questions in a statistics book in its original print form or online with SuperBook. Versions 1 and 2 reflect the results of formative evaluation and redesign. About half of the time difference between versions 0 and 1 is attributable to faster code, the result to improved user–system interaction protocol.

been achieved (Furnas, Landauer, Gomez, & Dumais, 1987; Gomez, Lochbaum, & Landauer 1990), and a nice formal model of the value of fisheye views has been stated and verified (Furnas, 1986). When this "theoretical" understanding was applied to the design of the SuperBook™1 text browser, the zero-order version (before testing and redesign) was probably better, from a usability perspective, than previous "seat-of-pants" designs, but not by very much. On the other hand, three short, empirical, formative design-evaluation cycles reduced average information retrieval times by over 50% and increased success rates by about 25%. This progression is shown graphically in Figure 5.1.

One kind of important design information discovered by empirical testing is exemplified by an observation made in the first evaluation of an attempt to add on-screen graphics to the browser. When pictures came up automatically, they sometimes covered the table of contents, making it impossible to continue search by the most effective method, posting keyword hits against the outline. This flaw illustrates the problem of complexity; so many things can happen in the interaction of a human with a machine that it is impossible to anticipate everything that can go wrong. It is hard to imagine any "theory" that would help.

---

1. SuperBook is a trademark of Bell Communications Research, Inc.

What does one do in such a situation? Well, one approach is to use human empathy and intuition to model the phenomenon; humans can perform immensely complex, nonlinear, fuzzy, satisficing cognition, so maybe they can put themselves in the place of other humans, and in the place of theories, and generate, perhaps unconsciously, the understanding needed for design. Some such process seems to be required in the use of scenario techniques as described by Carroll in this volume, the heuristic evaluation methods demonstrated by Nielsen and Molich (1990), or even the "theory-based walkthrough" method proposed by Lewis, Polson, Wharton, and Rieman (1990). It would appear to be the only basis for hope in the hermeneutic and contextual research positions (Wixon, Holtzblatt, & Knox, 1990) where not only theory but systematic data collection and analysis as well are rejected.

Another approach is to rely primarily on empirical methods. "But," the interlocutor will respond, "there is no such thing as a purely empirical method. An interface never steps into the same river twice, so in using the results of an evaluation study you necessarily generalize; thus use some implicit theory to tell what situation and design variations are unimportant." "Got me!" admits the philosopher, "and I must be using the same 'intuitive theory' approach I have lately ridiculed, *but*," he hastens to add, "I am minimizing the risk by reducing the scope of theory." (It's just about what situations are very similar, and other kinds of theory would have to do that as well as the fancier things they attempt.)

Let me add an example of more constructive design guidance resulting from empirical testing. In one of Dennis Egan's "formative evaluation" studies of the SuperBook browser, college-student subjects wrote "open book" essay exams (Egan et al., 1990). Half the students were using a normal printed paper textbook on a statistics topic. The others were using the automatically generated SuperBook on-line version of the same book. The SuperBook students averaged scores 1.5 standard deviations higher than those using the original print text, roughly the difference between an A− and a C grade.

Closer analysis of the data revealed that the SuperBook students had all found a particular section of the text that had much of the information needed for a good answer. At first we jumped to the conclusion that the superior search facilities of the on-line version were responsible for its advantage. But Egan is too careful an empiricist to let the matter rest so easily. He ran a control study with users of the paper book watched by video, and discovered that they just as often found the relevant page as did the SuperBook users! Moreover they got to the relevant page just as quickly, and spent the same amount of time examining it. It appears that the reformatting – rearrangement and highlighting – of the page, or perhaps the search context in which it was found, caused one group of users to notice and absorb the information where the others passed it over. In SuperBook the section containing user search terms is promoted to the top of the "page," the relevant context is conveyed by the dynamically updated hierarchical heading structure displayed just above the text, and the typographical emphasis created by the author for linear reading is largely suppressed. We now call this "dynamic page recomposition," and list it as a feature.

This single empirical data point suggests some very interesting directions for future design experiments. One intriguing aspect of the situation is that many designers and critics have supposed that it would be optimal to reproduce print composition as exactly as possible in electronic browsers, the rationale being that we have no supportable basis for improving on the well-evolved art and conventions of print design. I leave it to the reader to judge whether the apparently counterintuitive lead of Egan's finding is likely to generalize, and to what extent similar leads have come or are likely to come from "cognitive theory" as usually imagined. Wright (1987) remarked that psycholinguistics had offered almost no guidance to text design. I would add that, up to now at least, theoretical work on discourse analysis, natural-language processing, or information retrieval has not either.

Some Useful Theory Will Be of Familiar Homely Kinds, and Have Minor Impact

The examples I mentioned included Fitts's Law, Hick's Law, the "Power" Law of practice, and various laws of visual and auditory perception. I do not want to push the radical pessimist view too far. To be sure, some important phenomena of behavior have been captured by tidy theories that hold widely, and we should certainly apply them where we can and pray for more. My favorite example is Fitts's Law. In designing the browser we used mouse-actuated "soft buttons" for several functions, and we think we improved the speed of operation in a late version by moving buttons closer to the point from which they would usually be operated and making their active target area larger. We probably saved tens of milliseconds per 5-minute browse. This really is not bad, as such things go; it's often not done in commercial systems, and is economically worthwhile in our expected applications, which have large multipliers. I think saving small fractions of a second by optimal button placement is probably a good illustration of the real but limited impact that traditional psychological theory can have if diligently applied.

And I believe that there could be many more profitable applications of known psychological principles. Let me give just a few more examples to communicate the flavor. Color psychophysics prescribes uses of color coding for graphic data presentation that are quite at variance with common practice. Hue is a metathetic as opposed to a prothetic continuum (Stevens & Galanter, 1957), meaning that hue differences will not map onto a one-dimensional monotonic scale of subjective quantity, and thus should not be used to indicate degree, as in temperature or altitude, as they often are.

Another example from our laboratory is the derivation from Hick's Law for decision time that hierarchical menus should be made as flat as possible, a prediction confirmed by our own and others' empirical tests (Landauer & Nachbar, 1985; Tullis, 1985.). Barnard, in this volume, describes some additional documented success stories in which theory from laboratory-based psychology has driven design and invention.

However, let us be realistic. Even the best examples of theory applications have produced only small quantitative and/or local gains in usability. Moreover, it seems likely that the design improvements they suggest would often have also been suggested by observations of trial users. Where such tests were not done, it is hard to prove that they would have substituted for theory. But if one watched users trying to hit small, distant keys, interpret red as "low," or work their way through deep menu hierarchies, it would not be surprising if one reached the same conclusions dictated by the relevant theories. And because usability evaluation studies will always be needed to catch the infinite variety of flaws and interaction effects (Landauer, 1987; Landauer & Galotti, 1984) not foreseeable by theory, it may be more efficient to skip the theory stage entirely.

More Useful "Theories" Will Be of New but Mundane Kinds

Examples here are data-based simulations, qualitative understanding of task performance factors, or empirical generalizations about user needs and characteristics. For discussion, let us take the information retrieval research as an example again. Early on, a set of empirical studies was done to measure the variation in terminology applied by different people in forming "keyword"-style indexing terms, category labels, and command names for several different domains (Furnas, Landauer, Gomez, & Dumais, 1983, 1987). The statistical characterization of these data was translated directly into a numerical simulation model that could be used to predict the empirical probability distributions of correct and erroneous hits when representative users pose queries against data bases in which the objects are named by various schemes. For example simulations showed that rich indexing – by collecting keywords from large numbers of potential users instead of single indexers, or by full-text indexing – expectedly improves recall (the proportion of wanted things found) by factors of two to five without much of a decrease in precision (the proportion of found things wanted). Several completely separate empirical studies at Bellcore (Gomez et al., 1990), and elsewhere (e.g., Good, Whiteside, Wixon, & Jones, 1984) have produced remarkably similar results for success rates of prototype command or information retrieval interfaces as a function of "pointer" vocabulary size. Although quantitative model predictions have not been made, experimentally observed search success for SuperBook is about 25% better than for comparable paper books with good but much smaller indexes. And a prototype "adaptive index" in which user words are monitored and added semiautomatically quickly produced very large gains in access success for users of an on-line directory (Furnas, 1985).

   This sort of "theory" is different from what has usually been dignified by that title in psychology or computer science, and from what proponents of theory in HCI like Newell and Card (1985) seem to have in mind. But my belief is that it can be widely very useful. The central characteristic of such theory is that it is empirically based modeling of user behavior in a task for which a computer tool may be designed. Such models answer the question: Given a particular performance goal and general method, how often will representative users do what? In the example, the task was finding information by offering query words to match index words. If the task were spelling correctly, one might collect data on how often typical users in typical situations of composition or copy typing omit, substitute, or transpose particular letters or position-specific *n*-grams, or, in more detail, how often each misspelled word in a large sample was a mutation of what other words. Then simulations could reveal how well various schemes for spelling correction would work. Astonishingly, to my knowledge no such empirical modeling approach has ever been used to construct spelling correctors (cf. Kernighan, Church, & Gale, 1990), designers having depended instead on ad hoc "metrics" of the differences between strings – for example, the distances between letters on keyboards, or crude point scores for omissions, deletions, and transpositions.

Empirical models also both offer opportunity for qualitative understanding of important aspects of HCI – for example, that information retrieval fails very frequently because of vocabulary differences – and can generate useful descriptions of user characteristics and needs, such as how many spelling errors at what time cost do most people make, which can point the way to needed design features and functions.

But Direct Empirical Modeling and Formative Evaluation Are Enough

Distributional data on task behavior, simulations accomplished by simple calculations on them, naturalistic observations of current task performance and prototype use seem most inelegant and unexciting sources for technological progress. But they are, if not all, at least much of what is now needed as the basis of a vast range of new and wonderful artifacts. Computers and communications hardware and software are already extremely powerful and flexible. The reason they have been of so little utility – witness the fact that U.S. productivity has not improved during the information revolution, either globally or in most of the industries that have adopted it (Dertouzos, 1990) – is that they have not done much that is actually of significant net help to the user. For the most, past computer systems have been designed either (a) to mimic on a computer (but often less well) what we can already do some other way – for example, desktops and text on tiny screens for business tasks; (b) to do something you cannot do without a computer merely because you can (or because it's a challenge) – for example incomprehensible icons instead of words, or spaghetti tangles of links instead of searchable verbal descriptors (see Lenat & Guha, 1989, chap. 9, for a sad case history); or (c) on the basis of one or more programmer's unimproved hunch (the "wouldn't it be neat if . . ." design method) – for example, mouse-operated virtual calculators on the screen, or joint scheduling calendars (see Grudin, 1988, for a critique). Moreover, most actual system design is done by software engineers and programmers whose attention and creative energies are rightly focused on the mechanism, on how to write the program efficiently and elegantly, how to maximize performance and maintainability – not on usefulness or usability.

Thus what we really stand in need of is a usefulness-and-usability–oriented design discipline. The few successful computer and HCI inventions, such as spreadsheets, to date have come from lucky hunches, discovered useful essentially by market-selection factors, not from product ideas obviously good from the start but hard to achieve. Contrast the new functions provided by computers with those that motivated the development of better light sources, faster vehicles, or long-distance communication. But just intending to do right and paying attention to usefulness and usability will not suffice. What is badly needed or dramatically desirable in information-using human activities is not as obvious as it has been in these other fields.

Similarly, evaluating whether an invention or new design is superior, or even acceptable, is not as easy in HCI as it is in most engineering disciplines. The inventor can tell whether a steam engine works better than the last model by personal observation. Personal observation of one's own system is one of the worst ways to assess usability. We need a reliable and valid feedback signal, an "objective function," with which to measure success and guide evolution. Here modern psychological science can serve us well. Psychologists know how to observe, record, and analyze behavioral data, how to get behavioral data to yield valid conclusions. They know what to do and not do with single-case, single-observer impressions, and how to overcome biased intuition and the persuasive force of anecdote and social compliance. There is no reason in this age of science to rely solely on the noisy and inefficient informal evaluations that have shaped much of the technical advance of the past (Carroll, this volume) in all fields, but most especially the creation of cognitive tools.

The fact that disciplined investigation can easily disclose what people cannot do well and suggest ways in which a computer could help them is not widely appreciated. But the mundane empirical methods and models I have discussed can do this very effectively. The step from the level of understanding provided by such empirical studies to the creation of new cognitive tools can sometimes be a short one. Rich indexing is just one example of something a computer could easily do for people once it was known that is was needed. There are many more opportunities for similar innovations that will not be identified by deep or elegant general theory of the kind I believe to be impossible, but by simple empirical analysis of what is wrong with the way things are.

Another necessary component of success in HCI will be a way to deal with the complexity of the HCI system, with the certainty that there will be many things wrong with any initial design. Even if a new design includes genuinely valuable innovations, the "nuggets" of gold may be entirely hidden in the dirt. Fortunately, there is a straightforward methodology that works extremely well to separate the good aspects from the bad – iteratively test, analyze, and revise. This is a familiar and powerful expedient in almost all fields of engineering and design (and certainly HCI is either engineering or design). Wings and cars are tested in wind tunnels, beams in stress tests, ships in model tanks, building designs in balsa models and renderings, computer programs by compilation and exercise. That there has been so much resistance to the test-cycle approach to computer usability defies understanding.

Possibly to belabor the obvious, the point is that if human–machine behavior is too complex to design or predict from theory, as I claim, then initial designs will always have unexpected properties. By the usual statistics of evolutionary processes, almost all of these unexpected properties are likely to be undesirable, and only a few will be improvements over past designs. Insofar as the defects and novel advantages of the new design are large, they will be noticeable on the basis of a moderate amount of observation. So far, practical experience, as well as some experimental evidence, suggests that tests with 2 to 10 users usually reveal most glaring flaws, and sometimes offer strong guidance for positive improvements (Egan et al., 1990; Good et al., 1984; Nielsen, 1989; Tesler, 1983). Thus hope for major progress without the aid of strong theory is quite justified.

Let me bring this brief case for empiricism to a close by reviewing the history of one case of reasonably successful HCI invention and design. I take my text from the design of SuperBook on the grounds that it has eventuated in the deployment of a system that is demonstrably better than the preexisting noncomputerized technology. This is a surprisingly rare accomplishment in HCI (and in computer applications generally). In the domain of textual information access and use there is a clear baseline, ordinary paper and print books. Insofar as computer-based text systems have been evaluated against comparable book technology, they have either lost badly or barely tied, both in formal studies (Egan et al., 1990; review in Shneiderman, 1987; Weyer, 1982) and in commercial experience. Interestingly, this negative comparison is at least as true of existing hypertext systems (McKnight, Dillon, & Richardson, 1989). SuperBook, in the version currently being deployed by telephone companies, by contrast, results in much more efficient use of textual information than is obtained by experienced users with the familiar high-quality paper documents from which the on-line SuperBook version is automatically generated.

How did SuperBook get this good? Figure 5.2 depicts the history of the information retrieval and display research work in Bellcore's Cognitive Science group. Theoretical work is indicated by underlining, empirical data or analysis by plain type, principles and methods by straight bold, prototypes and systems by italics. The empirical contributions include true experiments, systematic observations, empirical modeling of indexing schemes, tests against standard data bases of queries and targets, formative evaluations of prototypes, and acceptance testing of a product. For this line of work, we still lack data on how resulting products are actually used in large-scale office environments. As previously shown in Figure 5.1, the prior "fundamental" research on which the first version of SuperBook was based led to a design that was somewhat (not reliably) better for accuracy but reliably slower than print. That was actually good compared to previous on-line text systems, especially since part of the slowness was the fault of the development language. But in the most important sense it was a complete failure. It is not our job to produce clever computer applications that reduce productivity However, analysis of the good and bad properties of that initial version, and two more design revision cycles based on similar observations produced a very large improvement.

I hardly want to claim that this experience will be repeated everywhere. But at least in this one case, I believe it was clear that the two essential ingredients for success were (1) a good analysis of what people needed to achieve their goals that prior technology did not provide well enough (rich indexing with good disambiguation, good contextual and organization support for orientation and navigation), and (2) iterative formative evaluation of designs to remove the flaws and

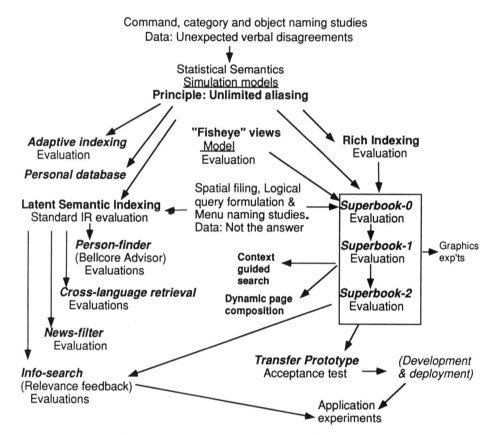

Figure 5.2. Schematic history of work on textual information in Bellcore's Cognitive Science group. Plain text indicates empirical data collection and analysis, boldface indicates principles and methods, italics prototypes and products. Theories and models are indicated by underlined text.

improve the flows (better interaction protocol, controls, dialog, screen design, code.)

Received cognitive theory found only a very minor role. Furnas's "degree-of-interest" function (1986) provided a theoretical rationale for the dynamic table of contents, although similar hierarchical TOCs have been invented without its help. Similarly Fitts's Law was in our minds when we positioned and sized the soft buttons and scroll bars, but did not make a major contribution. Our empirical work on "statistical semantics" leading to the principle of "unlimited aliasing" caused us to choose full-text indexing where it has often been eschewed (especially in other hypertext systems). We have not yet incorporated a true adaptive index because we have not yet learned how to implement it well in the text-browser environment. (Version 2 SuperBook does have a synonym creation facility, but that's quite different, and inferior; it makes two terms equivalent rather than adding a pointer from a term to a single object.)

There were some other lines of work that also contributed useful insights. One was research on the use of traditional data base query expressions (Greene, Devlin, Cannata, & Gomez, 1990; Greene, Gomez, & Devlin, 1986). It showed that most people have enormous difficulty composing logical information descriptors even though they have no trouble choosing appropriate data from a table. This suggested using a method other than boolean queries for disambiguating the results of full-text search. The invention of "context-guided search" – posting hits against the expandable table of contents – was an expression of this insight. There was also considerable research done on the creation and labeling of menu graphs for ad hoc information collections, to the conclusion that menus alone are not a general solution (Dumais & Landauer, 1984), and on spatial cues for filing and retrieval, to the conclusion that screen location is almost worthless for more than a handful of items (Dumais & Wright, 1986). In addition, of course, the literature on HCI and information retrieval contains many reports of empirical observations and experience on which we drew. This is not the place for a review of this literature, but relevant work is cited in the papers that are referenced here, and much of it is reviewed in Dumais (1988).

Another cognitive-tool invention that arose from the same starting observations and "statistical semantics" analyses was Latent Semantic Indexing (LSI). Latent Semantic Indexing uses a powerful statistical method for noise reduction that has been widely applied in signal processing to reduce significantly the "synonym" problem in word-based search. We also have not yet found a completely satisfactory way to combine LSI with a browser, although explorations continue. To reach the prototype system stage, LSI went through a separate series of formative design evaluations and improvements. In this case, early evaluations were based on standard query and relevance judgment data bases; more recent ones involve laboratory studies. While we made use of previous empirical comparisons of various accessory techniques for automatic indexing (e.g., how best to preweight terms), the extensive *theoretical* literature of information retrieval, linguistics, cognitive psychology of language, and computational natural language processing has been virtually no help at all. If anything, I expect the theory–applications relation to supply a benefit in the other direction. Latent semantic indexing seems to capture important aspects of human relevance judgments (see Deerwester, Dumais, Furnas, Landauer, & Harshman, 1990). It does so by using statistical methods to acquire an abstract "deep structure" representation of word meanings from the analysis of large amounts of representative text. Who knows, perhaps this model will lead the way to a new theory of human meaning representation and acquisition.

Perhaps the most important new technique in SuperBook is the posting of term-search hits against the table of contents. We're not entirely sure where this idea came from, although knowledge of the value of full text indexing along with the awareness that it would carry with it the need for disambiguation, was certainly important. And our and others' research showing that logical query expression is very difficult to learn and use, plus results from our statistical semantics work (Gomez et al., 1990) indicating that it will not give good results anyway, discouraged the use of boolean queries. However, this feature, which we now call *context-guided search,* was first introduced as an empirical design experiment. It was formative evaluation that led to the realization of its power and to refining it and making it a central interactive tool.

For me, the lesson of our work on information access is clear. Not coincidentally, it reflects my view of HCI in general. That is, the empirical methods of task and performance analysis and simulation coupled with formative design evaluation are sufficient and strong guides; theory is a weak adjunct. The field, if it is to succeed, should put its effort into the former.

References

Card, S. K., Moran, T. P., & Newell, A. (1983). *The psychology of human–computer interaction.* Hillsdale, NJ: Lawrence Erlbaum Associates.

Deerwester, S., Dumais, S. T., Furnas, G. W., Landauer, T. K., & Harshman, R. (1990). Indexing by latent semantic analysis. *Journal of The American Society for Information Science 41, 391–407.*

Dertouzos, M. (1990). Redefining tomorrow's interface. In J. C. Chew & J. Whiteside (Eds.), *Proceedings of CHI '90: Human Factors in Computing Systems* (p. 1). New York: ACM.

Dumais, S. T. (1988). Textual information retrieval. In M. Helander (Ed.), *Handbook of human–computer interaction.* Amsterdam: Elsevier Science Publishers.

Dumais, S. T., & Landauer, T. K. (1984). Describing categories of objects for menu retrieval systems. *Behavior Research Methods, Instruments and Computers, 16,* 242–248.

Dumais, S. T., & Wright, A. L. (1986). Reference by name vs. location in a computer filing system. *Proceedings of the Human Factors Society 30th Annual Meeting* (pp. 824–828).

Egan, D. E., Remde, J. R., Gomez, L. M., Landauer, T. K., Eberhardt, J., & Lochbaum, C. D. (1990). Formative design-evaluation of SuperBook. *ACM Transactions on Information Systems, 7,* 30–57.

Furnas, G. W. (1985). Experience with an adaptive indexing scheme. In L. Borman & B. Curtis (Eds.), *Proceedings of CHI '85: Human Factors in Computing Systems* (pp. 185–191). New York: ACM.

Furnas, G. W. (1986). Generalized fisheye views. In M. Mantei & P. Orbeton (Eds.), *Proceedings of CHI '86: Human Factors in Computing Systems* (pp. 16–23). New York: ACM.

Furnas, G. W., Landauer, T. K., Gomez, L. M., & Dumais, S. T. (1983). Statistical semantics: Analysis of the potential performance of keyword information systems. *Bell System Technical Journal, 62,* 1753–1806.

Furnas, G. W., Landauer, T. K., Gomez, L. M., & Dumais, S. T. (1987). The vocabulary problem in human–system communications. *Communications of the ACM, 30,* 964–971.

Gomez, L. M., Lochbaum, C. C., & Landauer, T. K. (1990). All the right words: Finding what you want as a function of richness of indexing vocabulary. *Journal of the American Association for Information Science 41, 547–559.*

Good, M. D., Whiteside, J. A., Wixon, D. R., & Jones, S. J. (1984). Building a user-derived interface. *Communications of the ACM, 27,* 1032–1043.

Greene, S., Gomez, L. M., & Devlin, S. J. (1986). A cognitive analysis of database query production. *Proceedings of the Human Factors Society 30th Annual Meeting* (pp. 9–13).

Greene, S. L., Devlin, S. J., Cannata, P. E., & Gomez, L. M. (1990). No IFs, ANDs, or ORs: A study of database querying. *International Journal of Man–Machine Studies, 32*, 303–326.

Grudin, J. (1988). Why CSCW applications fail: Problems in the design and evaluation of organizational interfaces. *Proceedings of CSCW '88 Conference on Computer-Supported Cooperative Work* (p. 85–93). New York: ACM.

Kernighan, M., Church, K., & Gale, W. (1990). *A spelling correction program based on a noisy channel model.* Helsinki, Finland: COLING.

Landauer, T. K. (1987). Relations between cognitive psychology and computer system design. In J. M. Carroll (Ed.), *Interfacing thought: Cognitive aspects of human–computer interaction* (pp. 1–25). Cambridge, MA: MIT Press.

Landauer, T. K., & Galotti, K. M. (1984). What makes a difference when? Comments on Grudin and Barnard. *Human Factors, 26*, 423–429.

Landauer, T. K., & Nachbar, D. W. (1985). Selecting from alphabetic and numeric menu trees using a touch screen: Breadth, depth and width. In L. Borman & B. Curtis (Eds.), *Proceedings of CHI '85: Human Factors in Computing Systems* (pp. 73–78). New York: ACM.

Lenat, D. B., & Guha, R. V. (1989). *Building large knowledge-based systems.* Reading, MA: Addison-Wesley.

Lewis, C., Polson, P., Wharton, C., & Rieman, J. (1990). Testing a walkthrough methodology for theory-based design of walk-up-and-use interfaces. In J. C. Chew & J. Whiteside (Eds.), *Proceedings of CHI '90: Human Factors in Computing Systems* (pp. 235–242). New York: ACM.

McKnight, C., Dillon, A., & Richardson, J. (1989). A comparison of linear and hypertext formats in information retrieval. Paper presented at Hypertext II Conference, York, England.

Newell, A. (1989). *Unified theories of cognition: The 1987 William James lectures.* Cambridge, MA: Harvard University Press.

Newell, A., & Card, S. K. (1985). The prospects for psychological science in human–computer interaction. *Human–Computer Interaction, 1*, 209–242.

Nielson, J. (1989). Usability engineering at a discount. In G. Salvendy & M. J. Smith (Eds.), *Designing and using human–computer interfaces and knowledge based systems* (pp. 394–401). Amsterdam: Elsevier Science Publishers.

Nielsen, J., & Molich, R. (1990). Heuristic evaluation of user interfaces. In J. C. Chew & J. Whiteside (Eds.), *Proceedings of CHI '90: Human Factors in Computing Systems* (pp. 249–256). New York: ACM.

Shneiderman, B. (1987). *Designing the user interface: Strategies for effective human–computer interaction.* Reading, MA: Addison-Wesley.

Tullis, T. S. (1985). Designing a menu-based interface to an operating system. In L. Borman & B. Curtis (Eds.), *Proceedings of CHI '85: Human Factors in Computing Systems* (pp. 79–84). New York: ACM.

Weyer, S. A. (1982). The design of a dynamic book for information search. Doctoral dissertation, Stanford University, Palo Alto, CA.

Wixon, D., Holtzblatt, K., & Knox, S. (1990). Contextual design: An emergent view of system design. In J. C. Chew & J. Whiteside (Eds.), *Proceedings of CHI '90: Human Factors in Computing Systems* (pp. 329–336). New York: ACM.

6
The Task–Artifact Cycle
John M. Carroll, Wendy A. Kellogg, and Mary Beth Rosson

One of the most appealing aspects of human–computer interaction (HCI), and also one of the most vexing, is the commitment – pursued energetically through the 1980s – to produce an intellectually rich applied psychology that can proactively support the design of usable computer equipment. Part of the appeal, of course, is that the general case throughout the history of technology is that science has provided uncertain and indirect support to practical endeavor (Basalla, 1988; Hindle, 1981; Laudan, 1984; Morrison, 1974). Difficult problems are inevitably the most attractive ones.

Chutzpah notwithstanding, the ambition of theory-based design in HCI has been frustrated to a great extent. Through the 1980s, many efforts presumed a simple one-way relationship between science and technology (the traditional notion of "technology transfer"). They focused on applying rather thin examples of information-processing psychology, reducing the user's performance and experience to counts of low-level tokens, ignoring the user's prior knowledge, task context, and goals. They also incorporated rather thin views of technology. They did not take seriously the fact that design is a process with a well-established practice that can only be impacted if it is understood in intimate detail. (For a dramatic statement of this approach, see Newell & Card, 1985; for analysis of its limitations, see Carroll & Campbell, 1986, 1989).

Currently, a reanalysis of HCI as a practical and scientific endeavor is underway. This reanalysis incorporates (at least) these three aspects: (1) reconceiving the relationship between psychological science and HCI design to be one of interaction, (2) integrating richer and more diverse areas of psychology into HCI, and (3) taking the process and products of design more seriously. Many of the papers in this volume contribute to this reanalysis. For example, diSessa argues that some scientifically important issues can be effectively pursued only by building artifacts with particular properties (see also Anderson, 1987). Norman argues that the science of psychology must itself incorporate the artifacts people use into its accounts of human activity and experience. Many of the chapters stress the point that the HCI area exists at all because of the practical and urgent need for better computer tools, tools that enhance human performance, experience, and growth (Bannon & Bødker, Brooks, Henderson, Karat & Bennett, Landauer, and Pylyshyn, all in this volume).

Our work in the User Interface Institute is much influenced by the current reanalysis of HCI. Our particular commitment is to develop HCI science and theory (in the sense of conceptual frameworks and analytical tools) that can find immediate application in HCI design. This commitment has many more entailments than we can discuss here. One that we shall focus on is the principle that theories of HCI should be ontologically minimized with respect to the extant design domain (Carroll, 1990a). That is, our approach urges that we take seriously as scientific objects the objects that are of obvious practical importance in the current practice of HCI. An ontologically minimized HCI science starts with the extant ontology of HCI practice and embellishes this only as necessary to facilitate conceptual and practical progress. (It contrasts, for example, with the "cognitive description" approach to HCI in which the ontology of cognitive psychology is imported wholesale into HCI to provide descriptive vocabulary for usability phenomena; see Carroll, 1989a). Our hope is that such a contextually grounded approach can advance the ambitious commitment of HCI: to provide an intellectually rich applied psychology that proactively supports the design of usable computer equipment.

In this chapter we explore the idea that lessons from the history of technology can be applied to understanding current issues in HCI. We first examine a general pattern in the evolution of technology, taking the development of the steam engine as an illustration. We then describe how this pattern, as instantiated in HCI technology evolution, can provide a framework for a more pertinent science of HCI. We reconsider the Training Wheels system as an illustration of this. Efforts to develop science in HCI have for the most part proceeded as if technology evolution had no history and provided no precedents. This insularity may itself explain the lack of success the field has had in understanding and enhancing its own practice.

The Evolution of Technology: An Example

Psychologists and computer scientists are apt to worry as they ponder the limited impact that science has had on HCI design. Psychologists are well conditioned to the charge that psychology is not a "real" science (i.e., not like physics). And computer scientists have heard too often that any science with "science" in its name is no science at all. Most work on the history of technology has, fortunately, focused on physics, and therefore does not add to or suffer from this imperialistic stereotyping. Generally speaking, the method that historians and philosophers use in this area is to select paradigm cases of significant technological advances and ask how and why they developed as they did. In our discussion of the steam engine, we will follow Basalla (1988), to which the reader is referred for lively discussion of this and many other examples.

Emulation, Deduction, Detail, and Iteration

There are two major mythologies about technology development. One is that our scientific understanding of nature is systematically applied to yield our technology; the second is that, whether science-based or not, technological innovations occur through the heroic acts of individuals. The facts are quite different: Design and development proceed chiefly by emulation of prior art; deduction from scientific principles has always played a minor role. Moreover, details of both the design and its context are critical determinants of viability. A "major" innovation typically depends on a variety of more modest innovations, craft techniques, and even happenstance. Finally, design is an iterative process. Major innovations rarely if ever emerge full-blown; they are incrementally synthesized over time. Every emulation, every modest detail alters, in a sense creates, the context for subsequent invention (see Basalla, 1988; Hindle, 1981; Laudan, 1984; Morrison, 1974).

As is well known, James Watt produced a steam engine in 1775. In the popular myth, Watt was inspired by observing steam rushing from a boiling tea kettle. In an awesome moment, he envisioned the mechanism for steam power and its many applications. The actual development of steam power, however, was quite different from this heroic myth. Watt worked for eleven years to complete his first steam engine, and he continued to develop aspects of the basic design for more than a quarter century after 1775. But perhaps most striking is the fact that steam engines had been in routine use in England for fifty years *before* Watt even began his work. Indeed, the development of Watt's first steam engine was instigated and guided by his personal experience repairing one of these earlier engines.

The type of steam engine Watt had repaired was invented by Thomas Newcomen, an English ironmonger, in 1712. Newcomen's engine was an atmospheric steam engine: It made critical use of the weight of the atmosphere to generate power. In Newcomen's design, an upright, steam-filled cylinder fitted with a piston is cooled by sudden injection of cold water into its interior. This causes the steam in the cylinder to condense, creating a partial vacuum. The weight of the atmosphere then forces the piston to plunge downward through the cylinder, delivering the engine's power stroke. When the piston reaches the bottom of its stroke, steam from an attached boiler is reinjected, equalizing the pressure above and below the piston, and allowing the weight of the mechanism to which the piston is connected by a walking beam to lift it back to the top of the cylinder again.

Newcomen's engine also did not emerge through a single, heroic act. It required ten years of development work. Moreover, it incorporated ideas, techniques, and mechanical elements drawn from many sources. Basalla (1988, p. 37) notes that some of its elements have their origins in thirteenth-century China. Newcomen's technique for creating a partial vacuum by cooling steam may have been adapted from an apparatus built by Denis Papin in the 1680s in France (perhaps by way of a steam-driven pump designed by the Englishman Thomas Savery in 1699 – though it is likely that Savery's pump never actually worked; see Cardwell, 1972, pp. 59, 69). Papin was interested in practical applications of vacuums, which had become of considerable scientific interest through the work of Galileo Galilei, Evangelista Torricelli, Blaise Pascal, and Otto von Guericke, among others. He placed a small amount of water into the bottom of a cylinder, forcing a piston through the cylinder by hand until it rested on the surface of the liquid. The cylinder was then heated, creating steam and causing the piston to rise. When the piston reached the top of the cylinder, Papin removed the flame and threw cold water on the cylinder. The steam condensed, creating a partial vacuum and allowing the weight of the atmosphere to push the piston down.

Who Invented the Steam Engine?

So who invented the steam engine? And what was the process of invention like? Papin did not build an engine suitable for any application. Newcomen did build a practical engine, but in fact his engine was used almost exclusively for one application, pumping water out of mines. Watt built an engine that found diverse application in virtually every context of 19th-century life.

Papin used a very small and crude cylinder and piston (a mere 2.5 inches in diameter). Steam alone raised the piston in the cylinder, which was very slow and inefficient. Moreover, he performed critical portions of the "engine" function by hand (opening and closing the cylinder's valves, cooling the cylinder by throwing water on it).

Newcomen's first engine had a cylinder diameter of 21 inches; subsequent models had cylinders 5 to 6 ft in diameter. Newcomen made use of the weight of the pump machinery that the engine drove in order to raise the piston in the cylinder by means of a walking beam pivot, connected on one side to a pump rod and on other to a piston rod. He produced steam in a separate boiler (instead of within the cylinder) and alternately injected steam and cold water into the cylinder by means of an automatic valve gear that he invented, and which was capable of producing 12 to 14 engine cycles per minute. Newcomen's valve mechanism automatically expelled leaked air through a snifting valve balanced with an eduction valve that expelled spent steam.

Watt broke with both Papin and Newcomen by relying solely on steam pressure: His engine alternately injected steam at each end of a closed cylinder, forcing the piston first one way and then the other. This produces two power strokes per cycle, instead of one. Watt also discarded the approach of alternately heating and cooling the cylinder: He used a separate boiler, like Newcomen, for producing steam, but also used a separate chamber for condensing spent steam. In the 1780s and 1790s he developed better means for producing smooth rotary motion from his engines. Newcomen's engine produced up and down motion that was suitable for pumping mines but not for more general industrial applications.

Clearly, the invention of the steam engine must be seen as a process of development and redevelopment. In the period 1800 to 1830, engines with more than one cylinder and with higher-pressure steam injection were developed, improving efficiency by a factor of 2 or 3. Indeed, as Basalla (1988) observes, the early 19th-century hot-air engines, the electric motor, and the internal combustion engine all were based directly on the steam engine. Each case represents an alternate way of moving the piston rod. This process of invention was chiefly realized through direct emulation: It is likely that Newcomen learned of Papin's apparatus from an English-language description published in 1697 (Basalla, 1988, p. 95) and it is established that Watt was directly guided by his own working experience with the Newcomen engine.

By far the most significant ingredient for the invention of the steam engine was the crafts tradition associated with producing machinery. Much of this would have been tacit knowledge and skill; indeed, a modern project to rebuild a Newcomen engine from specifications alone encountered a variety of difficulties (Cardwell, 1972, pp. 68, 71–72). According to Basalla's (1988, p. 92) analysis, the only contribution from science was the idea of a vacuum. This concept was quite important to Papin, but after having been incorporated into his apparatus, it seems an open question whether the concept played any role as such for Newcomen and Watt.

The development of the steam engine also illustrates the importance of details and context. The initial 21-inch cylinders and pistons for the Newcomen engine required special production and fitting techniques. But even with its better pistons and cylinders, the Newcomen engine could not have become successful technology without Newcomen's walking beam and automatic valve gear. The walking beam emulated and synthesized known mechanical techniques, but in a novel way. The automatic valve gear was even more novel and critical to ever achieving as many as 12 to 14 engine cycles per minute. The Newcomen engine also depended on the cumulating contributions of others – for example, around 1767 John Smeaton refined techniques for cylinder boring and developed means of using leaked air to insulate cylinder walls, allowing efficiency improvements on the order of 2 to 3 (Cardwell, 1972, pp. 79–84).

However, even the mechanically complete Newcomen engine needed a suitable application. Pumping water out of mines is not glamorous but it was a very important application in the 18th century and it allowed the technology to rapidly disseminate throughout the world. It was also quite opportune: The coal mined on site could be used to fuel the engine's boiler. As Gomory (1983) put it, pumping mines offered an ecological "niche" for the steam engine, an application in which the technology could survive to be refined and redeveloped.

This point is critical with respect to the heroic myth of Watt and the tea kettle. Without the technological and cultural preparation afforded by 60 years of successful development and application of the Newcomen engine, Watt's steam engine could never have caused the technological revolution it did. Basalla's book is full of examples like this.

The Evolution of Tasks and Artifacts in HCI

Technological evolution in HCI follows the general pattern evident in the example of the steam engine: HCI technology (workstation hardware, operating systems, application programs, user interface displays, and so forth) typically emerges through an extended process of development and redevelopment. Emulation plays a major role in this process, scientific deduction a relatively minor role. Details of design and of the context of application play critical roles in viability. The myth of the heroic inventor is also very evident in popular conceptions of HCI, from the garage geniuses of the 1970s to the recent legal debates over ownership of user interface "look and feel."

A striking example is the emergence of what are now called "direct manipulation" interfaces (Hutchins, Hollan, & Norman, 1986; Shneiderman, 1982). This interface style was first implemented in running systems in the mid-1960s (Engelbart & English, 1968; Sutherland, 1963). During the next decade, a variety of seminal developments were made, chiefly by emulation and synthesis (most notably the effort at Xerox PARC). Many detailed contributions directed, facilitated, and perhaps even limited the development of these interfaces – for example, the early emphasis on closed applications instead of tool sets, the use of mouse pointers instead of touch screens, the focus on text-processing applications instead of graphics. In the late 1970s, the first commercial products employing direct manipulation interfaces appeared.

In the mid-1980s, scientific analyses of direct manipulation were developed. These accounts were also seminal HCI work and have played major roles in focusing additional research interest on this interface style. The point being stressed here is merely that the original direct manipulation interfaces owed little or nothing to scientific deduction, since in fact the impact went the other way round. Analogous points could be made regarding other innovations in HCI, for example, spreadsheet systems and object-oriented programming. Indeed, it seems typical in HCI for new ideas to be first codified in exemplary artifacts and only later abstracted into discursive descriptions and principles (Carroll, 1989b; Carroll & Campbell, 1989).

One reason for this is the sheer speed of the HCI development process. Even major innovations like direct manipulation can be realized technologically, and indeed put into use, far faster than they can be assimilated to scientific theories and conventionally explained. This has served to enhance the practical importance of emulation as the chief instrument of technological continuity and development. Waiting for science to take the lead in HCI over the past 25 years would have substantially impeded technological progress in the field.

A second reason for the importance of emulation is the sheer complexity of HCI development, in particular, the complexity of reciprocal impacts between human experience and endeavor on the one hand, and the viability and direction of HCI technology on the other. HCI impacts people more diversely and more personally than any other new technology in history. It is changing our work, our play, and the way we prepare supper; it is changing education, transportation, communication, and manufacturing. And it is doing this continuously and rapidly. These impacts contribute to the stress of modern life (perhaps we have no contemporary Luddites only because the immense breadth of impact provides no single target) and they make HCI design very difficult.

The evolution of HCI technology is a coevolution of HCI tasks and HCI artifacts: A task implicitly sets requirements for the development of artifacts to support it; an artifact suggests possibilities and introduces constraints that often radically redefine the task for which the artifact was originally developed. For example, electric typewriters altered office tasks, word processors altered them again, desktop publishing systems altered them still more. In each case, changed tasks themselves suggested new needs and opportunities for further change. This dynamic relation, the task–artifact cycle, circumscribes the development activities of human–computer interaction (Figure 6.1).

Our commitment to developing HCI science and theory that can find immediate application in HCI design suggests the straightforward extension of the task–artifact cycle as a framework for research and theory building in HCI. In particular, we propose to adapt the manifest task–artifact cycle to be a framework for what Wright (1978) called an "information flow" between science and application. Wright urged that science play a more closely coordinated and proactive role in analyzing applied solutions to practical problems in order to enable more refined subsequent solutions (see also Barnard, this volume). For HCI we envision perhaps

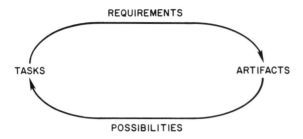

Figure 6.1. The task–artifact cycle: the manifest structure of technology evolution in HCI.

even more closely coordinated activity consisting in the principled analysis of artifacts, tasks, and situations of use as these are designed and developed in the
practical context of the task–artifact cycle. Our specific approach to this attempts to
codify and integrate important objects and practice in the field, entities that already
have an independent existence: design rationale, scenario-based design, and the
psychology of tasks.

Design Rationale

A design rationale is a detailed description of the history and meaning of an artifact. For example, it can enumerate the design issues that were considered during a
design process, along with the argument and evidence brought to bear on them,
dependencies on and implications for other issues, and the final decision that was
taken (e.g., Conklin & Begeman, 1988). This kind of design rationale has already
been employed specifically to understanding HCI technology (MacLean, Young, &
Moran, 1989).

One can also develop nonhistorical design rationales, descriptions that seek to
characterize the underlying import of aspects of the final design, but without necessarily detailing any process behind that final result. Such a design rationale could be
useful for organizing system maintenance and enhancement work (particularly
when the system maintainer is not the original designer; Biggerstaff, 1989). This
kind of design rationale has also been developed for understanding the operative
psychological claims embodied in HCI technology (as distinct from claims the
designers might have wished to embody in their work, that is historically speaking,
but which they may or may not have successfully embodied in it; Carroll & Kellogg,
1989; Kellogg, 1990).

Of course, the informal practice of rationalizing a significant design project is
well known in the recent HCI literature (e.g., Smith, Irby, Kimball, Verplank, &
Harslem, 1982). However, it is, perhaps understandably, often difficult in such
commentaries to separate the designers' intentions from actual achievements. Because the issues are informally articulated and argued, it is even difficult finally to
lay out the intentions very precisely. Taking design rationale seriously offers us a
chance to make this analytical work more methodologically sound, and perhaps

ultimately more useful. MacLean et al. (1989) suggest that a comprehensive design rationale, encompassing many possible histories, would be a very effective tool for evaluating tradeoffs in future designs.

Design rationale is a particularly well-suited tool for constructing descriptions and abstractions within the context of technological evolution. Unlike conventional scientific descriptions, the level of detail for a design rationale is understood to be expandable: For some purposes it suffices to summarize the key design issues from a development process or to extract the leading claims embodied in a final design. For other purposes, virtually any detail of the design process, any feature of final product, may be critical – for example, when we attempt to understand the evolving role of an artifact in a human social system (Bannon & Bødker, this volume). Because design rationale is understood as a workspace for representation, a dynamic viewing of an artifact, it is also particularly well suited to the iterative nature of the design process.

Scenario-based Design

Scenario-based design is a task-oriented technique for envisioning an artifact in use *before* it is built. In this method of designing, one begins with a list of user questions. These can be analytically generated, gathered empirically, for example by interviewing prospective users, or gleaned from direct observation of use (most design, after all, is redesign in some sense). These questions are elaborated into scenarios: descriptions of the tasks people might undertake to address the questions. The set of scenarios is successively elaborated, ultimately incorporating device-specific details and other work context articulating exactly how particular tasks will be accomplished.

A comprehensive set of such user interaction scenarios is a representation of the design (Carroll & Rosson, 1990). It provides the same basic information captured by traditional textual representations (so-called functional specification documents). The objects of the system are enumerated and defined (e.g., the objects of the user interface comprising a graphics window), as are the functions (e.g., a user can access the window contents). But instead of splitting out the individual objects and functions (e.g., in a list), their roles in the design as a whole are emphasized by embedding them in user scenarios; perhaps more important from the standpoint of the design process, their role in the design emerges from a process of considering contexts of use.

In fact, user interaction scenarios are now frequently incorporated into traditional textual product specifications. In practice, it is often noticed that the example scenario provides more effective guidance than the specification it is only meant to illustrate. One can ponder the future of the traditional specifications given these circumstances. Indeed, the increasing use of diverse media (graphics, video, simulation) for building scenario-based design representations is making functional specifications even more peripheral.

Like design rationales, user interaction scenarios already play a variety of roles in HCI design. For example, a set of scenarios is a critical requirement for the design of task-oriented user instruction and other documentation (e.g., Carroll, 1990b). We know of one case in which a scenario, originally added to a functional specification document purely as an illustration, later became the basis of the user tutorial for the system (little else in the specification document had any useful life after the implementation).

A second arena of further use for scenario design representations is in evaluation. Any thorough usability evaluation must begin from a set of user interaction scenarios. Typically these are produced very late in the design process, or perhaps produced generically for a class of applications (e.g., Roberts & Moran, 1983). However, if a system has been functionally specified by a set of user interaction scenarios, these are clearly the most appropriate possible starting point from which to develop usability evaluations. Thus, the kind of design representation a set of scenarios provides yields very specific support to the iterative process usability testing and redesign.

Like design rationale, user-interaction scenarios are a particularly well-suited tool for the context of technology evolution. They are appropriately open-ended with respect to the detail they incorporate: Even at the end of the design process, the original list of user questions is a succinct representation of the system. However, the fully expanded user scenarios can also include the important particulars of user situations that can be so critical (Suchman, 1987; Whiteside & Wixon, 1987). Scenarios also support design-by-emulation by providing a representation that amounts to a simulation of the artifact itself: A textual scenario is expanded into a storyboard of sequenced drawings plus description, and the storyboard can be expanded into a video simulation (Vertelney, 1989) or a scenario machine (Carroll & Kay, 1988; McKendree & Carroll, 1987).

The Psychology of Tasks

The task–artifact framework for HCI that we are proposing is sketched in Figure 6.2 (from Carroll, 1990a). In essence, we suggest that the extant techniques of scenario-based design and design rationale be recruited more systematically into the extant task–artifact cycle. The requirements that human experience, endeavor, and aspiration place on technology are developed through a process of scenario-based design: to express tasks as artifacts. The possibilities (and of course the problems) for human activity afforded by new technology are analyzed by developing design rationales for artifacts: to understand artifacts as tasks. This is our proposal for an ontologically minimized HCI: a science better integrated with its corresponding field of application.

At the vertex of this task–artifact cycle we position the psychology of HCI tasks, an admittedly eccentric term to distinguish what we have in mind from the establishment paradigm of psychology (in the United States), namely the thin information-processing psychology that was extensively imported into HCI in the 1980s to little effect. The kind of science base we imagine is contextualized: Information-processing psychology rests on the dubious assumption that if we understand laboratory tasks that are devoid of practical meaning we will have achieved a general understanding, not limited to just a single meaningful context. This is probably

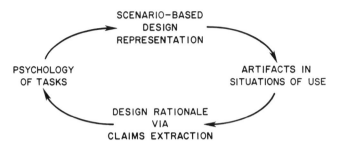

Figure 6.2. The task–artifact framework for integrating research and practice in HCI.

about half right: These analyses are in many cases not applicable to a single meaningful context in human experience.

The psychology of tasks rests on detailed taxonomies of human task and artifact domains: Understanding direct manipulation interfaces may indeed not generalize to understanding command interfaces, but an understanding of direct manipulation interfaces should (at least) support the design of direct manipulation interfaces. Of course, one objective of the task psychology is to articulate relationships among human activities so that, for example, we can anticipate how an understanding of given tasks and artifacts can be generalized and extended. But of perhaps greater importance for design pragmatics and responsibility is the aim to remain grounded in real situations of human endeavor and enriched by concern with the broader issues of human development.

This science base is to some extent already available. It has been developed in the "action theory" of German work psychology (Frese & Sabini, 1985; Frese, Ulich, & Dzida, 1987; Greif, this volume; Volpert, in press) and in Russian "activity theory" (Bannon & Bødker, this volume; Leont'ev, 1978; Vygotsky, 1978). It is developed in contemporary American psychology in the work of Cole (1990), Norman (1986, 1988), and Scribner (1984). Analyses of human activity within these traditions emphasize possibilities for self-regulation, and therein for greater engagement, satisfaction, growth, freedom, and dignity. For example, Volpert (in press) argues that task environments should be designed to promote personal development by providing greater scope of action, opportunities for initiative taking, varied postures, actions, experiences, the manipulation of real objects, and direct interpersonal cooperation. And Greif (this volume) argues that even at very fine grains of analysis, there is never "one best way" for a human to perform a task.

This view of the sort of science base that is appropriate for HCI is implicit in a variety of current views of HCI, a fact well illustrated in this volume. For example, Brooks, Pylyshyn, and Landauer discuss the need and importance of a *descriptive* science of HCI, by which they mean a descriptive psychology of HCI tasks, grounded in taxonomic analysis of tasks (Brooks and Pylyshyn) or in direct empirical modeling of particular tasks (Landauer). Norman and Payne develop the point that to understand human activity and experience we must understand how artifacts mediate and structure this activity and experience.

The objects and techniques reified in the framework in Figure 6.2 offer a special leverage and cohesion to HCI as a practical science and a science of practice. They support the central role of emulation in design and accommodate the need for arbitrarily detailed descriptions of artifacts and their situations of use. They offer the prospect of a systematic, science-based HCI practice that efficiently adds value to design work.

In summary, we believe that the task–artifact framework can be effective and integrative with respect to many other developments in current HCI. In other words, we are encouraged that we can use the history of technology and the current practice of HCI technology to frame and direct the development of a pertinent science of HCI. However, we are committed to the view that such proposals are best made through specifics. In the balance of this paper, we develop an example to illustrate how design rationale and scenario-based design can work together within the task–artifact framework for research and practice in HCI.

Reconsideration of Training Wheels

A simple illustration of the task–artifact cycle as a framework for HCI research and development can be drawn from reconsideration of the Training Wheels interface, a reduced-function training environment for a stand-alone text editor (Carroll & Carrithers, 1984). The key characteristic of this interface is that it "blocks" the consequences of problematic user actions. Thus, if the first-time user selects Merge Tasks, a message is returned that the function is not available in the Training Wheels interface. The user is spared the further prompting involved in merging data, spared the effort of recovering from a thwarted data merge and able to try another selection. This simple technique has been found to facilitate initial and continuing learning (i.e., learning advanced functions like Merge Tasks after Training Wheels are removed; Catrambone & Carroll, 1987).

Extracting Claims from the Displaywriter

A starting point for the Training Wheels task–artifact cycle is an enumeration of psychological claims embodied in the Displaywriter interface: The Training Wheels interface was originally implemented for the Displaywriter. These claims are best understood in the context of usage scenarios; an artifact is seen as having psychological consequences for a user involved in a particular task. The selection of these scenarios may result from prior analysis of related systems, an analysis of critical tasks for the system of interest, or from direct observation of system use. Table 6.1 presents some Displaywriter claims organized by scenarios that were developed from observations of users learning to use the system.

What Can I Do?   Users working opportunistically, wondering what they can do with the Displaywriter, are guided to discover basic word-processing goals (creating, revising, and printing documents) by the fact that the first-listed menu item on

Table 6.1. *Psychological claims of Displaywriter*

What can I do?	How to type–print	Parameter loop
menu item names and organization facilitate goal identification *(but can also suggest many inappropriate goals)*	menu item names and organization support analogical subgoal mappings *(but some subgoals may be obscured by analogical reasoning)*	standard "option change" and "finish" prompts cue and simplify menu interaction *(but user may not yet have seen the other menus that use this technique, and may assume it indicates something specific about this situation)*
	prominent positioning of core functionality in menus makes appropriate subgoals more salient	the option change prompt conveys the procedure for changing options *(but it may be interpreted as a directive by users who are confused or unsure)*
	the menu and prompt sequence (Typing Tasks, Document Name, Diskette Name, Create or Revise) comprise a self-evident action path *(but departures from the action path may be hard to interpret)*	highlighting the option change prompt makes the possibility of changing options more salient *(but makes the finish prompt and the possibility of not changing options less salient)*
	accomplishing a task that you already understand and want to do is intrinsically motivating *(but failing to accomplish such a task may be more keenly frustrating)*	continued highlighting of the option change prompt suggests the continuing appropriateness of changing options *(but may make it harder to recognize that it is also OK to finish)*
		returning to the Create or Revise menu is adequate feedback that an option change attempt is successful *(but may not be enough feedback for users who are unsure or confused)*

the first-displayed menu is "Typing Tasks." The other choices are less familiar-sounding and less canonical to word processing (Work Diskette Tasks, Program Diskette Tasks, Spelling Tasks, Feature Tasks, Key-to-Print Task, Merge Tasks). The Displaywriter implicitly supports the user's opportunistic sense-making efforts through this menu design.

However, the claim is also linked to a specific tradeoff, namely that the various menu choices might also suggest inappropriate goals to the user. For example, Spelling Tasks seems familiar and canonical to word processing (though it turns out not to be useful until one already has created some documents). Some of the other choices might seem intriguing even if not familiar. What is Merge Tasks all about? Users who opportunistically try these functions sometimes disappear into complex and inappropriate menu hierarchies.

How to Type–Print?   New users of text-processing equipment want to type and print simple documents immediately (Mack, Lewis, & Carroll, 1983). In many cases, they already know a lot about documents and they engage this knowledge as they initiate, execute, and evaluate various learning activities. For example, in learning to use the Displaywriter, learners first encounter the Task Selection menu; at the top of this menu is the selection Typing Tasks. For the learner motivated to type a document, this is a natural choice. At the top of the Typing Tasks menu is the selection Create Document; selecting it evokes the document name prompt, cueing the user to type a document name in the input field, and then the work diskette prompt, cueing the user to specify where the document to be created will be stored. When the document name and diskette name have been specified, the system displays the "Create or Revise" menu. This menu presents a variety of further options: changing document formats, engaging stored alternate formats, storing documents with comments, and so on. The user can merely press the Enter key to accept default options and go to the Typing Area, a workspace for creating and editing text using typewriting keyboard functions and keypress editing commands. Thus, to create a document, the user needs only to select the first-listed menu items and accept defaults. In this way, the Displaywriter makes the most basic word-processing task simple to do.

The design of the Displaywriter embodies several psychological claims pertaining to the basic type-and-print task. For the user pursuing the type-and-print goal, the menu names and organization support analogical subgoal mappings: The user can use prior knowledge about typing and printing in the real world to decide what to do in the Displaywriter situation. For example, one creates a document before revising it. However, users relying on analogical reasoning may have difficulties with components of the type–print task that are not suggested by their real world knowledge: They must specify a unique name for a document and the name of a work diskette on which to store it before even typing a single character; they must come to understand that "printing" in the Displaywriter consists of first queuing a print request and then operating the printer to get output.

The Displaywriter prominently positions the appropriate type-and-print subgoals in its menus, which makes the components of this basic task more salient. To get to the Typing Area, for example, the user needs to select the first-listed menu item on the first two menus and to accept default option settings on the third. The Displaywriter's menu and prompt sequence for the type-and-print task also embodies a claim to being a self-evident action path; each selection is to follow self-evidently from the situation created by the immediately preceding selection. However, if an incorrect selection is nevertheless made, the Displaywriter provides no mechanism for helping the user to recognize this or to recover and return to the correct menu and prompt sequence. This lack of error support trades off with the provision of implicit support for the correct action sequence.

A fourth claim the Displaywriter makes about typing and printing is that accomplishing a task that you already understand and want to do is intrinsically motivating. By assumption, the user is already familiar with the physical counterpart to this task and therefore can appreciate the satisfaction of completing the task. The downside here is that failing to accomplish such a task may be all the more frustrating since one may have entertained the expectation of success.

Parameter Loop.   The parameter loop scenario describes a problem situation often experienced by learners when they encounter the Create or Revise menu on their way to typing a document (Carroll & Carrithers, 1984); this scenario can be viewed as a subscenario of the basic "how to type–print" task.

In this scenario, a highlighted "option change" prompt at the bottom of the Create or Revise menu says, "Type YOUR CHOICE; press ENTER." The first-time user should ignore *all* the choices, but the prompt is visually salient, and users invariably do select an option to change by typing its ID letter and pressing Enter. For example, they might type a *c* and press Enter to select the option "Change Alternate Format." This initiates a subdialog to specify parameters for the selected option. When the subdialog is finished, the Create or Revise menu is redisplayed, including the highlighted option-change prompt, because for any given document, a user might well wish to change several or even all of the listed options.

On being returned to the Create or Revise menu, new users often worry that they *need* to specify further options, or that they have specified an option incorrectly. Accordingly, they specify and respecify, even *re*respecify particular options. The highlighted prompt, of course, continues to direct them to type their choices. We call this pattern of user behavior the parameter-loop error (Carroll & Carrithers, 1984). All the while, a *non*highlighted "finish" prompt is also displayed saying, "When finished with this menu; press ENTER." That is, at any time the user can leave the Create or Revise menu merely by pressing Enter without a new choice. But it often takes many parameter loops for people to try this.

In the context of the parameter-loop scenario, the design of the Displaywriter embodies several psychological claims: the parameter-loop error seems to derive from downside tradeoffs of these claims. The Displaywriter implements the Create or Revise menu with its standard "option change" and "finish" prompts, as described previously. Thus, the Create or Revise menu works just the same as, for example, the Print Document menu. The psychological rationale for this design is that standard prompts can cue and simplify menu interaction. However, when the new user first encounters the Create or Revise menu, the fact that the prompts are "standard" provides no leverage.

The key functionality of the Create or Revise menu is the options. Hence, it is important for the interface to convey to the user that these options can be changed. This rationale is reflected in the characteristics of the option-change prompt: The prompt text "Type YOUR CHOICE; press ENTER" describes the first step toward changing an option; highlighting the prompt makes the possibility of making such a change salient to the user. As we have reported, the prompt does have this effect. The downside is that a user who is unsure or confused may see the prompt as directive; highlighting it also diminishes the relative salience of the finish prompt – inviting the parameter-loop error.

When the user selects an option on the Create or Revise menu, for example Change Alternate Format, the Displaywriter brings up a specialized menu for that parameter (i.e., the alternate format). When the user finishes with this specialized menu (by pressing Enter), the system redisplays the Create or Revise menu, at which point the user can press Enter to go to the Typing Area or make another choice to specify another option parameter. It is important for the system to convey to the user that other options can be selected and changed. The Displaywriter attempts to convey the continuing possibility of changing options by continuing to highlight the option-change prompt when the user is returned to the Create or Revise menu after having changed an option. The downside of this approach is that it becomes relatively harder for users to recognize that they also can decide *not* to change further options, that they can follow the unhighlighted "finish" prompt and merely press Enter to go to the Typing Area.

After an option change attempt, the user is returned to the Create or Revise menu. This return is the feedback the system provides to the user that the option-change attempt was successful. This is a very efficient control: The return indicates both the completion of the preceding option change and the possibility of further option changing. The Displaywriter embodies the claim that the return is adequate feedback, but for the unsure or confused user this may be false. The user may see the return to the Create or Revise menu as evidence that nothing was accomplished, that the option change failed and must be reattempted (hence, again, the parameter-loop error).

Building up the Psychology of Tasks

The analysis of psychological claims embodied in the Displaywriter design displayed in Table 6.1 is incomplete. Continuing this sort of analysis, we would seek to enumerate all the important user-interaction scenarios for the Displaywriter and the claims it embodies pertaining to each. This is clearly an open-ended type of description. In a gross sense, Table 6.1 does capture the key learning scenarios (deciding what can be done, doing it, making an error while doing it). But the list can easily be extended. There are other basic tasks: printing a document (including operating an attached local printer), finding and revising a document one has previously created and stored, changing margins, printing multiple copies, and so on. There are several other important Displaywriter error scenarios, such as misspecifying a diskette name and accidentally queuing multiple print jobs.

Indeed, to capture very fine, but possibly very important details about Displaywriter interactions, we would need to incorporate specific episodes of user interaction, graphically illustrating exactly how given important interaction phenomena arose. One can envision this level of detail as codified in video recordings of user interactions exemplifying various claims and tradeoffs. Such details are essential in a psychology of real interaction tasks, and essential to establishing a science base rich enough to be of serious use in design.

It is important to stress the situational details incorporated into the psychology of tasks, because conventional notions of science tend to focus so reflexively on the abstractness and generality of scientific analysis. But a science base for the design of interactions also must include means for abstraction. The Displaywriter is an office-information system and a word-processing system: User scenarios, psychological claims, and interaction episodes from the Displaywriter also illustrate tasks, problems, and techniques of these more abstract classes.

The Displaywriter scenarios in many cases can also be viewed as instantiating more abstract scenario schemata. For example, the type-and-print scenario with respect to text-processing systems is analogous to the arrange-a-meeting scenario for shared calendar systems. Both are core scenarios for the application domain, and presumably exercise the core application function of a domain tool. One might imagine a science base with a "core scenario" abstraction annotated with claims analyses of core functionality in a variety of systems. A designer might reason from this base to a new domain, determining what the core functionality should be, and carrying over the claims constructed for existing artifacts (e.g., increasing the perceptual prominence of basic tasks).

As another example, consider the parameter-loop problem. This scenario might be characterized more generally as one in which users choose task customization over acceptance of a default-action path. The highlighting scheme of the Displaywriter supports this choice process. For a system in which task customization is likely even for the most basic learning tasks, this might be a productive scenario. For the Displaywriter, the scenario led to severe problems. Ironically, by the time a Displaywriter user is ready to experiment with changing document options, the assistance provided by highlighting the option-change prompt may be completely gratuitous.

The psychology of tasks is a science base that can be visualized as a multimedia, relational data base. Materials from claims analyses, from video protocol studies of user interaction, and from design rationale information about the Displaywriter are all indexed in this repository by hardware and software categories, by application domain, by intended-user category, and by psychological claims and tradeoffs. Users can query, browse, and contribute to this data base through the course of their design and analysis work.

Developing Scenarios for the Training Wheels Interface

The psychology of tasks supports an initial specification of the Training Wheels interface: scenarios of learning, of learning text-processing equipment, or of learning the Displaywriter can be used as a design representation for redesigning or enhancing the Displaywriter. The claims developed for any given scenario can drive design thinking by posing and helping to answer questions: How will this scenario be supported in the changed design? Will the new design make the same claims? Can the tradeoff for a claim be reduced, or removed? Productive scenarios (e.g., how to type–print?) may simply be streamlined or used as models for analyzing other system tasks (e.g., editing a document). More troublesome scenarios, like the parameter-loop problem, can expose general or specific problems with a design and lead to design responses, in effect reworking the scenario so that it supports productive activity.

In scenario-based design, a set of scenarios is developed by collecting typical and critical user episodes through direct observation and through analytically elaborating and interrogating scenarios already incorporated into the task psychology. Thus, the general type-and-print scenario (part of which is developed for the Displaywriter) might have already been part of our understanding of the task of learning to use a text-processing system. When it is incorporated into the design representation for the Training Wheels interface, it is of necessity specialized for the Displaywriter learning situation (referring to specific menus, selections, and system states). The parameter-loop scenario might also be a basic pattern in our task psychology, or it might be a discovery made by watching people struggle with this aspect of the Displaywriter.

Enhancement or redesign of a system can begin with a scenario-based claims analysis of a prototype or of an existing system, such as that we have presented for the Displaywriter. The scenarios relevant to an already existing system are likely to have continued relevance for an enhanced version. In some cases, however, a design may change so substantially that some usage scenarios no longer make sense (e.g., some piece of functionality may be removed). A more likely situation is that the new design will have additional scenarios: In the case of Training Wheels, for example, a new scenario of critical importance arises when a user moves from the training system to the full-function Displaywriter.

In many cases, designers will be able to use the claims analyses of existing systems in a proactive fashion, reasoning about the claims to generate new design ideas. Most claims have two pieces, the claim itself and a downside or tradeoff; one way to develop design enhancements is to look across the claims, trying to enhance their consequences while reducing their downsides. For this to be successful, of course, the analysis must encompass the entire set of claims, rather than addressing individual claims case by case.

Consider the third claim of the "how to type–print?" scenario, that the menu and prompt sequence comprise a self-evident action path (see Table 6.1). In trying to reduce the downside of the claim (that departures from the path may be hard to interpret), a designer might imagine removing from Displaywriter menus the function choices that are not relevant to the type–print goal; this preempts the problem of path departures.

For some situations, hiding function in this way may be an excellent technique for assisting users down a task path: We have found it to be an effective technique for filtering Smalltalk's enormous class library for new users (Rosson, Carroll, & Bellamy, 1990). However, although the technique does eliminate the unwanted digressions, it brings with it two *new* downsides. Because some functionality is being hidden, there is the possibility that in some situations, the reduced set will be so small as to be disconcerting to the user. For the Displaywriter, this downside is a serious consideration, as hiding choices not relevant to type–print would lead to some menus having just a single choice, others being entirely empty. A second downside is embodied in the dissimilarity between the reduced function menus in the training system and the full-function menus in the nontraining system; this dissimilarity may reduce learners' ability to transfer to a normal usage situation.

A better solution in this case might be to use a technique that does not modify menu content, but rather dims (or in some other way marks) choices that are not currently available. Such a technique would address many of the problems observed in Displaywriter learning situations, problems implied by the downsides of the claims. In general, it should prevent departures from the appropriate action path, increase their chance of success, and so forth. And it does not carry with it the new downsides associated with function hiding.

However, although such a marking technique does indeed address many of the downsides of the Displaywriter claims, it fails to capitalize on the type–print claims themselves. So, for example, because the correct path would be uniquely "marked" at many choice points, the claim about the menu and prompt sequence being a self-evident action path is weakened: It becomes less important whether users can reason what to do in a sequence, because the system literally shows them. Similarly, the role of analogical reasoning in generating subgoals is diminished. Weakening these claims is especially costly in this training situation, where a paramount goal must be to provide practice with reasoning and decision processes that will carry over into the nontraining usage situation.

Similar reasoning applies to the parameter-loop scenario. One might imagine removing the option-change prompt, or somehow reducing its salience to the new user. But if these strategies were followed, the revised system would no longer capitalize on the original claims, those having to do with the Displaywriter prompt conventions, and conveying to users that changing options is an important subgoal to think about.

These considerations might lead one to imagine a different technique, one in which users are encouraged to use analogical reasoning, to benefit from the self-evident nature of Displaywriter action paths, and to realize that changing options for a document is a possibility, but in which the consequences of any incorrect decisions deriving from these realistic reasoning processes are minimized. An example of this is the error blocking technique employed in the Training Wheels interface.

Extracting Claims from the Training Wheels Interface

The task–artifact cycle is by assumption an unending process of innovation, refinement, analysis, and requirement setting. Just as the psychological design rationale for the Displaywriter was incorporated into the task-psychology science base and guided the design of the Training Wheels interface, so an analysis of the Training

Wheels interface can be a further discovery representation for the psychology of tasks.

Claims embodied in the Displaywriter may or may not be embodied in the Training Wheels interface. Some claims may be preempted by the design changes. Other claims may be "inherited" by the new design, with no change in usability consequences. Still others may reappear, but in a slightly different form. In particular, the tradeoff of a claim may have been altered, such that its downside cost has been reduced, or that an entirely new tradeoff has emerged.

In an analysis of an enhanced design, an important step is a reconsideration of the claims of the original artifact – indeed, as we suggested earlier, these claims are likely to be the driving force for many of the new design ideas. However, it will almost certainly be the case that the new artifact will embody additional claims, claims entrained by the novel aspects of the design.

Table 6.2 displays an analysis of the psychological claims embodied in the Training Wheels interface, organized under the key learning scenarios that the system supports. The analysis is based on the three scenarios from which the original Displaywriter claims were developed, as well as a fourth scenario reflecting the situation in which a user who has used the Training Wheels interface begins using the full system.

What Can I Do?   As for the Displaywriter, the Training Wheels interface embodies the claim that the menu items and organization will help a user figure out what to do. However, in the new design, a user who has not yet articulated the appropriate goal is blocked from utilizing functions inappropriate to the type-and-print goal. This implicitly guides the user toward identifying the appropriate goal.

Notice that this design change results in a new tradeoff. In the Displaywriter, we observed that the user might become attracted to inappropriate menu items, and perhaps disappear into Spelling Tasks. In the Training Wheels interface this possibility is preempted: Spelling Tasks is a blocked selection. The user who selects it would receive a "blocking" message "Spelling Tasks is not available on the Training Displaywriter." Indeed, the only working menu selection available in this system state is Typing Tasks. The downside of the Training Wheels design is that the available functions might not satisy a given user in a given circumstance: This is a central gamble of the Training Wheels design.

How to Type–Print.   The user who has already articulated the appropriate type-and-print goal is blocked from mapping inappropriately into Displaywriter system functions. For example, the user is prevented from utilizing any function but Typing Tasks on the Task Selection menu. In this way, the user is guided to an analysis of type-and-print as a sequence of operations starting with the selection of Typing Tasks. This mitigates the tradeoff associated with this claim for the full Displaywriter system: Although analogical reasoning may not lead to a complete understanding of a task's components, problems stemming from an incomplete understanding are minimized (for example, users are prevented from requeuing a document already on the print queue; Carroll & Carrithers, 1984).

Table 6.2. *Psychological claims of Training Wheels error blocking*

What can I do?	How to type–print	Parameter loop	Using the full system
menu item names and organization facilitate goal identification *(but some identifiable goals are blocked)*	menu item names and organization suggest analogical subgoal mappings *(but some spurious mappings are possible)*	blocking option changing suggests the possibility of not changing options *(but could discourage option changing later)*	exposure to full menus supports unintentional learning *(but could discourage selection of advanced function later)*
	accomplishing a task that you already understand and want to do is intrinsically motivating *(but failing to accomplish such a task may be more keenly frustrating)*	allowing commission of errors permits realistic planning for action *(but prolonged episodes of errors and blocked actions may become too complex to make sense of)*	a well-learned function subset supports further learning *(but could discline people to learn more)*
	less nested action sequences are more salient, facilitating plan formation *(but user may expect all tasks to be simple and shallow in structure)*	less distraction from error recovery episodes focuses the user's attention on correct actions *(but preempts opportunities to acquire and practice strategies for dealing with errors)*	practicing coherent kernel scenarios establishes integrated and contextualized skills *(but may inhibit generalization of skills to other contexts)*
	constraining a user's intention increases effectiveness of feedback by allowing feedback on goal mapping *(but the user may misconstrue the system's ability to diagnose intentions and offer intelligent assistance)*	blocking requested actions motivates further action *(but could cause frustration)*	a reduced device space constrains hypothesis generation *(but could limit the generality of generated hypotheses)*
		immediate feedback on blocked device states instigates evaluation while relevant intentions, plans, and actions are still active in memory *(but could also encourage nonplanful action)*	

The Training Wheels interface inherits from the Displaywriter the claims about prominent positioning of appropriate subgoals and the self-evident nature of the menu and prompt sequence. Because the Training Wheels interface does not alter any aspect of the Displaywriter design regarding these usability consequences, the new analysis does not represent these claims explicitly.

The Training Wheels interface also inherits the claim that accomplishing a task that the user already understands and wants to do is intrinsically motivating. However, to the extent that the error-blocking technique increases the chance that the user will be able to type and print a document, the Training Wheels interface reduces the downside of this claim, the possibility of frustration arising from a failure to accomplish such a task.

The Training Wheels interface embodies claims not inherent in the Displaywriter. The Training Wheels user is less often interrupted by error-recovery episodes while executing a task, because inappropriate selections are blocked. Thus, the resulting action path that accomplishes the type-and-print goal is relatively optimized and stereotyped. Such simple action sequences may be easily understood, recognized, and remembered by the learner; they may be easily integrated into the learner's repertoire of Displaywriter interaction plans. On the downside, this support may lead users to believe that all tasks will have a simple and shallow structure, a belief that may lead to frustration when the user leaves the training environment.

If the user has a specific and appropriate goal in mind, the simple blocking messages are quite effective supports for goal mapping – that is, for determining what action sequence will accomplish the goal. For example, a user trying to type and print who nonetheless selects the Change Alternate Format option on the Create or Revise menu gets the blocking message "Change Alternate Format is not available on the Training Displaywriter." In the context of the goal, this implies that choosing a new parameter for Change Alternate Format is not part of the appropriate action sequence, and the user's developing plan for typing and printing can be updated accordingly. At the same time, a user may misconstrue the system's ability to understand his or her intentions, and expect this sort of goal-relevant feedback to appear in other task situations.

Parameter Loop.   The Training Wheels interface inherits the claim regarding standard prompts embodied in the Displaywriter. However, as with the earlier claim regarding prominence of goal-relevant menu items, it does not alter the usability consequences of this claim.

The Displaywriter claims regarding the content and highlighting of the option-change prompt are also present in the Training Wheels interface: The Create or Revise menu still offers users an opportunity to set options, and the prompt indicating that possibility is still highlighted. But in the training system, these claims are "countered" by the error-blocking technique. Although the highlighting may invite a user to change an option, and the continued highlighting may suggest the continuing appropriateness of this goal, the blocking of any attempted option change suggests that this is *not* an appropriate goal. Indeed, the error blocking in this scenario makes a new claim, that not changing options is a reasonable goal. The training system might be seen as providing support for interpreting the highlighted prompt: It may at some point be appropriate to respond to this invitation, but not now. The downside of this claim is that users may learn to ignore this particular prompt, and not attempt to change options later on.

The Training Wheels interface embodies a variety of additional new psychological claims for the task scenario of making the parameter-loop error. The user *can* make an error in the Training Wheels system – for example, by selecting unnecessary options on the Create or Revise menu. Only the *consequence* of errors is blocked, not the opportunity to commit errors in the first place. The user goes through a realistic decision-making process to determine a correct goal mapping. Any incorrect mapping is clearly flagged by error blocking but without further consequence. The claim is that this aids users in evaluating inappropriate subgoals and actions. Of course, blocking errors does not tell the user what *to* do; a long sequence of attempted but blocked actions could become too complex to make sense of.

Blocking access to irrelevant functions purports to control the potential distraction of developing and pursuing erroneous plans. Because there are no false starts, action sequences are less deeply nested and relatively stereotyped across previous and subsequent attempts. This increases the chance that learners will notice what they are doing as they practice kernel scenarios (typing and printing). It becomes more likely that these action sequences will become saved in the plan repertoire. Of course, by blocking errorful paths, the training system also removes the opportunity for learning to deal with errors, to recognize and recover from them.

Recall that when an inappropriate selection is made, not only is it blocked, but also the user receives a message " . . . is not available on the Training Displaywriter." The immediate feedback seeks to support an evaluation of the just-attempted action while the relevant goals, plans, and action are still in memory. On the downside, it could foster a reflexive, nonplanful style of action by users, in which they simply make selections without thinking about them, relying on the system's feedback to make the "right" choice.

Finally, the Training Wheels interface embodies the claim that thwarting a user action will motivate further action. The claim could be true, but it could also be the case that blocking requested actions is frustrating to users, particularly when they do not fully understand the rationale for an action being blocked or if they experience a series of blocked attempts. This tradeoff is another central gamble inherent in the design of the Training Wheels interface.

Using the Full System. One of the primary roles of the Training Wheels interface was to make learning-by-doing more feasible for the Displaywriter. But this means that at some point there will be a learning transition from the Training Wheels version of the system to the full-function system. The Training Wheels interface embodies several claims about why this transition to the full system might be facilitated. Some of these claims have already been discussed. For example, the first two claims in the parameter-loop scenario pertain to this transition. We considered them in that scenario because their consequences are more important and more specific to the parameter-loop error. It is often the case that claims arise in the context of more than one user scenario.

Table 6.2 lists additional claims for the transition to the full system. First, the Training Wheels user has throughout been exposed to the actual full-system menus of the Displaywriter. Selecting a menu item might have led only to a blocking message, but the item was displayed and selectable. This made it possible for users to learn about the full system function unintentionally: "Spelling Tasks is not available in the Training Displaywriter" invites the inference that there is a function called Spelling Tasks available in some Displaywriter. Of course, at the same time, users may learn to avoid these blocked functions, and so be less likely to use them when they are available.

The Training Wheels interface also embodies the claim that a well-learned subset of system function can provide a foundation for further learning. The Training Wheels user has used only some of the Displaywriter function (that needed for creating and printing a document), but that subset is something from which to build. Because fewer functions and system states have been encountered, users may be better able to recognize and make sense of regularities in their learning experience. The scaffolding provided by this subset should be enhanced by the fact that it represents not just any subset but the core function of the application domain. The tradeoff here is that users may come to feel satisfied with this core subset, and on moving to the full system may attempt to use the well-learned function to address all their task needs, rather than learning more about the system.

The Training Wheels design also asserts that practicing kernel scenarios establishes basic skill components as parts of meaningful wholes. Thus, the typing and printing scenario incorporates the subtask of making a menu selection; the learner who practices typing and printing necessarily practices menu selection and experiences that basic skill as meaningful. Indeed, it is possible to imagine a basic skill whose learning is so well integrated into a meaningful task context that its generalization to other task contexts is inhibited.

Finally, the reduction in the number of possible system states, in consequence of error blocking, admits of fewer possible explanations for actions and consequences in an episode, and hence constrains the user's evaluation of an interaction. The tradeoff here is that these explanations might be too narrow to be of use when the user must deal with the full system.

Science-based Design

The Training Wheels example shows how the task–artifact cycle can be enhanced as a framework for HCI design practice by scenario-based design and psychological design rationale. A point we want to stress in describing this framework is that it affords scientific development; the psychology of tasks cum artifacts grows through the regular-science mechanisms of cumulation and abstraction. Two aspects of this are particularly important: the generalization of scenarios into what one might call user concerns and the generalization of system techniques into what one might call design strategies.

User Concerns

The analysis of Training Wheels as a structure of psychological claims in scenarios builds up the psychology of tasks. At the lowest level of abstraction, we can analyze claims embodied in specific scenario instances – for example, we could save a video clip of a particular user trying to cope with a particular parameter-loop problem. We can also abstract such particulars into *types;* Tables 6.1 and 6.2 illustrate this middle-level abstraction of the parameter-loop scenario.

Through further abstraction, middle-level scenarios can become instances of particular concerns that users might have. For example, a concern users frequently seemed to have in the parameter-loop scenario was what we might call the Did that work? concern. In the particular case of the parameter-loop scenario, this concern often led users to redundantly specify option changes. Other concerns can be identified – for example What can I do now? or What does this do? In the context of the parameter-loop scenario, these concerns make reference to users' difficulty in recognizing *not* changing options as possible action, and to the allure of unfamiliar but easily accessible function.

More abstractly still, the psychology of tasks incorporates general scenarios and issues of people engaging in activities with interactive artifacts (e.g., Norman, this volume): perhaps *learning about the system* or *recovering from errors.* It incorporates general issues and scenarios of work activity and human development (e.g., Greif, this volume; Volpert, in press): perhaps *personally restructuring one's work, collaborating with others,* or *learning by discovery.*

The psychology of tasks develops through cumulation and abstraction of scenarios. The analysis of particular task–artifact cycles codifies key scenarios associated with specific applications. It articulates the specific concerns users have, the fluencies and difficulties they encounter in pursuing these scenarios. Through abstraction, broader concerns are identified. In this way, the psychology of tasks can serve as a starting point for scenario-based design and the next excursion around the task–artifact cycle.

Design Strategies

A complementary way to develop the psychology of tasks is through a perspective on interface techniques as instantiations of design strategies. One way to do this is to look at techniques that make similar contributions to tasks, but do so in different ways. Training Wheels error blocking, for example, is similar to menu dimming as employed in the Macintosh (Carroll & Kellogg, 1989) and to function hiding as employed in the Bittitalk browser (Rosson et al., 1990) in that all three techniques help users to accomplish tasks by limiting the range of functions immediately available.

But the three techniques differ in their approach to managing the possibility of a user pursuing inappropriate function. Bittitalk browser function hiding can be viewed as an *attack* strategy; it preempts the possibility of pursuing inappropriate function by removing it from the interface. Macintosh menu dimming attempts to *mitigate* the problem; it reduces the chances that it will occur, and if it does occur, the consequences to the user are negligible. Training Wheels error blocking demonstrates an *exploit* strategy; it allows the problem to occur, but then uses its occurrence to the user's advantage (see Carroll & Rosson, 1987, for further discussion of these design strategies.).

We do not yet know whether interface techniques like function hiding, error blocking, and menu dimming will always be associated with particular design strategies. But we do know that the details of the situation of use and the design are critical for fully appreciating how a strategy works in a particular case. For example, the Training Wheels design seeks to exploit user errors in multiple ways. Users who select an inappropriate function are prevented from pursuing it; as articulated in the design rationale for Training Wheels (Table 6.2), error blocking allows the error to be exploited, because it supports useful inferences (e.g., that the selected function is not part of the task). But Training Wheels exploits such errors in another way by preserving the Displaywriter interface, including problematic features such as the biased highlighting on the Create or Revise menu that contributes to the parameter-loop error. In Training Wheels, when the parameter-loop error is made, the learner experiences the disparity between what *ought* to be done in that particular situation (e.g., bypass option changes) and what *seems necessary* from the interface display (i.e., "Type YOUR CHOICE; press ENTER"). If Training Wheels had not preserved this aspect of the Displaywriter design, this further opportunity to exploit learner errors would have been lost.

Developing the psychology of tasks through the abstraction of scenarios and system techniques entails at least two important consequences for using the task–artifact cycle as a framework for HCI design practice. The psychology of tasks cumulates and integrates knowledge of designs and their psychological consequences, backed up by a repository of detailed and contextualized examples of specific design situations. Moreover, the abstractions in the psychology of tasks like user concerns and design strategies can serve as indexes into the repository of specific examples. The psychology of tasks may thus enable us to map our understanding of scenarios like type-and-print and the parameter-loop error into other domains, for example, to designing a shared calendar system. Of course, the greater the abstraction, the greater the inductive risk. But when the task psychology is applied in scenario-based design, we are likely to want to take these risks in order to be able to systematically build from what we already know.

Can HCI Theory Be Usable?

Paradigm cases of the evolution of technology, like the steam engine, reveal a complex, iterative process of emulation and synthesis in which the details of solutions and contexts of use cast long shadows. This pattern raises challenging questions regarding the commitment of HCI to produce practical and intellectually rich theory. In this chapter our strategy was to clarify and augment the evident organization of current HCI design practice, a reiterating cycle of discovering and defining and understanding tasks people want to do, need to do, or might do, and then designing, developing, and analyzing artifacts to support tasks.

We conjecture that were this process better understood, articulated, and critiqued, more deliberately managed, it might serve both designers and users better. Our commitment to taking the context of technology development and use seriously leads us to the project of building what we have called an ontologically minimized HCI in which research abstractions and techniques are justified, even initially, on grounds of design pragmatics. We believe that this approach can make good on the commitment of HCI to produce an intellectually rich applied psychology that can proactively support the design of usable computer equipment.

More than this, however, we believe this work can contribute a more adequate conception of psychology itself. The detailed importance of the artifacts people use and the task environments in which they use them is not an eccentricity of HCI. It is the touchstone of the complex and dynamic world in which humans exist. Psychology has chronically been distracted by quirks like behaviorism and mentalism, but there have also always been strong voices urging more serious conceptions of experience and activity (in recent years, and from very different perspectives, James Gibson and Herbert Simon are examples). No one, of course, can predict revolutionary change in science, but today more prominently even than in the past, this urging for a more seriously grounded psychology resounds. The development of high-visibility areas like HCI will no doubt play a large role in the contemporary resolution of this perennial issue in psychology.

A key to facilitating this development in HCI, and in psychology itself, will be more adequate grounding of programmatic discussion. It is perplexing that discussions of methodological and ontological issues rarely include decent examples. Arguments are frequently pursued only in the most general terms, sometimes tiny "throw-away" examples are tossed off on the spot to flesh out a point, and realistic examples are pointed to rather than developed. This approach is chronic in psychology, where until recently it was bad manners to notice that experimental situations bore no relevance to real experience. In a design domain like HCI, it is all the more baffling that frameworks for integrating science and practice should be boldly sketched, but without the least effort at exemplification. We feel that working out examples is critical for ensuring that pithy abstracts and aesthetic sketches are ever made adequately operational.

The Training Wheels system was not developed using the tools and techniques we described here (though to a great extent these tools and techniques merely make explicit what was implicit in the original design process and rationale; see Carroll, 1985, 1990b; Carroll & Carrithers, 1984). Our goal was to show how the psychology embodied in the Displaywriter design and its contexts of use could play a proactive role in the task–artifact cycle. We have demonstrated this possibility, not merely asserted it. Our ongoing work includes a variety of "model farm" projects in which we are serving as our volunteers, employing scenario-based design for various interactive tools and environments, developing usability design rationales for these, and then redesigning (Bellamy & Carroll, 1990; Carroll, 1990b; Carroll & Rosson, 1990; Carroll, Singer, Bellamy, & Alpert, 1990).

History and practice in HCI design and development are far more systematic and successful than even a decade ago. We no longer must, and indeed no longer can, merely imagine a priori frameworks for infusing psychological science into this activity. This is not to say that HCI does not need a better model of itself or that HCI practice could not possibly make better use of psychology. Rather, it is to say that proposals for achieving either of these goals should start inside the practice and should build from the practical success and toward the practical problems.

Acknowledgment

We are grateful to Stephen Payne, Kevin Singley, and Linda Tetzlaff for comments on a prior draft of the paper.

References

Anderson, J. R. (1987). Methodologies for studying human knowledge. *Behavior and Brain Science, 10,* 467–505 (with commentary).

Basalla, G. (1988). *The evolution of technology.* New York: Cambridge University Press.

Bellamy, R. K. E., & Carroll, J.M. (1990). Redesign by design. In D. Diaper, D. Gilmore, G. Cockton, & B. Shackel (Eds.), *Human–Computer Interaction: Interact '90.* Proceedings of the Third IFIP Conference on Human–Computer Interaction (Cambridge, August 27–31). Amsterdam: North-Holland.

Biggerstaff, T. J. (1989, July). Design recovery for maintenance and reuse. *IEEE Computer, 22* (7), p. 36–49.

Cardwell, D. S. L. (1972). *Turning points in Western technology.* New York: Science History Publications.

Carroll, J. M. (1985). Minimalist design for active users. In B. Shackle (Ed.), *Proceedings of First IFIP Conference on Human–Computer Interaction: Interact '84* (London, September 4–7). (pp. 39–44). Amsterdam: North-Holland.

Carroll, J. M. (1989a). Evaluation, description and invention: Paradigms for human–computer interaction. In M. C. Yovits (Ed.), *Advances in computers* (Vol. 29, pp. 47–77). Orlando, FL: Academic Press.

Carroll, J. M. (1989b). Feeding the interface eaters. In A. G. Sutcliffe & L. A. Macaulay (Eds.), *People and computers V* (pp. 35–48). London: Cambridge University Press.

Carroll, J. M. (1990a). Infinite detail and emulation in an ontologically minimized HCI. In J. C. Chew & J. Whiteside (Eds.), (pp. 321–327). *Proceedings of CHI '90: Human Factors in Computing Systems.* New York: ACM.

Carroll, J. M. (1990b). *The Nurnberg funnel: Designing minimalist instruction for practical computer skill.* Cambridge, MA: MIT Press.

Carroll, J. M., & Campbell, R. L. (1986). Softening up hard science: Reply to Newell and Card, *Human–Computer Interaction, 2,* 227–249.

Carroll, J. M., & Campbell, R. L. (1989). Artifacts as psychological theories: The case of human–computer interaction. *Behaviour and Information Technology, 8,* 247–256.

Carroll, J. M., & Carrithers, C. (1984). Training Wheels in a user interface. *Communications of the ACM, 27,* 800–806.

Carroll, J. M., & Kay, D. S. (1988). Prompting, feedback, and error correction in the design of a scenario machine. *International Journal of Man–Machine Studies, 28,* 11–27.

Carroll, J. M., & Kellogg, W. A. (1989). Artifact as theory-nexus: Hermeneutics meets theory-based design. In K. Bice & C. H. Lewis (Eds.), *Proceedings of CHI '89: Human Factors in Computing Systems* (pp. 7–14). New York: ACM.

Carroll, J. M., & Rosson, M. B. (1987). The paradox of the active user. In J. M. Carroll (Ed.), *Interfacing thought: Cognitive aspects of human–computer interaction.* (pp. 80–111) Cambridge, MA: MIT Press/Bradford Books.

Carroll, J. M., & Rosson, M. B. (1990). Human computer interaction scenarios as a design representation. *Proceedings of HICSS-23: Hawaii International Conference on System Sciences* (pp. 555–561). Los Alamitos, CA: IEEE Computer Society Press.

Carroll, J. M., Singer, J. A., Bellamy, R. K. E., and Alpert, S. R. (1990). A view matcher for learning smalltalk. In J. C. Chew & J. Whiteside (Eds.), *Proceedings of CHI '90: Human Factors in Computing Systems* (pp. 431–437). New York: ACM.

Catrambone, R., & Carroll, J. M. (1987). Learning a word processing system with guided exploration and Training Wheels. In J. M. Carroll & P. P. Tanner (Eds.), *Proceedings of CHI + GI '87: Human Factors in Computing Systems and Graphics Interface* (Toronto, April 5–9), (pp. 169–174). New York: ACM.

Cole, M. (1990). Cultural psychology: A once and future discipline? Paper presented at the Nebraska Symposium, 1989.

Conklin, J., & Begeman, M. L. (1988). gIBIS: a hypertext tool for exploratory policy discussion. *CSCW '86: Proceedings of the Conference on Computer Supported Cooperative Work* (pp. 140–152). New York: ACM.

Engelbart, D., & English, W. (1968). A research center for augmenting human intellect. *Proceedings of Fall Joint Computer Conference, 33(1).* 395–410. Montvale, NJ: AFIPS Press.

Frese, M., & Sabini, J. (Eds.), (1985). *Goal directed behavior: The concept of action in psychology.* Hillside, NJ: Lawrence Erlbaum Associates.

Frese, M., Ulich, E., & Dzida, W. (Eds.), (1987). *Psychological issues of human–computer interaction in the workplace.* Amsterdam: North-Holland.

Gomory, R. E. (1983). Technology development. *Science, 220,* 576–580.

Hindle, B. (1981). *Emulation and invention.* New York: New York University Press.

Hutchins, E., Hollan, J., & Norman, D. A. (1986). Direct manipulation interfaces. In D. A. Norman & S. Draper (Eds.), *User centered system design: New perspectives on human–computer interaction.* Hillsdale, NJ: Lawrence Erlbaum Associates.

Jones, J. C. (1970). *Design methods: Seeds of human futures.* New York: Wiley.

Kellogg, W. A. (1989). *Extracting psychological claims from artifacts in use* (Research Report RC 15511). Yorktown Heights, NY: IBM T. J. Watson Research Center.

Kellogg, W. A. (1990). Qualitative artifact analysis. In D. Diaper, D. Gilmore, G. Cockton, and B. Shackel (Eds.), *Human–Computer Interaction: Interact '90.* Proceedings of the Third IFIP conference on Human–Computer Interaction (Cambridge, August 27–31). Amsterdam: North-Holland.

Laudan, R. (1984). Introduction. In R. Laudan (Ed.), *The nature of technological knowledge: Are models of scientific change relevant?* (pp. 1–26). Dordrecht: Reidel.

Leont'ev, A.N. (1978). *Activity, consciousness, and personality.* Englewood Cliffs, NJ: Prentice-Hall.

Mack, R. L., Lewis, C.H., & Carroll, J. M. (1983). Learning to use office systems: Problems and prospects. *ACM Transactions on Office Information Systems, 1,* 254–271.

McKendree, J. E., & Carroll, J. M. (1987). Impact of feedback content in initial learning of an office system. In H.-J. Bullinger & G. Shackel (Eds.), *Proceedings of Second IFIP Conference on Human–Computer Interaction: Interact '87 (Stuttgart, September 1–4),* (pp. 855–860). Amsterdam: North-Holland.

MacLean, A., Young, R. M., & Moran, T. P. (1989). Design rationale: The argument behind the artifact. In K. Bice & C. H. Lewis (Eds.), *Proceedings of CHI '89: Human Factors in Computing Systems* (pp. 247–252). New York: ACM.

Morrison, E. (1974). *From know-how to nowhere.* Oxford: Blackwell.

Newell, A., & Card, S. K. (1985). The prospects for psychological science in human–computer interaction. *Human–Computer Interaction, 1,* 209–242.

Norman, D. A. (1986). Cognitive engineering. In D. A. Norman & S. Draper (Eds.), *User centered system design: New perspectives on human–computer interaction.* Hillsdale, NJ: Lawrence Erlbaum Associates.

Norman, D. A. (1988). *The psychology of everyday things.* New York: Basic Books.

Roberts, T. L., & Moran, T. P. (1983). The evaluation of text editors: Methodology and empirical results. *Communications of the ACM, 26,* 265–283.

Rosson, M. B., Carroll, J. M., & Bellamy, R. K. E. (1990). Smalltalk scaffolding: A case study in minimalist instruction. In J. C. Chew & J. Whiteside (Eds.), *Proceedings of CHI '90: Human Factors in Computing Systems* (pp. 423–429). New York: ACM.

Scribner, S. (Ed.), (1984). Cognitive studies of work. *Quarterly Newsletter of the Laboratory of Comparative Human Cognition, 6*(1,2).

Shneiderman, B. (1982). The future of interactive systems and the emergence of direct manipulation. *Behavior and Information Technology, 1,* 237–256.

Smith, D. C., Irby, C., Kimball, R., Verplank, B., & Harslem, E. (1982, April). Designing the Star user interface. *Byte, 7*(4), 242–282.

Suchman, L. (1987). *Plans and situated actions.* Cambridge: Cambridge University Press.

Sutherland, I. E. (1963). Sketchpad: A man–machine graphical communication system. *Proceedings of the Spring Joint Computer Conference, 23,* 329–346. Montvale, NJ: AFIPS Press.

Vertelney, L. (1989). Panel abstract for "Drama and personality in user interface design." In K. Bice & C. Lewis (Eds.), *Proceedings of CHI '89: Human Factors in Computing Systems* (pp. 107–108). New York: ACM.

Volpert, W. (in press). Work design for human development. In R. Budde, C. Floyd, R. Keil-Slawik, & H. Zullighoven (Eds.), *Software development and reality construction.* New York: Springer-Verlag.

Vygotsky, L. S. (1978). *Mind in society: The development of higher mental processes* (M. Cole, V. John-Steiner, S. Scribner, & E. Souberman, Eds.). Cambridge, MA: Harvard University Press.

Whiteside, J., & Wixon, D. (1987). Improving human–computer interaction – a quest for cognitive science. In J. M. Carroll (Ed.), *Interfacing thought: Cognitive aspects of human–computer interaction* (pp. 337–352). Cambridge, MA: Bradford Books/MIT Press.

Winograd, T., & Flores, F. (1986). *Understanding computers and cognition: A new foundation for design.* Norwood, NJ: Ablex.

Wright, P. (1978). Feeding the interface eaters: Suggestions for integrating pure and applied research on language comprehension. *Instructional Science, 7,* 249–312.

7

Bridging between Basic Theories and the Artifacts of Human–Computer Interaction

Phil Barnard

Psychological ideas on a particular set of topics go through something very much like a product life cycle. An idea or vision is initiated, developed, and communicated. It may then be exploited, to a greater or lesser extent, within the research community. During the process of exploitation, the ideas are likely to be the subject of critical evaluation, modification, or extension. With developments in basic psychology, the success or penetration of the scientific product can be evaluated academically by the twin criteria of citation counts and endurance. As the process of exploitation matures, the idea or vision stimulates little new research either because its resources are effectively exhausted or because other ideas or visions that incorporate little from earlier conceptual frameworks have taken over. At the end of their life cycle, most ideas are destined to become fossilized under the pressure of successive layers of journals opened only out of the behavioral equivalent of paleontological interest.

In applied domains, research ideas are initiated, developed, communicated, and exploited in a similar manner within the research community. Yet, by the very nature of the enterprise, citation counts and endurance are of largely academic interest unless ideas or knowledge can effectively be transferred from research to development communities and then have a very real practical impact on the final attributes of a successful product.

If we take the past 20-odd years as representing the first life cycle of research in human–computer interaction, the field started out with few empirical facts and virtually no applicable theory. During this period a substantial body of work was motivated by the vision of an applied science based upon firm theoretical foundations. As the area was developed, there can be little doubt, on the twin academic criteria of endurance and citation, that some theoretical concepts have been successfully exploited within the research community. GOMS, of course, is the most notable example (Card, Moran, & Newell, 1983; Olson & Olson, 1990; Polson, 1987). Yet, as Carroll (e.g., 1989a,b) and others have pointed out, there are very few examples where substantive theory per se has had a major and direct impact on design. On this last practical criterion, cognitive science can more readily provide examples of impact through the application of empirical methodologies and the data they provide and through the direct application of psychological reasoning in the invention and demonstration of design concepts (e.g., see Anderson & Skwarecki, 1986; Card & Henderson, 1987; Carroll, 1989a,b; Hammond & Allinson, 1988; Landauer, 1987).

As this research life cycle in HCI matures, fundamental questions are being asked about whether or not simple deductions based on theory have any value at all in design (e.g. Carroll, this volume), or whether behavior in human–computer interactions is simply too complex for basic theory to have anything other than a minor practical impact (e.g., see Landauer, this volume). As the next cycle of research develops, the vision of a strong theoretical input to design runs the risk of becoming increasingly marginalized or of becoming another fossilized laboratory curiosity. Making use of a framework for understanding different research paradigms in HCI, this chapter will discuss how theory-based research might usefully evolve to enhance its prospects for both adequacy and impact.

Bridging Representations

In its full multidisciplinary context, work on HCI is not a unitary enterprise. Rather, it consists of many different sorts of design, development, and research activities. Long (1989) provides an analytic structure through which we can characterize these activities in terms of the nature of their underlying concepts and how different types of concept are manipulated and interrelated. Such a framework is potentially valuable because it facilitates specification of, comparison between, and evaluation of the many different paradigms and practices operating within the broader field of HCI.

With respect to the relationship between basic science and its application, Long makes three points that are fundamental to the arguments to be pursued in this and subsequent sections. First, he emphasizes that the kind of understanding embodied in our science base is a *representation* of the way in which the real world behaves. Second, any representation in the science base can only be mapped to and from the real world by what he calls "intermediary" representations. Third, the representations and mappings needed to realize this kind of two-way conceptual traffic are dependent upon the nature of the activities they are required to support. So the representations called upon for the purposes of software engineering will differ from the representations called upon for the purposes of developing an applicable cognitive theory.

Long's framework is itself a developing one (1987, 1989; Long & Dowell, 1989). Here, there is no need to pursue the details; it is sufficient to emphasize that the full characterization of paradigms operating directly with artifact design differs from those characterizing types of engineering support research, which, in turn, differ from more basic research paradigms. This chapter will primarily be concerned with what might need to be done to facilitate the applicability and impact of basic cognitive theory. In doing so it will be argued that a key role needs to be played by explicit "bridging" representations. This term will be used to avoid any possible conflict with the precise properties of Long's particular conceptualization.

Following Long (1989), Figure 7.1 shows a simplified characterization of an applied science paradigm for bridging from the real world of behavior to the science base and from these representations back to the real world. The blocks are intended to characterize different sorts of representation and the arrows stand for mappings between them (Long's terminology is not always used here). The real world of the use of interactive software is characterized by organizational, group, and physical

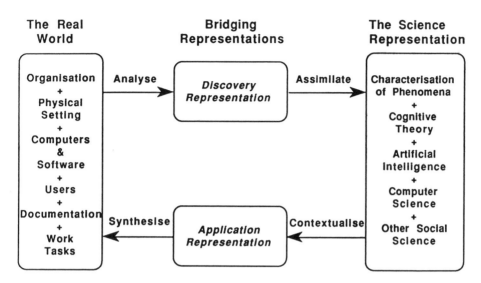

Figure 7.1. A view of an applied science paradigm (modified from Long, 1989).

settings; by artifacts such as computers, software, and manuals; by the real tasks of work; by characteristics of the user population; and so on. In both applied and basic research, we construct our science not from the real world itself but via a bridging representation whose purpose is to support and elaborate the process of scientific discovery.

Obviously, the different disciplines that contribute to HCI each have their own forms of discovery representation that reflect their paradigmatic perspectives, the existing contents of their science base, and the target form of their theory. In all cases the discovery representation incorporates a whole range of explicit, and more frequently implicit, assumptions about the real world and methodologies that might best support the mechanics of scientific abstraction. In the case of standard paradigms of basic psychology, the initial process of *analysis* leading to the formation of a discovery representation may be a simple observation of behavior on some task. For example, it may be noted that ordinary people have difficulty with particular forms of syllogistic reasoning. In more applied research, the initial process of analysis may involve much more elaborate taxonomization of tasks (e.g., Brooks, this volume) or of errors observed in the actual use of interactive software (e.g., Hammond, Long, Clark, Barnard, & Morton, 1980).

Conventionally, a discovery representation drastically simplifies the real world. For the purposes of gathering data about the potential phenomena, a limited number of contrastive concepts may need to be defined, appropriate materials generated, tasks selected, observational or experimental designs determined, populations and metrics selected, and so on. The real world of preparing a range of memos, letters, and reports for colleagues to consider before a meeting may thus be *represented* for the purposes of initial discovery by an observational paradigm with a small population of novices carrying out a limited range of tasks with a particular word processor (e.g., Mack, Lewis, & Carroll, 1983). In an experimental paradigm, it might be represented noninteractively by a paired associate learning task in which the mappings between names and operations need to be learned to some criterion and subsequently recalled (e.g., Scapin, 1981). Alternatively, it might be represented by a simple proverb-editing task carried out on two alternative versions of a cut-down interactive text editor with ten commands. After some form of instructional familiarization appropriate to a population of computer-naive members of a Cambridge volunteer subject panel, these commands may be used an equal number of times with performance assessed by time on task, errors, and help usage (e.g., Barnard, Hammond, MacLean, & Morton, 1982). Each of the decisions made contributes to the operational discovery representation.

The resulting characterizations of empirical phenomena are potential regularities of behavior that become, through a process of *assimilation,* incorporated into the science base where they can by operated on, or argued about, in terms of the more abstract, interpretive constructs. The discovery representations constrain the scope of what is assimilated to the science base and all subsequent mappings from it.

The conventional view of applied science also implies an inverse process involving some form of application bridge whose function is to support the transfer of knowledge in the science base into some domain of application. Classic ergonomics–human factors relied on the handbook of guidelines. The relevant processes involve *contextualizing* phenomena and scientific principles for some applications domain – such as computer interfaces, telecommunications apparatus, military hardware, and so on. Once explicitly formulated, say in terms of design principles, examples, and pointers to relevant data, it is left up to the developers to operate on the representation to *synthesize* that information with any other considerations they may have in the course of taking design decisions. The dominant vision of the first life cycle of HCI research was that this bridging could effectively be achieved in a harder form through engineering approximations derived from theory (Card et al., 1983). This vision essentially conforms to the full structure of Figure 7.1.

The Chasm to Be Bridged

The difficulties of generating a science base for HCI that will support effective bridging to artifact design are undeniably real. Many of the strategic problems theoretical approaches must overcome have now been thoroughly aired. The life cycle of theoretical enquiry and synthesis typically postdates the life cycle of products with which it seeks to deal; the theories are too low level; they are of restricted scope; as abstractions from behavior they fail to deal with the real context of work and they fail to accommodate fine details of implementations and interactions that may crucially influence the use of a system (see, e.g., discussions by Carroll & Campbell, 1986; Newell & Card, 1985; Whiteside & Wixon, 1987). Similarly, although theory may predict significant effects and receive empirical support, those effects may be of marginal practical consequence in the context of a broader interaction or less important than effects not specifically addressed (e.g., Landauer, 1987).

Our current ability to construct effective bridges across the chasm that separates our scientific understanding and the real world of user behavior and artifact design clearly falls well short of requirements. In its relatively short history, the scope of HCI research on interfaces has been extended from early concerns with the usability of hardware, through cognitive consequences of software interfaces, to encompass organizational issues (e.g., Grudin, 1990). Against this background, what is required is something that might carry a volume of traffic equivalent to an eight-lane cognitive highway. What is on offer is more akin to a unidirectional walkway constructed from a few strands of rope and some planks.

In *Taking artifacts seriously* Carroll (1989a) and Carroll, Kellogg, and Rosson in this volume, mount an impressive case against the conventional view of the deductive application of science in the invention, design, and development of practical artifacts. They point both to the inadequacies of current information-processing psychology, to the absence of real historical justification for deductive bridging in artifact development, and to the paradigm of craft skill in which knowledge and understanding are directly embodied in artifacts. Likewise, Landauer (this volume) foresees an equally dismal future for theory-based design.

Whereas Landauer stresses the potential advances that may be achieved through empirical modeling and formative evaluation, Carroll and his colleagues have sought a more substantial adjustment to conventional scientific strategy (Carroll, 1989a,b, 1990; Carroll & Campbell, 1989; Carroll & Kellogg, 1989; Carroll et al., this volume). On the one hand they argue that true "deductive" bridging from theory to application is not only rare, but when it does occur, it tends to be underdetermined, dubious, and vague. On the other hand they argue that the form of hermaneutics offered as an alternative by, for example, Whiteside and Wixon (1987) cannot be systematized for lasting value. From Carroll's viewpoint, HCI is best seen as a design science in which theory and artifact are in some sense merged. By embodying a set of interrelated psychological claims concerning a product like HyperCard or the Training Wheels interface (e.g., see Carroll & Kellogg, 1989), the artifacts themselves take on a theorylike role in which successive cycles of task analysis, interpretation, and artifact development enable design-oriented assumptions about usability to be tested and extended.

This viewpoint has a number of inviting features. It offers the potential of directly addressing the problem of complexity and integration because it is intended to enable multiple theoretical claims to be dealt with as a system bounded by the full artifact. Within the cycle of task analysis and artifact development, the analyses, interpretations, and theoretical claims are intimately bound to design problems and to the world of "real" behavior. In this context, knowledge from HCI research no longer needs to be transferred from research into design in quite the same sense as before and the life cycle of theories should also be synchronized with the products they need to impact. Within this framework, the operational discovery representation is effectively the rationale governing the design of an artifact, whereas the application representation is a series of user-interaction scenarios (Carroll, 1990).

The kind of information flow around the task–artifact cycle nevertheless leaves somewhat unclear the precise relationships that might hold between the explicit theories of the science base and the kind of implicit theories embodied in artifacts.

Early on in the development of these ideas, Carroll (1989a) points out that such implicit theories may be a provisional medium for HCI, to be put aside when explicit theory catches up. In a stronger version of the analysis, artifacts are in principle irreducible to a standard scientific medium such as explicit theories. Later it is noted that "it may be simplistic to imagine deductive relations between science and design, but it would be bizarre if there were no relation at all" (Carroll & Kellogg, 1989). Most recently, Carroll (1990) explicitly identifies the psychology of tasks as the relevant science base for the form of analysis that occurs within the task–artifact cycle (e.g. see Greif, this volume; Norman this volume). The task–artifact cycle is presumed not only to draw upon and contextualize knowledge in that science base, but also to provide new knowledge to *assimilate* to it. In this latter respect, the current view of the task artifact cycle appears broadly to conform with Figure 7.1. In doing so it makes use of task-oriented theoretical apparatus rather than standard cognitive theory and novel bridging representations for the purposes of understanding extant interfaces (design rationale) and for the purposes of engineering new ones (interaction scenarios).

In actual practice, whether the pertinent theory and methodology is grounded in tasks, human information-processing psychology, or artificial intelligence, those disciplines that make up the relevant science bases for HCI are *all* underdeveloped. Many of the basic theoretical claims are really provisional claims; they may retain a verbal character (to be put aside when a more explicit theory arrives), and even if fully explicit, the claims rarely generalize far beyond the specific empirical settings that gave rise to them. In this respect, the wider problem of how we go about bridging to and from a relevant science base remains a long-term issue that is hard to leave unaddressed. Equally, any research viewpoint that seeks to maintain a productive role for the science base in artifact design needs to be accompanied by a serious reexamination of the bridging representations used in theory development and in their application.

Science and design are very different activities. Given Figure 7.1, theory-based design can never be direct; the full bridge must involve a transformation of information in the science base to yield an applications representation, and information in this structure must be synthesized into the design problem. In much the same way that the application representation is constructed to support design, our science base, and any mappings from it, could be better constructed to support the development of effective application bridging. The model for relating science to design is indirect, involving theoretical support for engineering representations (both discovery and applications) rather than one involving direct theoretical support in design.

The Science Base and Its Application

In spite of the difficulties, the fundamental case for the application of cognitive theory to the design of technology remains very much what it was 20 years ago, and indeed what it was 30 years ago (e.g., Broadbent, 1958). Knowledge assimilated to the science base and synthesized into models or theories should reduce our reliance on purely empirical evaluations. It offers the prospect of supporting a deeper understanding of design issues and how to resolve them. Indeed, Carroll and Kellogg's (1989) theory nexus has clearly developed out of a cognitive paradigm rather than a behaviorist one. Although theory development lags behind the design of artifacts, it may well be that the science base has more to gain than the artifacts. The interaction of science and design nevertheless should be a two-way process of added value.

Much basic theoretical work involves the application of only partially explicit and incomplete apparatus to specific laboratory tasks. It is not unreasonable to argue that our basic cognitive theory tends only to be successful for modeling a particular application. That application is itself behavior in laboratory tasks. The scope of the application is delimited by the empirical paradigms and the artifacts it requires – more often than not these days, computers and software for presentation of information and response capture. Indeed, Carroll's task–artifact and interpretation cycles could very well be used to provide a neat description of the research activities involved in the iterative design and development of basic theory. The trouble is that the paradigms of basic psychological research, and the bridging representations used to develop and validate theory, typically involve unusually simple and often highly repetitive behavioral requirements atypical of those faced outside the laboratory.

Although it is clear that there are many cases of invention and craft where the kinds of scientific understanding established in the laboratory play little or no role in artifact development (Carroll, 1989b), this is only one side of the story. The other side is that we should only expect to find effective bridging when what is *in* the science base is an adequate representation of some aspect of the real world that is relevant to the specific artifact under development. In this context it is worth considering a couple of examples not usually called into play in the HCI domain.

Psychoacoustic models of human hearing are well developed. Auditory warning systems on older generations of aircraft are notoriously loud and unreliable. Pilots don't believe them and turn them off. Using standard techniques, it is possible to measure the noise characteristics of the environment on the flight deck of a particular aircraft and to design a candidate set of warnings based on a model of the characteristics of human hearing. This determines whether or not pilots can be expected to "hear" and identify those warnings over the pattern of background noise without being positively deafened and distracted (e.g., Patterson, 1983). Of course, the attention-getting and discriminative properties of members of the full set of warnings still have to be crafted. Once established, the extension of the basic techniques to warning systems in hospital intensive-care units (Patterson, Edworthy, Shailer, Lower, & Wheeler, 1986) and trains (Patterson, Cosgrove, Milroy, & Lower, 1989) is a relatively routine matter.

Developed further and automated, the same kind of psychoacoustic model can play a direct role in invention. As the front end to a connectionist speech recognizer, it offers the prospect of a theoretically motivated coding structure that could well prove to outperform existing technologies (e.g., see ACTS, 1989). As used in invention, what is being embodied in the recognition artifact is an integrated theory about the human auditory system rather than a simple heuristic combination of current signal-processing technologies.

Another case arises out of short-term memory research. Happily, this one does not concern limited capacity! When the research technology for short-term memory studies evolved into a computerized form, it was observed that word lists presented at objectively regular time intervals (onset to onset times for the sound envelopes) actually sounded irregular. In order to be perceived as regular the onset to onset times need to be adjusted so that the "perceptual centers" of the words occur at equal intervals (Morton, Marcus, & Frankish, 1976). This science base representation, and algorithms derived from it, can find direct use in telecommunications technology or speech interfaces where there is a requirement for the automatic generation of natural sounding number or option sequences.

Of course, both of these examples are admittedly relatively "low level." For many higher level aspects of cognition, what is *in* the science base are representations of laboratory phenomena of restricted scope and accounts of them. What would be needed in the science base to provide conditions for bridging are representations of phenomena much closer to those that occur in the real world. So, for example, the theoretical representations should be topicalized on phenomena that really *matter* in applied contexts (Landauer, 1987). They should be theoretical representations dealing with extended sequences of cognitive behavior rather than discrete acts. They should be representations of information-rich environments rather than information-impoverished ones. They should relate to circumstances where cognition is not a pattern of short repeating (experimental) cycles but where any cycles that might exist have meaning in relation to broader task goals and so on.

It is not hard to pursue points about what the science base *might* incorporate in a more ideal world. Nevertheless, it does contain a good deal of useful knowledge (cf. Norman, 1986), and indeed the first life cycle of HCI research has contributed to it. Many of the major problems with the appropriateness, scope, integration, and applicability of its content have been identified. Because major theoretical perestroika will not be achieved overnight, the more productive questions concern the limitations on the bridging representations of that first cycle of research and how discovery representations and applications representations might be more effectively developed in subsequent cycles.

An Analogy with Interface Design Practice

Not surprisingly, those involved in the first life cycle of HCI research relied very heavily in the formation of their discovery representations on the methodologies of the parent discipline. Likewise, in bridging from theory to application, those involved relied heavily on the standard historical products used in the verification of basic theory, that is, prediction of patterns of time and/or errors. There are relatively few examples where other attributes of behavior are modeled, such as choice among action sequences (but see Young & MacLean, 1988). A simple bridge, predictive of times or errors, provides information about the user of an interactive system. The user of that information is the designer, or more usually the design team. Frameworks are generally presented for how that information might be used to support design choice either directly (e.g., Card et al., 1983) or through trade-off analyses (e.g., Norman, 1983). However, these forms of application bridge are underdeveloped to meet the real needs of designers.

Given the general dictum of human factors research, "Know the user" (Hanson, 1971), it is remarkable how few explicitly empirical studies of design decision making are reported in the literature. In many respects, it would not be entirely unfair to argue that bridging representations between theory and design have remained problematic for the same kinds of reasons that early interactive interfaces were problematic. Like glass teletypes, basic psychological technologies were underdeveloped and, like the early design of command languages, the interfaces (application representations) were heuristically constructed by applied theorists around what they could provide rather than by analysis of requirements or extensive study of their target users or the actual context of design (see also Bannon & Bødker, this volume; Henderson, this volume).

Equally, in addressing questions associated with the relationship between theory and design, the analogy can be pursued one stage further by arguing for the iterative design of more effective bridging structures. Within the first life cycle of HCI research a goodly number of lessons have been learned that could be used to advantage in a second life cycle. So, to take a very simple example, certain forms of modeling assume that users naturally choose the fastest method for achieving their goal. However, there is now some evidence that this is not always the case (e.g., MacLean, Barnard, & Wilson, 1985). Any role for the knowledge and theory embodied in the science base must accommodate, and adapt to, those lessons. For many of the reasons that Carroll and others have elaborated, simple deductive bridging is problematic. To achieve impact, behavioral engineering research must itself directly support the design, development, and invention of artifacts. On any reasonable time scale there is a need for discovery and application representations that cannot be fully justified through science-base principles or data. Nonetheless, such a requirement simply restates the case for some form of cognitive engineering paradigm. It does not in and of itself undermine the case for the longer-term development of applicable theory.

Just as impact on design has most readily been achieved through the application of psychological reasoning in the invention and demonstration of artifacts, so a meaningful impact of theory might best be achieved through the invention and demonstration of novel forms of applications representations. The development of representations to bridge from theory to application cannot be taken in isolation. It needs to be considered in conjunction with the contents of the science base itself and the appropriateness of the discovery representations that give rise to them.

Without attempting to be exhaustive, the remainder of this chapter will exemplify how discovery representations might be modified in the second life cycle of HCI research; and illustrate how theory might drive, and itself benefit from, the invention and demonstration of novel forms of applications bridging.

Enhancing Discovery Representations

Although disciplines like psychology have a formidable array of methodological techniques, those techniques are primarily oriented toward hypothesis testing.

Here, greatest effort is expended in using factorial experimental designs to confirm or disconfirm a specific theoretical claim. Often wider characteristics of phenomena are only charted as and when properties become a target of specific theoretical interest. Early psycholinguistic research did not start off by studying what might be the most important factors in the process of understanding and using textual information. It arose out of a concern with transformational grammars (Chomsky, 1957). In spite of much relevant research in earlier paradigms (e.g., Bartlett, 1932), psycholinguistics itself only arrived at this consideration after progressing through the syntax, semantics, and pragmatics of single-sentence comprehension.

As Landauer (1987) has noted, basic psychology has not been particularly productive at evolving exploratory research paradigms. One of the major contributions of the first life cycle of HCI research has undoubtedly been a greater emphasis on demonstrating how such empirical paradigms can provide information to support design (again, see Landauer, 1987). Techniques for analyzing complex tasks, in terms of both action decomposition and knowledge requirements, have also progressed substantially over the past 20 years (e.g., Wilson, Barnard, Green, & MacLean, 1988).

A significant number of these developments are being directly assimilated into application representations for supporting artifact development. Some can also be assimilated into the science base, such as Lewis's (1988) work on abduction. Here observational evidence in the domain of HCI (Mack et al., 1983) leads directly to theoretical abstractions concerning the nature of human reasoning. Similarly, Carroll (1985) has used evidence from observational and experimental studies in HCI to extend the relevant science base on naming and reference. However, not a lot has changed concerning the way in which discovery representations are used for the purposes of assimilating knowledge to the science base and developing theory.

In their own assessment of progress during the first life cycle of HCI research, Newell and Card (1985) advocate continued reliance on the hardening of HCI as a science. This implicitly reinforces classic forms of discovery representations based upon the tools and techniques of parent disciplines. Heavy reliance on the time-honored methods of experimental hypothesis testing in experimental paradigms does not appear to offer a ready solution to the two problems dealing with theoretical scope and the speed of theoretical advance. Likewise, given that these parent disciplines are relatively weak on exploratory paradigms, such an approach does not appear to offer a ready solution to the other problems of enhancing the science base for appropriate content or for directing its efforts toward the theoretical capture of effects that really matter in applied contexts.

The second life cycle of research in HCI might profit substantially by spawning more effective discovery representations, not only for assimilation to applications representations for cognitive engineering, but also to support assimilation of knowledge to the science base and the development of theory. Two examples will be reviewed here. The first concerns the use of evidence embodied in HCI scenarios (Young & Barnard, 1987; Young, Barnard, Simon, & Whittington, 1989). The second concerns the use of protocol techniques to systematically sample what users know and to establish relationships between verbalizable knowledge and actual interactive performance.

Test-driving Theories

Young and Barnard (1987) have proposed that more rapid theoretical advance might be facilitated by "test driving" theories in the context of a systematically sampled set of behavioral scenarios. The research literature frequently makes reference to instances of problematic or otherwise interesting user-system exchanges. Scenario material derived from that literature is selected to represent some potentially robust phenomenon of the type that might well be pursued in more extensive experimental research. Individual scenarios should be regarded as representative of the kinds of things that really matter in applied settings. So for example, one scenario deals with a phenomenon often associated with unselected windows. In a multiwindowing environment a persistent error, frequently committed even by experienced users, is to attempt some action in an inactive window. The action might be an attempt at a menu selection. However, pointing and clicking over a menu item does not cause the intended result; it simply leads to the window being activated. Very much like linguistic test sentences, these behavioral scenarios are essentially idealized descriptions of such instances of human–computer interactions.

If we are to develop cognitive theories of significant scope, they must in principle be able to cope with a wide range of such scenarios. Accordingly, a manageable set of scenario material can be generated that taps behaviors that encompass different facets of cognition. So, a set of scenarios might include instances dealing with locating information in a directory entry, selecting alternative methods for achieving a goal, lexical errors in command entry, the unselected windows phenomenon, and so on (see Young, Barnard, Simon, & Whittington, 1989). A set of contrasting theoretical approaches can likewise be selected and the theories and scenarios organized into a matrix. The activity involves taking each theoretical approach and attempting to formulate an account of each behavioral scenario. The accuracy of the account is not at stake. Rather, the purpose of the exercise is to see whether a particular piece of theoretical apparatus is even capable of giving rise to a plausible account. The scenario material is effectively being used as a set of sufficiency filters and it is possible to weed out theories of overly narrow scope. If an approach is capable of formulating a passable account, interest focuses on the properties of the account offered. In this way, it is also possible to evaluate and capitalize on the properties of theoretical apparatus that do provide appropriate sorts of analytic leverage over the range of scenarios examined.

Traditionally, theory development places primary emphasis on predictive accuracy and only secondary emphasis on scope. This particular form of discovery representation goes some way toward redressing that balance. It offers the prospect of getting appropriate and relevant theoretical apparatus in place on a relatively short time cycle. As an exploratory methodology, it at least addresses some of the more profound difficulties of interrelating theory and application. The scenario material makes use of known instances of human–computer interaction. Because these scenarios are by definition instances of interactions, any theoretical accounts built around them must of necessity be appropriate to the domain. Because scenarios are intended to capture significant aspects of user behavior, such as persistent errors, they are oriented toward what matters in the applied context. As a quick and dirty methodology, it can make effective use of the accumulated knowledge acquired in the first life cycle of HCI research, while avoiding some of the worst "tar pits" (Norman, 1983) of traditional experimental methods.

As a form of discovery bridge between application and theory, the real world is represented, for some purpose, not by a local observation or example, but by a sampled set of material. If the purpose is to develop a form of cognitive architecture, then it may be most productive to select a set of scenarios that encompass different components of the cognitive system (perception, memory, decision making, control of action). Once an applications representation has been formed, its properties might be further explored and tested by analyzing scenario material sampled over a range of different *tasks,* or *applications domains* (see Young & Barnard, 1987). At the point where an applications representation is developed, the support it offers may also be explored by systematically sampling a range of design scenarios and examining what information can be offered concerning alternative interface options (AMODEUS, 1989). By contrast with more usual discovery representations, the scenario methodology is not primarily directed at classic forms of hypothesis testing and validation. Rather, its purpose is to support the generation of more readily applicable theoretical ideas.

Verbal Protocols and Performance

One of the most productive exploratory methodologies utilized in HCI research has involved monitoring user action while collecting concurrent verbal protocols to help understand what is actually going on. Taken together these have often given rise to the best kinds of problem-defining evidence, including the kind of scenario material already outlined. Many of the problems with this form of evidence are well known. Concurrent verbalization may distort performance and significant changes in performance may not necessarily be accompanied by changes in articulable knowledge. Because it is labor intensive, the observations are often confined to a very small number of subjects and tasks. In consequence, the representativeness of isolated observations is hard to assess. Furthermore, getting real scientific value from protocol analysis is crucially dependent on the insights and craft skill of the researcher concerned (Barnard, Wilson, & MacLean, 1986; Ericsson & Simon, 1980).

Techniques of verbal protocol analysis can nevertheless be modified and utilized as a part of a more elaborate discovery representation to explore and establish systematic relationships between articulable knowledge and performance. The basic assumption underlying much theory is that a characterization of the ideal knowledge a user should possess to successfully perform a task can be used to derive predictions about performance. However, protocol studies clearly suggest that users really get into difficulty when they have erroneous or otherwise nonideal knowledge. In terms of the precise relationships they have with performance, ideal and nonideal knowledge are seldom considered together.

In an early attempt to establish systematic and potentially generalizable relationships between the contents of verbal protocols and interactive performance, Barnard et al., (1986) employed a sample of picture probes to elicit users' knowledge of tasks, states, and procedures for a particular office product at two stages of learning. The protocols were codified, quantified, and compared. In the verbal protocols, the number of true claims about the system increased with system experience, but surprisingly, the number of false claims remained stable. Individual users who articulated a lot of correct claims generally performed well, but the amount of inaccurate knowledge did not appear related to their overall level of performance. There was, however, some indication that the amount of inaccurate knowledge expressed in the protocols was related to the frequency of errors made in particular system contexts.

A subsequent study (Barnard, Ellis, & MacLean, 1989) used a variant of the technique to examine knowledge of two different interfaces to the same application functionality. High levels of inaccurate knowledge expressed in the protocols were directly associated with the dialogue components on which problematic performance was observed. As with the earlier study, the amount of accurate knowledge expressed in any given verbal protocol was associated with good performance, whereas the amount of inaccurate knowledge expressed bore little relationship to an individual's overall level of performance. Both studies reinforced the speculation that it is specific interface characteristics that give rise to the development of inaccurate or incomplete knowledge from which false inferences and poor performance may follow.

Just as the systematic sampling and use of behavioral scenarios may facilitate the development of theories of broader scope, so discovery representations designed to systematically sample the actual knowledge possessed by users should facilitate the incorporation into the science base of behavioral regularities and theoretical claims that are more likely to reflect the actual basis of user performance rather than a simple idealization of it.

Enhancing Application Representations

The application representations of the first life cycle of HCI research relied very much on the standard theoretical products of their parent disciplines. Grammatical techniques originating in linguistics were utilized to characterize the complexity of interactive dialogues; artificial intelligence (AI)–oriented models were used to represent and simulate the knowledge requirements of learning; and, of course, derivatives of human information-processing models were used to calculate how long it would take users to do things. Although these approaches all relied upon some form of task analysis, their apparatus was directed toward some specific function. They were all of limited scope and made numerous trade-offs between what was modeled and the form of prediction made (Simon, 1988).

Some of the models were primarily directed at capturing knowledge requirements for dialogues for the purposes of representing complexity, such as BNF grammars (Reisner, 1982) and Task Action Grammars (Payne & Green, 1986). Others focused on interrelationships between task specifications and knowledge requirements, such as GOMS analyses and cognitive-complexity theory (Card et al., 1983; Kieras & Polson, 1985). Yet other apparatus, such as the model human information processor and the keystroke level model of Card et al. (1983) were primarily aimed at time prediction for the execution of error-free routine cognitive skill. Most of these modeling efforts idealized either the knowledge that users needed to possess or their actual behavior. Few models incorporated apparatus for integrating over the requirements of knowledge acquisition or use *and* human information-processing constraints (e.g., see Barnard, 1987). As applications representations, the models of the first life cycle had little to say about errors or the actual dynamics of user–system interaction as influenced by task constraints and information or knowledge about the domain of application itself.

Two modeling approaches will be used to illustrate how applications representations might usefully be enhanced. They are programmable user models (Young, Green, & Simon, 1989) and modeling based on Interacting Cognitive Subsystems (Barnard, 1985). Although these approaches have different origins, both share a number of characteristics. They are both aimed at modeling more qualitative aspects of cognition in user–system interaction; both are aimed at understanding how task, knowledge, and processing constraint intersect to determine performance; both are aimed at exploring novel means of incorporating explicit theoretical claims into application representations; and both require the implementation of interactive systems for supporting decision making in a design context. Although they do so in different ways, both approaches attempt to preserve a coherent role for explicit cognitive theory. Cognitive theory is embodied, not in the artifacts that emerge from the development process, but in demonstrator artifacts that might support design. This is almost directly analogous to achieving an impact in the marketplace through the application of psychological reasoning in the invention of artifacts. Except in this case, the target user populations for the envisaged artifacts are those involved in the design and development of products.

Programmable User Models (PUMs)

The core ideas underlying the notion of a programmable user model have their origins in the concepts and techniques of AI. Within AI, cognitive architectures are essentially sets of constraints on the representation and processing of knowledge. In order to achieve a working simulation, knowledge appropriate to the domain and task must be represented within those constraints. In the normal simulation methodology, the complete system is provided with some data and, depending on its adequacy, it behaves with more or less humanlike properties.

Using a simulation methodology to provide the designer with an artificial user would be one conceivable tactic. Extending the forms of prediction offered by such simulations (cf. cognitive complexity theory; Polson, 1987) to encompass qualitative aspects of cognition is more problematic. Simply simulating behavior is of relatively little value. Given the requirements of knowledge-based programming, it could, in many circumstances, be much more straightforward to provide a proper sample of real users. There needs to be some mechanism whereby the properties of the simulation provide information of value in design. Programmable user models provide a novel perspective on this latter problem. The idea is that the designer is provided with two things, an "empty" cognitive architecture and an instruction language for providing it with *all* the knowledge it needs to carry out some task. By programming it, the designer has to get the architecture to perform that task under conditions that match those of the interactive system design (i.e., a device model). So, for example, given a particular dialog design, the designer might have to program the architecture to select an object displayed in a particular way on a VDU and drag it across that display to a target position.

The key, of course, is that the constraints that make up the architecture being programmed are humanlike. Thus, if the designer finds it hard to get the architecture to perform the task, then the implication is that a human user would also find the task hard to accomplish. To concretize this, the designer may find that the easiest form of knowledge-based program tends to select and drag the wrong object under particular conditions. Furthermore, it takes a lot of thought and effort to figure out how to get round this problem within the specific architectural constraints of the model. Now suppose the designer were to adjust the envisaged user-system dialog in the device model and then found that reprogramming the architecture to carry out the same task under these new conditions was straightforward and the problem of selecting the wrong object no longer arose. Young and his colleagues would then argue that this constitutes direct evidence that the second version of the dialog design tried by the designer is likely to prove more usable than the first.

The actual project to realize a working PUM remains at an early stage of development. The cognitive architecture being used is SOAR (Laird, Newell, & Rosenbloom, 1987). There are many detailed issues to be addressed concerning the design of an appropriate instruction language. Likewise, real issues are raised about how a model that has its roots in architectures for problem solving (Newell & Simon, 1972) deals with the more peripheral aspects of human information processing, such as sensation, perception, and motor control. Nevertheless as an architecture, it has scope in the sense that a broad range of tasks and applications can be modeled within it. Indeed, part of the motivation of SOAR is to provide a unified general theory of cognition (Newell, 1989).

In spite of its immaturity, additional properties of the PUM concept as an application bridging structure are relatively clear (see Young et al., 1989). First, programmable user models embody explicit cognitive theory in the form of the to-be-programmed architecture. Second, there is an interesting allocation of function between the model and the designer. Although the modeling process requires extensive operationalization of knowledge in symbolic form, the PUM provides only the constraints and the instruction language, whereas the designer provides the knowledge of the application and its associated tasks. Third, knowledge in the science base is transmitted implicitly into the design domain via an inherently exploratory activity. Designers are not *told* about the underlying cognitive science; they are supposed to discover it. By doing what they know how to do well – that is, programming – the relevant aspects of cognitive constraints and their interactions with the application should emerge directly in the design context.

Fourth, programmable user models support a form of *qualitative* predictive evaluation that can be carried out relatively early in the design cycle. What that evaluation provides is not a classic predictive product of laboratory theory, rather it should be an understanding of why it is better to have the artifact constructed one way rather than another. Finally, although the technique capitalizes on the designer's programming skills, it clearly requires a high degree of commitment and expense. The instruction language has to be learned and doing the programming would require the development team to devote considerable resources to this form of predictive evaluation.

Approximate Models of Cognitive Activity

Interacting Cognitive Subsystems (Barnard, 1985) also specifies a form of cognitive architecture. Rather than being an AI constraint-based architecture, ICS has its roots in classic human information-processing theory. It specifies the processing and memory resources underlying cognition, the organization of these resources, and principles governing their operation. Structurally, the complete human information-processing system is viewed as a distributed architecture with functionally distinct subsystems each specializing in, and supporting, different types of sensory, representational, and effector processing activity. Unlike many earlier generations of human information-processing models, there are no general purpose resources such as a central executive or limited capacity working memory. Rather the model attempts to define and characterize processes in terms of the mental representations they take as input and the representations they output. By focusing on the mappings between different mental representations, this model seeks to integrate a characterization of knowledge-based processing activity with classic structural constraints on the flow of information within the wider cognitive system.

A graphic representation of this architecture is shown in the right-hand panel of Figure 7.2, which instantiates Figure 7.1 for the use of the ICS framework in an HCI context. The architecture itself is part of the science base. Its initial development was supported by using empirical evidence from laboratory studies of short-term memory phenomena (Barnard, 1985). However, by concentrating on the different types of mental representation and process that transform them, rather than task and paradigm specific concepts, the model can be applied across a broad range of settings (e.g., see Barnard & Teasdale, 1991). Furthermore, for the purposes of constructing a representation to bridge between theory and application it is possible to develop explicit, yet approximate, characterizations of cognitive activity.

In broad terms, the way in which the overall architecture will *behave* is dependent upon four classes of factor. First, for any given task it will depend on the precise configuration of cognitive activity. Different subsets of processes and memory records will be required by different tasks. Second, behavior will be constrained by the specific procedural knowledge embodied in each mental process that actually transforms one type of mental representation to another. Third, behavior will be constrained by the form, content, and accessibility of any memory records that are needed in that phase of activity. Fourth, it will depend on the overall way in which the complete configuration is coordinated and controlled.

Because the resources are relatively well defined and constrained in terms of their attributes and properties, interdependencies between them can be motivated on the basis of known patterns of experimental evidence and rendered explicit. So, for example, a *complexity* attribute of the coordination and control of cognitive activity can be directly related to the *number* of incompletely proceduralized processes within a specified configuration. Likewise, a *strategic* attribute of the coordination and control of cognitive activity may be dependent upon the overall amount of *order uncertainty* associated with the mental representation of a task stored in a memory record. For present purposes the precise details of these interdependencies do not matter, nor does the particularly opaque terminology shown in the rightmost panel of Figure 7.2 (for more details, see Barnard, 1987). The important point is that theoretical claims can be specified within this framework at a high level of abstraction and that these abstractions belong in the science base.

Although these theoretical abstractions could easily have come from classic studies of human memory and performance, they were in fact motivated by experimental studies of command naming in text editing (Grudin & Barnard, 1984) and performance on an electronic mailing task (Barnard, MacLean, & Hammond, 1984). The full theoretical analyses are described in Barnard (1987) and extended in Barnard, Grudin, and MacLean (1989). In both cases the tasks were interactive, involved extended sequences of cognitive behavior, involved information-rich environments, and the repeating patterns of data collection were meaningful in relation to broader task goals not atypical of interactive tasks in the real world. In relation to the arguments presented earlier in this chapter, the information being assimilated to the science base should be more appropriate and relevant to HCI than that derived from more abstract laboratory paradigms. It will nonetheless be subject to interpretive restrictions inherent in the particular form of discovery representation utilized in the design of these particular experiments.

Armed with such theoretical abstractions, and accepting their potential limitations, it is possible to generate a theoretically motivated bridge to application. The idea is to build approximate models that *describe* the nature of cognitive activity underlying the performance of complex tasks. The process is actually carried out by an expert system that embodies the theoretical knowledge required to build such models. The system "knows" what kinds of configurations are associated with particular phases of cognitive activity; it "knows" something about the conditions under which knowledge becomes proceduralized, and the properties of memory records that might support recall and inference in complex task environments. It also "knows" something about the theoretical interdependencies between these factors in determining the overall patterning, complexity, and qualities of the coordination and dynamic control of cognitive activity. Abstract descriptions of cognitive activity are constructed in terms of a four-component model specifying attributes of configurations, procedural knowledge, record contents, and dynamic control. Finally, in order to produce an output, the system "knows" something about the

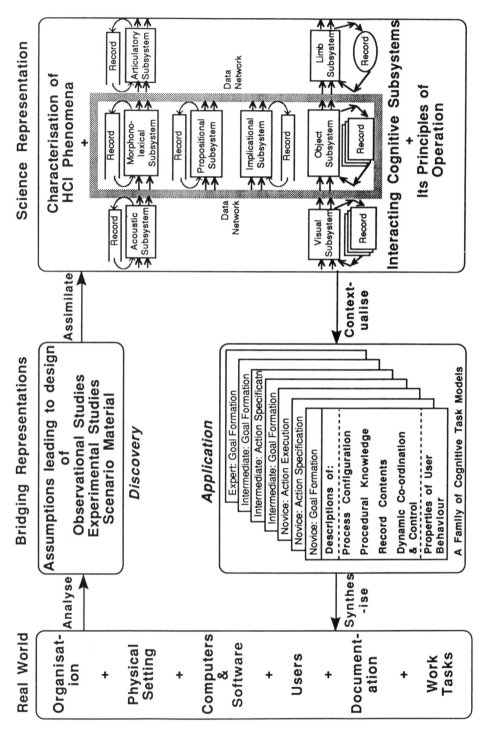

Figure 7.2. The applied science paradigm instantiated for the use of interacting cognitive subsystems as a theoretical basis for the development of an expert system design aid.

relationships between these abstract models of cognitive activity and the attributes of user behavior.

Obviously, no single model of this type can capture everything that goes on in a complex task sequence. Nor can a single model capture different stages of user development or other individual differences within the user population. It is therefore necessary to build a set of interrelated models representing different phases of cognitive activity, different levels and forms of user expertise, and so on. The basic modeling unit uses the four-component description to characterize cognitive activity for a particular phase, such as establishing a goal, determining the action sequence, and executing it. Each of these models approximates over the very short-term dynamics of cognition. Transitions between phases approximate over the short-term dynamics of tasks, whereas transitions between levels of expertise approximate over different stages of learning. In Figure 7.2, the envisaged application representation thus consists of a family of interrelated models depicted graphically as a stack of cards.

Like the concept of programmable user models, the concept of approximate descriptive modeling is in the course of development. A running demonstrator system exists that effectively replicates the reasoning underlying the explanation of a limited range of empirical phenomena in HCI research (see Barnard, Wilson, & MacLean, 1987, 1988). What actually happens is that the expert system elicits, in a context-sensitive manner, descriptions of the envisaged interface, its users, and the tasks that interface is intended to support. It then effectively "reasons about" cognitive activity, its properties, and attributes in that applications setting for one or more phases of activity and one or more stages of learning. Once the models have stabilized, it then outputs a characterization of the probable properties of user behavior. In order to achieve this, the expert system has to have three classes of rules: those that map from descriptions of tasks, users, and systems to entities and properties in the model representation; rules that operate on those properties; and rules that map from the model representation to characterizations of behavior. Even in its somewhat primitive current state, the demonstrator system has interesting generalizing properties. For example, theoretical principles derived from research on rather antiquated command languages support limited generalization to direct manipulation and iconic interfaces.

As an applications representation, the expert system concept is very different from programmable user models. Like PUMs, the actual tool embodies explicit theory drawn from the science base. Likewise, the underlying architectural concept enables a relatively broad range of issues to be addressed. Unlike PUMs, it more directly addresses a fuller range of resources across perceptual, cognitive, and effector concerns. It also applies a different trade-off in when and by whom the modeling knowledge is specified. At the point of creation, the expert system must contain a complete set of rules for mapping between the world and the model. In this respect, the means of accomplishing and expressing the characterizations of cognition and behavior must be fully and comprehensively encoded. This does not mean that the expert system must necessarily "know" each and every detail. Rather, within some defined scope, the complete chain of assumptions from artifact to theory and from theory to behavior must be made explicit at an appropriate level of approximation. Equally, the input and output rules must obviously be grounded in the language of interface description and user–system interaction. Although some of the assumptions may be heuristic, and many of them may need crafting, both theoretical and craft components are there. The how-to-do-it modeling knowledge is laid out for inspection.

However, at the point of use, the expert system requires considerably less precision than PUMs in the specification and operationalization of the knowledge required to use the application being considered. The expert system can build a family of models very quickly and without its user necessarily acquiring any great level of expertise in the underlying cognitive theory. In this way, it is possible for that user to explore models for alternative system designs over the course of something like one afternoon. Because the system is modular, and the models are specified in abstract terms, it is possible in principle to tailor the systems input and output rules without modifying the core theoretical reasoning. The development of the tool could then respond to requirements that might emerge from empirical studies of the real needs of design teams or of particular application domains.

In a more fully developed form, it might be possible to address the issue of which type of tool might prove more effective in what types of applications context. However, strictly speaking, they are not direct competitors, they are alternative types of application representation that make different forms of trade-off about the characteristics of the complete chain of bridging from theory to application. By contrast with the kinds of theory-based techniques relied on in the first life cycle of HCI research, both PUMs and the expert-system concept represent more elaborate bridging structures. Although underdeveloped, both approaches are intended ultimately to deliver richer and more integrated information about properties of human cognition into the design environment in forms in which it can be digested and used. Both PUMs and the expert system represent ways in which theoretical support might be usefully embodied in future generations of tools for supporting design. In both cases the aim is to deliver within the lifetime of the next cycle of research a qualitative understanding of what might be going on in a user's head rather than a purely quantitative estimate of how long the average head is going to be busy (see also Lewis, this volume).

Summary

The general theme that has been pursued in this chapter is that the relationship between the real world and theoretical representations of it is always mediated by bridging representations that subserve specific purposes. In the first life cycle of research on HCI, the bridging representations were not only simple, they were only a single step away from those used in the parent disciplines for the development of basic theory and its validation. If cognitive theory is to find any kind of coherent and effective role in forthcoming life cycles of HCI research, it must seriously reexamine the nature and function of these bridging representations as well as the content of the science base itself.

This chapter has considered bridging between specifically cognitive theory and behavior in human–computer interaction. This form of bridging is but one among many that need to be pursued. For example, there is a need to develop bridging representations that will enable us to interrelate models of user cognition with the formed models being developed to support design by software engineers (e.g., Dix, Harrison, Runciman, & Thimbleby, 1987; Harrison, Roast, & Wright, 1989; Thimbleby, 1985). Similarly there is a need to bridge between cognitive models and aspects of the application and the situation of use (e.g., Suchman, 1987). Truly interdisciplinary research formed a large part of the promise, but little of the reality of early HCI research. Like the issue of tackling nonideal user behavior, interdisciplinary bridging is now very much on the agenda for the next phase of research (e.g., see Barnard & Harrison, 1989).

The ultimate impact of basic theory on design can only be indirect – through an explicit application representation. Alternative forms of such representation that go well beyond what has been achieved to date have to be invented, developed, and evaluated. The views of Carroll and his colleagues form one concrete proposal for enhancing our application representations. The *design rationale* concept being developed by MacLean, Young, and Moran (1989) constitutes another potential vehicle for expressing application representations. Yet other proposals seek to capture qualitative aspects of human cognition while retaining a strong theoretical character (Barnard et al., 1987; 1988; Young, Green, & Simon, 1989).

On the view advocated here, the direct theory-based product of an applied science paradigm operating in HCI is not an interface design. It is an application representation capable of providing principled support for reasoning about designs. There may indeed be very few examples of theoretically inspired software products in the current commercial marketplace. However, the first life cycle of HCI research has produced a far more mature view of what is entailed in the development of bridging representations that might effectively support design reasoning. In subsequent cycles, we may well be able to look forward to a significant shift in the balance of added value within the interaction between applied science and design. Although future progress will in all probability remain less than rapid, theoretically grounded concepts may yet deliver rather more in the way of principled support for design than has been achieved to date.

Acknowledgments

The participants at the Kittle Inn workshop contributed greatly to my understanding of the issues raised here. I am particularly indebted to Jack Carroll, Wendy Kellogg, and John Long, who commented extensively on an earlier draft. Much of the thinking also benefited substantially from my involvement with the multidisciplinary AMODEUS project, ESPRIT Basic Research Action 3066.

References

ACTS (1989). Connectionist Techniques for Speech (Esprit Basic Research Action 3207), *Technical Annex*. Brussels: CEC.

AMODEUS (1989). Assimilating models of designers users and systems (Esprit Basic Research Action 3066), *Technical Annex*. Brussels: CEC.

Anderson, J. R., & Skwarecki, E. 1986. The automated tutoring of introductory computer programming. *Communications of the ACM, 29,* 842–849.

Barnard, P. J. (1985). Interacting cognitive subsystems: A psycholinguistic approach to short term memory. In A. Ellis, (Ed.), *Progress in the psychology of language* (Vol. 2, chapter 6, pp. 197–258). London: Lawrence Erlbaum Associates.

Barnard, P. J. (1987). Cognitive resources and the learning of human–computer dialogs. In J. M. Carroll (Ed.), *Interfacing thought: Cognitive aspects of human–computer interaction* (pp. 112–158). Cambridge MA: MIT Press.

Barnard, P. J., & Harrison, M. D. (1989). Integrating cognitive and system models in human–computer interaction. In A. Sutcliffe & L. Macaulay, (Ed.), *People and computers V* (pp. 87–103). Cambridge: Cambridge University Press.

Barnard, P. J., Ellis, J., & MacLean, A. (1989). Relating ideal and non-ideal verbalised knowledge to performance. In A. Sutcliffe & L. Macaulay (Eds.), *People and computers V* (pp. 461–473). Cambridge: Cambridge University Press.

Barnard, P. J., Grudin, J., & MacLean, A. (1989). Developing a science base for the naming of computer commands. In J. B. Long & A. Whitefield (Eds.), *Cognitive ergonomics and human–computer interaction* (pp. 95–133). Cambridge: Cambridge University Press.

Barnard, P. J., Hammond, N., MacLean, A., & Morton, J. (1982). Learning and remembering interactive commands in a text-editing task. *Behaviour and Information Technology, 1,* 347–358.

Barnard, P. J., MacLean, A., & Hammond, N. V. (1984). User representations of ordered sequences of command operations. In B. Shackel (Ed.), *Proceedings of Interact '84: First IFIP Conference on Human–Computer Interaction,* (Vol. 1, pp. 434–438). London: IEE.

Barnard, P. J., & Teasdale, J. (1991). Interacting cognitive subsystems: A systemic approach to cognitive-affective interaction and change. *Cognition and Emotion, 5,* 1–39.

Barnard, P. J., Wilson, M., & MacLean, A. (1986). The elicitation of system knowledge by picture probes. In M. Mantei & P. Orbeton (Eds.), *Proceedings of CHI '86: Human Factors in Computing Systems* (pp. 235–240). New York: ACM.

Barnard, P. J., Wilson, M., & MacLean, A. (1987). Approximate modelling of cognitive activity: Towards an expert system design aid. In J. M. Carroll & P. P. Tanner (Eds.), *Proceedings of CHI + GI '87: Human Factors in Computing Systems and Graphics Interface* (pp. 21–26). New York: ACM.

Barnard, P. J., Wilson, M., & MacLean, A. (1988). Approximate modelling of cognitive activity with an Expert system: A theory based strategy for developing an interactive design tool. *The Computer Journal, 31,* 445–456.

Bartlett, F. C. (1932). *Remembering: A study in experimental and social psychology.* Cambridge: Cambridge University Press.

Broadbent, D. E. (1958). *Perception and communication.* London: Pergamon Press.

Card, S. K., & Henderson, D. A. (1987). A multiple virtual-workspace interface to support user task-switching. In J. M. Carroll & P. P. Tanner (Eds.), *Proceedings of CHI + GI '87: Human Factors in Computing Systems and Graphics Interface* (pp. 53–59). New York: ACM.

Card, S. K., Moran, T. P., & Newell, A. (1983). *The psychology of human–computer interaction.* Hillsdale, NJ: Lawrence Erlbaum Associates.

Carroll, J. M. (1985). *What's in a name?* New York: Freeman.

Carroll, J. M. (1989a). Taking artifacts seriously. In S. Maas & H. Oberquelle (Eds.), *Software-Ergonomie '89* (pp. 36–50). Stuttgart: Teubner.

Carroll, J. M. (1989b). Evaluation, description and invention: Paradigms for human–computer interaction. In M. C. Yovits (Ed.), *Advances in computers* (Vol. 29, pp. 44–77). London: Academic Press.

Carroll, J. M. (1990). Infinite detail and emulation in an ontologically minimized HCI. In J. Chew & J. Whiteside (Eds.), *Proceedings of CHI '90: Human Factors in Computing Systems* (pp. 321–327). New York: ACM.

Carroll, J. M., & Campbell, R. L. (1986). Softening up hard science: Reply to Newell and Card. *Human–Computer Interaction, 2,* 227–249.

Carroll, J. M., & Campbell, R. L. (1989). Artifacts as psychological theories: The case of human–computer interaction. *Behaviour and Information Technology, 8,* 247–256.

Carroll, J. M., & Kellogg, W. A. (1989). Artifact as theory-nexus: Hermaneutics meets theory-based design. In K. Bice & C. H. Lewis (Eds.), *Proceedings of CHI '89: Human Factors in Computing Systems* (pp. 7–14). New York: ACM.

Chomsky, N. (1957). *Syntactic structures.* The Hague: Mouton.

Dix, A. J., Harrison, M. D., Runciman, C., & Thimbleby, H. W. (1987). Interaction models and the principled design of interactive systems. In H. Nicholls & D. S. Simpson (Eds.), *European software engineering conference,* (pp. 127–135). Berlin: Springer Lecture Notes.

Ericsson, K. A., & Simon, H. A. (1980). Verbal reports as data. *Psychological Review, 87,* 215–251.

Grudin, J. T. (1990). The computer reaches out: The historical continuity of interface design. In J. Chew & J. Whiteside (Eds.), *Proceedings of CHI '90: Human Factors in Computing Systems* (pp. 261–268). New York: ACM.

Grudin, J. T., & Barnard, P. J. (1984). The cognitive demands of learning command names for text editing. *Human Factors, 26,* 407–422.

Hammond, N., & Allinson, L. 1988. Travels around a learning support environment: rambling, orienteering or touring? In E. Soloway, D. Frye, & S. B. Sheppard (Eds.), *Proceedings of CHI '88: Human Factors in Computing Systems* (pp. 269–273). New York: ACM.

Hammond, N. V., Long, J., Clark, I. A., Barnard, P. J., & Morton, J. (1980). Documenting human–computer mismatch in interactive systems. In *Proceedings of the Ninth International Symposium on Human Factors in Telecommunications* (pp. 17–24). Red Bank, NJ.

Hanson, W. (1971). User engineering principles for interactive systems. *AFIPS Conference Proceedings, 39,* 523–532.

Harrison, M. D., Roast, C. R., & Wright, P. C. (1989). Complementary methods for the iterative design of interactive systems. In G. Salvendy & M. J. Smith (Eds.), *Proceedings of HCI International '89* (pp. 651–658). Boston: Elsevier Scientific.

Kieras, D. E., & Polson, P. G. (1985). An approach to formal analysis of user complexity. *International Journal of Man–Machine Studies, 22,* 365–394.

Laird, J. E., Newell, A., & Rosenbloom, P. S. (1987). SOAR: An architecture for general intelligence. *Artificial Intelligence, 33,* 1–64.

Landauer, T. K. (1987). Relations between cognitive psychology and computer systems design. In J. M. Carroll (Ed.), *Interfacing thought: Cognitive aspects of human–computer interaction* (pp. 1–25). Cambridge, MA: MIT Press.

Lewis, C. H. (1988). Why and how to learn why: Analysis-based generalization of procedures. *Cognitive Science, 12,* 211–256.

Long, J. B. (1987). Cognitive ergonomics and human–computer interaction. In P. Warr (Ed.), *Psychology at Work* (3rd ed.). Harmondsworth, Middlesex: Penguin.

Long, J. B. (1989). Cognitive ergonomics and human–computer interaction: An introduction. In J. B. Long & A. Whitefield (Eds.), *Cognitive ergonomics and human–computer interaction* (pp. 4–34). Cambridge: Cambridge University Press.

Long, J. B., & Dowell, J. (1989). Conceptions of the discipline of HCI: Craft, applied science and engineering. In A. Sutcliffe & L. Macaulay (Eds.), *People and computers V* (pp. 9–32). Cambridge: Cambridge University Press.

MacLean, A., Barnard, P., & Wilson, M. (1985). Evaluating the human interface of a data entry system: User choice and performance measures yield different trade-off functions. In P. Johnson & S. Cook (Eds.), *People and computers: Designing the interface* (pp. 172–185). Cambridge: Cambridge University Press.

MacLean, A., Young, R. M., & Moran, T. P. 1989. Design rationale: The argument behind the artefact. In K. Bice & C. H. Lewis (Eds.), *Proceedings of CHI '89: Human Factors in Computing Systems* (pp. 247–252). New York: ACM.

Mack, R., Lewis, C., & Carroll, J. M. (1983). Learning to use word processors: Problems and prospects. *ACM Transactions on Office Information Systems, 1*, 254–271.

Morton, J., Marcus, S., & Frankish, C. (1976). Perceptual centres: P-centres. *Psychological Review, 83*, 405–408.

Newell, A. (1989). *Unified Theories of Cognition: The 1987 William James Lectures.* Cambridge, MA: Harvard University Press.

Newell, A., & Card, S. K. (1985). The prospects for psychological science in human–computer interaction. *Human–Computer Interaction, 1*, 209–242.

Newell, A., & Simon, H. A. (1972). *Human Problem Solving.* Englewood Cliffs, NJ: Prentice-Hall.

Norman, D. A. (1983). Design principles for human–computer interaction. In *Proceedings of CHI '83: Human Factors in Computing Systems* (pp. 1–10). New York: ACM.

Norman, D. A. (1986). Cognitive engineering. In D. A. Norman & S. W. Draper (Eds.), *User centered system design: New perspectives on human–computer interaction* (pp. 31–61). Hillsdale, NJ: Lawrence Erlbaum Associates.

Olson, J. R., & Olson, G. M. (1990). The growth of cognitive modelling since GOMS. *Human Computer Interaction5*, 221–265.

Patterson, R. D. (1983). Guidelines for auditory warnings on civil aircraft: A summary and prototype. In G. Rossi (Ed.), *Noise as a Public Health Problem* (Vol. 2, pp. 1125–1133). Milan: Centro Richerche e Studi Amplifon.

Patterson, R. D., Cosgrove, P., Milroy, R., & Lower, M. C. (1989). Auditory warnings for the British Rail inductive loop warning system. In *Proceedings of the Institute of Acoustics, Spring Conference* (Vol. 11, pp. 5, 51–58). Edinburgh: Institute of Acoustics,

Patterson, R. D., Edworthy, J., Shailer, M. J., Lower, M. C., & Wheeler, P. D. (1986). Alarm sounds for medical equipment in intensive care areas and operating theatres. *Institute of Sound and Vibration (Research Report AC598).*

Payne, S., & Green, T. (1986). Task action grammars: A model of the mental representation of task languages. *Human–Computer Interaction, 2*, 93–133.

Polson, P. (1987). A quantitative theory of human–computer interaction. In J. M. Carroll (Ed.), *Interfacing thought: Cognitive aspects of human–computer interaction* (pp. 184–235). Cambridge, MA: MIT Press.

Reisner, P. (1982). Further developments towards using formal grammar as a design tool. In *Proceedings of Human Factors in Computer Systems Gaithersburg* (pp. 304–308). New York: ACM.

Scapin, D. L. (1981). Computer commands in restricted natural language: Some aspects of memory and experience. *Human Factors, 23,* 365–375.

Simon, T. (1988). Analysing the scope of cognitive models in human–computer interaction. In D. M. Jones & R. Winder (Eds.), *People and computers IV* (pp. 79–93). Cambridge: Cambridge University Press.

Suchman, L. (1987). *Plans and situated actions: The problem of human–machine communication.* Cambridge: Cambridge University Press.

Thimbleby, H. W. (1985). Generative user-engineering principles for user interface design. In B. Shackel (Ed.), *Human computer interaction: Interact '84* (pp. 661–665). Amsterdam: North-Holland.

Whiteside, J., & Wixon, D. (1987). Improving human–computer interaction: A quest for cognitive science. In J. M. Carroll (Ed.), *Interfacing thought: Cognitive aspects of human–computer interaction* (pp. 353–365). Cambridge, MA: MIT Press.

Wilson, M., Barnard, P. J., Green, T. R. G., & MacLean, A. (1988). Knowledge-based task analysis for human–computer systems. In G. Van der Veer, J-M. Hoc, T. R. G. Green, & D. Murray (Eds.), *Working with computers* (pp. 47–87). London: Academic Press.

Young, R. M., & Barnard, P. J. (1987). The use of scenarios in human–computer interaction research: Turbocharging the tortoise of cumulative science. In J. M. Carroll & P. P. Tanner (Eds.), *Proceedings of CHI + GI '87: Human Factors in Computing Systems and Graphics Interface (Toronto, April 5–9)* (pp. 291–296). New York: ACM.

Young, R. M., Barnard, P. J., Simon, A., & Whittington, J. (1989). How would your favourite user model cope with these scenarios? *SIGCHI Bulletin, 20 (4),* 51–55.

Young, R. M., Green, T. R. G., & Simon, T. (1989). Programmable user models for predictive evaluation of interface designs. In K. Bice and C. H. Lewis (Eds.), *Proceedings of CHI '89: Human Factors in Computing Systems* (pp. 15–19). New York: ACM.

Young, R. M., & MacLean, A. (1988). Choosing between methods: Analysing the user's decision space in terms of schemas and linear models. In E. Soloway, D. Frye, & S. B. Sheppard (Eds.), *Proceedings of CHI '88: Human Factors in Computing Systems* (pp. 139–143). New York: ACM.

8
Interface Problems and Interface Resources
Stephen J. Payne

Kinds of Psychology

For the sake of argument, we can consider current psychological research to belong to one of three paradigms, according to whether it is driven primarily by the exposure and scoping of phenomena, by the specification and application of general mental architectures, or by understanding the problems that people have to solve and the environmental resources that they may utilize to so do. Most experimental psychology is phenomenon-driven. A phenomenon, such as the recency effect, or semantic priming, is discovered in the laboratory (or, occasionally, noticed in every-day life and then confirmed in the laboratory), and then pursued relentlessly through a series of ever-more-intricate experiments, to discover its scope across experimental conditions. Typically, this research leads to isolated theories targeted at explaining specific phenomena. Theoretical development then progresses by the articulation of binary oppositions: Does episodic memory rely on a different system to semantic memory, or the same system? Is there one mental lexicon or two? Newell (1973), observing this pattern, complained that the game of 20 questions could never be won, as research would uncover more binary oppostions than it ever could resolve.

In place of phenomenon-driven psychology, Newell argued for the search for "models of control processes" – what today would be called cognitive architectures– which could be programmed to mimic intelligent human performance on a wide range of tasks while respecting known constraints on human information processing. His plea has been widely attended to, and several of the most influential current psychological theories are general architectures of this kind. Newell's SOAR and Anderson's ACT* are paradigm cases, and, though there are different emphases, connectionist mechanisms, such as pattern associators or the Boltzmann machine, are often described as candidate cognitive architectures.

Architecture-driven research runs into difficulties of its own. The first, and most significant is computational power. In order to capture the targeted range of empiri-cal phenomena, architectures may have to be so flexible as to provide very few constraints on algorithms for particular tasks, and therefore to supply very little empirical muscle. The second difficulty, somewhat ironically, is that architectures themselves tend to be shaped far more by some phenomena – their "signature phenomena" (Anderson, in press) – than by others within their broad explanatory scope. So architectures never really escape from the dilemmas of phenomenon-driven research. Anderson (in press) notes that ACT* was shaped by the fan effect (Anderson, 1983), and that SOAR was shaped by the power law of practice (Newell & Rosenbloom, 1981).

None of these criticisms insists that either phenomenon-driven or architecture-driven research should be abandoned. Some phenomena are intrinsically fascinating or economically important, and worth studying in their own right, whatever the limits on their broader theoretical significance. Likewise, the problems of cognitive architectures may yet be overcome, allowing architectures that are both sufficiently powerful and sufficiently limited to support meaningful explanations, without being constrained too heavily by the need elegantly to treat one particular phenomenon. Yet the weaknesses are apparent, and there is a third alternative, which overcomes many of these weaknesses.

The third approach maintains that to understand the way the mind works, one must understand the problems it solves and the environmental resources that can be exploited in the solution of these problems. A psychology driven from an analysis of problems and resources will still need to uncover phenomena and to posit mechanisms. But the phenomena will act as clues to the construction of accounts of how people solve their problems, and the mechanisms will be offered in the service of particular solutions.

I will call this problem/resource-driven approach "ecological" as it relies so heavily on an analysis of the problems persons face in their everyday environment. In my reading, the problem/resource orientation is a key aspect of Gibson's (1979) ecological approach to perception and of Neisser's (1978) prescription for memory research; but by adopting this label for the general orientation I do not wish to embrace all the implications that these authors derive, such as the rejection of mental processing (Gibson) or the preference for phenomena over theory (Neisser). Indeed, David Marr's (1982) work on vision, with its heavy emphasis on computation, and on theory, but its disenchantment with general mechanisms, is also ecological in the sense intended here, although from his philosophy, I am rejecting the exclusive emphasis on encapsulated elementary processing modules. Marr introduced the important idea of a "computational theory": a rather awkward term to denote that analyses of problems, analyses of what has to be computed, can themselves have theoretical status, indeed preeminent theoretical status, independent of algorithms or representations. Anderson (in press) has recently applied Marr's insight to the analysis of human memory, showing that several classical phenomena may best be explained at the computational level, independent of cognitive architecture.

As a final example of the ecological approach, I would cite aspects of Newell and Simon's (1972) approach to problem solving. A cornerstone of their work is to analyze in detail the structure of the problems that are being solved. Though Marr himself is dismissive of their work, he focuses his attack on the use of production systems. (From our standpoint, another problem is the exclusive focus on artificial puzzles.) But Newell and Simon's other major integrative idea – the problem space – is, it seems to me, a candidate computational theory in Marr's sense. The work reported in this chapter will use the problem space hypothesis as a framework for ecological analysis of artifacts.

Marr (1982) offers a persuasive analogy to argue for the ecological (problem/resource-oriented) approach. To understand how a bird flies, he notes, one cannot build a theory purely from studies of feathers and wings. Instead, one needs an account of aerodynamics, of what it means to fly, and of what it takes to fly. Only in terms of the aerodynamic theory can the structure of feathers and wings make sense.

Of course, the ecological approach also has its critics. One might be worried, for example, that different problems will need different theories, so that much of what psychologists have to say will not be very general. This is one of the frequent arguments for cognitive architectures – they express the common ground of many task-dependent theories. Another approach would be to bolster the power of task analysis – to develop a taxonomy of tasks, so that the relations between tasks and theories could be structured. The chapter will offer the beginnings of a move toward such a taxonomy for interface tasks. A different kind of response to the task–theory dilemma is simply not to worry. A theory of a single task, provided it is an important enough task, would be well worth having. The tasks of human–computer interaction are, for practical purposes, of just this kind.

Kinds of Human–Computer Interaction

Psychological research in HCI has been dominated by the first two orientations; it is typically either phenomenon-driven or architecture-driven. Phenomenon-driven research in HCI, like that in psychology, is fruitful but ultimately unsatisfying. Phenomenon-driven HCI exploits "usability phenomena," close siblings of standard psychological phenomena: Strong examples include stimulus–response compatibility and the improved learnability afforded by consistent over inconsistent design. These phenomena can be directly encoded as guidelines for design and as such have had a direct and important impact on real design work. Ultimately, however, the empirical scoping of these phenomena is an inadequate basis for application of the guidelines, as discussed by Barnard (this volume).

Architecture-driven HCI research began with Card, Moran, and Newell's (1983) model information processor and has progressed through Kieras and Polson's (1985) cognitive complexity theory and Barnard's (1987) interacting cognitive subsystems to Young, Green, and Simon's (1989) Programmable User Models. The assumption underlying all this work is that there are general cognitive constraints, which can be embodied in some general architecture and which can inform the design of devices. By definition, the architectures are independent of device use. Interacting cognitive subsystems (Barnard, 1987) model the flow of information processing between separate memory stores whether the task is using a word processor or recognizing words. GOMS models (Card et al., 1983; Kieras & Polson, 1985) describe how methods for performing routine tasks may be stored and run, whether the task is editing a document or pruning a rose bush. Programmable User Models (PUMs) (Young, Green, & Simon, 1989; Barnard, this volume) rely on SOAR (Laird, Newell, & Rosenbloom, 1987), the universal architecture mentioned already.

Indeed, this is surely a strength of these models. The mind can hardly have evolved special processing modules to cope with computer systems, so one might conclude that the important cognitive psychological constraints are surely generic. I resist this conclusion. Of course there are general constraints on human information processing, but, as the ecological approach suggests, the environmental constraints of problems and resources may be more important and carry more of the explanatory load. Simon's (1969) well-known ant parable, in which he argues that the complexity of an ant's path is produced by a simple mind processing a complex world, makes exactly this point, but the usual implication drawn by scientists of the mind is that the goal of specifying an architecture may, after all, be attainable. That conclusion may or may not turn out to be fine for long-term science. In the meantime, HCI needs to import some psychology, and my own guess is that the ecological approach will be the more fruitful.

Adopting an ecological approach entails a conclusion that has profound implications for the relationship between psychology and HCI and will overlook the rest of this essay: *Thought is shaped by tools.* This proposition, in various guises, has a long history in psychology, notably in Vygotsky's (1978) "instrumental psychology," and Bruner's similar orientation (e.g., Bruner & Olson, 1977–1978), but as Norman (this volume) points out, it has not entered the mainstream of cognitive science. The ecological approach insists on such a conclusion because it is so clear that tools change the tasks people perform, and thus the basic units of analysis for ecological psychology.

Accepting the tool dependence of thought constrains realistic application strategies for the role of psychology in HCI. It entails that HCI cannot be dealt with by taking psychological findings or theories off the shelf. Instead, we must try to understand why existing devices are good or bad, and to express this understanding so that it might be generalized to new designs. This conclusion is essentially the same as that reached by Carroll, Kellogg, and Rosson (this volume) but it has been reached by a separate route. They argue from a characterization of invention as emulation; I have argued from limitations on psychological theory.

The ecological approach to HCI also dictates the *kind* of artifact analysis that must be done: One must analyze the ways in which artifacts structure people's tasks. In this volume, Norman illustrates this kind of analysis by considering a simple checklist. Computational artifacts share this effect of task restructuring that checklists illustrate, offering users dramatically different resources, and thereby posing dramatically separate problems to users, problems that simply did not exist when the artifact was not there.

More complex artifacts set up a more complex web of resources and problems. The artifacts are useful only to the extent that they offer users new resources. In so doing they set the user new problems, but, in turn, the design of the artifact may offer resources for overcoming these artifact-centered problems. For example, a text editor gives writers the ability to swiftly edit trial sentences, but only if they can work out and remember the editing commands. Modern designs provide the user with a resource for this interface problem, in the form of visible menus and simple selection protocols. To analyze an artifact, then, is to analyze this interplay of interface problems and interface resources.

A Framework for Understanding How Artifacts Restructure Tasks

In his discussion of checklists, Norman (this volume) describes their effect on tasks at two levels. First, he analyzes the specific resources offered by a checklist, and the new problems that they pose. Then he abstracts to make general claims about the way any artifact may restructure a task: It can distribute actions across time or across people, and it can demand new actions.

This discussion raises an important issue for an ecological HCI: At what level of generality should artifact analyses be conducted? I believe that rather specific analyses will prove necessary to understand the functionality of artifacts, but that some relatively general analytic tools can be developed for some issues of user interface design, because such issues are often general across a wide range of artifacts.

The work that I report here is pitched at this more general level. The framework is derived from Newell and Simon's (1972) notion of a problem space, which underlies most attempts with cognitive psychology and artificial intelligence (AI) to understand goal directed behavior. The concept of search through a problem space was developed to treat simple puzzle-solving tasks. This is no accident – the problem space treatment of such tasks is made straightforward by the clearly discrete number of states, the clear definition of goal states, the readily itemized operators, and so on. This facile analysis is usually attibuted to the puzzle being "well-structured problems," but I believe there is another reason. In all such puzzles the user can act on and perceive the problem space directly; there is no mediating artifact.

To analyze the way artifacts restructure tasks, therefore, I suggest comparing situations of artifact use with the pure problem spaces of simple puzzle solving, and itemizing the additional complexities in the user's situation, and the additional resources that are made available. It seems plausible that this top-down analysis of the space of interface issues could converge with Carroll et al.'s (this volume) bottom-up notion of user concerns. Their most general example concern, What can I do, illustrates that artifacts often make the problem space operators obscure. In my work to date, I have concentrated on three such aspects of artifact mediation, but there are no doubt further aspects that are critical. The three aspects of artifact mediation considered in this chapter are:

The device represents the user's task domain, and the user operates on these representations, rather than directly on task objects.

Operators are not effected directly; an artificial language maps operators onto actions.

Actions are tightly coordinated with the system; their availability and interpretation are sensitive to the content and timing of system responses (which may be unknown in advance).

These aspects of device use are double-edged. Each poses a particular interface problem, especially a learning problem, but each provides new information-processing resources for the user (Payne, 1990). Furthermore, the design of the artifact may itself supply resources for the user to overcome the interface problems— for example the display design, as we will see, may help the user map from operations to actions.

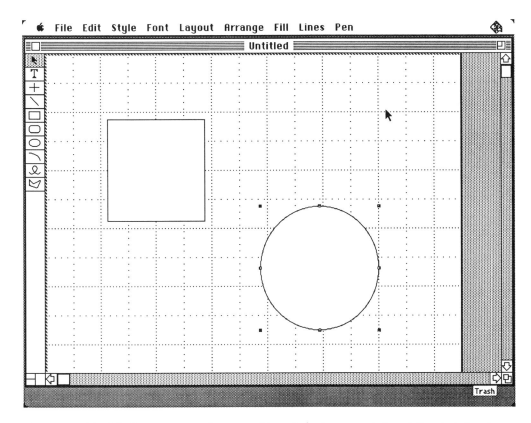

Figure 8.1. The MacDraw screen, after two objects have been created, and the circle has been selected.

The remainder of this chapter is structured as follows. The next three sections sketch attempts to understand each of these aspects and to provide simple limited models that express the understanding so that it might influence design. To provide some face validity that the models can be used to develop serious analyses of serious artifacts, and to flesh out the initial sketches, the models will then be used in conjunction to analyze a modern, popular application program.

Both to introduce the three minitheories and to illustrate their analytic potential, we will consider MacDraw, a direct manipulation drawing system that runs on the Apple Macintosh range of computers. Like many Macintosh applications, the user interface of MacDraw relies primarily on menus of tools and operations, together with direct manipulation of interface objects. Figure 8.1 shows the MacDraw display. The icons at the left are the object tools, and the menu-bar heads are pull-down menus used for file management and for editing object properties.

To introduce each of the minitheories, simple aspects of the MacDraw interface will be considered, with the emphasis on explaining the theories, through consideration of the artifact. Once each theory has been introduced, the emphasis will switch to explaining the usability of the artifact, through consideration and coordination of the theories. It should be admitted in advance that we will be considering the core of MacDraw, rather than the entire system. The central functionality is included in this core; additional interface frills are omitted in the interests of brevity.

The Device Model

Compare a display editor (such as VI) with a simple cut-and-paste editor (such as MacWrite). The display editor has separate commands for deleting words, deleting sentences, deleting paragraphs. The cut-and-paste editor allows all these to be achieved with a single command, for deleting strings. The two editors place different demands on the user's understanding. The conceptual entities (Greeno, 1983) in the appropriate problem spaces are different. Users of the cut-and-paste editor must construct the concept of a string, and the way it maps onto text objects.

This is an example of a very general interface problem for users. It reflects one of the fundamental ways in which devices restructure tasks – the conceptual objects that can be manipulated are changed. I suggest that this interface problem can be analyzed in terms of a device-oriented elaboration of Newell's problem space hypothesis, namely the yoked state space (YSS) hypothesis: The user of any device must construct and maintain at least two separate state spaces, the goal space and the device space, and a semantic mapping between them (Payne, 1987; Payne, Squibb, & Howes, 1990).

The goal space represents the "external" world that can be manipulated with the device. The minimal device space must be capable of representing all the states in the goal space. Device operators allow the user to transform states in the device space. The user's overall task is to accomplish a transformation in the goal space, but this can be achieved only by applying operators in the device space. Figure 8.2 sketches a yoked state space for the core functions of the MacDraw application. The goal space comprises a document of one or more drawings (to be more precise, line drawings with text). The user's task is to create and edit such documents. To do this, the user must construct a device space and learn how entities in this device space represent drawings and how operations in the device space can thus create and transform drawings. Figure 8.2 shows an example device space (which, as we shall see later, is rather too simple). The main conceptual entities of the device space are files and objects, where a file is defined as a set of objects in particular locations, and is in a particular state, according to whether it is saved, open, and active (there are cooccurrence restrictions here, in that only open files can be active, but these have been omitted from the description for simplicity). Objects are defined by their type, shape, size, fill pattern, and pen characteristics. A large number of operations act on these entities to create new instances and change existing ones.

The YSS is a kind of computational theory, in that it specifies a function to be computed, rather than an algorithm for its computation. It does not specify how the knowledge of goal space, device space, and so on are mentally represented; it just specifies what must be represented. The particular notation used in Figure 8.2 does

Goal Space

document = drawing*

Device Space

file = (object,location)*, file-state

object = obj-type,shape,size, fill-pattern, pen

obj-type = text / line / rectangle /   ellipse / arc / curve / polygon

file-state = saved?, open?, active?

Operations

open new file
save file
activate file
close file
print file

create object
reshape object
move object
change pen
edit text
change object-fill pattern
rotate object
duplicate object
delete object

Semantic Mapping

document --- file
drawing --- (object, location)*

Figure 8.2. A yoked state space model of MacDraw.

not, therefore, have any theoretical pretensions: The intent is simply to describe the important entities and their relationships economically. A more complete psychological account would address representation and algorithm, but the computational theory as is has important empirical consequences and allows interesting analyses of user interfaces.

One way to use YSS in analysis of artifacts is to specify the "ideal" understanding a user must construct in order to exploit the device, and to examine the learnability of this specification. Payne et al. (1990) do this for the kind of cut-and-paste editor already introduced, showing experimentally that the concept of a string, and its mapping onto text objects, is indeed a central aspect of learnability. A second analytic strategy is to consider the implications of a YSS for problem solving. A particular device space and semantic mapping will facilitate some goal space tranformations and hinder others. When considering such implications of the device model, it is important to look beyond the ideal specification to alternative device models that are weaker than the ideal understanding, but that may be readily available to users and lead to problems in use. In the work on text editors, Payne et al. (1990) showed that users who fail to construct the device space concept of a copy buffer will use inefficient copying methods.

Both these analytic stategies will be pursued below, to uncover conceptual difficulties with MacDraw.

The Interface Language

The second interface problem that is common to all computational artifacts is mapping operations onto actions. A user who has constructed a yoked state space will not be able to do anything with the device before learning how to translate device operations into specific action sequences. This aspect of user interfaces can be usefully treated as a language, whether the vocabulary is made of lexical items or actions, like pointing with a mouse.

The learnability of such a language was at one time a hot topic for HCI research, but has faded from fashion. Why? Partly, I suspect, because the field has become more ambitious, wishing to impact the global design of systems, rather than mere surface aspects of the interface (the chapters in this book tend to illustrate this ambition). Partly also, perhaps, because the success of menu-driven systems has mitigated some of the critical difficulties that were apparent with earlier command-language designs (Norman, 1981) and which motivated much of the research. Nevertheless, I believe that the interface language is still a major learnability problem in many systems, and still deserving of research attention.

About eight years ago, under the direction of Thomas Green, I embarked on a project to develop a notation that can formally describe interface languages, in a way that models the structure of the language as perceived by users. The main clue driving the model was the importance of "consistency" in the learnability of interfaces. We argued that many of the important aspects of consistency can be captured by a model of user knowledge that:

Identifies the "simple tasks" that can be routinely performed and that require no iterations or branching (these correspond to the operations in the device space);

Represents these simple tasks by sets of semantic components, reflecting a categorization of the available operations;

Rewrites simple tasks into action specifications, using the machinery of grammatical rewrite rules;

Simple tasks

                              Operation

Start new drawing   new

Close current drawing   close

Save current drawing   save

Print current drawing once   print

Rule schemas

Task [Operation] ->   action (point, "File"),
                            select [Operation]

select [Operation = new] -> action (drag, "New")

select [Operation = close] -> action (drag, "Close")

select [Operation = save] -> action (drag, "Save")

select [Operation = print] -> action (drag, "Print one")

Figure 8.3. A simple task–action grammar (TAG) of some MacDraw file operations. In this simple example, each simple task is defined by the value of a single feature, Operation. Rule schemas that contain unvalued features are expanded by assigning a value to the feature consistently throughout the rule. Action clauses, action (action-type, object), are the terminals of the grammar.

Marks the tokens in rewrite rules with semantic features from the task world (or from a model of semantic memory) to capture regularities in the task–action mappings.

    These ideas describe a computational theory of task–action mapping. The theory can be expressed as an attribute grammar, a task–action grammar (TAG; Payne & Green, 1986). A simple example is shown in Figure 8.3, which describes the mappings onto actions of the file operations in the MacDraw device model. This example shows a key principle – structural regularity in the relationship between tasks and actions can be captured by higher level rule schemas (in this case a single higher-level schema, marked with the task symbol, suffices).

    Task–action grammars illustrate the ecological approach by being constrained to illuminating a particular interface problem. Comparing their range of coverage over arbitrary user interface scenarios, with the coverage of universal architectures, as Young, Barnard, Simon, and Whittington (1989) do, is thus meaningless (as the authors recognize, but their figure 1 seems to deny). What may appear to be a weakness of TAG is, I would argue, a virtue. By narrowing their focus, task–action grammars can remain very simple and relatively concise, and yet still allow meaningful psychological insights. I hope that my subsequent MacDraw analysis makes good on this promise.

I do not mean to imply that TAG is without fault; it was initially proposed as a kind of base camp – more accurately, perhaps, a first excursion from Phyllis Reisner's (1981) base camp – and it has been gratifying that many people have taken up the assault, though on different routes (e.g., Hoppe, 1988; Reisner, 1990; Tauber, 1988). One particular weakness of TAG is relevant to the focus of this chapter: It neglects the vital role that the display can play as a resource for task–action mapping. This point is well demonstrated by the experiment of Mayes, Draper, McGregor, and Oatley (1988), who found that experienced users of MacWrite, a menu-driven user interface, could not recall the names of many frequently used menu items. This finding was replicated by Payne (1991) using an imagined task context to lessen the possibility that recall was artificially depressed by lack of goal-derived cues. Yet TAG assumes that users must learn and remember the precise mapping from operation to action, albeit in general schematic form where possible. To tackle this problem, Andrew Howes and I developed an extension to TAG – D-TAG, display-oriented task–action grammar (Howes & Payne, 1990).

D-TAG aims to analyze the way the display serves as a resource for the user in specifying operations. It uses simple formal extensions to the TAG notation, of which the most important is a display-item function, which we defined as follows:

> display-item (<task features> <display features>)
>
> retrieve the subset of objects in <current display> that have <display features>, then retrieve semantic definitions for each of these objects from <lexicon> and compare each of these definitions to <task features>. Return the best match. The function relies on two implicit parameters, a lexicon and a current display, which are not denoted in the task–action grammars.

Note that, once again, this is a (rather loose) computational theory. It specifies a function to be computed, not a particular representation and algorithm. Howes and Payne (1990) also suggest a scheme for representing display features as nested frames, each identified by some of the descriptors: "type" (e.g., icon menu), "location" (relative to the nesting frame, e.g., top) and "state" (e.g., highlighted). The key point is that display features must be capable of representing descriptions like "the item at the top of the left icon menu," as, informally, we have found that users often remember just this kind of detail.

Display-based rule schema

```
Task [Operation] ->      action (point, display-item(  [Operation],
                                                        [type=menu-bar]   ) ),

                         action (drag, display-item(   [Operation],
                                                        [type=menu-bar;
                                                            type=pull-down-menu;
                                                            location=below;
                                                                type=item]   )  )
```

Figure 8.4. A display-based rule schema for the MacDraw file operations. The display-item function is used to specify the objects of action clauses indirectly, by matching display items against task semantics. The display features are described by nested frames, each separated by a semicolon.

D-TAG allows descriptions of knowledge of interface languages that rely on the available information on the computer display. For example, Figure 8.4 shows a D-TAG description for the same MacDraw file operations as we considered previously. According to the grammar, the user knows that to execute each operation you must first point to the item on the menu bar that is semantically closest to the operation, then drag down to the item on the pull-down menu that is semantically closest. According to this model, then, the screen design of MacDraw allows such a user to perform these operations without ever memorizing the specific menu items, and thus brings the TAG model of competence into line with the results of Mayes et al. (1988).

Like the YSS model, TAG/D-TAG can be used for analysis in different ways. Ideal TAGs can be used to index learnability, by specifying a part of what the competent user needs to know. More heuristically, TAGs can be used to explore alternative perceived structurings of the interface and their implications. What happens, for example, when users fail to perceive certain regularities, or perceive bogus generalizations that are ultimately misleading?

Action and Interactivity

The final type of task restructuring noted previously is coordination with the device. The balance of the issue here is more toward the resources for action provided by the user interface than toward the problems it poses.

D-TAG only treats a limited part of that issue, knowledge of the mapping of operations onto actions. Another important issue was exposed in the simple experiments already noted (Payne, 1991). Experienced users of word processors are unable to report the precise effects of a frequently used operation, such as searching for a specified string, or deleting a word. They fail to remember aspects of the dialogue that are vital for the detail of action sequences. The obvious, simple conclusion is that users do not commit to memory things that they are able to pick up from the display as required. Nevertheless this "uncertainty of effects" phenome-

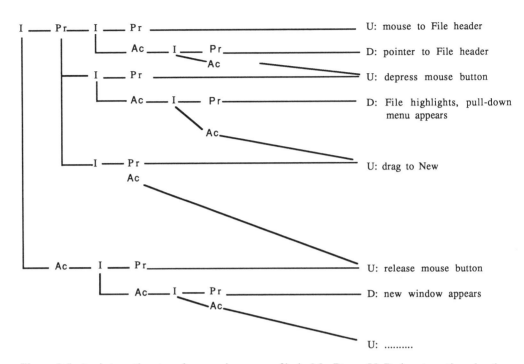

Figure 8.5. An interaction tree for opening a new file in MacDraw. U, D denote actions by the user and device respectively. Each unit interaction (I) is made up of a presentation (Pr) followed by an acceptance (Ac).

non has important implications for models of planning, suggesting a vital part of skill is the on-line interpretation of system responses, which must therefore play a much larger role than simple feedback.

I have recently begun an analysis of this feature of action at the user interface, by adapting Clark and Schaefer's (1987, 1989) model of human conversation to describe the way meaningful interactions are produced through coordinated presentations and acceptances (Payne, 1990). The key claim of this model is that interaction is structured into Unit Interactions of two phases, presentation, followed by acceptance. Both presentations and acceptances may be composed out of nested unit interactions and, in a sense, achieved collectively by user and device. What distinguishes HCI from human conversation, in this model, is that the criterion for eventual acceptance is not mutual grounding, but rather the user's sense that the interaction can be accounted for in terms of his or her current purposes. What distinguishes HCI from goal-driven action on some passive world is that this accounting process is done dynamically and incrementally, allowing the user to act meaningfully without fully articulating (at the time) goals or plans.

Figure 8.5 shows a simple interaction tree for the MacDraw new-file operation. The figure shows how the Interaction Tree model describes the interaction as a sequence and a hierarchy of unit interactions (denoted I). Each unit interaction begins with a presentation by either user (U) or device (D), and ends with an acceptance, to which both user and device may contribute, but which ultimately must be closed by the user accepting the role of the unit interaction by moving onto the next (shown by diagonal acceptance arcs). Interaction trees suggest that interaction exploits a tight coupling between user action and device responses, and suggests that many user actions primarily play a role of "accepting" previous actions.

The analytic ambitions of interaction trees are that, by displaying the conversational status of user actions and device responses, they may inform the design of these "low-level" aspects of the interface, which, I suspect, are central to the feel of the system. Unlike the TAG and YSS models, interaction trees cannot be used to describe the overall configuration of a user interface. Instead, the analyst may focus on the interaction design for particular use scenarios, or on describing actual observed interactions between a user and the machine.

An Analysis of MacDraw

The coverage of each of the three minitheories described previously is, as I keep stressing, strictly limited. This suggests that they might fruitfully be combined to provide a cumulation of insights into user interface designs. Our consideration of MacDraw file operations has already illustrated this potential, to an extent. But the most interesting usability aspects of MacDraw lie not in file handling, but in drawing. In this section, the problems and resources that are provided by the MacDraw drawing interface will be described at each level in turn.

Constructing a Device Model for MacDraw

Using MacDraw radically restructures the task of producing line drawings (compared with using pen and paper). At the highest level, the task changes from drawing to assembly – the user no longer has to draw shapes, rather, they are chosen, sized, and assembled into a complete drawing. How can we analyze this task restructuring? How can we understand its psychological consequences? The key feature of the device space for MacDraw is that it is object-centered. Graphic objects, like circles, rectangles, or text objects, can be created and modified by selecting from a repertoire of tools; drawings are simply arrangements of objects. To use MacDraw successfully, the user must appreciate the important, consistent nature of this object-based representation scheme (as is recognized by the user manuals, e.g., Claris Corporation, 1988). The user must also appreciate its limitations, which are not at first obvious, and which can cause problems to users who lack an adequate model of the device.

The simple device space for MacDraw shown in Figure 8.2 illustrates the central role played by the concept of an object. The fundamental point is that all sorts of geometric shapes are treated as objects, and that operations apply to any such objects. This allows powerful generalization, of the kind the string concept provides for text editing. Unfortunately, as we shall see, the simplicity of the conceptual model

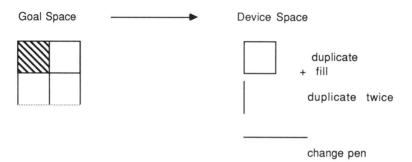

Figure 8.6. A troublesome drawing, with a possible construction trace.

shown in Figure 8.2 needs to be compromised to fully represent the device. The analysis of MacDraw usability will begin by considering the implications of the simple object-centered device model shown in Figure 8.2, which can be viewed as representing a minimal understanding required for use of the device. Next, inadequacies in this device model will be exposed, and the kind of elaborations that must be made to the model to capture the intricacies of the MacDraw design will be considered.

Mapping from the device space to the goal space takes on a rather different character with MacDraw than with text editing. In text editing, the goal space is a stable structure of relations between text objects: Paragraphs are always made out of sentences, which are always made out of words. Drawings are not so uniform: They may contain circles inside or outside squares, use unique shapes and shading patterns, and so on. It is therefore an ongoing problem for the user to map between the current goal state and MacDraw's device space, to instantiate the general semantic mapping shown in Figure 8.2.

The fact that most operations apply to any object allows powerful generalization, but it also constrains the semantic mapping, as all objects must have internally consistent attributes. Often, the user wants to specify an attribute for part of an object, but, because MacDraw knows nothing of object parts, this cannot be done.

The object-centered device model is also needed to explain a limitation on filling, which might otherwise frustrate the user. A space enclosed by a number of separate lines cannot be filled, as fill-patterns are properties of objects, not of pixel space.

These two inherent limitations of the rigid object-centered design of MacDraw both have important implications for the problem of mapping goal space drawings onto device space objects. To illustrate both issues economically with a single example, consider the task of creating the drawing shown in Figure 8.6. At first, this drawing might appear to be parsable into several different object configurations. But many of the most intuitive parses will simply not permit the drawing to be replicated. If the grid is created from horizontal and vertical lines (tempting, as the duplication operation means that each orientation would only need to be drawn once), then the cell could not be filled. If the grid is created out of four boxes, then the appearance of the bottom line cannot be changed. If the grid is parsed into a square containing a cross, then neither the cell nor the bottom line can be changed.

The only solution is to use a strange hybrid of boxes and lines. This troublesome semantic mapping is shown in Figure 8.6. Note how these problems might be compounded if the desired properties of the drawing are not all specified in advance. Certain edits of a drawing depend critically on its construction; the history of a design, as well as its final shape, influences possible future developments.

These points arise from the consistent object-centered design of MacDraw. They suggest that a user without a robust device model will often be misled. But other usability issues emerge because of quirks in the interface. The first quirky feature of the device space is that circles and squares are treated as special kinds of ellipse and rectangle respectively. These objects can be created by modifying the method for creating the more general object. The nature of these modifications is treated in the task–action grammar; the point at this level is that the user needs a particular conception of the space of geometric objects. A further quirkiness is that some objects are initially created as "frames," filled with nothing, others as "solids," filled with white. This difference is visible on the display, rather indistinctly, though it affects printed drawings only if objects overlap. It does, however, have implications for the selection of objects, as solids can be selected by pointing anywhere on their enclosed surface, whereas frames demand precise pointing to the outline.

Next, consider the grouping operation. The device space in Figure 8.2 suggests (as does the user manual) that grouping combines several objects into a single composite object, which then behaves just like any other object. However, the grouping operation in fact maintains the pregroup object structure (to implement ungrouping presumably), leading to a nasty inconsistency. If a polygon is made out of lines, and then grouped, the polygon can be moved and reshaped as if it were a bona fide object. But it cannot be filled, as the grouping operation only applies to the lines – the status of the space they surround is unchanged.

The final device space issues to be confronted concern the relationship between text objects and other "geometric" objects. In many respects, the text objects are like any others. This consistency has its upsides and its downsides. Text objects are created using a tool from the tool menu (although, obviously, the method of creation also involves typing), and they can be moved, rotated, and duplicated just like regular objects. Further, style changes must be applied to whole text objects: A single underlined word will necessitate dividing text into three separate objects–before the word, the word, and after the word.

However, text objects have some special properties, not shared by the others. First, text cannot be reshaped. If text is included in a grouped object, then that object can be reshaped, but the text will remain in the same size, and in the same position relative to the frame of the composite object. All the other objects will change relative dimensions, so that the overall effect can be unpredictable.

Second, there is a special kind of text object, called "paragraphs" in the user manual. A paragraph is created without selecting the text tool (see the discussion on D-TAG). It differs from standard text objects (called "captions" in the manual) in being fitted to the boundaries of a geometric object, if one is selected.

Third, text can be edited, using simple cut-and-paste edit functions. Editing, like creation, begins with selection of the text tool. By then pointing to an existing text

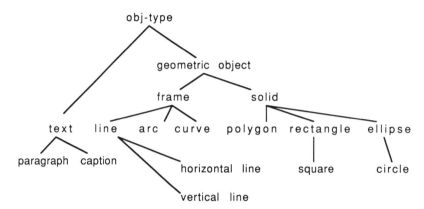

Figure 8.7. An elaborated concept of object type for the MacDraw device model.

object insertions and other edits can be accomplished. In fact, a full device model for MacDraw will contain a model for text objects similar to that described by Payne et al. (1990). However, if a text object is selected, before editing, and the text tool is not selected, the whole text object will be replaced by any new typing. Furthermore, this edit cannot be recovered.

All these properties of text objects must be understood to use MacDraw without difficulty. They can combine to produce behavior that, without the correct device model, is very hard to interpret. Imagine that one wishes to insert new text in text that is part of a grouped object. The user should realize that this cannot be done without ungrouping, as the change is not to the grouped object as a whole. However, a user with an incomplete model might fail to realize this limitation. What happens? A new text object is created, overlaying the first. This may result in the first being obscured, or, worse perhaps, if the "insert" is within a space in the original text, the failure to edit will go unnoticed until, say, the composite object is moved, and the new text object is left behind.

A very similar problem can result when the user wants to add new text immediately before or after an existing text object. Does this involve editing or creation? To choose between the two, the user must know that text objects are created with leading and trailing blanks on every line. Typing within the range thus defined will append to the existing object; typing outside these borders will create a new object.

To interact skillfully with MacDraw, then, the user needs to construct several elaborations on the device space of Figure 8.2, especially the object entity. Figure 8.7 gives a schematic of this more adequate, elaborate model of object types.

Task–Action Grammars of MacDraw

Task–action grammars of MacDraw have already been published by Payne and Green (1986), and Schiele and Green (1990). Payne and Green (1986) focused on the issue of "special" objects, circles, squares, horizontal and vertical lines, and "special" object movements, constrained to vertical and horizontal. In the MacDraw interaction language, both of these constraints are specified by holding down the shift key while performing the requisite action. However, as the TAG analysis by Payne and Green exposed, this consistency can be captured only if the shift-key depression interrupts the standard sequence of pointing and dragging. Payne and Green argue that this organizational conflict will lead many users to simply ignore (or never discover) the constrained form of movement.

A point worth noting in the current context is that Payne and Green's analysis relied on the concepts of "special" objects being available to the user. The device space and the task–action grammar are closely related. In particular, the device space specifies the granularity of simple tasks, and also provides semantic features for organizing the task–action mappings. (For an artifact analysis that rests on this chain of influence, see Payne, 1989.)

Howes and Payne (1990) use a D-TAG to analyze an inconsistency in the MacDraw interface. With all objects except text, creation of the object leads to automatic deselection of the object tool. With text, the tool remains selected until specifically deselected.

In the light of this previous work, the discussion of usability issues arising from a D-TAG analysis of MacDraw will be limited to some specific points, relating to some of those raised in the discussion of the device space. Figure 8.8 shows a partial D-TAG for the tasks of creating and editing objects. The D-TAG shows how tempting organizations of the language can produce inappropriate generalizations that will lead to errors in performance. Rules marked with an asterisk denote overgeneral schemas of this kind. Accurate performance requires knowledge of the more specialized forms marked with letters.

The first misgeneralization involves object creation. Almost all object creations begin with selection of the appropriate tool icon, which is done in a uniform way. The user might well be inclined to form a completely general creation schema (Rule 1), which cannot cope with the case of paragraph creation. The prediction is that users, especially those who do not read the manual, will rarely use paragraph text.

The second misgeneralization involves object modification. Again, almost all modifications begin with selection of the to-be-modified object. Furthermore, all "discrete" modifications, such as filling, rotating, flipping, changing font, and changing line width, can then be achieved by using a simple display-based rule (Rule 3). Unfortunately, as noted, text modification must begin with selection of the text tool, rather than a text object. Failure to encode this special case has very unpleasant results, as attempting to edit with a text object selected results in the replacement of that object. An appropriate task–action grammar therefore relies heavily on features of the more elaborate device space shown in Figure 8.7.

For the user who does construct an appropriate organization, note how closely related are the methods for editing and creating text. The organization of the task–action grammar thus compounds the potential problem noted previously, of inadvertent creation of new text objects.

Simple Tasks

	Obj-type	Effect	Features Change-type	Change
Create geometric object	geometric	create		
Create text caption	caption	create		
Create text paragraph	paragraph	create		
Change object shape	geometric	modify	cont	shape
Rotate object	any	modify	discrete	rotate
Flip object	any	modify	discrete	flip
Fill object	any	modify	discrete	fill
Insert text	text	modify	cont	insert

Rule Schemas

*1. Task[Effect=create, Obj-type]   ->   select tool
                                                create [Obj-type]

1a. Task [Effect=create, Obj-type = geometric] ->   select tool
                                                       action (point, val-from-goal)
                                                       action (drag, val-from-goal)

1b. Task [Effect=create, Obj-type=caption] ->   select tool
                                                     action (point, val-from-goal)
                                                     action (type, val-from-goal)
1c. Task [Effect=create, Obj-type=paragraph] ->   action (point, val-from-goal)
                                                     action (type, val-from-goal)

*2. Task [Effect=modify]   ->   select object
                                      modify [Change-type, Change]

2a. Task [Effect=modify, Obj-type=text] ->   select tool
                                                 action (point, val-from-goal)
                                                 action (type, val-from-goal)

2b. Task [Effect=modify, Obj-type=geometric, Change-type=discrete] ->
                                      select object
                                      modify [Change-type, Change]

3. modify [Change-type = discrete] ->

              action (point, display-item([Change],
                                            [type=menu-bar]   )),

              action (drag, display-item([Change],
                                            [type=menu-bar;
                                                type=pull-down-menu;
                                                location=below;
                                                    type=item]   ))

Figure 8.8. A partial D-TAG for MacDraw.

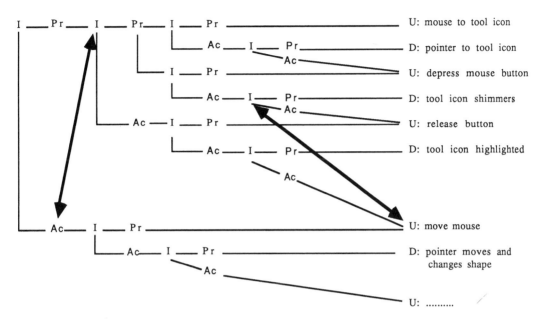

Figure 8.9. An interaction tree for MacDraw tool selection. Bold arcs show a misparsing error.

Interacting With MacDraw

The MacDraw D-TAG shows a role for the static aspects of the device's display, but it ignores the dynamics of device responses, which, I argue, play a big role in the specification of action. These aspects of interactivity can be approached with the interaction-tree notation, described previously. The interaction-tree notation is much less well developed than task–action grammars. Nevertheless, I feel that interaction-tree descriptions of MacDraw interaction patterns do throw some light on the interactivity of the interface.

Payne (1990) describes an interaction tree for MacDraw tool selection, showing how, and why, the device's response to a mouse-button depression on a tool icon can be misleading to novices. The point, briefly, is that button depression does not actually achieve anything, but MacDraw's shimmering tool icon suggests that it does, leading many novices to prematurely "accept" the selection presentation by moving (dragging) into the drawing area before releasing the mouse button to complete the tool selection. Figure 8.9 illustrates this problem with the interaction design, by showing the interaction tree for the ideal interaction sequence, and overlaying this with "parsing-error" arcs that describe a particular user's observed difficulty.

Figure 8.10 shows an interaction tree for selecting multiple objects. This method is not shown in the D-TAG. It is achieved by pointing to some place on the screen outside the perimeter of the multiple-object configuration, and dragging to "lasso" the entire configuration. In this case, the problem is that the device does not offer

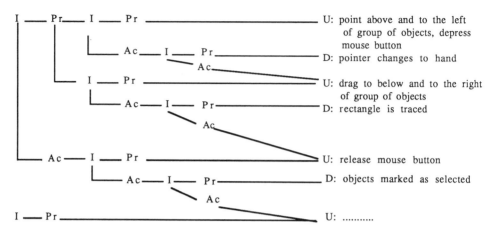

Figure 8.10. An interaction tree for selecting multiple objects.

rich enough feedback to allow the user's acceptance to be informed. The interaction tree suggests that the user's action of releasing the mouse button signals acceptance of a presentation that plays the role of selecting a set of objects. Yet the device does not display which objects have been selected until after this acceptance. Ideally, the interaction should be designed so that user acceptance can be delayed until after definite feedback about the objects that have been selected.

Finally, Figure 8.11 shows the interaction trees for both editing and creating text. The point here is that the detailed behavior of the device is identical in both cases. Of course, one does not really need to draw an interaction tree to illustrate this equivalence, but one does need to focus on the low-level interactivity of the design, and no existing models support such a focus. The lack of any perceptual distinction between editing and creating text exacerbated the possibility of inadvertent creation of new text objects when the intention is to edit an existing object (or vice versa). According to our analysis, this particular interface problem is reflected at all levels, from the concepts of the device space and the organization of action sequences to the dynamics of device interactivity.

Discussion

By analyzing one artifact through the filters of three separate minitheories, I hope to have illustrated how limited models driven through the analysis of problems and resources can be integrated. Because of their limited focus, the models provide complementary insights into the psychological implications of the user interface.

The case study illustrates, I hope, that one can analyze the ways in which artifacts restructure tasks. It thus instantiates the "application strategy" that was derived earlier in the chapter from a characterization of ecological psychology. To this point in the chapter, however, I have not directly addressed a central question for this book – how might psychology impact design? I have argued that the best strategy is

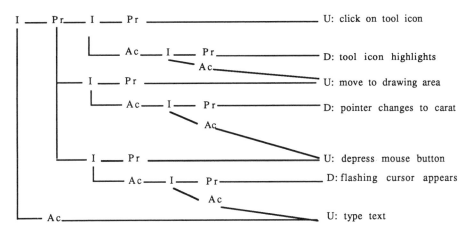

Figure 8.11. An interaction tree for editing or creating text objects.

to understand what is good or bad about existing artifacts, but I have said nothing about how such understanding might feed the design process. It is time to characterize such a vision, to make some case for the usefulness of problem/resource artifact analysis.

First, let us consider the class of design activities to which this research might be addressed. The most obvious target is redesign of existing systems. Our exposure of some potential usability difficulties with MacDraw illustrates how redesign might be driven by this kind of detailed artifact analysis. Since the analysis does not rely on empirical studies (except to test the validity of the points that arise), it can be targeted at what is often called "early evaluation," using interface specifications rather than prototypes or products. The redesign of specifications is surely cheaper than the redesign of products.

A different application focus arises from the focus of the models on analyzing the problems that users have to overcome. Such an analysis seems intuitively likely to speak to design of instructions or to other interface extensions designed to help users with these problems. In the case of MacDraw, for example, it seems plausible that instruction in the complexities of the device model could avoid many difficulties of interpretation. The user manual stresses the object model, but, to my mind, does not expose the shortcomings of this model, or the inconsistent departures from it. Users will doubtless discover some of these problems the hard way, and may be forced to build a more adequate device model through trial and error.

The experimental literature in HCI shows that instructional mental models might have beneficial effects (e.g., Bibby & Payne, 1990; Halasz & Moran, 1983; Kieras & Bovair, 1984; Payne, 1988) but nothing in that literature is able to offer specific guidelines for how to develop and convey such models. The YSS model is a constrained theory about the nature of device models. In unpublished work at the University of Lancaster, my colleagues and I have used the model to drive the design of successful instructions for a menu-driven computer system that allows remote diagnosis of faults in telephone circuits. Note that this system is removed from text editing and MacDraw, supporting the claim that the model is quite general.

Having identified a set of design activities that might be impacted, the second challenge is to package the analytical machinery so that it might be accepted into design practice (Carroll, in the introduction to this volume, calls this the applicability constraint).

The earliest work that I have described, that on task–action grammars, was driven by a simple infiltration strategy. Formalisms, like Backus Naur Form (BNF), already play an important role in some software engineering projects, for reasons that are well known and widely accepted in both software engineering and in theoretical psychology (e.g., Broadbent, 1987). It may be possible to exploit this existing niche in designers' everyday practice and value systems. TAG as a formalism is little more complicated than BNF, and the same thing is true of interaction trees, although they do not share such a well-known platform. And, though the work has not yet been done, it is easy to envisage packaging YSS descriptions in a simple uniform notation. Such simple notations may provide what Barnard (this volume) calls "application representations," packaging psychological knowledge into a tool for designers.

The status of this strategy today is, I believe, completely open. As far as I am aware, no designers outside the research community have used any of these models to analyze their designs, but this need not signal any general weakness in the idea. The particular notations could be deemed unsuitable or unusable in design contexts, or, as I strongly suspect is the case, they could be unknown. To test the strategy fully, some real effort would need to be made to sell the notations to designers. But perhaps a more direct impact on design practice could be sought by communicating to designers not the models themselves, but the design insights that the models generate. One might envisage a role for such models in the Carroll et al. scheme for supporting design emulation. The specific usability issues raised in the MacDraw analysis, for example, could be viewed as a kind of claims analysis. To use Barnard's terminology, the models might serve as a discovery representation for such claims analyses. In this role, it seems to me, these ecological minitheories offer a particular advantage. By focusing on interface problems and resources, they tend to result in analyses that cut across the individual features of an interface design. Many of the issues that emerge are caused by the configuration and interrelation of design decisions, rather than by the properties of some isolated feature. Carroll and Kellogg (1989) are aware that such interrelations are a vital contribution that artifact analysis needs to be targeted toward, but the current presentations of matrixes of claims, each tied to a concrete interface feature, tend to encourage undesired atomism.

Whichever of these two roles is envisaged for the limited models reported in this chapter (or their successors), their usefulness will depend on their ability to provoke insights into the design of artifacts that would otherwise not be readily apparent. It is a matter of fact that I had not noticed some of the usability aspects of MacDraw before undertaking the detailed analyses, and that I had not understood some of the others. To strengthen the case, further analyses of different artifacts must also succeed in uncovering and understanding aspects of usability. I fully expect such work to improve on the example models described in this paper.

Acknowledgments

MacDraw is a product of Claris Corporation. Version 1.96 was analyzed. Thanks to Jack Carroll, Robert Campbell, and Linda Tetzlaff for comments on a previous draft. Thanks to Andrew Howes and Thomas Green for discussions about MacDraw. Many of the ideas presented here were developed while the author was employed by the University of Lancaster, England. That work was supported by Alvey/SERC undergrant GR/D60355, a collaborative project with British Telecommunications plc.

References

Anderson, J. R. (1983). *The architecture of cognition.* Cambridge, MA: Harvard University Press.

Anderson, J. R. (in press). The place of cognitive architectures in a rational analysis. In K. Van Lehn (Ed.), *Architectures for intelligence.* Hillsdale, NJ: Lawrence Erlbaum Associates.

Barnard, P. J. (1987). Cognitive resources and the learning of human–computer dialogs. In J. M. Carroll (Ed.), *Interfacing thought.* Cambridge, MA: MIT Press.

Bibby, P. A., & Payne, S. J. (1990). *Learning about devices by internalizing instructional descriptions* (Research Report RC 15522). Yorktown Heights, NY: IBM T. J. Watson Research Center.

Broadbent, D. E. (1987). Simple models for experimentable situations. In P. E. Morris (Ed.), *Modelling cognition.* Chichester: Wiley.

Bruner, J. S., & Olson, D. R. (1977–1978). Symbols and texts as tools of intellect. *Interchange, 8,* 1–15.

Card, S. K., Moran, T. P., & Newell, A. (1983). *The psychology of human–computer interaction.* Hillsdale, NJ: Lawrence Erlbaum Associates.

Carroll, J. M., & Kellogg, W. A. (1989). Artifact as theory-nexus: Heremenutics meets theory-based designing. In K. Bice & C. Lewis (Eds.), *Proceedings of CHI '89: Human Factors in Computing Systems.* (pp. 1–14). New York: ACM.

Claris Corporation (1988). *MacDraw user manual.* Mountain View, CA: Claris Corporation.

Clark, H. H., & Schaefer, E. F. (1987). Collaborating on contributions to conversations. *Language and Cognitive Processes, 2,* 19–41.

Clark, H. H., & Schaefer, E. F. (1989). Contributing to discourse. *Cognitive Science, 13,* 259–294.

Gibson, J. J. (1979). *The ecological approach to visual perception.* Boston: Houghton Mifflin.

Greeno, J. G. (1983). Conceptual entities. In D. Gentner & A. Stevens (Eds.), *Mental models.* Hillsdale, NJ: Lawrence Erlbaum Associates.

Halasz, F. G., & Moran, T. P. (1983). Mental models and problem solving using a calculator. In *Proceedings of CHI '83: Human Factors in Computing Systems.* New York: ACM.

Hoppe, H. U. (1988). Task-oriented parsing – A diagnostic method to be used by adaptive systems. In E. Soloway, D. Frye, & S. B. Sheppard (Eds.), *Proceedings of CHI '88: Human Factors in Computing Systems.* New York: ACM.

Howes, A., & Payne, S. J. (1990, in press). Display-based competence: Towards user models for menu-driven interfaces. *International Journal of Man–Machine Studies.*

Kieras, D. E., & Bovair, S. (1984). The role of a mental model in learning to operate a device. *Cognitive Science, 8,* 255–273.

Kieras, D. E., & Polson, P. G. (1985). An approach to the formal analysis of user complexity. *International Journal of Man–Machine Studies, 22,* 365–394.

Laird, J. E., Newell, A., & Rosenbloom, P. (1987). SOAR: An architecture for general intelligence. *Artificial Intelligence, 33,* 1–64.

Marr, D. (1982). *Vision.* San Francisco: Freeman.

Mayes, J. T., Draper, S. W., McGregor, M. A., & Oatley, K. (1988). Information flow in a user interface: The effect of experience and context on the recall of MacWrite screens. In D. M. Jones & R. Winder (Eds.), *People and computers IV.* Cambridge: Cambridge University Press.

Neisser, U. (1978). Memory: What are the important questions? In M. M. Gruneberg, P. E. Morris, & R. N. Sykes (Eds.), *Practical aspects of memory.* London: Academic Press.

Neisser, U. (1985). The role of theory in the ecological study of memory: Comment on Bruce. *Journal of Experimental Psychology: General, 114,* 272–276.

Newell, A. (1973). You can't play 20 questions with nature and win. In W. G. Chase (Ed.), *Visual information processing.* New York: Academic Press.

Newell, A., & Rosenbloom, P. (1981). Mechanisms of skill acquisition and the law of practice. In J. R. Anderson (Ed.), *Cognitive skills and their acquisition.* Hillsdale, NJ: Lawrence Erlbaum Associates.

Newell, A., & Simon, H. A. (1972). *Human problem solving.* Englewood Cliffs, NJ: Prentice-Hall.

Norman, D. A. (1981). The trouble with Unix. *Datamation, 27,* 139–150.

Payne, S. J. (1987). Complex problem spaces: Modelling the knowledge needed to use interactive systems. In H. Bullinger & B. Shackel (Ed.), *Human–Computer Interaction: Interact '87.* Amsterdam: Elsevier Science Publishers.

Payne, S. J. (1988). Metaphorical instruction and the early learning of an abbreviated-command computer system. *Acta Psychologica, 69,* 207–230.

Payne, S. J. (1989). A notation for reasoning about learning. In J. Long & A. Whitefield (Eds.), *Cognitive ergonomics and human–computer interaction.* Cambridge: Cambridge University Press.

Payne, S. J. (1990). Looking HCI in the I. In D. Diaper (Ed.), *Human–Computer Interaction: Interact '90.* Amsterdam: Elsevier Science Publishers.

Payne, S. J. (1991, in press). Display-based action at the user interface. *International Journal of Man–Machine Studies.*

Payne, S. J., & Green, T. R. G. (1986). Task–action grammars: A model of the mental representation of task languages. *Human–Computer Interaction, 2,* 93–133.

Payne, S. J., Squibb, H., & Howes, A. (1990, in press). The nature of device models: The yoked state space hypothesis and some experiments with text editors. *Human–Computer Interaction.*

Schiele, F., & Green, T. R. G. (1990). HCI formalisms and cognitive psychology: The case of task–action grammar. In M. Harrison & H. Thimbleby (Eds.), *Formal methods in human–computer interaction.* Cambridge: Cambridge University Press.

Simon, H. A. (1969). *The sciences of the artificial.* Cambridge, MA: MIT Press.

Reisner, P. (1981). Formal grammar and design of an interactive system. *IEEE Transactions of Software Engineering, 5,* 229–240.

Reisner, P. (1990). What is inconsistency? In D. Diaper (Ed.), *Human–Computer Interaction: Interact '90.* Amsterdam: Elsevier Science Publishers.

Tauber, M. (1988). On mental models and the user interface. In G. C. van der Veer, T. R. G.

Green, J. M. Hoc, & D. M. Murray (Eds.), *Working with computers: Theory versus outcome.* London: Academic Press.

Vygotsky, L. (1978). *Mind in society: The development of higher mental processes.* (M. Cole, V. John-Steiner, S. Scribner, & E. Souberman, Eds.). Cambridge, MA: Harvard University Press.

Young, R. M., Barnard, P., Simon, T., & Whittington, J. (1989). How would your favourite user model cope with these scenarios? *SIGCHI Bulletin, 20(4),* 51-55.

Young, R. M., Green, T. R. G., & Simon, T. (1989). Programmable user models for predictive evaluation of interface designs. In K. Bice & C. Lewis (Eds.), *Proceedings of CHI '89: Human Factors in Computing Systems.* New York: ACM.

9
Inner and Outer Theory in Human–Computer Interaction
Clayton Lewis

The past decade has seen major effort by psychologists to contribute to the design of usable computer systems. Early on some psychologists, and some who encouraged them to get involved in design, hoped that existing psychological theory would provide ready answers to many problems in design. Over the years these hopes have not been realized, and it is now common, even for psychologists themselves, to argue that psychological theory has little to contribute, and that psychology as a discipline provides valuable methodology and a useful empirical orientation to design but little more. Barnard (this volume) also notes this view.

The purpose of this chapter is to consider whether this depreciation of the role of psychological theory has been carried too far. In particular, I consider arguments for and against the view that important advances in user-interface technology might develop from study of the mechanisms of mental processes.

Outer and Inner Theory

Although any role for psychological theory in design is controversial, as this book attests, those psychologists who continue to urge the value of theory mainly follow the lead of Card, Moran, and Newell (1983) in promoting approximate quantitative models of human performance as the interface between psychology and design. Rather than considering the arguments for and against this approach, I want to focus on a possibility that has been largely neglected – that discovery of the way in which mental processes are actually implemented could make possible improvements in user interfaces not to be obtained otherwise.

The kind of psychological theory stressed by Card et al. (1983) can be called *outer* theory: It describes what mental processes do, and how they are influenced by external factors, but does not describe how the processes are accomplished. By contrast, an *inner* theory describes the mechanisms underlying the processes, ideally in such a way that an outer theory could be deduced from the description.

The control of movement can be used to illustrate this distinction. Fitts's Law (Fitts, 1954), which has been useful in describing and comparing the performance of various pointing devices (Card, English, & Burr, 1978) is a piece of outer theory: It provides a good estimate of the time required to execute movements of given length and accuracy but says nothing about how movements are actually controlled. The work of Meyer and colleagues (Meyer, Abrams, Kornblum, Wright, & Smith, 1988) looks beneath the surface of Fitts's Law to discover the mechanisms whose operations produce the quantitative regularity described by the law. It appears that the relationship among length, accuracy, and speed is shaped by noise in the motor

154

system whose amplitude grows with the velocity of a movement. What are the prospects for the development of this kind of inner theory for other phenomena of interest in user-interface design, and what impact on design could be expected?

The optimistic view can be stated this way. Like the other sciences, psychology will push ahead, delivering insights into the mechanisms of mental processes. Because mental processes are fundamental to computer use, understanding how mental processes work will lead to important new ideas about how to exploit them. Designers will be able to avoid difficulties by steering around the causes of difficulties, and improve effectiveness by engaging the causes of effective performance. One might take medicine as a model: An inner theory of disease that tells us about germs is of tremendous value in avoiding infection. Inner theory of the immune system and the structure and function of viruses is of tremendous value in improving the effectiveness of the body's natural defenses.

The contrast between this story and a similar story featuring outer theory should be clear. Armed with an outer theory of mental processes that tells what they are, how long they take, and what results they will usually produce, but not how they work, designers would also be able to make progress, but more limited progress. Outer theories connecting yellow fever to swamps were useful, but not as useful as inner theories explicating the role of mosquitoes.

How does the inner theory story relate to stories in which theory of mental processes plays a peripheral role, as in the "ontologically minimized" HCI science advocated by Carroll, Kellogg, and Rosson in this volume? Again the parallel with medicine is useful. Although progress in medicine has been driven by the problem of disease and its relief, and though much medical practice has little theoretical basis, medicine has not progressed by cutting itself off from basic sciences such as biochemistry, but rather by seeking to extend explanations of observed phenomena of interest, such as Parkinson's disease, in such a way as to link up with theories of cell function and chemical processes in the nervous system. The inner-theory story for HCI to be considered here will follow medicine in this regard, asserting the value of inner theory in connecting up explanations across application areas and across levels of analysis within an area.

Many readers may be puzzled here. Isn't this inner theory story obviously right, trite, not worth discussing? But readers who have read to this point in this volume may be prepared for controversy. There are strong arguments to be faced.

Arguments Con and Responses Pro

Inner Theory Will Not Work in HCI because Theory Never Plays a Major Role in Any Engineering Discipline. The just-mentioned puzzled readers may be assuming that inner theory would be valuable in HCI by analogy to other disciplines where powerful theories in (say) physics provide the framework in which design takes place. Examination of real design practice shows the matter to be more subtle: Theory often follows application, for example, and much design is guided by empirical refinement of past attempts rather than by first-principles analysis. Carroll et al. (this volume) illustrate this situation for the development of the steam engine. But as Card (1990) points out, one can find examples that demonstrate a big role for theory as well as ones that do not. We have already considered the case of medicine, where it is obvious that a wide range of theoretical ideas, from germ theory to membrane chemistry, play a crucial role. New liquid-crystal displays use "designer molecules" whose desired structure is derived from theoretical models of the way in which molecules respond to applied fields (Walba et al. 1986) and which give performance superior to previously known materials. So there can be no simple argument against an important role for theory in HCI along these lines.

Inner Theory Will Never Have Much Impact on HCI because the Complexity of the Situation–User–System Aggregate Means That Unpredictable Interactions Swamp Any Predictable Main Effects.   According to this argument theory will not be as useful in HCI as in medicine or display design because the specifics of different design problems will dominate any general considerations. The riposte is that the main effects are important, even in context, and that knowledge of the main effects helps to determine a basic design, which can then be refined to deal with the interactions.

Inner Theory Will Not Work in HCI because We Don't Have Any.   It seems fair to say that there is no inner theory whatsoever in cognitive psychology that has success and support comparable with the germ theory of disease. This is a powerful argument but does not mean that we cannot get inner theories if we continue to try. Granting that we are no more skillful or diligent than our psychologist predecessors, we can still hope that we have gained some understanding of possibly useful abstractions for understanding mental processes, and that these will help us. We may also be encouraged by the success of inner theories of perceptual processes: Psychology as a whole is not completely lacking in inner theories.

We Will Never Have Inner Theories of Mental Processes because of the Complexity of the Implementation and the Self-regulation of the Cognitive System.   It seems likely that the mapping between mental processes and their realizations is highly indirect and implicit, so that the reductionist approaches that have been partially successful for perceptual systems will bog down. It will probably not be possible to put an electrode in the representation of a proposition. Less invasive and reductionist methods of study are thwarted by the ability of the system to regulate the impact of external manipulations. An experimenter cannot compel a subject to perform a task in a certain way and hence cannot be sure that two samples of performance reflect the same mechanisms even for the same task, let alone differing tasks. Resort to models seems the best response to these problems, accepting that theories tested only by modeling may never enjoy the clear support reductionist theories have in other areas. The problem of identifiability (Townsend, 1974) can further justify considerable skepticism about this approach: Radically different models can fit a given body of data. On the other hand, if model development leads to inner theories with accurate and useful implications for design, then the pudding has been proved by eating.

The Success of Inner Theories in Other Fields Will Not Be Repeated in HCI because We Cannot Isolate and Manipulate the Elements of the Cognitive System. This argument is related to but not identical with the last. This argument grants that we might have inner theories of mental processes but denies that we could then capitalize on them, because we cannot do what scientists and engineers have had to do to cash in on inner theory in other areas. Germs could be captured, cultured, and examined. The rare radioactive elements could be detected and isolated. The development of nuclear fission as an engineering reality from inner theory required an investment of truly staggering proportions even given the ability of chemists and physicists to analyze and reshuffle the natural arrangements of materials. We cognitive scientists have no such ability.

Genetics can supply a counter to this argument while not denying its force. It was possible to make good use of genetic theory long before the structures at lower levels of implementation were known and could be manipulated. Formulation of the idea of the gene and its role in inheritance did not await knowledge of its chemistry. Genetic engineering shows that much more can be accomplished when the lower-level structures can be isolated and manipulated, but it remains true that more limited insight and control were already very valuable.

Inner Theory Will Have Limited Impact in HCI because the Cognitive System Is Partially Decomposable. Newell and Card (1985) argue that the processes of interest in HCI behave in ways largely independent of their implementation. In their view, what is important about mental processes is that they manipulate symbols, not that they are implemented in flesh. Therefore worrying about the flesh will not help understand what is happening. The level of processing of interest to HCI is mainly that governed by bounded rationality – that is, the organism will act to accomplish its goals within the limits of its resources. So most of what one needs to know about cognition can be derived from task descriptions anyway. In this argument Newell and Card are applying to HCI influential but controversial ideas about cognitive science generally.

If the brain were a computer the argument would be solid: It is more than 99 44/100 percent irrelevant in programming a computer how the instruction set is implemented. Implementation knowledge is useful for sabotage but with very rare exceptions cannot be used to modify the behavior of the system via the programming interface. But there does not seem to be any close analog to the programming interface for the cognitive system. It may be that understanding the implementation would allow in effect new modes of programming or communication with the system. Inner theory of perception has in fact permitted this: Sightless patients can be given meaningful visual sensations via electrodes in the cortex.

Associative Models of Mental Processes Will Permit Us to Exploit Phenomena Like the Stroop Effect in Interface Design. Many researchers now believe that cognitive models should reflect the parallel, apparently associative architecture of the brain and have made contact between such models and HCI (Kintsch, 1988; Mannes & Kintsch 1988; Norman, 1988). Such models may go beyond current symbolic models in accounting for some cases in which underlying implementation constraints show through as limits on performance not apparent from task descriptions.

In the Stroop effect (Stroop, 1935; also see Jensen & Rohwer, 1966) subjects find it very difficult to name the color of ink in which color words are printed, if the words do not match the inks. This effect seems unmotivated in a decomposable cognitive architecture. Perlman (1984), following suggestions in Norman (1981), demonstrated that an analogous interference can occur in menus when the character used to select an item can conflict with the initial character of the item.

Despite the usefulness of Perlman's finding there are two reservations to be noted about this claim for inner theory. First, we do not now have a good inner theory of the Stroop effect. For example, it has been widely thought that differences in speed of processing of conflicting cues are important in the effect, but recent work by MacLeod and Dunbar (1988) questions this. Perlman's demonstration accordingly rests on reasoning by analogy from observations rather than on a theory.

Similar comments could be made about the application of Garner's ideas on stimulus structure to the design of displays, another candidate example of useful inner theory. Garner's observation (Garner, 1970) that the effect of redundant cues depends on whether the cues are "integral" or "separable," with elaborations distinguishing state- and process-limited behavior, was never made the basis of an inner theory. In any case the behavior of so-called object displays, in which separate data items are displayed as aspects of a single object rather than as separate display elements, seems better described in terms of emergent features of complex displays rather than in Garner's terms (Sanderson, Flach, Buttigeig, & Casey, 1989).

Returning to the Stroop effect and Perlman's counterpart, a second reservation about the example is that the effects are large but negative. While the avoidance of negative effects is important, one could hope for inner theory to open up new positive opportunities for design, and this example does not show that happening.

Inner Theory Will Never Contribute Much Beyond Bounded-rationality Theory because the Discrepancies Are All Negative. The Stroop effect is unmotivated in a bounded-rationality theory because performance is worse than it should be. If performance were good, it would be expected under bounded rationality, because good performance is what the rational system attempts to produce. So, at most, inner theories would help to steer around problems like Perlman's.

This argument overlooks two points. First, it is possible for performance to be irrationally good, at least in the sense that there are factors that can dramatically improve performance for which the rational basis is not apparent to us. John Thomas (personal communication) observed that popular literature is eagerly read voluntarily, whereas carefully written technical material is not read even with incentive. Julian Orr (1990) shows that technical material is maintained in a community of service representatives in the form of anecdotes in which the seemingly irrelevant human context of machine failures is carefully preserved. The situated cognition school (Suchman, 1987; see also Whiteside, Bennett, & Holtzblatt, 1988, and

Whiteside & Wixon, 1987) argues more generally that behavior is decisively influenced by contextual factors, especially social factors, that are beyond the scope of at least current bounded-rationality theory. Understanding of these influences could yield big improvements in HCI. Another case could be constructed from the work of Chase and Ericsson (1981) and others showing that prodigious short-term memory span is attainable under certain conditions. The general field of individual differences, in which presumably equally rational agents manage greatly different accomplishments, also suggests scope for insight into unusually good as well as unexpectedly poor performance. Of course, this argument does not establish any special role for inner theory, but it does show that bounded rationality does not monopolize the positive side of design.

A second ground for optimism about doing better than bounded rationality is that defects in mechanisms, as seen from one point of view, can be exploited as positive capabilities. A clear example is the apparent motion illusion. The visual system cannot distinguish actual motion from successive displays of related but discontinous images. This failure is in fact very useful: It makes cinematic and video presentations of motion possible. Again, this argument does not demonstrate a role for inner theory but it shows that seemingly negative effects can be turned to positive account. So even if associative inner theories succeed only in revealing limitations in the implementation of cognitive processes, these limitations may possibly be exploitable by positive design initiatives.

Successful Inner Theories of Cognition Would Be Disastrous for Humanity.
Just as the inner theories of physics have given people destructive powers they may be unable to control in the long term, it is possible that real insight into the mechanisms of cognition would make possible mind control, lives of fantasy, or other innovations distasteful to us. Although it is risky for us to judge what may be seen as desirable in the future (e.g., consider the attitude of educated Romans toward Christianity), it is necessary for researchers to consider whether they are striving for the realization of their worst nightmares, or whether the self-regulation of the cognitive system would permit some benign interventions while retaining its integrity.

Conclusion

These arguments, even though they can all be at least partially met, make it hard to trust in the inner-theory story for progress in HCI. The balance of experience so far in the field is against it, and there are additional arguments tending the same way. But the arguments do not rule out the possibility of benefit from inner theory, and the potential may lead some to invest in it. How might such an investment be managed?

Let us return once more to the example of medicine. As we saw earlier, progress in medicine has resulted from a mixed strategy, in which purely empirical, outer-theory work has coexisted fruitfully with basic research and basic science. The disadvantages of empirical work uninformed and unorganized by theoretical ideas, and theoretical work unconnected and perhaps unconnectable with practical concerns, can be avoided in the kind of partnership medical science and practice represent.

This model can be applied in HCI as well. The author, together with Stephanie Doane, Gerhard Fischer, Walter Kintsch, Andreas Lemke, and Peter Polson, participates in a cooperative research effort that links the development of cognitive theory with state-of-the-art design case projects. The ground rules of the effort are that the designers are obliged to analyze their design approaches from the perspective of the theory, and the theoreticians are obliged to extend the theory to address issues encountered by the designers that are not covered. The effort has led to better understanding of existing systems (see, e.g., Doane, Kintsch, & Polson, 1989) and a new method for evaluating interface designs (Lewis, Polson, Wharton, & Rieman, 1990). Contributions to design have been modest thus far; had they been more compelling, this chapter would be quite different.

This example of fruitful interplay between the study of theory and design work will perhaps suggest that attention to cognitive theory does not require that one turn away from other aspects of the larger HCI problem, as they are described in other chapters – for example, the nature and function of artifacts (Norman), or the way systems are used (Henderson; Bannon & Bødker). Rather, the approach that seems most likely to succeed in HCI is the one that remains most open to useful knowledge about all aspects of the problem.

It made sense for Watt to do what Watt did in incrementally refining the steam engine, little aided by theory, as recounted by Carroll et al. (this volume). But it also made sense for Priestley to do what he did at about the same time in discovering oxygen. The long term success of technology owes a debt not only to the practical engine builders but also to those who revealed the nature of air and its constituents. The needs of HCI are growing as the power and complexity of computing systems continue to grow, and we will be unwise to neglect any approach to meeting them.

Acknowledgments

I thank the workshop participants for useful comments, and especially John Bennett, Don Norman, and Jack Carroll for suggestions in the aftermath. I am grateful to the National Science Foundation and U.S. West Corporation for research support.

References

Card, S. K. (1990). Theory-driven design research. In C. R. McMillan (Ed.), *Applications of human performance to systems design* (pp. 501–509). New York: Plenum.

Card, S. K., Moran, T. P., & Newell, A. (1983). *The psychology of human–computer interaction.* Hillsdale, NJ: Lawrence Erlbaum Associates.

Chase, W. G., & Ericsson, K. A. (1981). Skilled memory. In J. R. Anderson (Ed.), *Cognitive skills and their acquisition* (pp. 141–189). Hillsdale, NJ: Lawrence Erlbaum Associates.

Doane, S. M., Kintsch, W., & Polson, P. (1989). Action planning: Producing UNIX commands. In *Proceedings of Eleventh Annual Conference of the Cognitive Science Society (Ann Arbor, August 16–18)* (pp. 458–465). Hillsdale, NJ: Lawrence Erlbaum Associates.

Garner, W. R. (1970). The stimulus in information processing. *American Psychologist, 25,* 350–358.

Jensen, A. R., & Rohwer, W. D. (1966). The Stroop color–word test: A review. *Acta Psychologica, 25,* 36–93.

Kintsch, W. (1988). The role of knowledge in discourse comprehension: A construction–integration model. *Psychological Review, 95,* 163–182.

Lewis, C., Polson, P., Wharton, C., & Rieman, J. (1990). Testing a walkthrough methodology for theory-based design of walk-up-and-use interfaces. In L. Borman & B. Curtis (Eds.), *Proceedings CHI '90: Human Factors in Computing Systems* (pp. 235–241). New York: ACM.

MacLeod, C. M., & Dunbar, K. (1988). Training and Stroop-like interference: Evidence for a continuum of automaticity. *Journal of Experimental Psychology: Learning, Memory and Cognition, 14,* 126–135.

Mannes, S. M., & Kintsch, W. (1988). Action planning: Routine computing tasks. In *Proceedings of 10th Annual Meeting of the Cognitive Science Society* (pp. 97–103). Hillsdale, NJ: Lawrence Erlbaum Associates.

Newell, A., & Card, S. K. (1985). The prospects for psychological science in human–computer interaction. *Human–Computer Interaction, 1,* 209–242.

Norman, D. A. (1988). *The psychology of everyday things.* New York: Basic Books.

Norman, D. A. (1981). Categorization of action slips. *Psychological Review, 88,* 1–15.

Orr, J., (1990). Sharing knowledge, celebrating identity: War stories and community memory in a service culture. In D. S. Middleton & D. Edwards (Eds.), *Collective remembering: Memory in society* (pp. 169–189). London: Sage Publications.

Perlman, G. (1984). Making the right choices with menus. In B. Shackle (Ed.), *Human–Computer Interaction: Interact '84* (pp. 317–321). Amsterdam: North-Holland.

Sanderson, P. M., Flach, J. M., Buttigeig, M. A., & Casey, E. J. (1989). Objects displays do not always support better integrated task performance. *Human Factors, 31,* 183–198.

Suchman, L. (1987). *Plans and situated actions: The problem of human–machine communication.* New York: Cambridge University Press.

Walba, D. M., Slater, S. C., Thurmes, W. N., Clark, N. A., Handschy, M. A., & Supon, F. (1986). Design and synthesis of a new ferroelectric liquid crystal family. *Journal of the American Chemical Society, 108,* 5210–5221.

Whiteside, J., Bennett, J., & Holtzblatt, K., (1988). Usability engineering: Our experience and evolution. In M. Helander (Ed.), *Handbook of human–computer interaction* (pp. 791–817). New York: North-Holland.

Whiteside, J., & Wixon, D. (1987). Discussion: Improving human–computer interaction – A quest for cognitive science. In J. Carroll (Ed.), *Interfacing thought: Cognitive aspects of human–computer interaction.* (pp. 353–365). Cambridge, MA: MIT Press.

10

Local Sciences: Viewing the Design of Human–Computer Systems as Cognitive Science

Andrea A. diSessa

The question of whether or not a body of scientific knowledge exists that can significantly inform the design of human–computer systems is in hot debate. My position is not so much that such knowledge already exists, but that it can now be generated. I claim that design can serve not only as an application of emerging cognitive principles but, more radically, that design can serve as a central part of the scientific work that generates those principles. Finally, I hope to show that the Boxer project group at the University of California, Berkeley, is helping to generate such principles and reaping benefit from them.

Introduction

This chapter emerges from two basic epistemological commitments. The first is that scientific progress is made in diverse ways. This is a stand against any sort of essentialism with respect to the scientific program, against the proposition that we can define once and for all what constitutes science. Although studies of science may well lead to interesting apparent generalities – Popper's falsifiability doctrine (Popper, 1962) may be a good example – we will inevitably find complexities and new wrinkles on how science progresses that make those principles dubious. Universal principles are particularly suspect with respect to normative attempts to assert what one must do in order to do science. The normative point of view is important here, for my interest in characterizing science is for the purpose of making better progress.

Indeed, my second epistemological commitment is that it is helpful to try to understand, in general terms, what we are doing in order to make better scientific progress. Thus though I am not particularly inclined to believe proposed universal descriptions of scientific progress, I am equally suspicious of the totally agnostic position that says "anything goes." Paul Feyerabend (1975) has produced wonderful evidence that simple, universal descriptions of science hardly capture the past, let alone the future. However, he has not convinced me that there is nothing at all special about science and that it is useless to try make judgments about better and worse ways to proceed based on some level of generality. I am advocating a kind of fieldwide metacognition for cognitive science as it relates to human–computer interaction, proposing that it is possible to know something about what we are doing and how it works.

This chapter has three parts. The first tries to describe at a general level the mode of work that I have chosen to pursue on human–computer interaction, and how and why it should work. The second part of the chapter tries to exemplify the program

162

by motivating a particular phase of research that we are just now entering. The third part describes some preliminary empirical results of this phase. The phase is a critical one for the program, which makes it interesting to consider, even though we are still at an early stage with respect to it.

A Kind of Science

Let us imagine that the following situation exists. Suppose a class of phenomena, the focus of a scientific inquiry, is tremendously rich and diverse – so diverse, in fact, that there may be no single set of principles that span it. This is hardly an unusual set of affairs. Think of the relation of physics to chemistry, and chemistry to biology. Physical principles are sufficient, in some sense, to explain chemistry, and chemistry may, in like manner, explain biology. Yet these are different sciences. They are different because reducing biology to chemistry or chemistry to physics is sometimes impractical. The more basic view is simply too complex to run on the higher-level questions. The sciences are different as well because reduction is sometimes unsatisfying. We may be able to understand how a metabolic path runs with chemical principles, but that does not tell us the path's function or its complex context that, altogether, creates life. We need to find more local purchase than any "in principle" reduction to basic principles.

Now, what I have in mind is more a breadth of phenomenology than a depth. Thus, the science pieces of interest, local sciences, may not relate in any even approximately reductionist way. Instead, they might cover distinct parts of the phenomenological landscape.

Suppose that we have managed to find some particular principles that apply to simplify and explain parts of the domain of interest. These principles may have a certain internal integrity so that we come to believe them in part for that integrity as much as for their empirical validation. Indeed, it might be that the application of the principles is rather problematic. This might particularly be true as we have rather weak instruments of empirical inquiry – physics without cloud chambers, astronomy without telescopes, and biology without microscopes. So we might know a little about bacteria in principle, but be hard pressed in any instance to know whether it is a bacterium or a virus that is at issue. With a great deal of effort we may be able to figure out which, and draw important inferences out of that – but careful and extensive study of the particular circumstance might be needed to do this.

Optimistically, this area of scientific inquiry might be described as a kind of "multi-Newtonian stew." There might be nuggets of clarity, but they are covered with a mushy opaque "sauce" that obscures so that it is hard to tell the meat from the potatoes.

The phenomena I am interested in here are cognitive. It may be a substantial overestimate of the situation to think we have anything remotely Newtonian to say about cognition. But perhaps we are beginning to build some little chunks of clarity. I don't think it is exaggerating to say that, as yet, we have rather poor instruments with which to look at cognitive objects. So, I am on firmer ground saying that the

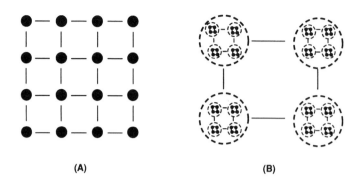

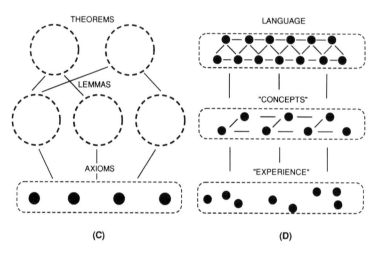

Figure 10.1. Types of organization in complex systems. (A) Flat, uniform organization. (B) Uniform hierarchy. (C) Reductionist hierarchy with uniform (proof) relations. (D) Layered approximate modules, with differing internal organizations.

application of whatever chunks we have may frequently be problematic, and may involve substantial work to find out if and how they apply.

There is a simple and fundamental reason, I believe, that cognitive phenomenology is diverse. It deals with knowledge, and knowledge comes frequently in systems having numerous pieces. If expertise consists of 50,000 chunks, how many possible organizations can one make with those? Let's list a few dimensions of variation, with Figure 10.1 serving to illustrate. Let us say the chunks go together in packages of some number of chunks. Each package defines a node in a hierarchical system, with some pattern of branching ratios in some number of layers. Now there may be nonhierarchical links, which may vary in density from the top to the bottom of the hierarchy. In fact, this is a two dimensional array of variation, because cross-links from any level may vary as a function of the level to which the links connect. If we consider the developmental history of such systems, we get another combinatorial explosion of possibilities. Of the nodes and links, what percentage are new in learning that system; what percentage are old? For the old elements, how are they separated from prior systems of which they were a part? What series of approximate, semistable organizations does the system go through as it evolves?

Perhaps I am being too restrictive in assuming relatively uniform nodes and a roughly hierarchical system. The system could be irregularly flat and clumpy. But such variations make the same point once again. Knowledge systems and their development must constitute a hugely diverse space of possibilities.

These arguments for the diversity of knowledge systems do not depend on details specifying the kind of objects that participate in knowledge systems, or on the particular relations involved. As long as there are very many entities, the conclusion that a large number of organizations might exist seems inescapable.

In what follows I will not make any remotely complete specification of the basic entities and relations involved in any knowledge system. Such specification belongs more properly to the (reductionist) specification of *cognitive architecture* (cf. SOAR, ACT*, etc.). Instead, I take the general lesson that a wide range of types of knowledge systems may exist and try to define classes that are each sufficiently homogeneous so that identifying a knowledge system as belonging to a class has useful consequences. I call these classes *knowledge architectures* because I believe we will ultimately understand them best in relation to a specification of the underlying cognitive architecture.[1]

Similarly, we need to say something about the dynamics of a knowledge system. Each architecture may have several *modes* of activity that are appropriate to it, each one, again, with substantial commonalties of performance features. Finally, we may want to say something about how these architectures develop, *learning modes*.

Examples may be helpful. One cluster of architectures and associated modes may correspond to what some are calling mental models and their use. The prototype for such an architecture would be that some very rich and well-developed knowledge system serves as a kind of framework and accessible "handle" on much less accessible knowledge. Thus, the ability of people to imagine and manipulate a relatively complex spatial state with little external support may serve as an input and output interface for much less articulate process knowledge about how things change in causal sequence. In using a mental model one might deliberately imagine a particular configuration of physical system objects, and "read out," via annotating one's expectations for change, how the system will evolve. People have intuitions about physical laws, but they may be able to access those intuitions only by imagining a situation and reading out their expectations for change.

A very similar kind of process may well be an important part of the trade for

---

1. I attempt a specification of a knowledge architecture in terms of organization on top of an underlying cognitive architecture in diSessa (in press).

designers of human artifacts. A graduate student at U.C. Berkeley, Susan Newman, has looked at designers of various sorts and finds a very particular mode, thinking with "scenarios," where the designer runs through, with some care, activities prospective users might undertake with the proposed artifact. The interpretation here is that scenarios make use of rich and relatively articulate capabilities to "set the scene" for artifact use; then the designer simply notices his or her own reactions and dispositions for action, and the consequences they might have for the design. The fact that this seems like a very natural thing to do should not hide the fact that the same main goal might be accomplished in rather different ways. For example, we might have a theory of human action that would take the place of the designer's personal reactions to the scenario setup. Or, the means of getting feedback on what people do might be completely empirical, as a human-factors approach tends to assume.[2] For an interestingly related use of scenarios as a self-conscious part of the design process, see Carroll, Kellogg, and Rosson (this volume).

Another (hypothetical) architecture may relate directly to understanding the process of design for human–computer sustems. An *aesthetic* (diSessa, in press) is a rich knowledge system that allows one to draw substantial conclusions. Yet it is limited in very particular ways. First, the system is relatively inarticulate. Everyday lexicon is not very helpful, and one might find oneself frequently at a loss for words in verbally describing situations from the point of view of this architecture. At best, it might have mental model interfaces (as already described) to solve access problems. Short of a vocabulary for describing the principles embodied in the knowledge system, one might only describe situations in which the principles act, and their consequences. Second, an aesthetic is sparse in the sense that relatively few elements apply to any problem situation, and when conflicts arise, conflict resolution is difficult within the system. Third, it is recognition driven and, by and large, is unsuitable to forming hypotheticals – that is, proposals for what knowledge from the system might be appropriate to a situation without actually being able to see that the knowledge applies and how it applies. The development of such knowledge systems might be a very different proposition than, for example, the development of skills à la Anderson's models of learning domains such as Lisp programming; standardized procedures for goal-based decomposition might simply not exist. Yet the intuitively important ability to make good judgments might essentially consist of having a particular well-developed aesthetic in this technical sense. A refined understanding of aesthetics and their learning modes might help us understand how designers exercise good judgment and how they acquire these skills.

Aesthetics may have modes of thinking that are characteristic of them. For example, lack of articulateness and data-driven characteristics may mean access to appropriate knowledge may be highly problematic. One may need to resort to very weak methods, such as repetitiously turning a problem over and over in one's mind,

---

2. The fact that using scenarios or mental models seems natural should not hide the fact that substantial expertise might be needed to run them effectively. For example, substantial knowledge might be needed to judge: the level of detail one needs in the scenario setup; how much care and attention is needed to be able to read out expectations; and how to compensate for idiosyncratic reactions, or those that are artifactual of a lack of care or inappropriate setting up of the scenario.

seeking insights as to how to think of it. Contrast these to weak problem-solving methods that assume the basic description is unproblematic, and something like search-through possibilities is the issue. Another characteristic mode might involve specific knowledge about how to modify problem situations so as more likely to cue relevant knowledge. How do designers develop a point of view toward a particular design from the specifics of the design situation?

Aesthetics may have social modes connected with them as well as individual ones. Unlike more familiar knowledge systems, say, physics expertise, experts in some particular aesthetic area may have a great deal of difficulty agreeing on an appropriate analysis of a situation. However, well-developed communal aesthetics may well converge in a case through extended argument, though it may be idiosyncratic to the situation rather than through general methods like proof. It would be an important characteristic of a communal knowledge system that arguments do generally converge, as opposed to either converging very quickly as with normal science (in Kuhn's sense), or not at all. Whether or not group design is possible may depend on the existence of communal aesthetics. Karat and Bennett (this volume), in particular, discuss the importance of understanding design as a group process, hence underlining the potential importance of group aesthetics.

Note from these examples that modes are not likely to be much like predictive user models. We do not need to specify all the details of actions taken in order to constrain our expectations about what will happen when a user tries to understand a system, or to interpret and draw implications when we finally see what is done. A prediction that a user might puzzle for some time about how a feature in a system works, consider several possibilities, and eventually converge on an appropriate interpretation *is* an important prediction even if it says nothing much about the specific considerations of the user.

It seems certain knowledge systems like aesthetics *might* exist. Yet, without well-developed characterization of the particular system, it would be very hard to tell one from a different architecture, where decisions might not just be slow due to access and articulation problems, but might be made on the basis of negotiation, politics, and social power structures instead of knowledge. Like differentiating a viral from a bacterial infection without highly refined tools, determining a knowledge system to be an aesthetic might take a great deal of effort.

With this preliminary sketch, I can now outline an approach to doing science that is appropriate to certain inquiries. "Principled design" might be a sufficient label. The outline is both an ingredients list and, perhaps, a rough chronology.

1.   Principles   The first need is a set of cognitive principles. I don't presume much about how one goes about developing such principles. However, in light of my preliminary comments, architectures and modes might be a prominent focus of them. Furthermore, we would in general like to have significantly more than empirical support for the principles. Thus, they might look more like mathematics in the sense that defining types, presumptions, and entailments constitutes the core of the principles, as opposed to empirical generalizations about the way things must work.

2.   Grounding   Roughly, we need to specify a corner of the stew of cognition for inspection and tune up our ways of viewing it. We need to work out what are the particular characteristics of the instances of generalizations specified in the principles (virus or bacterium). Particular characteristics might be critical to drawing design implications. This may be a data-intensive job, to identify specific knowledge elements and the cognitive ecology into which our principles may fit.

3.   Design   Based on principles and grounding we should be able to prescribe aspects of the design of some artifact that lead to particular objectives.

Here, all of a sudden, we are on less familiar scientific ground. Principles (or laws) and grounding (say, applicability conditions, correspondence principles, and the like) sound like science. But a central role for design in a scientific practice needs more comment.

One is tempted to consider design as part of the *application* of scientific principles rather than occupying a more central role in developing and testing the principles. But, popular lore aside, scientists *always* need to innovate as part of science. In particular, designing productive experiments is central to the practice. So it helps to think of design as developing and conducting a large experiment.

Assimilating design to the role of experiments in more paradigmatic science is not without its own difficulties. For example, design tasks are frequently large and encompass much more than seems within the scope of a testable scientific principle. The first response to this is that architectures and modes are simply not tiny and simple things to explore. We have come to understand in physics that some things cannot be explored with limited commitment of resources. You cannot explore quarks without an expensive accelerator. Similarly, to approach the kinds of things we are studying, we may need to engage in substantial activities, on the scale of the design of an artifact and extended study of its use.

Another reason design seems inappropriate to science is that design is usually driven by practical need, not scientific concerns. Indeed, there is necessarily some tension here. It is essentially certain that we do not have and cannot develop on short order principles for all practical problems (in human–computer interaction or any other cognitive arena). So some design will, indeed, not make sense as part of a scientific practice. Yet some, I claim, can make such sense.

On the other hand, there is a reason to join practical need and scientific need in the choice of design projects. If we accept the fact that a substantial scale of effort may be necessary to reach the issues of modes and architectures of knowledge systems, it would be well worth attempting to amortize that investment by having, at the same time, some likelihood of producing value other than scientific value. So we may look preferentially for design tasks that suit both scientific purposes and practical ones. Nuclear fusion may be an interesting area of relatively basic research. But it receives attention and funding in part for its promise of practical value.

Design may also serve a more formative role in this scientific program, that of an "intuition pump." Although it is not standardly recognized in the philosophy of science, I take it as a cognitive fact that the development, articulation, and sharpening of intuitive ideas concerning some class of phenomena is an important develop-mental mechanism. Sharp formulations and critical experiments emerge gradually from broader musings and explorations at a more intuitive level. The latter are almost always less public than the former, but that does not make them less impor-tant. So how do we develop, so as to pump for scientific effect, our own intuitions about cognitive architectures and modes? I suggest one of the best ways to engage in a broad range of design activities, including substantial formative work with users, focused on the modes and architectures of interest. Unlike, say, Newtonian mechanics, for which we all begin with a relatively uniform intuitive base, intuitions about cognition in contexts of the design of electronic artifacts must be developed. And fitting our presumption of many modes and knowledge architectures, it seems that it would have to be the case that intuition building and pumping is at least as local as the pockets of science that emerge from it.

4. Review Having completed the design, a designer may usually be sub-stantially done with his job. But for this new role, design itself is obviously insuffi-cient. Careful study of the operation of the design in use is vital. This study may have several outcomes. First, the design may fail for a number of reasons. The principles may be faulty. More likely they might turn out to be insufficiently speci-fied. A second type of failure might be in the grounding. On more careful study, it might turn out that the designed artifact works, but with some other knowledge, architectures, or modes.

The design process itself is fraught with complexities. For example, design is almost always a game of trade-offs and compromises. We might have made the wrong order of magnitude estimate of the effect of certain mechanisms – a pre-dicted, but expected-to-be-minor difficulty might turn out to be fatal.

Now, of course, the failure of the design might be most illuminating. From the standpoint of science (rather than more practical measures of success), there is only one reason to expect design failures to be less informative than successes. That is, if the principles and grounding are just not capable of specifying at least part of what we see in the design operation, then the design is a scientific failure. This is just as much true if the design is a practical success, but we still cannot see at least part of the reasons for its success.

In many scientific contexts, reviewing an experiment is a trivial affair. Your fusion works or does not. You get a meter reading as predicted, or not. In the case of principled design concerning psychological affairs, undoubtedly it will never be so simple. If the design is at all substantial, the behavior of users of the design will be complex, not predicted in detail. Sorting out what is working by the principles, what requires revision in the principles, and what might have been mistaken in the original grounding will require at least a substantial fraction, perhaps much more, of the effort that went into the principles and grounding of the original design.

To summarize: I have tried to specify a paradigm of doing science that does justice to what I take to be basic facts about trying to do cognitive research. It is a local scientific program in which, in addition to general principles, one needs sub-stantial work to ground those principles in the context of interest. The program entails four elements. First, one derives, by whatever means, general principles of cognitive operation. But general principles do not mean universally applicable principles. They might be quite specific to a limited set of knowledge architectures and modes of operation of those architectures.

Second, a substantial effort will have to be expended to ground those principles in a particular context (that of the intended use of the designed artifact), finding the instances of the objects of the principles, and the relevant characteristics of those objects so as to be able to make productive design decisions.

Third, designing by those principles constitutes another stage, one with multiple functions. In addition to specifying the characteristics of the system according to principles, working through a design may well generate substantial input for the other stages. Indeed, principles and grounding are unlikely to have been arrived at without careful consideration of the modes and architectures appropriate to the imagined designed system. The design process itself can serve as an intuition pump out of which principles and grounding emerge.

Finally, a substantial review of the way in which the design functions serves (optimistically) to validate and refine the principles and grounding, as well as to provide feedback on specific design decisions. At this stage of cognitive science, any design is bound by multiple sets of principles, over which, undoubtedly, we will have only partial control in the foreseeable future. Predicting success and failure by obvious standards may not be within range of our scientific inquiry. We hope only that the other factors impinging on the design do not dominate to the point that the action of our principles is invisible in the behavior of the designed system.

This program is a committed attempt at useful inner theories of human–computer interaction, to use Lewis's phrase (this volume). It addresses head-on some of the key difficulties he notes for producing such a theory. In particular, the problem of the sheer complexity of cognition is handled in each of the four steps. The principles are expected to be sufficiently abstract to encompass many unknown details, while still posing useful constraints for design. The issue of finding the principles in the detailed activity of users (grounding) is explicit. The program entails that "experiments" will be intrinsically complex and expensive, and that their review will need special, extended attention.

A Principled Design

We (the Berkeley Boxer Group) are about two thirds of the way through the principled design of a programming language we call Boxer. The system is intended to be significantly more than a programming language in the conventional sense. It is intended to be a "computational medium." That is, it is intended to function for people much in the way that written text functions for literate societies and individuals. This means the system is intended to provide a standardized core for a tremendous range of uses, from small and idiosyncratic ones for individuals, to much more specialized purposes (say, for subgroups) that might require a very substantial amount of planning and effort. The niche we are most interested in charting is education, written quite broadly. So, on the small end of things, we see children playing with our system or with programs written in it, or taking notes for school subjects, and so on. Teachers, we hope, will find uses from their own perspective – say, keeping and organizing course plans, grades, and so forth. They may also develop their own materials for students, or modify some that were supplied by colleagues or commercial sources. On larger scales curriculum developers and commercial suppliers might develop substantial systems in Boxer, corresponding to things like interactive books, or relatively highly tuned tools.

This image differs from more conventional images of the use of computers in education in that we envisage one integrated but multifunctional system at the root of all these uses. And that system includes the full means to create and modify within the system – programming. This is the reason we call it a reconstructible medium. Structurally, this means we want to deepen the available infrastructure for multiple uses of computers beyond a common interface, such as the Macintosh offers, to include the ability to create and alter the fundamental actions and interactions of the system. Functionally, this means that everyone will have at their fingertips the capability to create, modify, and interleave any subsystems built in Boxer, at least in principle. In contrast to a top-down society where experts and developers decide what is right for consumers, we are interested in shifting much of the initiative to users, so that they can invent and build to suit their own purposes, or so they can at least inspect and modify what is provided to them. Top-down may be just the right thing for much of our society. But where invention and personal actions are the very core of the enterprise, such as in education, computer systems need to be much more open.

There are two distinct levels at which this kind of design "lives." At the first level, it is well known that programming is a difficult enterprise. Not many individuals become expert enough for programming to serve them creatively. Comprehensibility of programming is, thus, the central scientific focus of our design. It defines the core of the discussion for the rest of this chapter.

I can give only cursory treatment to the second level. This is the social and cultural level that determines the uses and acceptance of something as broadly aimed as a computational medium. There are at least two pieces of this level. First and most important, from my point of view, are the activity structures that surround the medium. What diverse set of things can be done by individuals and groups that justify the substantial cost of adopting a broader basis for literacy, one which includes programming? It will not be sufficient that the medium does things currently done with written language and, indeed, with computers. A new medium must provide substantially more value to justify any change, let alone a change that introduces a major new skills component to literacy. This makes the design all the more tricky, for we are designing for new kinds of documents and activities, not just those as well known as programming. Indeed, the very meaning of programming will need to change from its present connotations involving esoteric expertise and great effort.

It is not clear that principled, scientific design is at all plausible at this social and cultural level, although surely we can and should be reflective about what might be possible and productive with a new medium. My own thoughts on this are sketched in diSessa (1990); see especially the discussion of tool-rich learning cultures. Yet success or failure of our efforts in anticipating future sociocultural activities and values is probably not under our scientific control.

Bannon and Bødker (this volume) are concerned with the importance of this level of design. I agree that microdesign of a system without some view of its intended use in a social context is extraordinarily limiting. Hence the notion of a computational medium and the social niches into which it will fall are central, guiding principles for us – principles that govern (a part of) our evaluation of the progress we are making. However, I believe that this view is complementary to other considerations rather than strictly alternative. Indeed, my claim here is that the knowledge system level can provide, for some systems, real help in the "juicier" parts of design without the radical epistemological shift Bannon and Bødker advocate.

The second major cluster of issues having to do with the adoption of a computational medium concerns the processes of change that might enable introduction of a new medium. Cynically, who makes how much money from it might dominate that discussion. But perhaps even that comment suggests we know more than we probably do about societal appropriation of innovation. In any case, it is time to get back onto the main track of discussion.

A Focus for Principled Design

How do we approach the issue of comprehensibility of programming languages so as to effect a better design? First, let us set some relevant parameters. We are not particularly interested in the first hour, or day, or probably even the first months. These may tell us something about the learnability of a system, but on the scale necessary to assess a computational medium, the first several months only begin to interest us. Of course, there may be insurmountable barriers right at the beginning. But if there are not, that still is insufficient for our purposes. Literacy with written text would probably fail anyone's test for learnability on the basis of early use by children. Similarly, ease of use and freedom from errors are not, by themselves, appropriate first-line measures. Again, written language is not particularly "user friendly," if by that we mean it is quickly learned and affords fluent and intuitive use in short measure.

On the high end, we are not interested in expertise as defined by current professional programming. The things people will be doing with a computational medium are not the same things professional programmers do. The scale of complexity in programming will not approach that of 50,000 line programs. The capability to design, comprehend, and modify diverse, small, but nontrivial programs is more central. My personal estimate is that our target lies largely within the range of programming that can be done in a day by an expert programmer (presuming an excellent, tool-rich programming environment). Note, this may be more than many would expect, especially those whose image of programming is C or Pascal. This scale happens, for example, to be about the maximum size program I have found useful to design and build for my own use in educational settings. Beyond that size, the effort committed per results attained, lack of feedback, and hence likelihood of dead-end designs seem just too much to endure.

These estimates put us into a most interesting context. It involves competence that, I believe, is within the range acquirable by ordinary people, judging by the complexity of things they demonstrably can learn – literacy, for example. It is centrally a cognitive context, significantly above the scale of skills learning in any conventional sense of that word, just as literacy is beyond decoding and encoding skills. On the other hand, there are clear limits in what has been achieved by ad hoc methods. This is not the place for a review, but, briefly, several months to a year or two does not seem sufficient to bring children to a reasonable understanding of the basic structures and functions of available programming systems, at least with common instructional techniques. See, for example, Pea (1986) and the section on difficulties, misconceptions, and bugs in Soloway and Spohrer (1989). If our intuitive designs have failed, the context may be right for a more scientific approach.

I have already alluded to arguments that significant social value might be achieved if we can overcome the programming learnability barrier. Thus, this constitutes an area where the expense of design may be amortized with some probability of practical as well as scientific payoff.

The key question that remains is: Can we establish plausible principles and grounding that are powerful enough to give us real design leverage in this area?

Principles for Programming Comprehensibility: Mental Models

The framework I have proposed for thinking about the design of comprehensible programming systems involves the construct of mental models, roughly in the vein mentioned earlier, as a class of knowledge architectures. Substantial work has been done within the last 10 years in this frame. Some of this work has concerned the understanding of physical devices for which people can internalize relatively easily a certain part of system state – most particularly spatial arrangements of two kinds: objects and connectivity, and the distributions of functional attributes. To illustrate, people can reason relatively easily about the topology of pipes, valves, and boilers in a steam plant. Furthermore, some other attributes of the plant are relatively easily internalizable. For example, people can reason qualitatively about temperature and its relation to processes such as boiling. What is less tractable is the behavior of a steam plant as a whole. See, for example, Gentner and Stevens (1983) and White and Frederiksen (1989) for relevant discussion of mental models.

To make the notion of mental model do work in the area of programming comprehension, I have found it necessary to distinguish different classes of models and to develop a design strategy based on an articulation of these multiple kinds of models together with a specification of appropriate and inappropriate modes of learning and of use for each. These ideas are treated in significantly greater detail elsewhere (e.g., diSessa, 1986). The view here is meant only to provide a sketch sufficient to illustrate principled design in a concrete context.

Structural Models

The first kind of model I call a structural model. The core niche for this model is as a context-invariant specification of the set of possible configurations of the computer (its state space in more technical terms) and the possible transitions from one state to another. This comes closest to what might be, in one version of a structural model, an internalizable image of the mechanism of the machine, at some appropriately abstract level, in which one can see how things will change on the basis of the current configuration together with a specification of input to the machine. Examples of such models are the stack model of RPN calculators (Young, 1981) and the "little man" model of program execution for Logo (diSessa, 1986).

The strengths of such a model are, first, its in-principle capacity to deal with any context of use of the system; and second, the cluster of advantages that can accrue to relatively compact and articulable knowledge systems in general, including stability and coherence. For example, a structural model may be coherent because the designer takes arbitrary amounts of time to *make* it coherent. And in contrast to an aesthetic, it is articulable because it is designed to be talked about.

The principle mode of use of structural models is to "run" the model in some situation to see the time-evolution of the system. Alternatively, one may reason in reverse, checking for plausible predecessor states to a given one, say, to reason what went wrong on the basis of characteristic effects of a bug.

Some plausible generalizations about the modes of learning and operation associated with structural models are possible. The most important ones I mention here and save others for contrasts with other types of models. Structural models will almost certainly be complex and difficult to learn. This is, on the one hand, an estimate of the minimal complexity of a fully functional programming language. On the other hand, it represents a general assessment of the capability of humans to appropriate such complex systems. Structural models, then, constitute a substantial and extended goal for learning a programming system, not an initial target or prerequisite to early use. To be sure, we would like to design structural models that are as easy to learn as possible, but there are limits to what can be expected in this direction.

These considerations of structural models may be irrelevant without being wrong. Some claim that programming languages can be designed so users need not be concerned with how the language works, but only with what they need to do with it. If this is correct, we designers simply need not worry about a comprehensible structural model or the learning trajectory thereof. It would be wrong to claim that multifunctionality represented in typical uses of a language requires a structural model. This would be a mistake in grounding, not in principles. There might still be other domains where structural models and their characteristics are important – electronics, for example. Again, local sciences may well have this mathematical characteristic of being conceivably irrelevant without being wrong. A failure in relevance might even be a success for the principles if we can find in the grounding exactly why they are irrelevant.

Retrenchment aside, "correct but irrelevant" is not a pleasant fate for principles of learnability, and I stand ready to defend the need for structural models for programming languages.

Functional Models

Structural models are context free. On the other hand, programming systems exist to be useful for particular applications, each of which comes with its own descriptive frame. Even very simple applications come with their own way of thinking about state and state transitions. Number crunching, for example, concerns constants, variables, algorithms, and less formal activities like collecting data and presenting answers. These all must be appropriately mapped into structures like variables, procedures, conditionals, and IO mechanisms. In problem contexts more remote from the structural turf of machines, the mappings may be much more complex. A physics program must represent, for example, the velocities and positions of multiple objects, but as well, it must represent topological relations such as contact between objects, and, perhaps the *logical relationship* between contact and the forces derived from that. A "computer psychiatrist" must represent *informal inferences* about another person's mental state.

The description of problems and solutions in terms proximal to their "native territory" I call *functional*. Of course, the central task of programming is to map functions into structures that are available or buildable in a language, structures that implement those functions. Topological or logical relationships and inferences must find their way into data structures and programming statements. This may require new decompositions of familiar problems and solutions.

With respect to learning modes, function is relevant in two related respects. First, beginners may well learn programming systems, at least in part, through solving problems with them. Thus, programming constructs may be first approached through the functions they perform in some early encounters with them. This is particularly true if the map from function to structure is relatively simple, at least from the point of view of the user. The tool is initially defined more by the job it accomplishes than the means by which it accomplishes that job, or the internal structural principles that allow the tool to work. A good example of a functional model that illustrates this is how most people understand a four-function calculator (Young, 1981). It is for them a device that just does simple arithmetic operations. Most users couldn't care less what internal registers and states actually implement this functionality.

Structures in a language become known as they implement *generic functionalities* – for example, a variable is a repository of data – for temporary storage or for communication among different portions of a program. And, stepping toward expertise, advanced users may accumulate complex chunks of language primitives, or strategies for producing complex chunks, that implement other abstract functionalities. The existence of this latter type of functional model (as a component of developing expertise, as opposed to early and preliminary versions of structural understanding) has been substantially documented, though with varying terminology such as plans or templates (Linn, Sloane, & Clancey, 1987; Soloway, 1985).

In comparison to structural models, functional ones have characteristic strengths and weaknesses. First, they are typically relatively more context specific than structural models. This makes them easier to use within their respective contexts, particularly for the task of invention. On the other hand, context specificity makes them less coherent, integrable, and extendible. Indeed, once one begins to write rather different sorts of programs, substantially different functional models may be needed. Compare stressing functional understanding of a four-function calculator by asking how one can perform unusual operations or recover gracefully from, say, a keystroke error. In contrast, a structural model "belongs to the language," not to its use, and thus is never, in principle, limited or obsolete. The applicability of structural concerns to a case is never in question, though that may be difficult to implement. To do so, one must instantiate all the relevant state in structural terms (not in problem-specific terms) and grind through the model's implications.

I can summarize the characteristics of these two models with typical scenarios of learning and use.

Structural models (in their entirety or even to the point of explaining everyday operation of the system) will in general be difficult to learn. They may, in fact, take many years to learn, and thus do not constitute the earliest goals for language learning. On the other hand, they are important for such capabilities as debugging, where function-specific expectations have gone awry, and for radical invention, where prior functional vocabulary is insufficient to the task at hand. For more expert programmers, structural models play an important role as a tightly integrated and hence easily regenerated core to programming understanding.

Some functional models may be important in early stages of learning programming. But they may not extend easily to very different contexts because they are phrased in more context-specific terms. Details of how a functional context is described and how the constructs of a language are mapped into that description are critical in judging the possibility of transfer. Routine and familiar programming will be done with a substantial component of functional models, and even experts will continue to develop a more and more diverse vocabulary to shortcut usually effortful use of structural models and the problems with nearly ab initio invention.

In contemporary research on learning programming, functional concerns (plans, goal/subgoal decompositions, templates) dominate structural concerns. Why might this be so? First, most researchers might focus more on early stages of learning than stages approaching expertise, where structural models are hypothesized to be most important. Second, they might be focusing on languages that are poorly designed by structural models' criteria, so little payoff would be in store for structural instruction. Third, functionally oriented researchers might be missing something essential. Fourth, I might be wrong. A Ph.D. thesis at U.C. Berkeley by Lydia Mann is in progress to sort some of this out.

Distributed Models

A third class of models is motivated empirically by noting how students explain to themselves early encounters with certain constructs of languages. In particular, students do not always wait for or listen to instructors' explanations for how a language works. Instead, they invent plausible explanations for why things are the way they are. These explanations are something like a learner's spontaneous versions of structural models. That is, learners try to provide general descriptions of language constructs that explain why and how they do what they do. Naturally, these descriptions will typically fall far short of the intended structural models, with much more diversity in their sources and unreliability in their transfer to other situations. Indeed, I call these *distributed models* to indicate the diverse and ad hoc principles that serve as a basis for them, and to indicate the diversity we can expect in the resulting collection of partial models. Some good examples of distributed models come from beginners' appropriating the natural language meaning of terms used in the language. IF and WHILE are reasonably close in meaning to English "if" and "while." This gives beginners a good head start. However, bugs result if understanding remains at the level of an analogy to natural language terms. Some beginners interpret IF to mean "whenever," and they do not understand that WHILE entails a very particular sequencing of test and action.

It is at our own peril that we ignore the formation of distributed models, whether they are productive or not, in understanding the sense that students are making of a computer system. We need to pay attention to these models primarily at the earliest stages of learning, optimistically to be able to engineer profitable ones but, as well, to know what kinds of specific teaching may be needed to overcome weaknesses in spontaneously generated models. A system well designed for distributed models will feel intuitively right. One not well designed will constantly surprise the user, even if, after the fact, its operation makes sense (structurally).

Although the specification of these expectations about the modes of operation of these different models is incomplete in various respects, variations may be relatively easily handled. For example, if means are found for producing relatively more comprehensible structural models (which we certainly intend), some reliance on functional models may be reclaimed. To the extent that this is possible, this shift toward reliance on structural models may well be quite desirable from the viewpoint of generality and transferability. However, from the point of view of routine invention and comprehension of routine code, functional models are not likely to be replaced.

In order to span a full set of conflicting needs – including ease of early learning and at the same time coherence in ultimate understanding; radical invention and at the same time everyday system use; debugging and routine invention; context-general and context-adapted comprehension of programming; and even effective explicit instruction along with enhanced uninstructed learning – it is important to design with multiple models in mind. Knowing the rough modes of learning and operation of models can help us to design them better individually, and also so they articulate better with complementary models.

Grounding

Some aspects of the grounding of these principles in the context of comprehensible programming systems have already been covered implicitly in the description of mental models. Rather than develop a more general description of mental models, I turned immediately to a level more apt to programming systems. In particular, I presumed some particular characteristics of programming systems in order to assert expectations. I assumed the system to be understood is substantially complicated so that complete structural models would be difficult to develop. In addition, I assumed a broadly inventive stance on the part of the user, that he or she would be involved in diverse undertakings in the role of inventor-modifier. If the system were to be used for a relatively narrow, highly tuned purpose, functional models might well dominate, and the need for structural models would be less pressing.

On the other hand some aspects of the grounding will necessarily be quite specific to the designed system. Judgments about the ability of users to use various models in various contexts will necessarily be affected by the effectiveness of the particular models at issue. We expect that there will be extreme cases where structural or functional models will clearly dominate a user's capability, but the middle ground depends on specifics and judgments. Most particularly, distributed models depend on specific prior knowledge that users have and may bring to the system, so the grounding in these cases will almost certainly be provided by empirical work. I defer details in grounding until I have laid out some of the specifics of our design, on which they depend.

Design

I cannot detail the full design of Boxer (consult, e.g., diSessa, 1985, 1987, for more extensive treatment). Instead, I briefly consider the central most strategic move to provide better models for Boxer. Then I describe a few other specifics of the design. These prepare for the last major section of the chapter, which begins the empirical review of Boxer's design.

The design of Boxer relies critically on human spatial–visual capabilities as the basis for both structural and distributed models. We intend the system to be comprehensible in substantial degree in that it will be visible; we intend the visible system to show as directly as possible the structure of the system. Users should have the impression of directly seeing and interacting with all the basic structures of the system. And fundamental relational structures of the system will be expressed by visible spatial organization. In Norman's terms (this volume), we seek to have only one effective representation unifying "surface" and "internal" representations. In a sense, there is no user interface that mediates.

Structural models will therefore be dense with spatial vocabulary. And in the similar way, users' spontaneous distributed models should centrally be in this same mode. Functional models, on the other hand, because they are tied to nonsystem descriptive frames, will often be much less tied to the visual–spatial orientation.

Because visual reasoning will play such an important role in the principled design of Boxer, it is important to situate such considerations carefully with respect to our modeling principles. In the first instance, the principles do not replace scientific understanding of visual reasoning capabilities and processes. It is, in fact, unfortunate that more is not known about these to serve as a better backdrop for designers' attempts to use models based on visual–spatial capabilities. The better the understanding of visual capabilities, the better grounded our modeling principles will be to Boxer's case. Short of comprehensive scientific theories of visual–spatial processing, I believe we have reasonable intuitive access to human capabilities of this type, which can be supplemented by empirical work focused on design-specific issues.

In complementary manner, understanding visual reasoning does not replace the modeling considerations. It is insufficient to say Boxer will be comprehensive because it provides good visualization since we are specifying in our modeling considerations what should constitute "good," and thus implicitly ruling out other uses of visual reasoning. So, for example, some may claim that iconicity and visual analogs of real world objects (desk tops, file folders, trash cans) are important to comprehensibility. We have rejected this in any direct sense for Boxer because it does not relate to our high-priority structural aims. Instead, we have attempted to use more abstract visual capabilities that relate directly to the underlying structure of Boxer programming rather than to make more directly functionally oriented comprehensibility moves. Similarly, we have consciously avoided purely graphical programming in Boxer in part because the choice of that kind of structure moves too far away from the uses we intend for Boxer, and it would thus afford too little functional modeling support. The most prominent decision in this context is to use a text-based surface representational form to join with a prominent class of uses of Boxer, as a hypertext, data base, personal information environment. To put this all more succinctly, we make structure rather than function visually accessible, but the structure we have chosen is designed to mesh with prominent system uses, thus affording functional comprehensibility.

Visual reasoning and modeling considerations are also distinct to the extent that we rely on models that are not visual. Although I will not highlight them here, essentially none of our designed functional models are visual, and some proportion of the distributed model considerations are also nonvisual. (One unanticipated example will show up in our empirical work, later in the chapter.) Finally, to clinch the case, we have obligated ourselves in the review of Boxer comprehensibility to show not just that it works, or even that it works because it is a visual programming language, but that it works in the way we say, via the power of designing appropriate models.

So what kinds of objects do we want to be the basis for Boxer? They should be visual for distributed early learning, and probably functionally motivated as well for the same reasons. Centrally, they must fit cleanly into the basic structural view of the system.

We chose boxes as the surface form of essentially all objects in Boxer. These are rectangular regions whose insides define them and their parts. Boxes are manipulable easily as a whole, their parts modified directly with text-editing functions. Readers may look ahead to figures to get the gist of Boxer's visual presentation. Boxes differ from windows in that they occupy (visually and semantically) a specific location in a spatial hierachy, they are always persistent across sessions, and they have specific functionality as objects in the programming language. Boxes and text are both the state readout of the system and the focus of a user's manipulation. Again using Norman's terms, boxes and text are "object symbols." And boxes represent a hierarchical place "intrinsically,"

There is a tremendous diversity of kinds of entities in most computer systems. Essentially all of Boxer's objects share a common representational form, the box. In contrast, lists, character strings, numbers, variables, fields, records, arrays, blocks, procedures, functions, environments, menus, message-passing objects, files, file directories, and so on, all may have diverse and subtly different representational forms. Some of these forms are quite uninformative about the internal structure of the object. In other cases *no* form is presented unless specifically requested. In contrast, Boxer has only two fundamental kinds of objects, data boxes and do-it boxes (and three subsidiary types, which I will not consider), that subsume all of the listed functionalities. Thus we have a tremendous compression of diversity to simplify structural comprehension. These are the only forms in which users see the structures of Boxer, and they are always immediately available for inspection.

Have we gone too far in emphasizing structure at the expense of function? Our principles, to the extent they have been developed, do not tell us precisely when the proper balance has been struck. But (1) they alert us to the central importance of structural concerns, (2) they provide a basis for knowing when we have gone too far (difficulties in early comprehension; or finding the system comprehensible, yet difficult to use for common tasks), and (3) they guide us in redesigning if we find these signs (perhaps we should diversify the set of basic types to match a wider range of functions).

The two box types themselves have simple functional root models. Data boxes are simply stuff of whatever form that one has around mostly for its informational value. Data boxes are inert, but "observed" and manipulated by other entities. The active entities in Boxer are do-it boxes, which are made with the intention of describing actions. In a sentence, we have data and do-it boxes for roughly the same reason natural languages have nouns and verbs.

Much of the diversity one needs in programming is provided in two basic ways. First, one may vary the internal structure of the box in ways that are easily described in naive terms. If you want a list, you put a number of items in spatial sequence in a data box (in "textual" order, left to right, top to bottom) and use functionally motivated accessors or mutators, primitives such as FIRST, BUTFIRST or ITEM 23 (of) X. If you want a two-dimensional array, you may use rows and columns, and accessors and mutators are included in the language to support this functionality of data. Similarly, if you want a block structure in a program, you put a do-it box in the midst of the code you are writing.

On the other hand, if you want a three-dimensional array, you either invent a way of representing it, or you just don't do it. Three-dimensional arrays were judged too much of a corruption of the basic two-dimensional structure to be supported. The general point is that functional variation (for noncentral functions) is frequently subordinated to structural simplicity.

Again it is appropriate to ask where the guidance in our theory is for the decision to abandon three-dimensional arrays. As with the function–structure balance, the theory alerts us to the threat three dimensions pose to the comprehensibility of the system, it provides an empirical focus for evaluating that threat (should we try to implement them, or should we find much easier structural comprehension of the simpler design, without them, than we expect), and possibly, it provides a basis for redesign (e.g., incorporating three dimensionality in the fundamental system structuring, rather than as a functionally motivated add-on). More than this would require comparative estimates of comprehensibility, which the theory at this stage cannot supply, but also comparative estimates of the value of three-dimensional arrays against their comprehensibility costs. The latter cannot be provided by modeling considerations as it resides in the social structures and values level of design toward which I make no pretense to contribute here.

The second general means of modifying the basic structural core to specific functional ends is through generic features associated with boxes that implement those specific functionalities. Thus any box may be named, and naming accomplishes the transition of a data or do-it object into a variable or defined procedure. Any box may be saved to disk (with or without a name), making it a file, and also making the surrounding box structure implicitly into a hierarchical file system. Naming and the totally unconstrained mix-and-match character of the system (you can put anything anywhere, do anything that you can do in one place anywhere else) automatically imply the easy implementability of more functionally tuned structures. A record with fields is simply a data box with named data subboxes. A local variable or subprocedure is simply a named data or do-it box located inside some particular other procedure.

Steps toward a Local Scientific Design Practice

A design pattern of which we found a number of instances in the design of Boxer is the "functional wedge-in." Thus, in some instances the root Boxer structural design could not be modestly corrupted to serve what we decided were necessary functionalities. For example, in dealing with multiple graphical objects, we judged a message-passing paradigm to be the simplest mode of interaction. So graphical objects can be "told" to execute some commands. But once added to graphical objects, we immediately made the capability entirely generic. Any box in Boxer may be told, thus creating a generic (though not highly tuned) message-passing capability.

A second "functional wedge-in" happened in the Boxer syntax. In order to obviate the need for users to learn special syntactic markers for a whole class of situations, we developed a system of "flavored inputs" that allows one to write syntax-free code. For example, TELL JOE MOVE_FORWARD X needs no special markers in Boxer, even though TELL treats its inputs very specially. The first input to TELL needs direct "object reference" to JOE, not access only to the information in JOE (thus, a copy is not sufficient), and the second input, the message for JOE, should not be executed in order to find a value. Executing inputs (call by value) is the standard in most programming languages (including Boxer) to achieve transparent function composition in the mathematical sense. We could have allowed TELL to remain special, tuned to its specific function. Instead we made the special features of TELL generic structure. We defined a system of input types that are structurally coherent, and generally accessible in any circumstances to (advanced) programmers for their own purposes.

The status of strategies like the functional wedge-in is interesting to consider. A positive interpretation is that these are the beginning of an engineering practice based on (local) scientific principles. Although invention and creativity will always remain as parts of design, other parts may begin to evolve into more routine problem solving based on principles. Standard and alternative methods together with applicability conditions should evolve. So should empirical means of establishing failure and thus the need for yet other strategies.

In this light, I can schematize the functional wedge-in. It is a strategy that applies when one needs specific functionally motivated variation, when existing structure provides inadequate functional models. In such a case, one invents a new structure tuned to the needed functionality. But having done so, one makes sure the new structure is generic and applies uniformly in the language so as to minimally corrupt the structural core. Typical failure patterns are that the new functionally motivated structure may either not serve its original function well enough, or may disturb to an unacceptable degree the structural integrity of the system. Alternate design strategies include reconsidering the need for the functionality in the first place, or "diffusing" the functionality, making it achievable not through specific functionally motivated structures but in a less effective (though less structurally threatening) way through multiple already existing or mildly extended system capabilities.

Consider a case where we rejected the functional wedge-in. Boxer does not have any browser or other overview capability, because we judged that threatened the "what you see is (always and exactly) what you have" character of the system. Browsing functionality can instead be diffused into, for example, simple box visibility control (expanding and shrinking boxes) and into the possibility of adding specific browsing capability, when needed, through programming.

I wish to make two general points about this humble example of an evolving design practice based on local scientific principles. First, the root intuition of the functional wedge-in may well be that in carefully considering the functions that artifacts are to serve, we can frequently reconceptualize their structure in more felicitous terms. Any designer worth his salt can hardly have missed this point. Yet, on the background of mental models, this intuition takes on a much broader scope and more bite. The listed considerations and strategies do not follow from the root intuition. Nor do the conditions under which the intuition is limited or irrelevant (e.g., invention is unimportant, thus structural models are also of limited importance). Such intuitions can hardly serve to orient the fundamental focus of design, as modeling considerations have for Boxer, nor are they up to the job of making difficult and sometimes controversial design decisions, like Boxer's concerning the importance of structural models in contrast to essentially any other programming system design.

The second point is once again about details and grounding as they relate to principles. Clearly a great number of unarticulated intuitions may be hidden under the banner of "judgment" in the decisions already discussed. But judgments employ *both* general and arbitrarily specific information about, say, the prior knowledge and the needs of users. At the general level, our mental model principles for design prepared us for design decisions such as this, focusing our attention on the diversity of functions for which a particular structure was intended, and to see whether the learning and use trajectories of the different aspects (structural–functional) were compatible. But even with empirically determined details, theory may play an important role. Consider the case of materials science where a critical strength parameter cannot be computed but must be measured. Still, the meaning of the parameter and our ability to draw implications from its having one value or another may well be drawn from theory. We need not worry that science is escaping us if particulars enter in, although we must make sure we do not mistake them for the science in our designs.

The bulk of the remainder of the chapter deals with the last of our four stages.

Review of a Principled Design

A Cognitive Benchmark for the Comprehensibility of Procedural Languages

There are a huge range of ways in which one may approach the evaluation of a design. So we add two important constraints to focus this work.

1.   Cumulative assessment technology   Unprincipled assessment of learnability leads to a lack of cumulativeness in the assessment process. If the grounds for assessment are unarticulated, there is no way to criticize and improve the means of assessment. Thus, we aim to contribute to a principled and therefore cumulative review technology. We view this as an especially central goal as no single individual or group is likely to "get it right," neither with respect to cognitive principles for design nor with respect to design assessment and review. A central need here is for the evaluation to feed back into the evaluation methodology as well as to reflect on learnability.

Principled assessment of learnability seems to be a new idea. In reviewing the literature, we would find only ad hoc attempts to access learnability of programming languages.[3] In particular, assessments typically blame or credit systems as a

3.   I am indebted to John Carroll for pointing out that a much closer parallel to our approach here exists in the design of interfaces, in contrast to programming languages. There, *usability specifications* (Carroll & Rossen, 1985) have become much more common practice. It seems to me the most salient confluences between our benchmarks project and the usability specification paradigm are: (1) a positive stance toward the application of psychological expertise in design; (2) a skeptical stance toward a priori and ungrounded (in the technical sense of this chapter) principles to evaluate comprehensibility; and (3) an integration of the development and application of principles into an ongoing design process (in the usability paradigm, subskills and behavioral prerequisite analysis substitute for cognitive modeling principles). The most salient differences are: (1) less expectation in the usability paradigm for the invariance of principles (subskills analysis) across multiple designs; (2) a more skills and behavior orientation as opposed to cognitive structure (as might appropriately

whole without articulating what aspects of the system are responsible. Or they "blame the learner" as being incapable of understanding programming structure. Among other effects, such global blame makes comparison across design strategies essentially impossible.

2. *Impartiality*   In an important sense, Boxer's whole design would be ungrounded unless we showed that in addition to the principles working, they work *better* than most present competitors, including a rather difficult competitor, unconstrained but expert intuitive design. There is no shortage of skepticism that we are near the time that basic cognitive principles can help in real and practical design problems. See, for example, Landauer's chapter (this volume). Such skepticism deserves some response.

So we want to define the turf of this review neutrally enough to allow some comparative assessments. In doing so, we accept that some of Boxer's more unusual and therefore interesting features will not be immediately reviewed.

In net, what we have in mind is a *cognitive benchmark* analogous to what has been established for more objective parameters of computer systems, performance with respect to definable speed and capability goals. We do not consider it a complete review, but a first step.

In the benchmark, we aim for a particular, reasonably modular target – initial structural understanding of a language, what users can come to understand about the system in roughly the first year of experience. The structural focus is appropriate since it is: (1) central to comprehensibility; (2) invariant across a broad range of uses of systems; and (3) beyond the earliest phases of understanding, hence at least somewhat indicative of eventual comprehension levels. Choosing structural understanding does mean, however, that our assessment will in principle be largely orthogonal to that which might be provided by dominantly functional views of what constitutes understanding of a programming language – for example, plan repertoire (Soloway) or the similarly functional view of programming skill provided by Anderson's ACT* motivated analyses.

Now, of course, the structural core of diverse systems may vary significantly. However, I believe that a reasonable commonality can be defined that is relatively invariant across many procedural programming languages. This core will have to do with the central constructs, variables, procedures, flow of control, and so forth that appear in various forms in all procedural languages.

Partitioning Blame

The centralmost organizing principle of the benchmark is partitioning blame. That is to say, we need to define and localize the causes for comprehensibility and the

reflect the difference between interface design and programming language design); (3) a focus on accountability and operational specifications rather than the more general scientific review; (4) perhaps a greater emphasis on the empirical basis of design (e.g., "design activity is essentially empirical," p. 13).

lack of it. In particular, before we even get to the programming language, we need to consider three other key parameters: The individual users; the instruction they are given; and the functional contexts in which they are learning programming. In the first case, past programming assessment has frequently blamed the victims in the sense that it claims people are intrinsically subject to all sorts of misconceptions about programming, including uncontrolled anthropomorphism, uncritical use of real world reasoning that does not apply to computer systems, and even defects in logical reasoning attainment (Nachmias, Mioduser, & Chen, 1986; Pea, 1986; Soloway, Ehrlich, Bonar, & Greenspan, 1982). We certainly do not mean to reject any of these explanations out of hand, but they are extremely difficult to evaluate in the absence of concerned focus on alternative "blames" such as instruction, or the language itself.

Many language learnability assessments make essentially no reference to instruction at all. Yet surely for something as complex as a programming language, the learning context is critical. "Learning context" may mean explicit instruction, although activities and cultural context are just as important. While simple and categorical assessments of instruction may not even be possible, especially in the case of negative outcomes we need to assure ourselves that a reasonable opportunity to learn was created.

The third non-language-specific consideration stems from the importance of functional models, even for (early stages of) structural comprehension. There is no doubt that the contexts in which programming problems are set affect the performance of programmers. For example, errors may display themselves in dramatically different ways if one is programming robot motions, or merely a mathematical model thereof. Therefore, attention to this dimension is important. As with looking at the issues of whether learners are somehow to blame, or their instruction, this is not the place for detail. Instead, we want to establish a commonsense context for evaluation that does not leave out obvious considerations in the way that much existing literature does.

Turning at last to the most obvious focus, language itself, we need to make at least two types of distinctions. First, we need some principled decomposition of the various things that exist in the language to understand or fail to understand. A substantial part of this can proceed on the basis of a rational analysis. A declared structural model can help us as well, though with some limitations imposed by our cross-linguistic intentions. Again, in this context I give only the flavor of how this analysis is proceeding in our project with a top-level decomposition:

Data structures and variables, both generic variables and input parameters. Assigning and fetching protocols.

Flow of control, including basic procedurality, conditional and iterative constructs and, at advanced stages, recursion (which, structurally, is only a special case of generic procedurability).

Interactions between data and control, particularly scoping and reference.

The programming environment as a separate focus: specifically, means of creating working structure (concretely or with files), inspecting that structure, executing it, interpreting responses (e.g., error messages), and changing and filing for retrieval.

The second type of distinctions involves different modes of encounter, in which different aspects of programming knowledge might be accessed. These categories, roughly, are playing a central role in our analysis:

Analysis (that is, reading code and predicting results). In general, the reliance on structural models as opposed to functional ones should be less and less as the familiarity of the program involved increases.

Synthesis. Again, we expect substantial shifts in knowledge used depending on whether this is a familiar situation involving routine invention (functional models) or radical invention (presuming more reliance on structural models).

Debugging. This is a context in which, in general, we might expect a great need for structural comprehension.

Learning–regeneration. I identified initial learning contexts as ones in which distributed models might be especially important. Very late development involves structural models particularly in remembering–regenerating partly forgotten aspects of the language on the basis of core generalities. This particular mode may play a minimal role in early language competence.

In principle, these distinctions effect a substantial partitioning of blame. We have intrinsic individual learning characteristics; instructional factors (learning context) and programming task context; functional, structural, and distributed considerations, for each identified feature of the language. Indeed, one could make this allocation of blame even more complicated in that, with a principled view of what the assessment instruments ought to be assessing, we have criteria for crediting or blaming *them* as well. Each assessment item should come with a testable rationale. Thus, for example, errors ought to exhibit appropriate consistency. If a learner exhibits failure of a particular structural understanding of one feature in one situation and not in another, that threatens the integrity of the items. Or more substantially, such inconsistency threatens the integrity of the framework for partitioning blame as it is currently specified.

To summarize, with a fully rationalized and well-articulated assessment technology, including a reasonable framework for identifying alternative targets of blame or credit, we hope to provide a first cast for an iterative and multigroup effort that is, at least in principle, up to the task of assessing the learnability of programming systems.

Having sketched the framework, it is time to bring the program back to modest, doable subprojects. I already mentioned that we have chosen to focus largely on structural understanding for individuals within their first year of experience with a system. In addition, our focus is in the age range from 11 to 14, with special emphasis on the lower end. We intend to handle learner characteristics modestly in that we hope for near complete success, so identification of intrinsic limitations of the learner should not be an issue. Similarly, we intend to document our instructional techniques sufficient to our aims, although without a substantial theoretical framework to describe instruction in broadly accepted neutral terms. There are, we hope, two aids here that will reduce stress on this aspect of the assessment. First, again, we wish to show the first substantially documented success in deep structural comprehension of a language. Given the state of the art, this should stand as a contribution in the form of an existence proof. Second, the emphasis on structural understanding means the assessment will be more instruction-oriented. At least some structural learning will depend critically on explicit instruction, which should make a focused exposition of the learning context easier than, say, distributed or functional models accumulated mainly through experience.

Finally, we hope to be able to sort out sufficient details about comprehensibility by looking through just three modes: analysis, syntheses, and debugging. And we hope to generate assessment items that contain these three modes in a relatively compact package, rather than having individual items for each. Indeed, it would be extremely difficult to categorize tasks logically as exclusively belonging to any one of these categories. Take, for example, structural understanding of X structure in the language for the purpose of synthesis. No doubt other language constructs will be used in combination with X; some functional comprehension will be involved in any context of use for X; and users do some on-line analysis and debugging in checking guesses for solution strategies. So the framework serves more an analytic purpose than strictly to categorize assessment items.

Review of Learnability of Boxer Scoping

We have carried out the first formative empirical stage of building the fully rationalized cognitive benchmark assessment.[4] This work was done largely by Berkeley computer science graduate student Chuen-Tsai Sun. The structural focus was scoping in Boxer, how names are connected to named entities.[5]

There were five children involved, 11 to 13 years old, with experience in Boxer ranging from a few months to just over a year. The school involved is located in Oakland, California. It is private and academically oriented, but has substantial student diversity. None of the students in the study had any instruction in Boxer scoping. Indeed, it is an important result that these students could have done substantial programming without developing a structural understanding of scoping. (Recall that too early a need for structural models was judged a serious, typical

---

4. Since the preparation of this manuscript a second preliminary study has taken place concerning variables. This will be reported elsewhere.

5. Admittedly, this may seem a somewhat esoteric place to start. Boxer is substantially more complex than many languages with regard to scoping because it allows the development of a very complex static scoping structure. However, we can still see in scoping important aspects of Boxer that do intersect with other languages. And, in fact, investigating a potentially problematic piece of Boxer rather than one where we felt we were on nearly unimpeachable grounds was essentially the motivation for starting with scoping.

problem.) We needed to have children who had basic notions of data, variable, and procedure under control in order to develop and test robust scoping knowledge.

The instrument developed was intentionally ambiguous in the sense that it was used simultaneously as a structured learning context and as a testing environment. Despite the importance of partitioning blame, the practical exigencies of creating manageably sized projects sometimes dominate. This, of course, leaves the study open to criticism and the need for more careful partitioning.

Our fundamental aim was to provide contexts in which the children could induce for themselves Boxer's model of scoping. Despite this, we were prepared to teach in circumstances where we believed instruction would be necessary. The instrument contained enough redundancy that we expected to see not only some of the natural learning progression but also its extension to similar tasks. These hopes proved founded; we both saw learning in process and got a reasonable sense for the ultimate state. In the future we expect to bifurcate the environment into one that embodies an exportable instructional progression and one that represents more purely assessment goals. Here, ambiguity with respect to these goals also affords an expositional economy in that the instruction will be more or less evident in the presentation of the assessment.

The student interviews took place over two or three sessions, involving a total of about 60 to 80 minutes time, with one student repeating the first half of the interview with a new partner. The interviewers maintained a relatively clinical stance, observing and asking for clarifications. But there were occasional instructional interventions.

Boxer's structural model for scoping can be presented as a sequence of propositions. I provide here summary aphorisms, judgments (subject to grounding by empirical work), and rejected alternatives that are intended to indicate some aspects of the design without the space necessary for extensive principle-based design arguments.

1. Boxes' interiors define scoping boundaries: Named objects, both procedure and data, are accessible by name within the box in which they are defined, and recursively in any subbox. [Reuse existing structure whenever possible to avoid structural proliferation. For example, use boxes to indicate scoping environments instead of any better-tuned alternative. Structures available for generic function, like scoping, should do initial jobs without requiring any structural comprehension. For example, the described regimen lets users have variables and procedures created in different microworlds (boxes) be accessible anywhere in their respective microworlds without any specific attention. Judgment: Scoping is hard; make it invisible if possible, but make sure it is visible when necessary. Reject alternatives that require specific attention, like textually defined lookup paths. Use space to represent system structural relations whenever spatial descriptions can adequately carry the required expressive burden. Make as many properties of system objects (boxes) as generic as possible, crossing even type boundaries (data, do-it).]
2. Names can be "shadowed": The hierarchically nearest superior box in which

there is an object with a certain name is the one accessed by that name. [Use "simplest possible" models when they do the basic job. In this case, "use the nearest one" is intended to be a learner-obvious guess at scoping (a distributed model), which is then refined slightly (nearest hierarchically superior) to mesh with box-hierarchy structure. "Shadowed" is intended as a metaphor of the sort even children can appropriate to explain to themselves the shadowing phenomenon.]

3. Copy and execute: The structural model for execution that we intend users to learn is that, on execution, a copy of the definition of the procedure replaces the name in the place of execution, and recursively. Thus, the visualizable image of execution is a series of nested boxes in the familiar Boxer sense. [First, there must exist a visualizable structural model of intraexecution state changes that completely accounts for sequence and scoping, among other features that effect state change. "Reusing structure" implies objects like procedure invocations are represented with the same structures that are used for static entities. "Copies" represents an accessible metaphor for procedure invocations.]

There are two scoping implications to the copy and execute model:

a. Procedures execute in place: Lookup for names interior to a procedure is from the place of execution. [Make sure frequently encountered implications of structural decisons are comprehensible in the situations in which they are encountered without using the full structural model. This lookup feature is a logical implication of the basic scoping and execution structure, but it is also natural and functional in its own terms.]

b. Dynamic scoping: Local variables are scoped upward through the dynamic hierarchy. [Minimizing structural variation implies scoping inside invocations should follow the same rules as scoping in the normally visible box hierarchy, hence is dynamic. Reject even only slightly more complicated alternatives that are better tuned to the circumstances in cases where comprehension is at all problematic; hence, reject lexical scoping, even though its modularity features make it a better alternative by functional standards. Make things more complex for experts rather than for those beginning to understand the structural model.]

In preparation for a discussion of results, I note four specific expectations. First, on the basis of strong spatial descriptive vocabulary, learners should be quite competent at developing their own personal ways of describing scoping rules. This amounts to asserting very strong distributed support for the structural model. In particular, we expected the process of looking up through the hierarchy of boxes to be a central part of spontaneous and instructed comprehension. On the basis of experience teaching Logo, we expected learners to anthropomorphize the search, describing it as being performed "by Boxer."

Second, we expected the normally visible portion of Boxer's scoping to be inducible by inspection from a sufficient set of examples, requiring no explicit explanation at all.

Third, we expected the dynamic part to need explicit instruction because it is ordinarily invisible. However, we expected dynamic scoping would be relatively easy to learn, as it is implied by the copy and execute rule, and it is the isomorphic extension to the dynamic context of the scoping rules for normal box hierarchy.

Finally, we did not count on or expect to see any functional modeling. It is not clear what would constitute accessible functional frames for scoping for children with the amount of experience with programming these have had. And the instruction–assessment made no pretense at supplying a useful context in which to explore scoping. Nonetheless, one especially precocious subject seemed to grasp some of the useful modularity implications of one aspect of Boxer scoping, as will be described.

The decision to use dynamic scoping in Boxer was one of the more difficult ones in Boxer's design. Other scoping regimens provide both for more efficient implementation and for more modular code. Nonetheless, this is a case where the requirement for a simple structural model won the day, and it is an instance where our scientific principles helped us make controversial and counterintuitive design decisions. The details of the argument for dynamic scoping are provided in diSessa (1985).

Some partitioning of blame beyond that implied in the propositions already presented will be evident in the analysis of results.

Results

Figure 10.2 shows a typical setup. The boxes marked "echo" are variables whose access are at issue. Other boxes, "cave" and "tunnel," are used as environments. (There is no structural distinction between variables and environments.) In Boxer, when the name of a variable such as "echo" is executed (by pointing and clicking with the mouse, or by using keystrokes to move the cursor and initiate execution), the accessed value is shown after a vertical bar at the end of the line on which the variable is executed. These fundamental environmental features were throughly understood by the children.

The boxes marked "dialog" are paraphrases of what children said on being asked what would happen in executing a particular "echo." There are a pair of interviewers, D and S. The children were run in pairs and triples so that much of the explanation would be among the children rather than between interviewer and child.

In Figure 10.2 we see a very early puzzle try and subsequent self-explanation. The child provides an explanation in terms of search and "first found." There are, of course, many ways to search. It is not clear which "first" is meant. Indeed, we found transient instability at early stages, indicating competing distributed models for "first."

Figure 10.3 shows self-correction on a mistaken guess. Here, inside "trap," one of the students had guessed the outside "echo" (the one previously seen to be accessed with the "echo" located just below the top variable). The children evi-

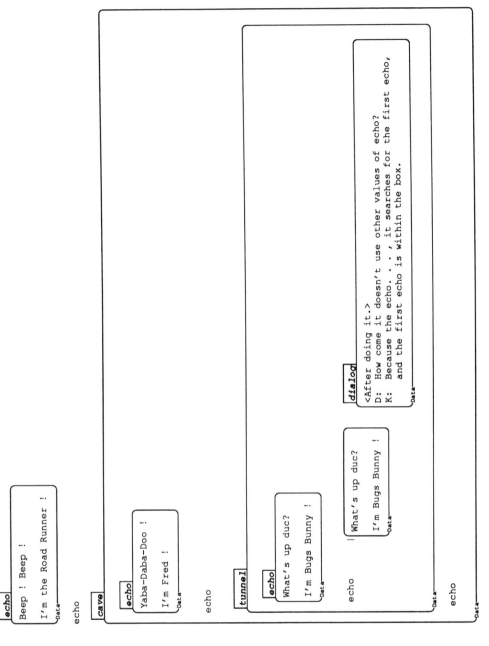

Figure 10.2. When "echo" is executed, which variable is accessed?

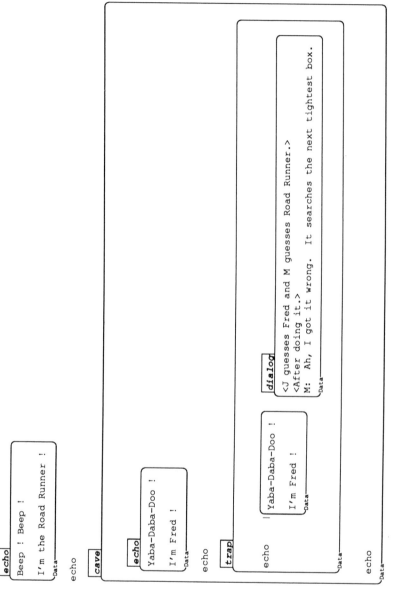

Figure 10.3. The echo variable containing "Fred" shadows the one containing the "roadrunner."

dently have appropriate descriptive language available and familiar to them, in this case, "tightest."

In these early stages, the children relied heavily on spontaneously applied visual strategies that sometimes failed. In particular, if a variable box was closed (shown small and grayed out), it was frequently ignored, whether for good or ill.

Figure 10.4 shows a more complicated case where both procedures ("santa") and variables ("stocking") are used. Here, J is confused, evidently looking to physically closer "santas" (with E. T. or a dinosaur to give) rather than hierarchically closer ones. However, J corrects herself, and M provides a correct rationale in terms of "not looking inside boxes." We have seen many children spontaneously suggest that Boxer should not look inside boxes, even before experience or instructional suggestion as to what should happen. This is a pleasant and unanticipated positive distributed model. Perhaps in this culture boxes are familiar means to keep things out of sight, to store them when unused. Thus, this distributed model may not be visual, except insofar as users recognize boxes from their appearance as being like storage places. In a few other instances students early on articulated quite precisely the criterion that the physically closest named object should be the one referenced (independent of hierarchy).

In Figure 10.5 M makes a wrong prediction. Note that this is the first problem that involves dynamic aspects of scoping. That is, though Figure 10.4 involved both procedures and variables, the effect of procedure execution in place is not visible; lookup from the place of the procedure definition (lexical scoping) provides the same prediction. Here, lookup of "santa" from the place of definition would yield a change in the "stocking" in "palace." Actually, lookup from the place of execution finds the "stocking" in the "garden."

M continued to mull over this puzzle, and in the context of the next puzzle he appeared to have solved it. He interrupted discussion of that puzzle to describe his insight, though it was not particularly relevant to the problem at hand. In the following quotation, note the level of abstractness of his discussion. Evidently his spatial reasoning capabilities are strong enough not to need any concrete, external support for his reasoning. That is, he described the situation verbally without any immediate physical prop to reason on or point to.

If it goes to a procedure outside its box, it will change the variable inside the original box, right? [Interpretation: If the procedure lookup finds a procedure outside the box where execution is taking place, still the variable lookup is from the place of execution.] If you have Box 1 inside Box 2, there is a procedure inside Box 2 [that] changes a variable, and you execute the procedure from Box 1, and if the variable is in Box 1 and Box 2 it will change the one in Box 1.

We found transfer of scoping rules to procedure variables located inside a procedure initially unproblematic. Children understood intuitively and immediately that local variables would be accessed on execution of that procedure in place of more global ones. For example, in Figure 10.6 the fact that the gift inside "batman" would be accessed on running "batman" rather than one outside was no problem.

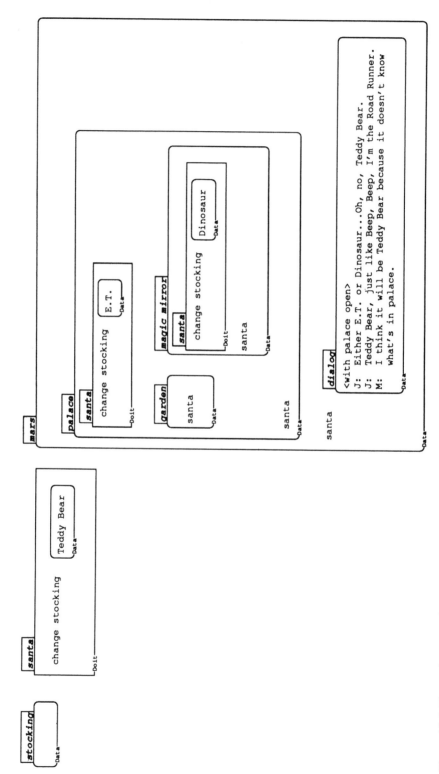

Figure 10.4. Boxer does not "look inside" boxes to access variables.

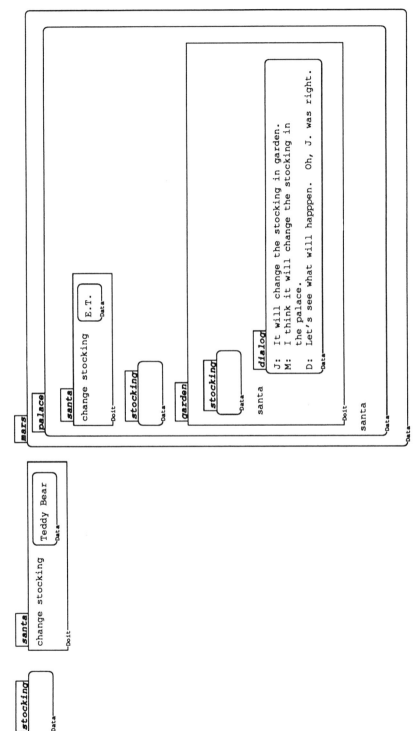

Figure 10.5. Variables from executed procedures are scoped from the place of execution (dynamic scoping).

195

196

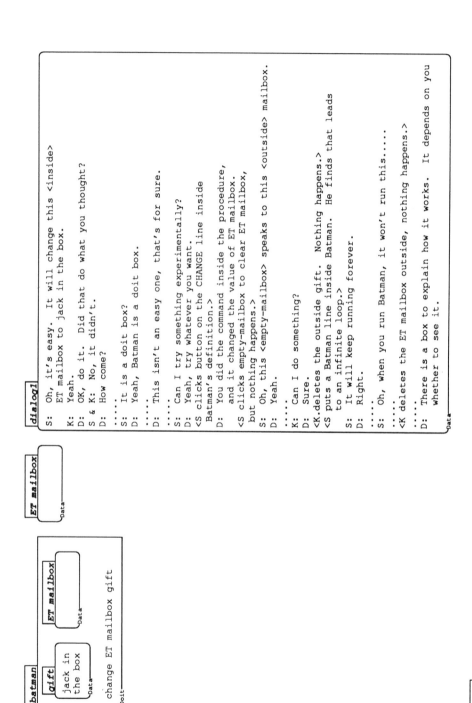

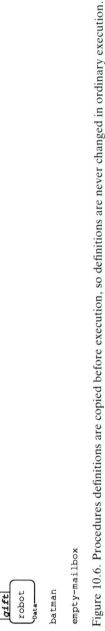

dialoq1

S: Oh, it's easy. It will change this <inside>
   ET mailbox to jack in the box.
K: Yeah.
D: OK, do it. Did that do what you thought?
S & K: No, it didn't.
D: How come?
.....
S: It is a doit box?
D: Yeah, Batman is a doit box.
.....
D: This isn't an easy one, that's for sure.
.....
S: Can I try something experimentally?
D: Yeah, try whatever you want.
<S clicks button on the CHANGE line inside
   Batman's definition.>
D: You did the command inside the procedure,
   and it changed the value of ET mailbox.
<S clicks empty-mailbox to clear ET mailbox,
   but nothing happens.>
S: Oh, this <empty-mailbox> speaks to this <outside> mailbox.
D: Yeah.
.....
K: Can I do something?
D: Sure.
<K.deletes the outside gift. Nothing happens.>
<S puts a Batman line inside Batman. He finds that leads
   to an infinite loop.>
S: It will keep running forever.
D: Right.
.....
S: Oh, when you run Batman, it won't run this......
.....
<K deletes the ET mailbox outside, nothing happens.>
.....
D: There is a box to explain how it works. It depends on you
   whether to see it.

batman

gift
jack in
the box

ET mailbox

ET mailbox

change ET mailbox gift

ET mailbox

gift
robot

batman

empty-mailbox

Figure 10.6. Procedures definitions are copied before execution, so definitions are never changed in ordinary execution.

Thus, initial stages of the structural model of scoping (those related directly to structure seen on the screen) appear to transfer unproblematically to initial stages of comprehending internal-to-execution scoping (which is not generally viewable). However, no notion of copy has been needed up to this point.

Figure 10.6 shows the point at which the children's spontaneous models broke down. As discussed, we had anticipated this and were prepared with modest direct instruction. "Batman" will only change the local variable "ET_mailbox" in the *copy* of that procedure made for execution. The children were very puzzled that nothing appeared to happen inside batman when it was executed by name (near the bottom of the figure), and they could offer no spontaneous explanation. Their persistence in the dialog seems quite a positive sign that they expect the system to be comprehensible, although they came to no resolution. The intervention that was made was to show a simulation that demonstrated the copy-and-execute model in action, showing changes being made in the copies.[6]

The copy-and-execute model was appropriated with some false steps and trepidation on the part of the children. Sometimes, several explanations were necessary before it was fully appropriated, although most of the explanations came from other children rather than the interviewers. A particularly interesting case was initiated by an explanation by an interviewer that the copies are not normally visible but come into and go out of existence very quickly. The pair of children interpreted "too quick to see" to say that the changes were, in fact, made in the procedure definition, but erased on conclusion of execution. This is a plausible model, but one that does not lead to Boxer's scoping rules (since lookup would be from the place of definition rather than from the place of invocation). It was especially interesting to see how the interviewers missed this misinterpretation in the discussion of the children. Episodes like this underscore for us how weak verbal explanations and discussion are compared with visual models and discussion based on disambiguation through pointing. They reinforce the fundamental Boxer heuristic of relying on visual models.

Figure 10.7 shows discussion by a pair of children while watching the copy-and-execute simulation. Figure 10.8 shows students discussing a new problem, at a stage we interpreted as near complete comprehension of the "changes in copies" issue.

The only clearly functional discussion of the series of interviews came in the discussion of the rationale for the copy rule. One of the interviewers offered that the copy rule existed because it would hardly be the right thing to have a procedure execution change the definition of the procedure, perhaps unbeknownst to the programmer. This invariance principle seemed to be compelling for at least one of the students, M, and he used it spontaneously to explain the copy rule.[7]

---

6. In fact, Boxer has a generic mechanism for showing the copy-and-execute model on any procedure. However, at the current stage of development, a simulation provided a pictorially clearer discussion piece.

7. Strictly, there are both functional and structural components of this explanation. The programming function is to have the behavior of definitions be constant, unless the definition is edited. The copy-and-execute model is one structural way to accomplish that.

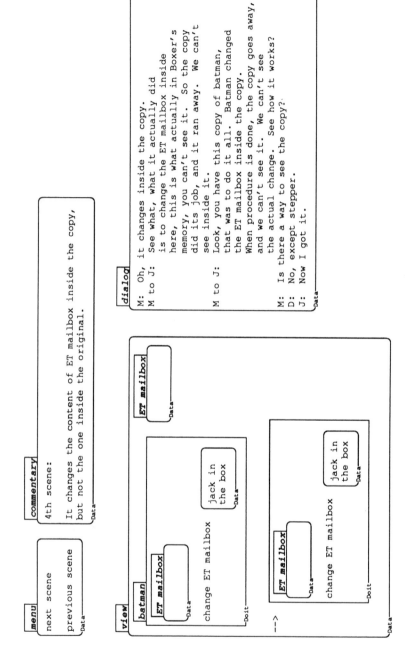

Figure 10.7. Students studying a model of Boxer copy and execute.

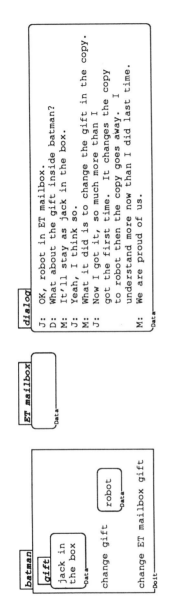

batman

gift
jack in
the box
└Data┘

change gift [robot]
         └Data┘

change ET mailbox gift
└Doit┘

ET mailbox
└Data┘

dialog

J: OK, robot in ET mailbox.
D: What about the gift inside batman?
M: It'll stay as jack in the box.
J: Yeah, I think so.
M: What it did is to change the gift in the copy.
J: Now I got it, so much more than I
   got the first time. It changes the copy
   to robot then the copy goes away. I
   understand more now than I did last time.
M: We are proud of us.
└Data┘

batman

empty-mailbox

Figure 10.8. Students solidifying their understanding of copy and execute.

In the end, all the children appropriated the copy-and-execute model and applied it successfully in novel problems, without help. In addition, they all seemed to find the puzzles quite engaging, despite a number of false steps. We interpret this to mean that developing an appropriate structural model was not trivial, but well within the range the children found acceptably challenging. After they saw how things worked, they considered the puzzles reasonable.

In all, we were extraordinarily pleased with this formative study. Our expectations about learning trajectory and when structural instruction would become necessary were on target. Distributed models were adequate to early stages of learning, and of the visual–spatial type we expected. Even unanticipated details like the expectation that Boxer should not look inside boxes have a natural place in the framework, as empirical grounding about the resources children have for distributed models.

Limitations

Clearly, there are limitations to this formative study. The "instructors" were expert, and the children probably atypical. As well, the integration of the model into more functional context has not been investigated. Nonetheless, especially because the children seem not to have any trouble articulating the model to themselves, we expect little difficulty with such transfer. The fact that Boxer's environment structure is essentially always visible also should support transfer because a prompt and support for model reasoning is always available.

This work is clearly in progress, and I cannot claim here to have thoroughly illustrated let alone validated the principled design program generally, or even in the case of the design of Boxer. But then, a central presumption of local sciences is that doing real science in a design context is difficult and requires long and complex research projects. In particular, I have had to suppress any real discussion of the evolution of our principles during the design process. Similarly, elaboration of the modeling considerations with sufficient grounding actually to make design decisions has been presented only telegraphically. Most critically, our formal review of Boxer has only begun, and scoping is only a small part of it. The scoping study did not show redesign on the basis of revised principles or grounding in part because the study validated our expectations to the level of detail intended. Finally and fundamentally, no one person or project can expect to validate principled design and the concept of local sciences presented here. I view a better test of such conceptions to be in their productive appropriation by a broader community.

Summary

I have argued that it is possible to view design as an essential part of a kind of science appropriate to this stage of the development of cognitive science in the service of human–computer interaction. The kind of science I envision involves developing *principles* and then doing the complex work necessary to *ground* the principles in contexts to which the principles are claimed to apply. Then, *design* is appropriate as a large-scale experiment to achieve feedback on the principles and grounding. Finally, the scientific use of design requires a more substantial and elaborate *review* of results than does design in nonscientific contexts.

I have argued that the essential characteristic of cognitive work that makes design an appropriate scale of experiment is that it involves, sometimes, the study of large knowledge systems. These systems may be of very diverse types, and involve many particulars so that elaborate grounding is necessary before experiments make sense. The task of describing knowledge architectures and modes of thought appropriate to particular architectures is put forward as a generic strategy for studying knowledge systems.

Abstract considerations about science often founder on the reality of everyday scientific practice. Thus I have taken pains to bring abstractions back, in stages, to specific scientific work. In particular, I reviewed the design of a programming system within the proposed framework for principled design. I discussed principles in terms of types of mental models (particular kinds of architectures) and how modes of their use should articulate in an effectively learnable artifact. Finally, I discussed one central framework for reviewing our design, proposing to produce a "cognitive benchmark," a principled basis for the assessment of the learnability of procedural programming systems. At this stage we have begun, in a small way, to validate aspects of the design. And more importantly, I claim we have begun to show the value of our principles in the work of children learning our system.

Acknowledgments

This work was supported in part by a grant from the National Science Foundation. The opinions expressed are those of the author and do not necessarily reflect those of the Foundation. The current grant number is MDR-88-50363.

I would like to thank Robert Campbell and Michael Leonard for substantial commentary and editorial suggestions concerning this paper. Jack Carroll provided insightful commentary that motivated a number of clarifications and extensions. Chuen Tsai Sun carried out most of the design of the scoping assessment, and Don Ploger contributed to its experimental execution.

References

Carroll, J. M., & Rosson, M. B. (1985). Usability specifications as a tool in iterative development. In H. R. Hartson (Ed.), *Advances in human–computer interaction* (pp. 1–28). Norwood, NJ: Ablex.

diSessa, A. A. (1985). A principled design for an integrated computational environment, *Human–Computer Interaction, 1*(1), 1–47.

diSessa, A. A. (1986). Models of computation. In D. A. Norman & S. W. Draper (Eds.), *User-centered systems design: New perspectives on human–computer interaction.* Hillsdale, NJ: Lawrence Erlbaum Associates.

diSessa, A. A. (1987). Reference and data construction in Boxer. In M. J. Tauber & P. Gorny (Eds.), *Visual aids in programming*. Heidelberg: Springer.

diSessa, A. A. (1990). Social niches for future software. In M. Gardner, J. Greeno, F. Reif, A. Schoenfeld, A. diSessa, & E. Stage (Eds.), *Toward a scientific practice of science education*, (pp. 301–322). Hillsdale, NJ: Lawrence Erlbaum Associates.

diSessa, A. A. (in press). Toward an epistemology of physics. *Cognition and Instruction*.

Feyerabend, P. K. (1975). *Against method*. London: NLB.

Gentner, D., & Stevens, A. (1983). *Mental models*. Hillsdale, NJ: Lawrence Erlbaum Associates.

Linn, M. C., Sloane, K. D., & Clancey, M. J. (1987). Ideal and actual outcomes from precollege Pascal instruction. *Journal of Research in Science Teaching, 25* (12), 467–490.

Nachmias, R., Mioduser, D., & Chen, D. (1986, April). *"Variable" – An obstacle to children learning programming,* Paper presented at the annual meeting of the American Educational Research Association, San Francisco.

Pea, R. D. (1986). Language-independent conceptual "bugs" in novice programming, *Journal of Educational Computing Research 2*(1), 25–36.

Popper, K. R. (1962). *Conjectures and refutations: The growth of scientific knowledge*. New York: Harper Row.

Soloway, E. (1985). From problems to programs via plans: The content and structure of knowledge for introductory LISP programming. *Journal of Educational Computing Research, 1* (2), 157–172.

Soloway, E., Ehrlich, K., Bonar, J., & Greenspan, J. (1982). What do novices know about programming? In B. Shneiderman & A. Badre (Eds.), *Directions in human–computer interaction*, Norwood, NJ: Ablex.

Soloway, E., & Spohrer, J. C. (1989). *Studying the novice programmer,* Hillsdale, NJ: Lawrence Erlbaum Associates.

Young, R. M. (1981). The machine inside the machine: Users' models of pocket calculators. *International Journal of Man–Machine Studies, 15,* 51–85.

11
The Role of German Work Psychology in the Design of Artifacts
Siegfried Greif

In the traditional view, the division of labor between science and application is simple. The task of science is to construct theories, which have to be evaluated by scientific criteria like precision, consistency, and empirical support. The task of applied research is to develop transformation rules for a deductive application of the theory. The remaining role of the practioner (e.g., a designer) is that of a well-educated scholar. He or she has to practice the theory precisely according to the transformation rules after having been being trained to use it correctly. Hugo Münsterberg (1912), who held a chair at Harvard, himself a scholar of Wilhelm Wundt, was one of the pioneers trying to apply knowledge from experimental psychology. He actively promoted the basic ideas of the traditional view and expected high economic returns from an application of experimental psychology. This deductivistic application paradigm has had many followers in the history of applied psychology. In the field of human–computer interaction (HCI) Card, Moran, and Newell (1983; Newell & Card, 1985), with their stimulating vision of the prospects for cognitive psychology through basic research and the construction of theoretical models, are a prominent example.

Carroll (1989; cf. Carroll, Kellogg & Rosson, this volume) has criticized the conventional view of theory-based design, because it has not been successful in HCI. The deductive application paradigm is problematic because practioners and especially designers in the field of HCI do not and in fact cannot assume the role of scholars. From a scientific and methodological point of view the traditional paradigm has run into trouble, because essential methodological problems (Brocke, 1978) have not yet been solved.

A first problem is that we may doubt if enough scientific theories are available that meet the standards and criteria as already mentioned. (This is, of course, not only a problem of the science of psychology, but of social and natural sciences in general.) A second difficult problem is the problem of applicability of the theory to different or varying laboratory and field conditions (often refered to as the problem of generalizability or validity). A third problem, less obvious but perhaps the most discouraging, is the development of transformation rules based on emprical evaluation research, which allow us to deduce precisely the practical applicability of the basic theory. (Phil Barnard in this volume refers to this problem from a different, refined approach of theory-based design).

As long as these three problems are not solved sufficiently it remains arbitrary which deductions and conclusions are drawn from theories. If it is based ultimately on arbitrary decisions, the vision of the deductive application paradigm has lost its consistency and brilliance. In the next section I will try to illustrate the difficulties of the traditional paradigm using the example of Card et al.'s (1983) models and application of experimental research results.

From the first publications German work psychologists like psychologists in other countries strongly rejected the GOMS model of Card et al. (1983) and related theoretical approaches. This sometimes emotional rejection of scientifically stimulating models can hardly be explained by neutral scientific arguments alone. Basic values and humanistic ideas seem to play a crucial role. In a subsequent section I will give a short outline of German action theory and its basic humanistic values showing where they are in conflict with Card et al.'s models. Bannon & Bøodker (this volume) draw upon activity theory and also favor a wholistic and value-oriented approach.

Although the next two sections essentially are written from an outer-theory approach (following Lewis' chapter in this volume; cf. also Floyd, 1987), the last section of the chapter tries to give an example of the process of artifact design. According to Lewis we could call this an inner-theory approach.

Experimental Problems of the Traditional Theory-based Design: The Example of GOMS and Keystroke-level Models

Few approaches have provoked as much criticism as the GOMS and keystroke-level models of Card et al. (1983). I will not try to give a summary of the implications for theory-based design. Newell and Card (1985) themselves have admitted essential difficulties. Several other important aspects are treated in other chapters of this book. But besides these shortcomings the validity of the basic experimentally founded standard reaction time models have seldom been questioned and tested by "hard experimental methods" as they call them. In the following I will shortly summarize the results of some experiments testing the validity of the basic reaction-time models and then discuss the implications for theory-based software design.

The validity and predictive value of reaction-time models cannot be sufficiently tested analyzing only the overall sum of the time components. In order to test all single components we have to apply well-balanced time series experiments with systematic variation of experimental factors and to test statistically all discriminable time components (for the details, cf. Greif & Gediga, 1987).

Using only the overall estimates of the sum of the time components our results seemed to support the models of Card et al., because the observed values did not exceed the predicted range. (They estimate the overall range by adding ranges. Consequently the overall range is very broad.) But if we examine single-time components we can find striking differences of the single mean-time parameters. For example our carefully trained subjects need about the same time for a first eye-movement operation of seeking a target position in a line of letters, which should be appropriate for the whole task.

In summary, our experimental results show that even for simple reaction-time tasks the data do not fit the model.

1. The subjects use various methods (some alternately) with very different keystroke-level structures. For one of the methods there is a clear and plausible

acceleration of the time functions depending on the length of the screening task.

2. The simple model of stable and additive time components is clearly inadequate. A minor deceleration of the mean systems-response time from 2 to 8 sec results in a dynamic acceleration of keystroke performance.

3. The time estimates found in our experimental results do not correspond to the parameters expected from the theoretical model. Relevant operations are left out in the model (e.g., a last test operation at the end of the task), which take substantial proportions of the observed overall time.

4. There is evidence of consciously conflicting microgoals, like the speed–accuracy conflict. Different methods are to be preferred if the goal is to minimize errors or to maximize speed. These conflicts cannot be modeled by constructing separate models for error tasks as the authors recommended.

Such results are not unexpected for experimental psychologists and they are essentially not new. In the last century, Donders (1868) used the same logic as Card et al. for analyzing reaction times. Our arguments basically follow the classic critique offered by James McKeen Cattell (1886): Even if it might be possible to describe the keystroke operations of a simple task under special context conditions and for a special group of subjects by additive factors, the generalizability and applicability of the additive model remains questionable.

Gediga and Wolff (1989) performed another set of time series experiments, where they tested the validity of basic assumptions of Fitts's Law and Hick's Law and the power law of practice using a mouse design. In summary of their results only Fitts's Law assuming that the moving time to a goal is a function of the distance of the goal and the target size can partly be supported. But it does not predict the movement time completely because it neglects a relevant component, the movement time *in* the target and the dynamics of the individual movement amplitudes. Hick's expectation of an augmented choice reaction time when the number of alternatives increases shows only minimal changes (max. 14 msec). At least for practical design problems, such small effects may be neglected. The power law of practice states that according to an increase of skill the processing time of a task shows a power function of decreasing time for the task depending on the number of trials. But at least for typical mouse movements, the individuals after few trials reach their skill maximum. These results again show how time parameters dynamically are depending on minimal task attributes. The predictions of basic models of experimental psychology that neglect such attributes seem to be very limited. It would therefore be misleading in the design of user interfaces to apply these models without additional consideration of task and context variations.

The Applicability Dilemma of Theory-based Design

The rationale of theory-based design is the application of theoretical models and parameter estimates established by experimental research. But if we apply the models and estimates without testing their applicability, we obviously risk completely wrong parameter values or even completely wrong models (cf. Carroll's similar position on the relevance of the details of the situation in use for application representations in Carroll, 1990). As the research examples in the field of HCI show, we can never be sure that the time parameters and models are applicable before we have tested their applicability. But if we have to test the validity of the theoretical model and eventually have to change it substantially *before* we can apply it, the validation study and not the model is the relevant base of design. Such an approach therefore should better be called "evaluation-oriented design" (or empirically controlled application). Shneiderman (1987) seems to favor this position.

The naive assumption of generalizability of experimental results has always been criticized. As every researcher knows, even for different laboratory contexts and measurement procedures the applicability of theoretical models may be very limited. Minor variations of task, context, and methods may result in unpredicted side effects that cannot be explained by the theory. The deductive application paradigm thereby loses it theoretical rationale.

This of course does not imply that experimental theories and laboratory experiments are useless for the design of artifacts. But the relationship between theory and practical application is more complicated and has to be redefined in a less naive form. In the next section I will try to show how in German work psychology humanistic values are applied as a heuristic conceptual framework for the evaluation of theories and artifacts design or of work and task design in general. But I am convinced that we have to develop inner-theory approaches, as Lewis (this volume) calls them, to understand the role of theory for design (cf. the example discussed in the last section). The task–artifact cycle as described by Carroll et al. (this volume) is an approach for understanding these interaction processes of artifact design.

German Action Theory and Work Psychology

Modern German psychology has been strongly influenced by integrative cognitive approaches based on concepts describing everyday actions, the so-called action theories. The book of Miller, Galanter, and Pribram (1960) has stimulated theory development fundamentally in the new phase of developing German action theories in the 1970s. Work psychologists like Winfried Hacker (Dresden, GDR before the German reunion), Eberhard Ulich (Zürich, Switzerland), and Walter Volpert (West Berlin, FRG) were among the first authors who apprehended and elaborated the theory and its application in the field and have published series of laboratory and applied research projects (cf. Hacker, 1986; Hacker, Volpert, & v. Cranach, 1982; Ulich, 1984; Volpert, 1975, 1990). Today we can observe differentiations of theoretical approaches depending on the field of application (see Frese & Sabini 1985, for an overview).

It is difficult to describe in a few words the essence of work psychological action theory, or action regulation theory as Volpert and Oesterreich (Oesterreich, 1981; Volpert, 1988) prefer to call it. There are some English translations treating special problems (Hacker, 1985, 1987; Hacker et al., 1982; Ulich, 1987; Ulich, Schüpbach, Schilling, & Kuark, 1990; Volpert, 1990) but good English introductions to the whole and complex theory are still missing. [And therefore the classical book of Miller et al. (1960) may still be recommended as an introduction.] In the following I will concentrate on the basic concepts and the central assumptions concerning human personality development.

Basic Concepts and Regulatory Models of Action Theory

Action can be defined as conscious, goal-directed behavior. Actions therefore always are related to concrete goals. The basic cybernetic model assumes that actions are controlled by a hierarchical network of mental regulatory processes and feedback loops (cf. the TOTE-units of Miller et al., 1960).

The lowest (sensorimotor) level of the hierarchical network of cyclic TOTE-units is the sequence of stereotypic movements or observable operations (e.g., eye and finger movement when typing a text). According to a basic assumption, conscious goals determine the whole regulatory process. The highest (intellectual) level according to Hacker (1986) can be defined by tasks or conscious action goals (e.g., "type a letter"). The intermediate level can be changed by the subgoals of the action goal or subtasks that are organized by coherent sequences of operations. The acting person may develop a verbal label or concept through inner speech to signify the subtask (e.g., "type a word"). Hacker therefore calls this level the "conceptual level."

A problem of understanding German action theory is that it is difficult to assess and discriminate the mental processes and feedback loops of individual subjects directly. For example, whether typing a letter, a word, or a sentence is a coherent subtask may depend on the proficiency of the typist. (For the beginner finding a letter on the keyboard is a conscious subtask, while for the expert typing letters and words may become automated and subconscious processes.) Therefore it is difficult to define and assess the regulatory levels operationally. In consequence there has been much debate about the adequate number of levels and how we can assess them.

Hacker (1986) assumes three functional levels (intellectual, conceptual, and sensorimotor regulation). Semmer and Frese (1985) add a fourth level (abstract thinking). Oesterreich (1981), from a somewhat different theoretical position analyzing the objective control of the individual over his work, discriminates five control levels. His highest control level is shown by a strategic decision over the establishment of a whole new action field (e.g., a new production line). The fourth level is the control and coordination of different subfields; the third is altered by decisions over subgoals in a defined action field. At the lower levels, the second and first, the individual is only allowed to control and plan a sequence of operations or merely the adequate performance of a given sequence. Volpert, Oesterreich, Gablenz-Kolakovic, Krogoll, and Resch (1983) have constructed an observation method (called VERA) by which well-trained observers can assess these levels consistently.

Between German action theorists there is consensus that the observable work behavior sequence can be predicted by some kind of hierarchical (or heterarchical) inner regulatory processes, where conscious goals, subgoals, and plans of the active individual and the operative cognitive representations of the tasks and environments determine the efficiency. But the methodological problems to access these theoretically postulated complex inner processes are apparent. The resulting difficulties to establish consensus over adequate research methods and the levels of regulation processes may explain why the role of the basic regulatory model has not been primarily to predict observable short-term regulatory behavior directly. Testable predictions are mainly concerned with the long-term outcome of work design, especially the development of active self-regulated individuals, who control and plan their activities competently and efficiently. The regulatory model therefore mainly should be understood as an idealized phenomenological background theory.

Our position is that the three- or five-level hierarchies are merely special cases of possibly more complex and dynamically organized heterarchic structures with conflicting goals and subgoals (conflicts between speed and accuracy processing tasks are an example). We therefore assume complex and dynamic changing inner regulation processes and the existence of different numbers of levels depending on the task and the subjective working steps and goals of the individual.

For the assessment of the subjective working steps and regulatory levels we have constructed a special version of individual log-file analysis and video confrontation interview called "heterarchic task analysis" (cf. Gediga, Greif, Monecke & Hamborg, 1989; Greif, 1990). For this method the subject is confronted with a log-file protocol and video film of its task performance (we prefer to use three cameras, one for the face, one for the screen, and one for the finger movements on the keyboard). There are similarities to the thinking-aloud technique applied by Carroll and Mack (1983). But in contrast we retrospectively ask the subject to tell us their action-related cognitions and the emotions they can remember. After this we try to assess the individual cognitive structures of working steps (or subjective tasks) of different hierarchical levels asking the subjects to sign precisely where in the keystroke protocol subtasks are ending. (The end of a subjective task is defined by the point in the task performance where the subject says he or she does not mind much to be interrupted – for example, by a telephone call.)

Applying this method of subjective task analysis we observed differences between individuals concerning the number and labels of the working steps and hierarchical levels of tasks and subtasks they are discriminating. The resulting individual task descriptions can be used for the design of task-oriented menus. Through experimental comparison studies of these and other menu structures we try to test the hypothesis that task-oriented structures based on individual concepts and knowledge help the user to develop a better mental model of the system and to perform complex tasks more easily.

Work and Artifact Design

Action theory integrates standard ergonomic design criteria but the central goal of work design in German action theory is to promote long-term well-being and human growth or personality development (i.e., the development of interests, skills, and general abilities). Following the results of series of field experiments, the

"Kings Way" of work design promoting human growth is to enlarge the control or activity latitude of the worker. In the past years more wholistic concepts have also been applied and empirically evaluated. An old humanistic ideal is a maximum self-determination and responsibility in the whole or "complete" task cycle, beginning with goal setting, decisions on means and procedures, social cooperation, perfor-mance, and output (called the "completeness" of the activities; cf. Hacker, 1987). Ulich (1987) with his concept of "differential and dynamic work design" in opposi-tion to Taylor's "one-best-way" design solutions considers individual differences and the dynamic development of humans through complex and demanding work activities. Lately he successfully applied "individualized system design" solutions (Ackermann & Ulich, 1987). The design goal of promoting long-term individual growth explains also why work and organizational psychologists are becoming more and more interested in developmental psychology and personality theories.

The design philosophy of promoting long-term well-being and human growth is applied also to the design of user interfaces. But an essential theoretical expectation is that the design of computer systems will be only meaningful if it is integrated in the design of the whole work activity of the employee. Following action theory, artifact design should always basically be work and activity design. Work activities are designed through the design of concrete tasks and tools. Task and artifact design therefore is the core of work-activity design, and instruments of work and task analysis – according to action theory – are the basic methods of designers.

Following action theory, basic criteria for task and artifact design are the enlarge-ment of control, complexity, and completeness (or meaningfulness) of the task supporting human growth and personality development. These criteria can be op-erationalized and assessed by elaborated methods of work and task analysis (cf. Oesterreich & Volpert, 1986). For a rich information flow between user and de-signer we should apply instruments of task analysis, which not only gather complete and precise log files but also stimulate the users to talk precisely and systematically about the task–artifact interactions and the accompanying cognitive and emotional processes. Our method of "heterarchical task analysis" (Gediga et al., 1989; Greif, 1990) is an approach that seems to stimulate this information flow. In typical design projects the individual user or the members of the whole work group of the employ-ees participate in the assessment and redesign process after a phase of information or training (Ulich, 1984). Floyd and Keil's (1983) concept of participative software design (Bannon & Bødker, this volume; cf. also Floyd, 1987; Keil-Slawik, 1990) is similar. But of course this is only a beginning assessment of task–artifact cycles for the development of a "psychological science of tasks" as Carroll demands it (this volume) or the development of action theory in the direction of a "task–action theory," which models and predicts the regulatory processes of individuals interact-ing with different types of tasks and artifacts.

Related Concepts and Models

Activity in comparison to action is a broad concept and refers to fields and series of actions and the long-term performance rooted in basic human motives. (The original

German term *Tätigkeit* is difficult to translate. Its meaning embraces "performance and field of activity.") Activity theory in Soviet psychology (Leontjew, 1973; Rubinstein, 1966; cf. Bannon & Bødker, this volume) is often cited as the general philosophical background of action theory. But German action theory in the field of work often concentrates more on the concrete tasks and action design at the workplace.

There are obvious similarities between action theory and Newell and Simon's (1972) or Card et al.'s (1983) model human processor and their definitions of goals, operations, and methods (or strategies) or cyclic feedback looks describing the cybernetic process of hierarchical regulatory processes of the sequences of human operations. But German action theorists at the same time reject GOMS and keystroke-level models and criticize them as too mechanistic. Action theorists, influenced by Gestalt theory, assume that the inner regulatory processes adapt much more flexibly to task and context conditions and especially to the resulting performance feedback in the process itself. If they also use computer analogies, these models are applied merely in a metaphoric sense or for heuristic and descriptive purposes. The relation between the regulatory process model and work and artifact design is therefore more complicated.

The action theory models of human performance are based also on humanistic values (see subsequent discussion). Despite many similarities, this difference may explain the criticism of the models and methods of time and motion studies of Card et al. (1983).

The Relevance of Humanistic Roots: Artifact Design for Human Growth

The historical roots of our modern humanistic ideals of scientific rationality, practical useful knowledge, freedom and moral responsibility, aesthetic experiences, individuality, and especially the education of our rich interests and abilities go back to the so-called new humanism of the 18th century (cf. Blättner, 1968). In this phase in England, in the Netherlands, and in Germany, a new self-consciousness stemming from the achievements of the developing universities arose. It resulted in a movement of becoming independent from the "Imitatio" of the over 1,000-year-old authority of the Roman language and culture. The vision was to go back to the basic roots of the predominant Roman culture, which were found in ancient Greek philosophy and ideals.

This humanistic movement had a strong and universal impact on our Occidental cultures and education through the new and expanding school and university system. Especially Wilhelm v. Humboldt's humanistic reform of the whole educational system influenced the basic divisions of school and university. He defined the ideals of universities as institutions of free scientific work, universal knowledge, and self-education.

The great and long pedagogic impact of these basic values in education may explain why these goals are familiar in all countries of Occidental culture origin. It may also explain why modern psychological (and also engineering) work design concepts are similar in their basic goal criteria, even if they stem from different countries and different theoretical backgrounds (Ulich & Clegg, 1989).

The engineer Frederick W. Taylor (1911) who founded the "Scientific management" movement has also been influenced by these humanistic values (Greif, 1987). He explicitely cites the values of growth of the abilities of workers and healthy working conditions. Following the utilitarian "branch" of humanism (esp. Jeremy Bentham and John Stuart Mill), he promoted the idea of applying scientific knowledge for universal economic growth and "the greatest happiness to the greatest number of people." He translates the hedonistic duality of pleasure and pain into money and punishment as primary motivating forces. The essential differences in comparison with other approaches based on the same humanistic roots are his simplification of human motivation, his idea that for tasks there is always "one best way" (in terms of energy costs and task time), and his concept for the division of intellectual and manual work. It was his firm belief that only managers (based on scientific knowledge) are intellectually able to plan and organize work activities. The part of the workers is the manual performance of given tasks following the "one best way" defined by management principles based on scientific research.

Numerous psychological–theoretical approaches, directions, and subdisciplines of psychology (e.g., gestalt psychology and modern cognitive psychology, personality theories, developmental psychology, humanistic clinical psychology, humanistic organizational psychology) reflect the old humanistic ideals in different ways. German action theory, with its fundamental relations to gestalt psychology, applies the values of human growth and personality development in a direct way, assuming long-term positive impacts of the control, complexity, and completeness of tasks and action environments (see previous discussions). But also in the international field of industrial and organizational psychology there are many other theories and concepts, which directly relate to the same ideals. A well-known example is Maslow's (1954) motivation theory of the development of human needs from low-level physiological needs to the highest level of growth and self-actualization needs and its implication for humanistic and participative organization development concepts. Herzberg's (1966) job-enrichment concept also has to be mentioned here.

The implicit and seldomly questioned relevance of humanistic growth values for task and work design may explain why work and organizational psychologists in diverse countries and also German action theorists strongly rejected the GOMS and keystroke-level models of Card et al. (1983). These "one-best-way models" (cf. Greif & Gediga, 1987) resemble the models and time-and-motion studies of Frederick W. Taylor and his followers. Work psychologists of all countries have a long tradition criticizing Taylorism and the implicit mechanistic model of human functioning. But Taylorism is still prominent and has not been influenced much by such criticism. Only in the past decade with its fundamental changes of traditional mass production and division of work to small series and quality products and flexible high-technology organizations relying on high intellectual competences and flexibility of the workers have alternative humanistic concepts been adopted as an efficient organization model of modern industry (cf. Greif, Holling, & Nicholson, 1989).

It may be interesting to note that especially the basic goals of systems design provoked criticism of German work psychologists as they were formulated at that time: "to be efficient and easy to use . . . so that people in our society may realize the potential benefits of computer-based tools" (Card et al., 1983, p. vii; cf. also the approach of Kieras & Polson, 1985). In spite of many theoretical similarities to action theory, these basic goals and values had no chance to be accepted by German action theorists. From this argument it also seems plausible why other theoretical concepts like Norman's systematic frameworks and differentiated analyses of every-day actions (this volume) or Barnard's models (this volume) and especially Carroll & Mack's (1983) exploratory concepts of HCI received more and positive attention in German work psychology.

It seems to be obvious that values of human growth have also a constructive impact on artifact design in German work psychology. Value-oriented criteria are applied by evaluating qualitatively the explicit and implicit goals of theories and – operationalized through instruments of task and work activity analysis – form the practical goals of artifact and work design projects in the field. Designing work for long-term human growth, health, and efficiency could be a short summary of the basic humanistic goals of one of the biggest international research and development funds in this field of the world, the West German Research and Technology Minis-tery program "Humanization of Working Life" (now renamed "Work and Technol-ogy"). Volpert (1990), who is one of the leading psychological authorities in this program, lately has formulated 10 basic "human criteria" for the design of work facilitating human development as basic values especially for artifact design. The "individual System (iS)" (see subsequent discussion), an artifact we constructed in Osnabrück (in a project funded by the research program mentioned), can too be interpreted as an application of human-growth values.

Theories Are Tools for Thought: Theoretical Concepts and Interpretation of an Example Artifact Design Process

Theories Are Artifacts

If we have to abandon the traditional deductive view and try to develop new approaches analyzing the relationship between scientific theory and practical appli-cation, we have to start with our understanding of the basic function of theories and experiments. From a historical and psychological point of view, we may consider theories and experiments also as artifacts or social constructs, which obviously have an existence apart from their scientific, empirical, and practical evaluation accord-ing to criteria like precision and consistency or practical utility. In addition to the analysis of task–artifact cycles (cf. Carroll et al., this volume), implicit and explicit humanistic values have to be incorporated, if we wish to explain why theories are rejected or applied to work and artifact design. Theories may be apprehended as more or less stimulating tools for thought that give us a framework for analyzing theoretical or practical problem-solving processes in the task–artifact cycle in a systematic way. Stimulating and well-documented experiments may have values beyond scientific evaluation in that they elicit our curiosity and demonstrate how we can operationalize or measure basic theoretical concepts and how we can suc-ceed in controlling task behavior or effecting common goals.

After a review of theories and design concepts in the field of work and organizational psychology and their role in science and application, we found (Greif et al., 1989) that in the history of work and organizational psychology we could not identify systematic positive relations between the scientific value of theories and their relevance for practical design. McGregor's (1960) humanistic management theory is a good example. Its basic assumptions express human-growth values and have never been proved scientifically. Even well-documented practical failures and hard criticism of leading scientists (cf. Miner, 1980) did not reduce its diffusion as an influential management philosophy. Several other theories in the field like Argyris's (1964) integrative organization theory and German action theory are much too complex and can never be supported completely by empirical and practical evaluation.

Only small-range theories formulated directly as instructions for managers – for example, the goal-setting theory of Locke (1968) – have been validated by a substantial body of supporting research studies. Goal-setting theory assumes simply that a manager who cooperatively defines concrete and difficult action goals with his subordinates motivates them to invest efforts to reach these goals. The simplicity of this assumption no doubt has facilitated the diffusion of the theory. I would not argue that the experimental confirmation studies of such assumptions are completely trivial. But as many researchers and practitioners soon have found out, the simple assumptions and practical consequences of Locke's theory are not always valid. In contrast the complex differentiations in for example, Argyris's theory between types of organizations and environments and their systemic relations to organizational structures and processes seem to be less vulnerable by case studies and specific context conditions. For a future survival as a stimulating framework, the theory of Locke therefore has at least to be enlarged to incorporate relevant moderating context conditions. This may provide an interesting example and analogy of short-term advantages and long-term problems of small-range artifact design theories of design rules, which are so simple that they are easily comprehensible and testable.

Theories as Artificial Tools for Thought

Even if they are complex, scientific theories, methods, and experiments simplify practical problem conditions (cf. Barnard, this volume). It would be therefore naive if the designer would trust too much in theories and theoretical design concepts if he wants to solve practical design problems. He should know – and this is an application problem shared by all social, natural, and technical sciences – that theories are idealized representations of reality or artificial tools for thought. The function of theoretical simplification is to reduce the infinite complexity of reality and to help us define problems and expected consequences. Therefore the designer normally will not succeed as a practical problem solver without actively changing the theory to adapt it to his problem and the practical situation and context condition.

In other words theories are frameworks that more or less systematically guide processes of problem solving. The practical success of the designer (from an inner theory perspective; cf. Lewis's distinction in this volume) therefore depends not only on the quality of the theory but also on his knowledge of the task and application situation, together with his theoretical background knowledge, theoretical creativity, and – last but not least – his practical and social competences in marketing the artifact. The resulting design process may be either a systematic application procedure with well-defined steps and criteria or merely an open exploratory activity. But even if the major influence of a theory in artifact design is merely to stimulate creative exploratory activities, we should not undervalue the relevance of theory for the concrete artifact. In the subsequent passages I will try to give an example to illustrate the meaning of these very abstract statements.

Artifact Design, Articulate and Tacit Theoretical Knowledge

The position that theories are frameworks that more or less systematically guide processes of problem solving seems to be a scientifically very weak position in comparison to the traditional deductive paradigm of theory-based design, outlined in the first part of this chapter. But as several chapters in this volume have shown, the deductive paradigm has failed. Standing before the gap between theory (in the sense of articulate theoretical knowledge) and artifact design, we can discriminate between the following groups of relations between artifact design and theory (cf. Carroll et al.'s division in this volume):

1. Artifact design as an open problem-solving process (without systematic design guidelines)
    1a. related to articulate theoretical knowledge
    1b. based on tacit knowledge
2. Artifact design with application of systematic design guidelines
    2a. related to articulate theoretical knowledge
    2b. based on tacit knowledge

The Card et al. (1983) approach and their model human processor is an attempt at artifact design applying systematic design guidelines that are explicitly related to theoretical assumptions (Group 2a). Examples of their design rules are "reduce learning time" or "minimize movement time" (applying design implications of Fitts's Law for mouse movements; see previous discussion). In the field of work psychology the action theoretical guidelines of Hacker (1986) or Volpert (1990), as mentioned previously, and the application of theory-based instruments of work and task analysis aiming at human growth and well-being through work design cannot be incorporated in this group of theory-oriented design system because they are only heuristic guidelines. (An example of a design rule is "enlarge decision latitude and action-oriented knowledge of the users.") Carroll's (1990) application representations and Barnard's solution (this volume) bridging the gap between theory and artifact design by applying refined systematic design rules belong to Group 2b. Other examples are applications of systematic principles of quality control without explicating the theoretical bases (see the iS example in this chapter; and Gediga, 1989).

The fundamental question, whether it is possible to construct design rules or to design artifacts with no rationale or theoretical concepts in mind (based either on everyday reasoning or on scientific theories), refers to our division between the subgrouping a and b in our classification (artifact design based on articulate and tacit theoretical knowledge). In the workshop discussions there was much debate on this question. Carroll's (1989) example of a wheelwright designer who long after constructing wagon wheels retrospectively published his "design theory" (referring to articulate technological expertise that only exists as tacit knowledge at the time when he constructed the wagon wheels) is very impressive. It shows that we have to mistrust retrospective theoretical reconstructions of artifact designers, especially if the time passed is very long. But from the example it does not follow that the wagon-wheel designers at the real time before and in the process of constructing carts had no tacit theoretical claims (naive or elaborated assumptions, right or wrong propositions) in their minds. Like Carroll we can assume that the designer always has some – at least spurious – rationale in mind. Therefore, we may assume that designers always use or develop either articulate or tacit theoretical knowledge in the design process.

Designers may understand artifact design as an open and creative problem-solving process without rules ("anything goes"). The major difference between Group 1 and 2 is that in the first no systematic design rules have been applied to artifact design. But what about creative productions that result from heuristic guidelines or application of systematic problem-solving procedures (cf. Amabile, 1983, and the TRIAD Design Project, 1990)? As long as they do not include systematic design rules such solutions would still belong to the first group. What is important is the theoretical fundamentals of artifact design. Therefore, it is a difference if the design solution is based on general problem-solving rules or specific artifact design decisions deducted from theoretical knowledge. (But since artifact design based on problem-solving processes in the future may incorporate design rules, the divisions may become more complicated. Such examples have to be classified as further combinations of the major groups. Because the essence of the classification is only to clarify possible ideal alternatives, such cases would not neutralize our assumption of different types of relations between artifact design and theory.)

Open problem-solving procedures may be related in different ways to scientific theory. Theoretically derived definitions may be applied to define the problem. Theoretical assumptions can be used as background knowledge. The problem-solving task can also be to change and adapt a given theory to a special problem and specified situation or context conditions (cf. the "difficult requirements" mentioned by Carroll, 1990). Because cases of theory-oriented problem-solving processes have not been documented in software artifact design, we will now concentrate on an example.

Software Artifact Design as a Theory-oriented Problem-solving Process: The Construction of a "Genetic Growing System" as an Example

At the Work and Organizational Psychology Unit, University of Osnabrück, we have conducted several evaluation studies in the field of computer training based on the assumptions and design concepts of Carroll and Mack (1983; Carroll, 1985). Günter Gediga (1989) in one of our larger projects constructed a prototype multifunctional office software system called the "individual System (iS)," applying systematic rules of quality control and methods of task and activity analysis (Gediga et al., 1989). We presented our artifact at the ORGATECH 1988 in Cologne and and the CeBIT '89 in Hannover. I think it could be an interesting (and realistic) example for artifact design as an open problem-solving process related to articulate theoretical knowledge. The theoretical fundamentals (Greif & Keller, 1990), the practical training (Greif, 1986) and design principles (Greif, 1989), and the research (Gediga et al., 1989; Greif & Janikowski, 1987; Mangel & Lohmann, 1988; Müller, 1989) have been described elsewhere. In the following I will concentrate on the process of design and the role of theory, but a short summary of our theoretical questions and the resulting concepts are necessary.

First Phase: Adapting a Computer Training Concept

The first discussions with my students concentrated, I remember well, on the implications of design concepts for human well-being and growth. What interested me most about the research of Carroll and his co-workers on human exploration was that they give us an alternative to mechanistic models of human–computer interaction and learning (see previous discussion). When we started our research and application projects we therefore choose to begin with studies on the application of exploratory learning concepts within the field of computer training of Carroll and Mack (1983) and Carroll (1985) and tried to design "Minimal Manuals" and "exploratory environments" for supporting active exploratory learning. It reinforced us that other colleagues were working with a similar perspective, like Yvonne Waern (1986) and Michael Frese and his co-workers (cf. Frese et al., 1989).

   A theoretical and practical problem that was of central importance from our first phase was the design of "exploratory environments" in the sense of software systems, where the complexity and the risks of errors are artificially lowered for training purposes. Carroll's (1985) concept of Training Wheels where menu functions are blocked for beginners until the subjects have learned to master the simpler training versions for us was a concrete operationalization of the concept. But in the beginning of our research we had simply no resources for the modification of existing software systems and therefore we had to concentrate on the design and evaluation of training principles.

   Similar to Carroll and Mack (1983) in the first phase we tried to evaluate an exploratory learning concept by developing Minimal Manuals and using tasks that require self-organized problem solving. But of course our ambition was not simply to replicate the studies of Carroll and Mack. In our discussions we found several open conceptual and methodological problems with their approach. Especially we could not see how from sometimes obviously chaotic processes clear mental models may develop and how coping with the reported fears of failure may be supported. The theoretical background knowledge of action theory and the research on the practical value of heuristic orientation models, and also our background knowledge in the field of stress at work and training, have influenced the resulting modifications of our training concept of "Exploratory Learning by Errors" as we have called it (cf. Greif, 1986, 1989).

From the introduction we make our subjects familiar with the fact that making errors when working with computer systems in unavoidable. The basic theoretical concept is to redefine errors as learning situations for which emotional and cognitive coping strategies have to be developed. Coping mechanisms for feelings of anxiety and panic can be learned by applying principles of "Stress Inoculation Training." (The basic idea of this cognitive behavior-modification approach is to "inoculate" the subjects against stress reactions at the workplace by stepwise confronting them with manageable stress and error situations in the learning process.)

Instead of relying on on-line help systems, we encourage our trainees to seek and give personal social support in the training setting. We see this as the basis of a personal help network for trainees when they return to their organizations. The training situation can thus facilitate the establishment of long-term learning partnerships and group meetings of organization members exchanging knowledge about the efficient and productive use of the computer system. These meetings can be the nucleus of special Quality Circles. Because such Quality Circles guided by the former trainer make innovations at work more likely and because the costs for these meetings are comparatively low, any organization can utilize and benefit from the readiness of most trainees to engage in such knowledge exchange.

Another special tool we designed as an alternative to on-line help systems are "Orientation Posters" (cf. Greif, 1989). These posters show pictographic maps of the basic structure and procedures to operate the system for major tasks (e.g., starting or ending the system, creating new files, and printing files). Our theoretical claims were that such Orientation Posters support the subject so they can develop adequate mental models of the structure of the system, give a useful orientation for systematic planning of tasks, especially solving problems resulting from errors; and help learners to remember the structure and procedures. (We routinely test the long-term efficiency of our training seminars after two or three months.)

With our modified concepts we conducted several experiments much in the line of Carroll and Mack's work (cf. Greif, 1989; Greif & Janikowski, 1987; Mangel & Lohmann, 1988). In general the results were promising. The exploratory learning groups showed better performance results on the more complex tasks or exploratory tasks. But the results were not completely consistent. There were differences between the results of different experiments even if we applied the same type of tasks. Some experimental groups did not produce the theoretically expected results. We therefore focused on the optimization of the training and software design, evaluation concepts and generalizability problems (previously discussed), and how we could identify the relevant context conditions or individual differences that in the opinion of our trainers played a crucial role explaining the results.

Second Phase: Elaborating the Theoretical Bases and Design of a "Genetic Growing System"

For a discussion of the theoretical problem of our design we got support from the developmental psychologists of our department (Heidi Keller and Axel Schölmerich have to be mentioned here) who were at that time not familiar with the field of software design but are well-known experts on the exploratory behavior of children. Our discussions of theoretical issues for our approach to artifact design resulted in three major topics.

First, the central concept of stimulating exploratory learning by "exploratory environments" (Carroll & Mack, 1983) and minimalist design (Carroll, 1985) should be explicated more precisely. As developmental research shows, we can follow Berlyne's (1960) view that in general it is complexity and novelty that stimulate exploratory activities and motivate knowledge acquisition. In general curiosity and knowledge acquisition in exploratory environments should be supported by designing stimulating tasks that are complex and new for the individual (in balance with the individual level of tolerance of ambiguity and competencies).

Second, time is a crucial variable for exploratory learning. In experimental and developmental research normally exploratory behavior is evaluated by a longer amount of time spent on a task. It is a theoretically intriguing question why an exploratory learning approach that follows Carroll and our results should take less training time in comparison to instruction methods. Theory would suggest that speeding the process of knowledge acquisition by exploratory learning will have negative effects on the resulting cognitive schemata.

Third, following from our practical experiences and developmental psychological research, we claim that we have to contrast different exploratory styles. Because different styles of exploration have different theoretical functions in the process of knowledge acquisition and because we wanted to support the learning process differentially, our idea was to support different types of exploratory behaviors and design special training resources for relevant subgroups (especially novices with learning difficulties). The resulting questions were: How can we identify individual different exploratory styles and how can we adapt our training design to take account of individual differences in the design of our training concept?

Because here we are primarily interested in the theoretical interpretation of the design process, in the following I will not describe the resulting theoretical concepts (cf. Greif & Keller, 1990) and research in detail (cf. Gediga et al., 1989; Greif, 1989). But some explanations may be necessary to understand the solutions.

Functionality and Simplicity of Artifacts in Use

For the design of artifacts in use as efficient work tools, "functionality" is an essential goal. Functionality of a tool may be defined by the safety with which the user is able to master the whole task with the tool. For a precise operationalization of the degree of functionality, task analysis is the major instrument. It is necessary to analyze the safety of all relevant components of the task, the safety of all possible sequences and of the overall performance process.

The perceptual control of a software system may depend on the quality of the graphic design of information presentation. (Aesthetic design and pictograms may help to emphasize and process informations easily.) For designing safe motor control of a tool we have to analyze the ergonomic properties of the input devices, especially time, precision, and harmony of the control movements (e.g., the keyboard and mouse movements).

Following Frese's (1987) distinction between complexity and complicatedness (i.e., dysfunctional complexity), we always should avoid complicatedness. A functional work tool composed of few well-designed parts often is safer than complicated systems. Because simple systems can be handled and mastered more easily by different people, "minimalist design" should in general be preferred for artifacts in use. But by definition the functionality depends on the ability to master the system and therefore we have to regard the competencies and knowledge of the individual user by specifying the meaning of "simplicity." For an expert programmer a complex command may be simple and functional because he or she can master it. For user groups with low programming knowledge the circumstantial menu-selection format may be much safer and therefore more adequate. Another relevant aspect is the balance between task and tool complexity. Not only a system that is too complex but also a tool that is too simple for efficient mastering of complex problems may be dysfunctional.

Minimalist and Maximalist Design of Learning Environments

Functionality as we defined it is a goal for artifacts in use. But we should not conclude that it has the same relevance for the design of learning environments. As mentioned previously, we have to consider Berlyne's theory of the role of complexity and novelty for stimulating knowledge acquisition processes. In order to find a consistent conceptual solution for the design of learning environments, we have to refine the concept of "exploratory environment" and minimalist design. The claim of minimalist design is to limit error for novices by initially blocking functions and thereby reducing the complexity and novelty of the environment. This should be an adequate solution for subjects, who are overloaded and unable to cope with the complex and novel task. But we have to keep in mind that according to Berlyne (1960) subjects with a higher tolerance of ambiguity and competence to cope with complex computer environments will react to simple systems with lower motivation and less acquisition of new knowledge. Following theory we should prefer a design that enlarges complexity, novelty, and even higher risks of errors or a "maximimalist design" in the sense that the individual learner always should try to cope with an environment of maximal manageable complexity. The design of learning environments therefore should not concentrate on a blocking of functions but on a stepwise enlargement of complexity or opening menu functions and also efficient command inputs for the growing user. Because Carroll (1985) during the learning process stepwise enlarges the Training Wheels functions and subsequentially presents the full-system functions, there may be no relevant practical differences between "minimalist" and "maximalist design." It is more the theoretical focus that differs.

But if we focus on maximal instead of minimal complexity and novelty, this may also stimulate different practical design solutions. For example, we have designed special "exploratory tasks" where the learners explicitly get no support from manuals and on-line help information or we try to stimulate exploratory knowledge acquisition by surprising error situations and the like. Developmental psychological and exploration theory helped us to elaborate such seemingly chaotic design solutions, which in our experience normally are avoided by designers and professional trainers. Tacit knowledge favors the design of simple and safe learning environments.

In the United States the idea of consciously designing complex learning environments may be a provocative position, as some comments in our workshop revealed. Because the general rule is to reduce complexity, several colleagues asked me if I really assume that it is good to enlarge complexity? And my answer was "Yes, for the design of learning environments." It is essential, of course, that the individual is able to manage the complexity and that learning processes that can be practically useful for managing complex problems on the job are stimulated. The complexity of the learning tasks should mirror the overall or long-term complexity of the practical task demands.

Genetic Growing Systems

We found an early example showing how to solve the mentioned problems by a stepwise enlargement of the complexity of a software system. Palme (1983) has designed a prototype data-base system encouraging user-knowledge growth that begins with a simple menu and stepwise grows to a complex menu and command system. Ideal examples of the basic rationale are object-oriented programming systems and especially the Boxer programming language and environment of diSessa (this volume). Systems that from a developmental psychological perspective (cf. Campbell, Carroll, & DiBello, 1989) support the natural process of user growth may be called "Genetic Growing Systems." The essential principle of Genetic Growing Systems is a facilitation of the natural development of cognitive schemas.

On the levels of Genetic Growing Systems users should be able to do simple but complete tasks. Complex tasks cannot be managed adequately by software systems with a structure that is too simple and functions that have only very limited combination and application possibilities. Complex tasks on the other hand demand knowledge of complex menu stystems or even knowledge of the syntax of condensed commands (normally the most efficient solution for professionals).

Günther Gediga (1989) in our MBQ project[1] has developed a prototype genetic-growing software system. This multifunctional office system is called the "individual System (iS)", since the individual can adapt it to his or her preferences and tasks following Ackerman and Ulich's (1987) principles of individualization of design.

In an experiment where we selected typists with no prior computer experience, the subjects trained with the Genetic Growing System had enormous benefits in comparison with those trained with a standard system (Greif, 1989). These results of course reinforced our confidence that we have succeeded to design a useful

---

1. The German title of the project is "Multifunktionale Bürosoftware und Qualifizierung (MBQ)" (Multifunctional Office Software and Qualification). The project is funded by the West German Minister of Research and Technology, "Humanization of Working Life" (now "Work and Technology") program.

artifact. But supporting our theoretical expectations following Berlyne (1960), Müller (1989) in one of our experiments with the system also found that the reduction of complexity by a Genetic Growing System for subjects with background knowledge may lower motivation and even hinder an optimal process of knowledge acquisition. For the training of student groups, especially students with prior computer experiences (e.g., DOS knowledge) and high competencies to cope with complexity (measured by a questionnaire), we recommend the use of the highest complexity level of the system from the beginning.

Time and Self-regulation of Exploration

Exploration and new situations processing new information are demanding activities. So the individual needs pauses, intervals of inactivity, or diversions in order to restore capacities or to find relief from a sustained mental load. Often periods of exploration are phased to prevent fatigue from becoming aversive. Teaching groups of novices (normally with eight participants) at a predetermined pace in our early studies we could observe typical reactions of monotony of the fast-learning subjects. Several developmental studies have demonstrated that the duration of the interaction with the new situation influences the accuracy and amount of recalled knowledge (cf. Herman & Siegel, 1978). Children who are allowed to explore new surroundings by themselves and at their own pace acquire more information about their spatial settings and a better spatial representation than children who were guided by an adult and who therefore passively explored their surroundings. This idea is supported by theories that conceptualize cognitive development as being closely related to and dependent on motor acts (Gibson, 1979).

These theoretical insights pushed us to change our training concept to a time schedule that is strictly self-regulated by the individual learner. Only in the beginning the trainer explains the training concept to the learning group and actively instructs them how to work with the first level of the system, following the learning task descriptions and the resources that can be used if the individual wishes. The individual also has to decide when to progress to the next level and group of tasks. The trainer in the process of learning is available to help if consulted.

A theoretical claim is that self-regulated exploration has an additional effect of eliciting positive emotional feelings and self-evaluations of competence and efficacy. These emotional qualities might themselves facilitate further exploratory knowledge acquisition, creativity, and role innovation (cf. West & Farr, 1990).

Conclusions

The development of our prototype "individual System (iS)" is an example of software artifact design, interpreted as an open problem-solving process related to articulate theoretical knowledge. It shows how theoretical concepts and assumptions in a very concrete way can be relevant for design decisions, even if they are applied merely as frameworks that seemingly not very systematically guide the complex and dynamic processes of problem solving in artifact design projects. But following Wertheimer's (1945) famous psychological analysis of scientific exploration our example may confirm that especially in deciding between different design solutions and coping with complex inconsistencies, theoretical framework guides our decisions. Therefore we would infer that even in an open problem-solving process the role of scientific or everyday theories can be crucial, especially at the choice points of artifact design. But it is not a single theoretical model that we have applied in a direct way. A rich psychological background stimulated our problem-solving processes. In this way the complex theoretical background may well be called "a mother of invention" (Landauer, 1987) for artifact design.

Artifact design following an open problem-solving approach is not the only way bridging the gap between theory and artifact design. We distinguished among the following idealized alternatives:

1. Artifact design as an open problem-solving process (without systematic design guidelines)
    1a. related to articulate theoretical knowledge
    1b. based on tacit knowledge

2. Artifact design with application of systematic design guidelines
    2a. related to articulate theoretical knowledge
    2b. based on tacit knowledge

The action theory work design guidelines of Hacker (1986) or Volpert (1988), mentioned earlier, may be seen as an approach to be classified between 1a and 2a because they show how we can bridge the gap between scientific theory and practical design by systematic, theory-related methods of work and task analysis combined with general heuristic work and software design guidelines. The emerging applied research and development in task and artifact design and the application of systematic design guidelines with and without explication of theoretical claims should according to Carroll et al. (this volume) be interpreted by task–artifact cycles following his perspectives developing a "psychology of tasks" or as I would prefer an interdisciplinary "task–action theory."

But we should not build up an artificial competition between the two approaches of artifact design with systematic design guidelines and artifact design as an open problem-solving process. The problem-solving approach perhaps merely describes the typical beginning phase of opening a new field for scientific research and technological construction. As I know from the beginning of the work of Walter Volpert and Rainer Oesterreich, before they succeeded in developing their systematic instruments, they had to go through an intensive theory-related problem-solving process. If in the field of artifact design until now we have only few theoretically systematic design guidelines, this in my opinion shows that we are still in a phase of constituting the new field of artifact design, applying and *developing* psychology and other sciences for the artifact design task (cf. chapter 1). Designing for product success and work design seems to be the future competition field of industry. Market analysis and the management of interdisciplinary design teams are crucial for success or failure of industrial organizations (cf. the evaluation of case studies by the TRIAD Design Project, 1990). The challenging future scientific task in the 1990s therefore will be to develop and apply better and more refined theory-related processes of professional design. But at the same time I believe that opening of new fields will always be a major task of scientific exploration and creative designers. And such open creative processes resulting in concrete and applicable artifacts also result in a definite sense of fun.

In this chapter the theoretical background frame was to consider scientific theories and artifact design as social constructs, which have an existence apart from their evaluation according to scientific or practical criteria. Historical or psychological descriptions and interpretations of the developmental processes of theories and artifact design are not an alternative to methodological approaches, defining and evaluating theories and artifacts. From a scientific standpoint, it may provoke criticism if we recommend explicitly applying and operationalizing cultural values as criteria of artifact design. But the relevance of humanistic growth values for artifact design and the way it is used in German action theory show that it may be an even greater problem to ignore relevant value-oriented criteria. A worthwhile perspective would be to formulate design philosophies that explicitly consider common and different cultural backgrounds.

References

Ackermann, D., & Ulich, E. (1987). The chances of individualization in human–computer interaction and its consequences. In M. Frese, E. Ulich, and W. Dzida (Eds.), *Psychological issues of human–computer interaction in the work place* (pp. 131–146). Amsterdam: North-Holland.

Argyris, C. (1964). *Integrating the individual and the organization.* New York: Wiley.

Amabile, T. M. (1983). *The social psychology of creativity.* New York: Springer.

Berlyne, D. E. (1960). *Conflict, arousal and curiosity.* New York: McGraw-Hill.

Blättner, F. (1968). *Geschichte der Pädagogik* (13th ed.). Heidelberg: Quelle & Meyer.

Brocke, B. (1978). *Technologische Prognosen.* Freiburg: Alber.

Campbell, R. L., Carroll, J. M., & DiBello, L.A. (1989). Human–computer interaction: The case for a developmental approach to expertise. Jean Piaget Society, June 1–3, Philadelphia, PA.

Card, S. K., Moran, T. P., & Newell, A. (1983). *The psychology of human–computer interaction.* Hillsdale, NJ.: Lawrence Erlbaum Associates.

Carroll, J. M.(1985). Minimalist design for the active user. In B. Shackle (Ed.), *Human–Computer Interaction: Interact '84* (pp. 39–44). Amsterdam: North-Holland.

Carroll, J. M. (1989). Taking artifacts seriously. In S. Maass & H. Oberquelle (Eds.), *Software-Ergonomie '89* (pp. 36–50). Stuttgart: Teubner.

Carroll, J. M. (1990). Infinite detail and emulation in an ontologically minimized HCI. In J. C. Chew & J. Whiteside (Eds.), *Proceedings of CHI '90; Human Factors in Computing Systems* (pp. 321–327). New York: ACM.

Carroll, J. M., & Mack, R. L. (1983). Active learning to use a word processor. In W. E. Cooper (Ed.). *Cognitive aspects of skilled typewriting* (pp. 259–282). Berlin: Springer.

Cattell, J. M. (1886). The time taken up by cerebral operations. *Mind, 11,* 220–242, 377–392, 524–538.

Donders, F. C. (1868). Over de snelheid van psychische processen. Translated by W. G. Koster 1969. On the speed of mental processes. *Acta Psychologica, 30,* 412–431.

Floyd, C. (1987). Outline of a paradigm change in software engineering. In G. Bjerkes, P. Ehn, & M. Kyng (Eds.), *Computers and democracy–a Scandinavian challenge* (pp. 193–110). Aldershot, UK: Averbury.

Floyd, C., & Keil, R. (1983). Adapting software development for systems design with the user. In U. Briefs, C. Ciborra, & L. Schneider (Eds.), *Systems design for, with, and by the users* (pp. 163–172). Amsterdam: North-Holland.

Frese, M. (1987). Conceptual issues in the psychology of human–computer interaction. In M. Frese, E. Ulich, & W. Dzida (Eds.), *Psychological issues of human–computer interaction in the work place* (pp. 313–338). Amsterdam: North-Holland.

Frese, M., Brodbeck, F., Heinbokel, T., Mooser, C., Schleiffenbaum, E., & Thiemann, P. (1989). *Errors in training computer skills: On the positive function of errors.* Munich. Unpublished manuscript.

Frese, M., & Sabini, J. (Eds.). (1985). *Goal directed behavior: the concept of action in psychology.* Hillsdale, NJ.: Lawrence Erlbaum Associates.

Gediga, G. (1989). Das Funktionshandbuch zum iS. *Schriftenreihe Ergebnisse des Projekts MBQ,* special issue *15,* 1–134.

Gediga, G., Greif, S., Monecke, U., & Hamborg, K.-C. (1989). Aufgaben- und Tätigkeits-analyse als Grundlage der Softwaregestaltung. In S. Maass & H. Oberquelle (Eds.). *Software-Ergonomie '89* (pp. 80–88). Stuttgart: Teubner.

Gediga, G., & Wolff, P. (1989). On the applicability of three basic laws to human–computer interaction. *Schriftenreihe Ergebnisse des Projekts MBQ,* special issue *11,* 1–33.

Gibson, J. J. (1979). *The ecological approach to visual perception.* Boston: Houghton Mifflin.

Greif, S. (1986). Neue Kommunikationstechnologien–Entlastung oder mehr Stress? Beschreibung eines Computer-Trainings zur "Stress-Imunisierung." In K. H. Pullig, U. Schäckel, & J. Scholz (Eds.), *Stress in Unternehmen* (Reihe Betriebliche Weiterbildung, 8, pp. 178–200). Hamburg: Windmühle.

Greif, S. (1987). Humanisierung des Arbeitslebens und Sozialpsychologie. In J. Schultz-Gambard (Ed.), *Angewandte Sozialpsychologie* (pp. 169–185). Munich: Psychologie Verlags Union.

Greif, S. (1989). Genetic growing systems and self controlled training. HdA-MDA Work-shop, December 12 to 13, 1988, Stockholm. *Schriftenreihe Ergebnisse des Projekts MBQ,* special issue *9,* 1–20

Greif, S. (1990). Organisational issues and task analysis. In B. Shackel (Ed.), *Human factors for informatics usability.* Cambridge: Cambridge University Press.

Greif, S., & Gediga, G. (1987). A critique of one-best-way models in human–computer interaction. In M. Frese, E. Ulich, & W. Dzida (Eds.), *Psychological issues of human–computer interaction in the work place* (pp. 357–377). Amsterdam: North-Holland.

Greif, S., Holling, H., & Nicholson, N. (1989). Theorien und Konzepte. In S. Greif, H. Holling, & N. Nicholson (Eds.), *Arbeits- und Organisationspsychologie. Interna-tionales Handbuch in Schlüsselbegriffen* (pp. 3–18). Munich: Psychologie Verlags Union.

Greif, S., & Janikowski, A. (1987). Aktives Lernen durch systematische Fehlerexploration oder programmiertes Lernen durch Tutorials? *Zeitschrift für Arbeits-und Organisa-tionspsychologie, 31,* 34–99.

Greif, S., & Keller, H. (1990). Innovation and the design of work and learning environments: The concept of exploration in human–computer interaction. In M. West & J. Farr (Eds.), *Innovation and creativity at work* (pp. 231–249). New York: Wiley.

Hacker, W. (1985). Activity: A fruitful concept in industrial psychology. In M. Frese, M. Sabini, & J. Sabini (Eds.), *Goal directed behavior: The concept of action in psychology* (pp. 262–284). Hillsdale, NJ: Lawrence Erlbaum Associates.

Hacker, W. (1986). *Arbeitspsychologie. Psychische Regulation von Arbeitstätigkeiten.* Berlin: Deutscher Verlag der Wissenschaften.

Hacker, W. (1987). Computerization versus computer aided mental work. In M. Frese, E. Ulich, & W. Dzida (Eds.), *Psychological issues of human–computer interaction in the work place,* (pp. 115–130). Amsterdam: North-Holland.

Hacker, W. , Volpert, W., & Cranach, V., (Eds.) (1982). *Cognitive and motivational aspects of action.* Amsterdam: North-Holland.

Herman, J. F., & Siegel, A. W. (1978). The development of cognitive mapping of the large-scale environment. *Journal of Experimental Child Psychology, 26,* 389–406.

Herzberg, F. (1966). *Work and the nature of man.* Cleveland: World Publishing.

Keil-Slawik, R. (1990). *Konstruktives Design.* Berlin: Technical University. (Unpublished Habilitation.)

Kieras, D. E., & Polson, P. G. (1985). An approach to the formal analysis of user complexity. *International Journal of Man–Machine Studies, 22,* 365–394.

Landauer, T. K. (1987). Psychology as a mother of invention. In J. M. Carroll & P. P. Tanner (Eds.), *Proceedings of CHI & GI '87: Human Factors in Computing Systems and Graphics Interface (Toronto, April 5-9)* (pp. 333–335). New York: ACM.

Leontjew, A. N. (1973). *Probleme der Entwicklung des Psychischen.* Frankfurt, Main: Athenäum Fischer.

Locke, E. A. (1968). Toward a theory of task motivation and incentives. *Organizational Behavior and Human Performance, 3,* 157–189.

Mangel, I., & Lohmann, I. (1988). *Alternative Trainingsmethoden für ein Textverarbeitungsprogramm.* (Unpublished Diplomarbeit, Osnabrück.)

Maslow, A. H. (1954). *Motivation and personality.* New York: Harper.

McGregor, D. (1960). *The human side of enterprise.* New York: McGraw-Hill.

Miller, G. A., Galanter, E., & Pribram, K. H. (1960). *Plans and the structure of behavior.* New York: Holt, Rinehart & Winston.

Miner, J. G. (1980), *Theories of organizational behavior.* Hillsdale, Ill.: Dryden.

Müller, M. 1989. *Softwaregestaltung und Computertraining: Entwicklung und Evaluation eines mitwachsenden Softwaresystems auf der Basis eines explorationsfördernden Trainings.* (Unpublished Diplomarbeit, Osnabrück.)

Münsterberg, H. (1912). *Psychologie und Wirtschaftsleben.* Leipzig: Barth.

Newell, A., & Card, S. K. (1985). The prospects for psychological science in human–computer interaction. *Human–Computer Interaction, 1,* 209–242.

Newell, A., & Simon, H. A. (1972). *Human information processing.* Englewood Cliffs, NJ: Prentice-Hall.

Oesterreich, R. (1981). *Handlungsregulation und Kontrolle.* Munich: Urban & Schwarzenberg.

Oesterreich, R., & Volpert, W. (1986). Handlungstheoretisch orientierte Arbeitsanalyse. In J. Rutenfranz & U. Kleinbeck (Eds.), *Arbeitspsychologie* (pp. 43–73). Göttingen: Hogrefe.

Palme, J. (1983). A human–computer interface encouraging user growth. In M. E. Sieme & M. J. Koombs (Eds.), *Designing for human–computer communication* (pp. 139–156). London: Academic Press.

Rubinstein, S. L. (1966). *Sein und Bewusstsein* (3rd ed.). Berlin: Akademie-Verlag.

Semmer, N., & Frese, M. (1985). Action theory and clinical psychology. In M. Frese, M. Sabini, & J. Sabini (Eds.), *Goal directed behavior: The concept of action in psychology* (pp. 296–310). Hillsdale, NJ: Lawrence Erlbaum Associates.

Shneiderman, B. (1987). *Designing the user interface.* Reading, MA: Addison-Wesley.

Taylor, F. W. (1911). *The principles of scientific management.* New York: Harper & Row.

TRIAD Design Project, (1990). Designing for product success. Essays and case studies of the exposition at the CeBIT '90, edited by the Design Management Institute Boston. New York: Econ.

Ulich, E. (1984). Psychologie der Arbeit. In *Management-Enzyklopädie* (Band 7, pp. 914–929). Landsberg: Moderne Industrie.

Ulich, E. (1987). Individual differences in human–computer interaction: Concepts and research findings. In G. Salvendy (Ed.), *Cognitive engineering in the design of human–computer interaction and expert systems* (pp. 29–36). Amsterdam: Elsevier Science Publishing Company.

Ulich, E., & Clegg, C. (1989). Arbeitsgestaltung. In S. Greif, H. Holling, & N. Nicholson (Eds.), *Arbeits- und Organisationspsychologie. Internationales Handbuch in Schlüsselbegriffen* (pp. 101–109). Munich: Psychologie Verlags Union.

Ulich, E., Schüpbach, H., Schilling, A., & Kuark, J. (1990). Concepts and procedures of work psychology for the analysis, evaluation and design of advanced manufacturing systems: A case study. *International Journal of Industrial Ergonomics.* Special Issue on Human Aspects of Advanced Manufacturing Systems, *5*(1), 47–57.

Volpert, W. (1975). Die Lohnarbeitswissenschaft und die Psychologie der Arbeitstätigkeit. In W. Volpert & P. Groskurth (Eds.), *Lohnarbeitspsychologie* (pp. 11–169). Frankfurt, Main: Fischer.

Volpert, W. (1990). Work design for human development. In R. Budde, C. Floyd, R. Keil-Slawik, & H. Züllighoven (Eds.), *Software development and reality construction.* New York: Springer.

Volpert, W., Oesterreich, W., Gablenz-Kolakovic, Krogoll, T., & Resch, M. (1983). *Verfahren zur Ermittlung von Regulationserfordernissen in der Arbeitstätigkeit (VERA).* Köln: Verlag TÜV Rheinland.

Voss, H. G., & Keller, H. (1983). *Curiosity and exploration: Theories and results.* New York: Academic Press.

Waern, Y. (1986). Learning computerized tasks. In *Human Factors in Information Technology,* No. 8. Series issued by The Cognitive Seminar Department of Psychology, University of Stockholm (pp. 1–63).

Wertheimer, M. (1945). *Productive thinking.* New York: Harper & Brothers.

West, M., & Farr, J. (1990). *Innovation and creativity at work.* New York: Wiley.

12
Beyond the Interface: Encountering Artifacts in Use
Liam J. Bannon and Susanne Bødker

Strictly speaking, nothing is a tool unless during actual use.

The essence of a tool, therefore, lies in something outside the tool itself. It is not in the head of the hammer, nor in the handle, nor in the combination of the two that the essence of mechanical characteristics exists, but in the recognition of its unity and in the forces directed through it in virtue of this recognition. This appears more plainly when we reflect that a very complex machine, if intended for use by children whose aim is not serious, ceases to rank in our minds as a tool, and becomes a toy. It is seriousness of aim, and recognition of suitability for the achievement of that aim, and not anything in the tool itself that makes the tool.

–Samuel Butler, *Notebooks*

This chapter is written by two people who come from rather different backgrounds, yet who, at the same time, share similar concerns about the human–computer interaction (HCI) area. One of us has a background in computing and cognitive science, coupled with a long-standing interest in helping users in their interactions with technology. He became uncomfortable with the gap between current cognitive theories and their utility in designing better interfaces to computer systems. The other person has a background in software engineering and computer systems design. In her search for a deeper understanding of issues in HCI, she came across the cognitive science framework, but she too felt that its methods did not provide much help for concrete design in real-life situations.

In many ways our personal histories reflect some of the developments within the HCI area – the search for more theoretical frameworks, and the subsequent realization of the gap between current theoretical formulations and actual situations of use. We can be seen as both insiders and outsiders to the mainstream, primarily Anglo-American, HCI–cognitive science tradition in several respects: One of us is trained in cognitive science, one is not; one did studies in Scandinavia, one primarily in North America.

Because both of us are concerned with making more useful and usable computer applications, we decided to look further for frameworks to help us. In this chapter we try to expose some of the problems we encountered in our joint effort to understand the HCI area and contribute to it, and to discuss some of the tensions and alternative viewpoints that we met on the way. The chapter does not contain a solution to the problems of HCI. Rather, it contains a dialog with ourselves about the matters of our concern, and we invite the reader to join this dialog: Our focus is on technology in use, where we emphasize the setting in which a piece of technology is used. We do not think that artifacts per se can be usefully studied in isolation. They need to be studied in their use settings. These use settings are developed over time, historically; they are not static and unchanging. For this reason the history of technology as well as of the organization of work become very important to us when we consider the (re)design of computer artifacts for people. What we do here is similar to Christiane Floyd's (1987) enterprise in her paper on software engineering perspectives. She invites us to join her in a comparison of what she identifies as two perspectives in software engineering, and a discussion of the limitations as well as the utility of these differing perspectives. We do not think that it is possible to uniquely identify the voices raised in this paper. They are all of us, or part of our mutual discussion. We invite readers to share with us their experiences in the field, their practice, and any examples of how theory has influenced their practice.

In this chapter, we provide a brief overview and critique of the descriptions and concepts that are currently used in the HCI area coming primarily from the cognitive science tradition, as they seem to embed within them certain assumptions that are overly limiting. Then we look at some recent arguments for reorganizing our conception of the field, or extending the field, coming primarily from within the field itself (as presently constituted). The next section presents a more elaborated "activity-theoretical" framework as one possible alternative, or perhaps complementary, framework that may give a richer depiction of the HCI field. Then we return to look more specifically at the different theoretical viewpoints, especially in regard to their reframing of issues in the field, relating the different emphases to another field, software engineering. This section tries to summarize some of the main points made in a form that can serve as a basis for future discussion.

Setting the Scene: The Current Framework of Cognitive Science and HCI

The Current State of Cognitive Theory

Over the past 30 years, the dominant view of human nature portrayed in psychology and allied disciplines, at least in the English-speaking world, has been a cognitivist, rather than a behaviorist, physiological, or phenomenological one. Cognition is seen as "information-processing psychology." People are regarded as "informavores" to use George Miller's term, and the study of human thinking and problem solving is commonly regarded as being concerned with representations in the head and the processes that run over them.

The idea of a distinct multidisciplinary research program labeled cognitive science has a somewhat more recent origin, although its principal proponents come from within the cognitive psychology discipline, with some support from artificial intelligence (AI) research, linguistics, and philosophy. Although other disciplines such as anthropology, sociology, and neurophysiology are also mentioned, their influence has been marginal. Enough authors have been exploring this field of cognitive science recently that we can simply quote a spokesperson for this new field. Bernsen (1988) talks of this discipline as follows:

It consists in the general idea that intelligent agents should be looked upon as information-processing systems, that is, as systems receiving, manipulating, storing, retrieving and transmitting information. . . . A central tenet is that there exists a level of description of intelligent systems at which the organization and use of knowledge is described functionally in computational or information-processing terms independently of the nature of the physical implementation of the system.

From this definition we see an emphasis on a multidisciplinary activity, spanning a wide variety of fields, that has supposedly in common an interest in the study of intelligence, and mechanisms whereby it can be realized, whether in natural or artificial organisms. Thus a key idea is the essential similarity of processes that are behind human and artificial "reasoning." Pylyshyn is most explicit about this: "my proposal amounts to a claim that *cognition is a type of computation*" (1984, p. xiii; our emphasis). This view has led many researchers in the field to build computer models of human thought processes that are taken to be strongly equivalent to the actual processes that are used by people in their comprehension and understanding of the real world.

A number of people from within the cognitive science community have admitted there are problems in the cognitive science approach as just outlined. Donald Norman, one of the pioneers in the field, as early as 1980 wrote a paper that outlined some of the shortcomings of the newly formed cognitive science "discipline" (Norman, 1980). Despite the fact that the paper was written over a decade ago, we think it is well worth revisiting today, to look at some of the questions raised, as many of these issues have not been satisfactorily addressed by current cognitive science theories.[1] Norman's paper argues that the human information processor is an animate organism and that this places constraints on what kind of cognitive system we have evolved. In all likelihood this natural cognitive system will thus be very different from the kinds of AI models we have been building to represent human thinking. In discussing his growing dissatisfaction with the model human information processor that lies at the heart of the cognitive science tradition, he notes (1980, p. 2) that:

The problem seemed to be in the lack of consideration of other aspects of human behavior, of interaction with other people and with the environment, of the influence of the history of the person, or even the culture, and of the lack of consideration of the special problems and issues confronting an animate organism that must survive as both an individual and as a species.

Despite this admission, the rest of the paper does not really develop these themes. However, alternative materialistic theories of human and societal development

1. Norman has recently returned to this issue with a paper at the 11th Cognitive Society Conference (August 1989) entitled "Four (More) Issues for Cognitive Science" – viz. connectionism, the relation to biological and clinical issues, the role of applied cognitive science, and the deficiencies of a disembodied theory of cognition. We do not have the space to go into these themes here, but the last two show a continued shift toward a more central role for social and environmental influences on cognition. See also his chapter in this volume.

exist that *do* take these issues into account (see our subsequent discussion), but such approaches, with a couple of notable exceptions (e.g., Cole, John-Steiner, Scribner, & Sonberman, 1978; Wertsch, 1985) have not had much support within the academic cognitive community in North America and England.

A common reply to this call for a richer understanding of human cognitive functioning from others in the community has been to claim that we cannot study everything at once, that we have to decompose problems, and simplify situations so that the power of our experimental methods can be brought to bear on these issues. The importance of actual practice is not recognized, the individual is still set up against the social, much cognition is still regarded as "in the head," and the laboratory is still seen as the appropriate place to learn about how people understand and act in the world. We continue to parcel out aspects of "problems" as defined by the traditional disciplines, to different disciplinary studies, in an effort to "divide and conquer." The argument we wish to make is that our most widely accepted methods for "carving Nature at its joints" have hacked our "person acting in a setting" (Lave, 1988) into a disembodied ratiocinator that bears little resemblance to a person acting (often cooperating with others) in a situation in the world, which is what we wish to understand.

Exemplars of the kinds of problems investigated by the psychological research community in this tradition concern laboratory investigations of puzzles, games, and so forth (Newell & Simon, 1972). Their "protocol analysis" research methodology, involving subjects' talking aloud during the problem session, provides a rich corpus of material from which the subjects representation of the problem and steps in solving the problem can be deduced. However, these studies tend to analyze individuals without reference to their community, or their history, performing on a task designed by the experimenter in an unfamiliar environment. The "problem" is defined and valued by the experimenter, not by the subject, who is then expected to perform in certain ways. In some experimental manipulations, even the very nature of the task, or the required behavior, may not be clear to the subject. The question of how "subjects" make sense of the game in which they are playing, trying to discover the "rules of the game" – that is, what the experimenter is after – is often not explicitly discussed in these studies. Performance is measured relative to a certain "ideal," rational model of problem solving, and the deviations of subjects from this abstract logic are noted.

It is presumed that the fundamental mental mechanisms posited to underlie human behavior in such prescribed domains can later be extended, without major modification, to more real-world activities. So the assumption is that "problem solving" is a generic cognitive activity that has a similar form across a wide variety of domains, from acting in a psychology experiment to everyday cognitive activities. It is also usually assumed, implicitly, that this activity is located "in the head" of the individual. These assumptions, which have been continually rejected by certain "borderline" groups, have once again come under serious attack from a variety of researchers. (For a major critique of the framework surrounding much experimentation in human information-processing psychology, see Lave, 1988.) Our purpose in this chapter is not to develop these arguments as to how the accepted paradigm is flawed, but rather to note that this conceptual framework has often been imported into applied cognitive research on HCI without question, limiting the utility and usability of many HCI studies that are grounded in these assumptions. To the extent that mainstream theory does not give an adequate account of how people think and act in the everyday world, basing the design of artifacts on such limited research studies may not be the most fruitful approach to adopt.

Concern for a more integrated, holistic approach to human thought and action in the world has led some people to search for a different theoretical framework as the basis for our experimental and observational studies. Some psychologists have found inspiration in the materialist philosophy expounded by Marx and Engels that emphasizes praxis as the basis for human development. The work of the Russian psychologists Vygotsky and Leontiev are examples (Leontiev, 1978, 1981; Vygotsky, 1978). In this paper, we will try to say a little more on some of these issues. However, before presenting this framework, let us investigate how the cognitive science tradition has influenced the applied field of HCI, as it is this topic that we wish to develop through theoretical reformulations.

The Field of Human–Computer Interaction

What constitutes the field of human–computer interaction? Our concern stems from the problem of where the boundaries of the field are, or should be, and why it might be of importance (Bannon, 1985). The HCI label appears to be self-explanatory – that is, anything to do with people interacting with computers – yet it has been interpreted more narrowly as simply the study of user interfaces, which seems an extremely limited view. Carroll and Campbell (1989) discuss a number of claims as to what HCI is, and end up with the claim: "HCI exists to provide an understanding of usability and of how to design usable computer artifacts." We support this switch from viewing HCI as a domain, to thinking of it as more of a design discipline that has as its goal the provision of more usable (and useful) artifacts.

From the point of view of the software practitioner, or designer, in the workplace today, HCI is often viewed as the province of human factors, or ergonomics personnel, who might be involved in user task analyses and perhaps later in display and layout considerations. Within this framework certain design guidelines might be taken into account, and basic physiological and perceptual capabilities of the person recognized as forming constraints on the ultimate system. But this role of traditional human factors is very limited. Research emphasis is on evaluation of existing systems, and not on supporting the whole process of design, or suggesting new designs.

A more recent view, as shown in the development of the Xerox Star system, is to involve people concerned with HCI from the outset of the design phase. Rather than the interface being an afterthought, it is seen as an integral part of the whole system, determining the whole design. "We have learned from Star the importance of formulating the fundamental concepts (the user's conceptual model) before software is written, rather than tacking on a user interface afterward. . . . It was designed before the functionality of the system was fully decided." This view stresses "the crucial importance of a task analysis – the analysis of the task performed by the user, or users prior to introducing the computer system. Task analysis involves establishing who the users are, what their goals are in performing the task, what information they use in performing it, what information they generate, and what methods they employ" (Smith, Irby, Kimball, Verplank, & Harslem, 1982). Such task analyses do not always appear to be successful, and the standard acceptance of the utility of task analyses in the design of computer systems has been questioned by many researchers on systems development, particularly in Scandinavia (Bødker, 1987; Ehn & Kyng, 1984). Because the issue has theoretical as well as practical ramifications, we will pursue the topic briefly here.

A Critical Look at Task Analysis

Task analysis, as it has traditionally been conducted in HCI, as well as in traditional systems design more generally, is based on the idea that a description, containing all necessary information to build the computer application, can be made of the sequence of steps that it takes for a human being (in interaction with a computer) to conduct a task. This task analysis contains a detailed description of each step of the individual user's interaction with the computer application – for example, as inputs and outputs.

Similarly, in traditional systems design, the total information processing of the organization is described this way. What we often hear, when a computer application fails to function according to the needs and wishes of the users, is that the initial task or flow analysis was "not good enough." In our experience there is always something more that ought to have been included. Therefore, we might ask ourselves whether it is the very idea of making these kinds of specifications that is the problem (see Bødker, 1987; Ehn & Kyng, 1984) rather than inaccurate or incomplete analyses.[2] The major issue is exactly what we can describe in such a description, a problem that has different impacts in the design process. When we make task descriptions we make observations or perhaps interview workers about what they are doing. In the first case we often make observations without knowing the practice that we are studying, and in the second we capture people's explicit knowledge, or breakdown knowledge in Winograd and Flores's (1986) terms. In neither of these cases are we capable of catching the tacit knowledge that is required in many skilled activities, or the fluent action in the actual work process – that is, we believe that we will never be able to give a full description of a task. Nor can we ask the person to predict how he or she might act in a possible future situation. The person will not know until it is done; it is, if you will, "triggered" by the actual

---

2. Critiques of task analysis can be, and partly have been, made from different theoretical platforms: Ehn (1988) makes a critique based on the Wittgensteinian ordinary language tradition, Bødker (1987) from human activity theory. These analyses have been inspired by Winograd and Flores (1986) among others.

conditions met at the moment of acting, by the meeting with the real environment, not by any quantifiable set of conditions determined beforehand.

Even though it is possible to get to know something about the tacit knowledge of a person for certain purposes, neither the person herself nor any observer can predict which knowledge comes into play in a specific activity of use. This means that when we make task descriptions they will be of only future explicit – but not tacit – knowledge. Even these descriptions are problematic, however, as often the users cannot understand their own work from these descriptions. In the UTOPIA[3] project in the early 1980s, for instance, we spent several hours explaining WYSIWYG computer text composition to a typographer (we of course did not have such a system available), who was otherwise well trained in computer-supported composition. After several hours he remarked that we had just forgotten one thing in our presentation: What did the formatting codes that went into the file look like, totally missing the most important point about WYSIWYG – that the codes were not there at all! Similar observations have been made by many people who work with user interfaces design – for example, Wasserman (1981), who suggests that users try out prototypes to experience what the design is about. At the same time, Wasserman's idea is to do separate design of the user interface, once the functionality of the system is established. This, we find, introduces yet another problem, which will be discussed in the following.

The Problems of Separating the User Interface from the Application

Wasserman's way of doing design is one contribution to the larger question: According to what principles should user interfaces be designed, and who should do the design – software engineers, psychologists, perhaps the users themselves? Some have argued for the need to separate the interface design, for consistency and efficiency reasons, from the rest of the design, and perhaps hand it over to user interface specialists (see, e.g., Draper & Norman, 1984). On the surface this might have certain advantages. One could concentrate expertise about HCI, one could ensure a consistent interface across applications, or one could experiment with a variety of interface styles without affecting the functionality of the system, but there are serious dangers to it, as we are now beginning to realize.

What makes a good interface, viewed from the user's side, is often the fact that there is a good conceptual model behind the system that is made apparent in the system image (Norman, 1986). This requires a good understanding of the task domain for which the application is being developed, and for how users currently conceptualize the domain. Getting this part of the design right is the key to a usable system. A danger is that "user interface experts" may not have the required domain knowledge to be able to form these good domain models, and may spend their time on much narrower issues, such as dialog style choices. Good design should come from an understanding of how the application will be used and thus there is a

---

3. This project was concerned with the development of quality computer tools to assist graphics workers in laying out text and graphics for full-size newspaper production.

danger in further separating the application designer from the user, which could be the logical outgrowth of the approach favoring separability.[4]

Designers of User Interface Management Systems (UIMSs) are also becoming aware of problems in the separation of the interface from the semantics of the application. The issue is that we may neglect the importance of the semantics of the domain in determining how the interface needs to be, and concentrate on lexical and syntactic features that are (to the user) not as important (see Bødker, 1987; Tanner & Buxton, 1985). An experience from the Utopia project (Bødker, Ehn, Romberger, & Sjögren, 1985; Ehn & Kyng, 1984) illustrates this: In the page makeup tools designed by the UTOPIA project, the following examples of requirements for the computer application were given:

1. Text can be represented as characters if the font size is over 14 points; otherwise it is to appear as gray lines on the screen.
2. The page is to be shown in a limited number of distinct reduction–magnification scales. (This is intended to help the user judge the appearance of the page on the basis of what can be seen on the display screen.)
3. An article can be placed on the page ground in a variety of ways. The user can use a new kind of tool, the "ruler," which allows the text to "float" into the empty space on the page under direct control of the user, or use various kinds of "paper paste-up" techniques.

Requirements 1 and 2 are clearly about the interface. At the same time, they have strong implications for which functions the typographer has to do when using the tool – for example, whether he can do proofreading of text at the same time as he is working on the overall page. Requirement 3 is apparently about functions. At the same time, if we did not apply some kind of direct manipulation interface, the first of the mentioned functions in 3 would not be possible. The design of functions and the interface cannot be separated from each other in this example. And similarly, the hardware and software choices are equally important.

There is a lot of talk about the user interface, but what exactly *is* the interface? Where do we draw the boundary? We allude to this in the title of our chapter – "Beyond the Interface" – as the goal of building usable systems may be better served by focusing on the task domain, and not on the details of the interface per se.[5] Being provocative, perhaps the very concept of HCI as a distinct topic or discipline concerned with user interfaces needs to be rethought, and emphasis moved from surface similarities of systems, in terms of interaction style, to under-

---

4. As we will see, an activity theoretical framework supports the notion that the application should determine the interface, which is the point argued here.

5. Interestingly, Rosson, Maass, and Kellogg (1988) in their interview survey of software designers quote some designers angrily replying to this question of interface separability, as follows: "never separate the user interface and the rest of the application. There is no module for the interface, that's stupid . . . the computer should never make the user feel that there is something between him and the things he is dealing with."

standing their use. Are there ways, in what is currently considered HCI, of achieving this?

Reframing HCI Issues from Within

In looking at work that falls under the HCI label, we can see a number of different premises, not always articulated. The HCI area can be seen as an applied domain for the testing of general cognitive theories. The focus is on the theory or model, rather than on building better interfaces per se. Other researchers, especially those in commercial settings, are more driven by applied concerns, and wish to make a difference in our design of interfaces now, whether or not there is a clear "theory" behind the changes. The idea that solid theory spills down into applied practice, a not uncommon belief, has been shown to be quite untrue for many domains (see Carroll, 1989, for examples). To date, the HCI research contribution has been more to criticize current design practice for not paying enough attention to users (e.g., Gould & Lewis, 1985), or to offer rather general and often not very usable guidelines (e.g., Rubinstein & Hersh, 1984; Shneiderman, 1987), or to speculate on alternative ways of doing things in HCI without much practical grounding (e.g., many of the articles in Norman & Draper, 1986).

It is generally accepted today that "Design is where the action is" to quote a memorable phrase of Allen Newell's. This is echoed in a comment by Carroll and Campbell (1989): "Impact on design practice is the touchstone of a successful approach to HCI." So how can cognitive science HCI work impact design? Newell and Card (1985) argue that what is needed to really help designers are specific calculational models of users that can be utilized in practical design. The argument about the practicality and utility of such calculational models in general, and especially the claim that this is the most important, if not the only way in which psychology and cognitive science can contribute to design, has been rather exhaustively discussed (Carroll & Campbell, 1986; Newell & Card, 1985, 1986) and we will not rehash it here, other than to voice support for a "science" of HCI that is broader than that conceived in the pathbreaking, but limited work of Card, Moran, and Newell (1983).

Many cognitive science–oriented HCI groups are currently active in "user modeling," looking at the structure, content, and dynamics of user cognition at the interface. Much work in the area continues the GOMS model tradition of Card et al. (1983), extending it in various ways. While meeting with limited success in very narrow domains, there are acknowledged to be a number of rather serious problems in trying to extend the technique. The question is whether these problems are ones that can be overcome, or whether they are fundamental barriers to the use of such an approach in actual design situations. Our view tends toward the latter, as these are ideal models of what users should do, not what they actually do, and they cover a very narrow range of user activities (see the chapter by Greif in this volume for more detailed comment).

In this regard, the recent wave of interest in Programmable User Models (PUMs) (Young, Green, & Simon, 1989) that are based on a generalized architecture of human cognition seem to be also unduly narrow. Rather than moving designers closer to actual users, such a device, if it existed, would seem to support the view that real contact with users was unnecessary, as the designer could just program the PUM in order to understand the "human constraints." The very vision of a PUM seems to us a rather abstract view of human activity in the world, and to imply a rather strange relationship between designers and users. As Reisner (1987) notes in her discussion of earlier modeling work, such user modeling can never replace prototyping and actual empirical user testing, although it might have a role at a certain stage in the design of a new system.[6]

Even within the cognitive science–HCI world, there are voices raised in concern at the level of adequacy of our theoretical accounts, and the low level of generalizability of many experimental results. For a good example of this, we would note the comments of Gray and Atwood (1988) in their review of *Interfacing Thought* (Carroll, 1987), a collection of papers on cognitive science and HCI. This is quite rightly seen as an excellent collection that captured the state of the art (and science) not so long ago. They note that "there are no examples of developed systems and no discussion of designing in the 'real world' in this collection." Perhaps particularly damning, in the light of our concern for developing theory that can be used by designers, is the comment by the reviewers that they are reluctant to encourage designers to read the book, as "the book will not convince the skeptical designer of the relevance of the cognitive sciences" (Gray & Atwood, 1988). Within the book itself, the comments of the discussants, Reisner, and Whiteside and Wixon, also sound some warning bells about the lack of relevance of much of the work for practical design activities. One positive step in linking cognitive science models to real situations is the recent scenario work of Young and others (Young & Barnard, 1987; Young, Barnard, Simon, & Whittington, 1989). This attempt to make the very narrow cognitive theories more relevant to real contexts is an interesting one, though it should not be regarded as a substitute for actual testing, as there will always be abstractions from the real situation that may appear trivial yet have important consequences.

Besides the critique of the limited applicability of the models developed by cognitive science–HCI research to date we also have had critique of our experimental manipulations from within the field. For example, in several recent papers, Landauer (1987a, 1987b) has decried the poverty of many of our experimental manipulations, and attempts to push psychology out of the laboratory setting in order to be more directly relevant to human needs in the workplace. He notes: "There is no sense in which we can study cognition meaningfully divorced from the task contexts in which it finds itself in the world." Yet this admission is not followed in practice. Whiteside and Wixon (in Carroll, 1987) give some nice examples of how far removed some of the cognitive science work is from real world situations. It is

---

6. Our focus is on how to design usable artifacts that are satisfying for users to work with, and we believe that this requires design to have its origins in the work process. Of course, there may be some benefit to having a designer program a user model; our argument here has to do with how central a role these models should play in the overall design process, relative to other activities.

this lack of appreciation of the use setting that is, in our view, a major problem with much of the cognitive science–HCI work to date.

A First Look at Artifacts

Recently, Carroll and his colleagues have developed an account of HCI that focuses on the nature of the computer artifacts created for use, and they analyze the psychological theory "embedded" in the artifact (e.g., Carroll, 1989a, 1989b; Carroll & Campbell, 1989; Carroll & Kellogg, 1989). It is claimed that this approach overcomes the problems with the earlier "human factors" and "cognitive description" paradigms in HCI (Carroll, 1989a).

Carroll argues that we should view the artifacts created by designers as HCI theories, which can be abstracted from the artifact (see Carroll, Kellogg, & Rosson, this volume, for further details on how this is done). In our view, the idea that artifacts embody theories is not as novel as is suggested in Carroll and Campbell (1989).[7] However, Carroll and Kellogg (1989) go on to develop this idea in more detail than has been done elsewhere, in trying to show the specific psychological claims made by specific artifacts. Although the idea is interesting, the results of this approach, or the example analyses so far presented, of HyperCard and the Training Wheels approach, do not seem to us particularly enlightening. We think this is partly due to the form of the analysis that is done, trying to fit the psychological claims into a very general goals, planning–acting, evaluation framework. We are not at all clear on how such analyses can contribute to inventing better artifacts, which is one of the claims made for this approach. Indeed, despite the claim that these analyses are done in the context of the "task–artifact" cycle, it appears that the analyses are too focused on the artifact, and not on the artifact in use. More recent work in this tradition (Carroll et al., this volume) addresses some of our criticisms – for example, using scenarios as the basis for claims extraction rather than generic analyses – but it remains to be seen whether it will be sufficient.

Can we put an artifact under the spotlight and discern its uses, never mind its design rationale? We think this is extremely problematic. For the artifact reveals itself to us fully only *in use*. A good example of this point comes from an area such as archaeology, where people must try to make up a theory of what a thing is, apparently based only on the object itself. A closer analysis, however, shows that this is not usually the case. Despite the inability to observe the artifact in actual use, researchers pay particular attention to the local context of the artifact, in terms of the location of the artifact on the site (e.g., the kitchen, garbage dump) and the objects that are physically copresent with it. This is why archaeologists are so concerned about *not* removing objects from their setting until all such analyses are

---

7. For example, Buxton (1986) gives an amusing account of the underlying model of the human user that might be inferred from an analysis of existing artifacts – at the perceptual-motor level – and in the same collection Bannon (1986) notes how all artifacts contain a theory of the user (and of the task domain) with reference to the KISS (Keep it Simple, Stupid) and "idiot-proof" design philosophies that were implicit in some HCI work.

completed.[8] They also consult old manuscripts for references to uses of the object, for drawings of activities with the tool in use, and so forth. The artifact is thus interpreted always as an object that is used by people to perform activities. Without analyzing it in its setting we are bound to overemphasize other aspects of the artifact that may not be crucial in the use setting. Thus, as many authors have argued, *a tool is what it is used for.*

In the understanding of artifacts, we would also like to emphasize the importance of studying the development of the artifact over time. Artifacts rarely spring into existence all at once, but are shaped by previous experiences over the years. Indeed, a general criticism of much HCI work is that it neglects development aspects, both of user competencies and of the tools themselves. The framework adopted by Carroll and colleagues for analyzing artifacts, while informative, seems to undervalue, in our view, analyses of the history of the artifact, and of the actual situations of use, both intended and, perhaps even more important, unintended (from the perspective of the original designer). To summarize, aspects of the "artifacts as theory" argument seem to fit into our own conceptions of what a reconstituted HCI field might usefully contribute to design, though we are not as optimistic as Carroll and others that such studies will inevitably lead to an important role for psychologists in inventing new ideas for artifacts (Carroll, 1989a) based on these analyses.

Bridging the Gaps

Other recent work in HCI – for example, the paper by Thomas and Kellogg (1989) – has attempted to bridge the gap between current HCI work and practical design. They acknowledge the problems of traditional human factors studies conducted in the laboratory, and discuss how to extend them into the world.[9] They talk of the "ecological gaps" caused by bringing studies into the lab, both by omission of factors in the real world, and by the addition of new elements in the testing situation that do not correspond to real world eventualities. They discuss the "user gap," based on individual differences, and motivations, which is often not addressed, and the "task gap," where the laboratory task may not generalize to actual work situations. But that's not all! There is the "problem formulation gap," which has to do with how the user realizes that a particular tool is appropriate for a task. There is the "artifact gap" where the application may not fit into other applications. The "extensionality gap" refers to the difference between brief laboratory use of a tool in an experiment and continuing use over perhaps years in a work setting. And perhaps one of the most important kinds of gaps from our point of view, due to their

---

8. See Larsen (1987) for a more extended account of archaeological methods that supports our description. His paper is concerned with the role of the archaeological metaphor in human memory studies, but the descriptions of archaeological work are quite relevant for our context here.

9. We do not mean to imply that nobody in the HCI community had addressed this issue before. The earlier work of people such as Gould, Lewis, and others at IBM and Whiteside and his colleagues at DEC should certainly be noted. See the chapters on usability by Gould and by Whiteside, Bennett, and Holtzblatt, both in Helander (1988), for a review of some of this work.

importance and diversity, is what Thomas and Kellogg refer to as "work-context gaps" concerning the social setting, the culture of the workplace, and so on.

Our interest in this particular paper here is not simply from the identification of the particular problems, useful as these are, as we believe that most of them have been stated before by a number of people in different contexts, but rather for other reasons: that it was written by people from within the HCI culture itself, that it was published in the widely read *IEEE Software* magazine, and that the authors have tried to "bridge the gaps" they have identified by offering some hints to researchers and designers. While we support the general concerns expressed in the paper, we are interested in whether another perspective on the "problems" of HCI might throw a different light on some of these issues, by reframing some of the questions. This need not imply the abandonment of existing techniques and theories, but rather the willingness to consider other theoretical frameworks and how they might recast some of the HCI questions. To keep to the "bridging" metaphor, if we walked up the road a little, maybe we would find some stepping stones across the "gaps," and thus not need to build all of the bridges in the first place. The next section gives a brief introduction to one such alternative approach, and attempts to show how it might be a useful basis for theory and practice in a reformulated HCI discipline.

Reframing HCI Issues from without

As we have seen, many attempts have been made to reframe issues from within the field of HCI. For us, the problem seems to be that most of these attempts appear to be "add-ons" or minor revisions to the traditional theoretical basis, driven by a growing concern for practical use of the theory. The question we are raising here is whether it is possible to come up with alternative theories that might give a coherent framework for understanding HCI as something inherently social, as an example of an aspect that traditional cognitive science–based HCI does not seem to be able to handle. What we are looking for are frameworks that start out from the praxis of a certain community, at the same time as they allow for an analysis of aspects that have been found of importance in traditional HCI. There have been a number of critiques of standard information-processing psychology and artificial intelligence research as a suitable framework for understanding human activity. For example, Lave (1988) provides a strong critique of the underlying assumptions in both cognitive psychology and anthropology and argues for a new understanding of human cognition that sees it as distributed across people and settings. Her account emphasizes the importance of praxis in understanding cognitive activities. From a somewhat different perspective, Suchman (1987) provides an insightful critique of various models of human reasoning that assume that a planning framework is adequate to understand human actions in settings. The book by Winograd and Flores (1986) presents yet another critique of current theoretical frameworks, arguing from a hermeneutic perspective that totally rejects the commonly accepted Cartesian, rationalist position underlying most Western theoretical frameworks.

As an example of an alternative framework, we will look at human activity theory as developed most thoroughly by the Soviet psychologist A. N. Leontiev, with its roots in the earlier work of the polymath L. S. Vygotsky. Vygotsky was, just like we are, developing his framework in reaction to the empiricist tradition that treated the human as a passive, reactive organism. More precisely, he wanted to develop a psychology that charted its way between the Scylla of behaviorism and the Charybdis of mentalism. In Hegel and Marx he found elements of a social theory of human activity, a historical view of human consciousness, and the concept of human praxis, which served as a basis for his theoretical reformulation of the field. (See Kozulin, 1986, for a useful historical account of the "activity theory" concepts that we utilize here.) The first thing to note is that this "theory" is a very general philosophical framework for understanding the development of human culture and individual personality based on dialectical materialism. It has ontogenetic and phylogenetic aspects. For these reasons it has also been referred to as the sociocultural or sociohistorical school.

There are many interpretations and also some more specific elaborations of human activity theory.[10] Raeithel (in press) provides a useful, more philosophically oriented introduction to the central tenets of this school. The books by Wertsch (1981, 1985) and Cole and Maltzman (1969) provide a useful introduction to this framework for Anglo-American readers. Also, for further background on the work of Vygotsky, the collection of papers in Vygotsky (1978) is a useful starting point. Our interpretation is primarily inspired by the writings of Engeström (1987), Karpatschof (1984), and Hydén (1981).

Central Tenets of Human Activity Theory – Mediation and Praxis

The fundamental concept in Soviet psychology as presented by Leontiev and others is to understand the dialectical relations between the development of the individual and the society in which the person exists. Aspects of the individual are not granted privileged status as they are within the Western rationalistic Cartesian model, but are to be explained as outgrowths of primarily social forces, some of which may become internalized over time. The theory takes its starting point in *human activity* as the basic component in purposeful human work.

In human activity theory, the basic unit of analysis is human (work) activity. Human activities are driven by certain needs where people wish to achieve a certain purpose. This activity is usually mediated by one or more instruments or tools (the concept of mediation is central to the whole theory). According to Kozulin (1986): "the main thing which distinguishes one activity from another, however, is the difference of their objects."

Because of the abstractness of these concepts, or rather their relative unfamiliar-

---

10. For example, the work of the German action theorists Hacker, Volpert, and others is a case of a specialization of the general activity theory framework that focuses on actions as the central organizing level for understanding human behavior but is compatible with the general framework of activity theory as we outline it here. See the articles in Frese and Sabini (1985) and Greif (this volume) for further information on this action perspective.

ity in the Anglo-American context, we have attempted to give a rather simple set of examples in the next few pages to try and give some insight into how the theoretical framework makes us view the world and human activity in the world in a different light to that of the standard view. It must be realized that what follows is a gross oversimplification, and interested readers are referred to other texts for elaboration of the theoretical perspective.

For example, the carpenter uses a saw and a hammer to produce a house out of wood and the like; the teacher uses language, books, pictures, and maps to teach her pupils geography. However, the carpenter building a house is not alone in the world. He works together with other carpenters, as well as with other building workers. The ensemble of carpenters divides the work between them. The ways of doing work, grounded in tradition and shared by a group of carpenters, nurses, or the like, we call practice or praxis. When getting trained as a carpenter or nurse one gets to share this praxis. At the same time each individual who holds a praxis continues the praxis, and he or she changes it as well, by coming up with new ways of doing things. It is this praxis that allows us to talk about more than just individual skills, knowledge, and judgment, and not just about a "generic" human being. In other words, we can talk about the appropriateness of a certain tool for a certain praxis.

Human beings always participate in various activities. If we look at a nurse working in a ward, he or she is part of the activity of getting the whole organizational machinery of the hospital going, the activities of caring for certain kinds of patients, and so on. These collective activities are structured according to the praxis of the particular society in which they take place. We need not go back many years to note that much of the caring done in hospitals today was done earlier by individual families at home. In most societies the division of labor has caused a separation between the needs of the individual and the purpose of the activity in which the person takes part: The nurse cares for others to earn a living, not because they are the people the nurse cares about per se.

Human beings mediate their activity by *artifacts:* The carpenter uses a hammer to drive a nail, the nurses use language and records to coordinate their actions toward the patients and each other. Tools, means to divide work, norms, and language can all be seen as artifacts for the activity: They are made by humans and they mediate the relations among human beings or between people and the material or product in different stages. One of the major contributions of Vygotsky was that he also viewed language and symbol systems as psychological tools for developing the human condition. Artifacts are there for us when we are introduced into a certain activity, but they are also a product of our activity, and as such they are constantly changed through the activity. This "mediation" is essential in the ways in which we can understand artifacts through activity theory.

Comparing this view to the view of artifacts in traditional HCI, we see two important points: If we want to study artifacts we cannot study them as things, we need to look at how they mediate use. Artifacts are not just means for individuals, they also carry with them certain ways of sharing and dividing work. Furthermore the artifacts have no meaning in isolation; they are given meaning only through their incorporation into social praxis (Ilyenkov, 1977). It is not until they have been incorporated in praxis that they can be the basis for thought and reflection.

So far we have looked at the *collective* side of human activity. Each activity is conducted through actions of individuals, directed toward an object or another subject. Building a house takes place because the carpenters carry the plywood, drive the nails, and cut the wood. Nursing is done by the nurses feeding patients, giving injections, and measuring temperatures. An action such as measuring a patient's body temperature contributes to the research activity or the caring activity, depending on our perspective. Activity is what gives meaning to our actions, though actions have their own goals, and the same actions can appear in different activities.

Each action that a human being conducts is implemented through a series of operations. To drive a nail means to hold and direct the hammer toward the nail, to hold the nail, to know the speed and angle of the hammer needed when hitting the nail. Giving an injection means noting the condition of the patient, finding the vein, and so on. Each operation is connected to the concrete physical or social conditions for conducting the action, and it is "triggered" by the specific conditions present at the time – for example, we know, without being conscious of it, that to secure a large nail (which is needed to hold a heavy piece of wood) we need a large hammer. These operations, which allow us to build houses or do nursing without thinking consciously about each little step, are often *transformed actions* – that is, we conduct them consciously as actions in the beginning. Through learning we transform them into operations, but on encountering changed conditions, we may have to reflect on them consciously again, and thus make former operations once more into conscious actions.

Two Views on Artifacts – As Things versus in Use

Artifacts, in a human activity framework, have a double character: They are objects in the world around us, which we can reflect on, and they mediate our interaction with the world, in which case they are not themselves objects of our activity in use. We use tools such as a hammer and saw through operations, where they are not objects of our activity.[11] Activity theory is not alone in this point of view. Polanyi (1967) talks about focal and subsidiary awareness, Winograd and Flores (1986) (borrowing from Heidegger) speak about ready-to-hand and present-at-hand. But what does it mean for our understanding of artifacts? In normal use situations our handling of artifacts is done through operations, and is not conscious to us. The carpenter focuses his attention on driving the nail, whereas he holds the hammer and moves it through operations. In certain situations the fluent hammering stops, the hammer does not respond to the actions of the carpenter, and it becomes an object in itself. To hold it and to move it require conscious actions, which prevent

---

11. In this regard, it is interesting to note that the meaning of the word *tool* is more transparent in other languages. For instance, the Danish word for tool is *Værktøj* and the German *Werkzeug*, which means "work clothes" or "work stuff" (the category *tøj/zeug* being a more general one than clothes, encompassing also, e.g., vehicles and military equipment).

the carpenter from focusing on the nail. To put it simply, an artifact works well in our activity if it allows us to focus our attention on the real object, and badly if it does not. However, even when we have difficulties with artifacts, people are adept at developing "new" operations that "work around" the problems, so that activities can be performed.

If we accept this perspective on the nature of artifacts we then need to study artifacts-in-use, not in isolation. And we need to study specific contexts of use, where the workers have a certain praxis. For example, we do not get to know much about how goldsmiths hammer from studying ordinary household hammering. Let us take an example from the HCI field: We need to study word-processor use in the hands of skilled secretaries, not in the hands of undergraduate college students. The praxis of the users is important. Here is the real meaning of "user-centered" system design.

Within this framework, artifacts are seen as historical devices that reflect the state of praxis up until the time that they are developed. This praxis in turn is shaped by the artifacts used, and so on. Artifacts can be characterized as *crystallized knowledge,* which means that operations that are developed in the use of one generation of technology are later incorporated into the artifact itself in the next. Continuing our carpentry example, we could imagine a world where the carpenters had only one kind of hammer. The skilled carpenters develop a repertoire of different ways of using this hammer, based on the size of the materials, the difficulty of striking the different nails, and so on. Sooner or later they start teaching their apprentices that there are these different ways of doing hammering, and later again, different hammers and nails start to evolve. Thus, to learn something about the present shape and use of an artifact, a historical analysis of artifacts as well as of praxis is important. Bærentsen (1989) gives interesting examples of how operations in one generation of weapon technology are reflected in artifacts developed in the next generation.

Switching focus back to HCI issues, we see that the activity approach puts emphasis on the use of computer applications, rather than simply the nature of the interface per se. The framework stresses that praxis within the application domain is important to understand the computer application, in design as well as in use. For example, as a psychologist or computer scientist, visiting a trade show, I am not able to "see" the user interface of a page makeup system, the way competent typographers who have been taught to use the system in their daily work do. The way we see the computer application, or the user interface if we like, is not primarily determined by our individualistic needs and understanding, but through the praxis, as typographer, psychologist, or designer, into which we have been trained. It is this switch in focus that gives a very different flavor to the activity-theory approach in contrast to traditional HCI studies of undifferentiated "users," where little or no attention is made to this aspect of the user experiences.

A Second Look at Artifacts in Use

A conclusion of our previous discussions is that a human activity approach to analysis of artifacts must include the actual praxis of use, as well as the specific material, social, and historical setting of that use. Engeström (1987), looking more widely at change processes in organizational settings, presents the following type of analysis of a work activity. His starting point is in a problem situation, where there is a reason for somebody to want a change (in our case, for somebody to want a new computer application). The idea is to look for contradictions within the activity and between this activity and surrounding activities, because they constitute the basis for change: He looks at contradictions in how tools, objects, subjects are seen, for example, so that a point-of-sales (POS) system is seen at the same time as a tool for the individual cashier to compute the total that the customer owes, and a tool for management to compare the cashier's work and wages with those of other workers. He suggests studying contradictions between, for example, the tools currently used and the object created, or the norms that are part of praxis and the division of work – for instance when a secretary is trying to produce a report containing an advanced layout with pictures using only a primitive text editor and some glue. Engeström discusses contradictions between this activity and different desired activity – for example, the secretary, again, may not be allowed to do advanced layout although he or she wishes to do so – and about contradictions between this activity and one of the activities that produced the tools, or materials. These contradictions are not necessarily observable in the activity at the same time, but looking for them in an analysis seems useful. We have not yet seen developed a more detailed analysis of HCI based on these contradictions, but we find that certainly these examples give hints as to the relevance of such an analysis. They explain something about why the artifact may not work, which we would not have found out by just analyzing the steps in an actual interaction process. For instance, if we had just looked at the text editor out of context, we would never have understood that it was inefficient in use, exactly because the secretary actually used it (and wanted to use it) differently from what was originally intended by the designers. Based on the analysis of Engeström we claim that artifacts are used differently from the original intentions, and this is why the need for new artifacts arises.[12]

Returning to an analysis of artifacts, we can start out from what kinds of contradictions the artifact is involved in. The following questions can be asked for each artifact: What is the object of the activity or actions in which the artifact is used? What is the outcome produced to be used for? To what extent is the artifact primarily dividing work, an instrument or tool of the actual production, or an enforcement of norms according to which we live? Let's look at the POS system again: Depending on our perspective, the object can be the serving of a customer, in which case, for example, the receipt that the customer gets is of importance, as is the service that the salesperson is able to provide. A more Tayloristic look at the same situation could suggest that the object is to get as many customers through the sales line as possible with the least effort. The most efficient way of registering sales and producing bills becomes important. There is also the management view of this same system: Management needs to divide work so that all customers get the same

---

12. This raises interesting questions about the nature of design, redesign-in-use, tailorability of systems, etc., which cannot be developed here. See Henderson (this volume) for further discussion.

treatment, so management may want to know which of the salespersons are too slow, relatively speaking. The outcome is a collection of statistics on percentage utilization of terminals and cashiers. The analysis in other words is not just a psychological analysis, but an integrated one of social relations, division of work, and so on.

As designers of computer applications, we also want a closer look at the artifacts in use, in particular at computer applications. In Bødker (1987, 1989) it is argued that when we look at computer applications, it is a good idea to look for conditions for the activity, which are set up through the artifact. The idea is that ideally, in the use situation, the user should direct operations, but not actions toward the computer artifact, in order to proceed smoothly, and not perform actions that require constant attention. In particular we should look for conditions for operations toward the artifact and for operations toward subjects or objects through the artifact. In the analysis where we are looking for these conditions, it is important to note where mediation breaks down and the user is forced to direct actions toward the artifact, because this will tell us where the conditions are inappropriate. The conditions that we are looking for can be divided into physical conditions that support the physical adaptation of the artifact to the user (e.g., the layout of the keyboard), handling conditions (e.g., the way menus work), and conditions for operations toward an object or a subject through the artifact (e.g., how formating is done on a text document).

This approach focuses on how the computer application appears to its user in use. It suggests that we ought to talk about human operation of a computer application rather than that of human–computer interaction (Bødker, 1987).[13] What we want is software and hardware supporting the human operation of the computer application in a specific type of use activity, constituting some of the material conditions for triggering specific operations in a specific use situation. This study must be done within the frame of certain activities carried out within a certain praxis. The role of praxis within groups or ensembles in the theory makes it possible to deal with human–computer interaction not just concerning an individual user but for groups who share a praxis.

Using human activity theory we see that there is a difference between the use situation where the computer-based artifact is operated while focusing on some other object or subject (e.g., when the secretary is using a word processor), and the design situation where the computer-based artifact is one of the objects and outcomes (e.g., when we are designing the word processor). What does this double role mean for the design activity?

Implications for Design

Design of artifacts in this framework can be viewed as a process in which we determine and create the conditions that turn an object into an artifact of use. The

---

13. A further distinction between artifacts as tools and machines may be relevant for a more fine-grained discussion, but we must omit this discussion here as it would lead too far from our current focus.

future use situation is the origin for design, and we design with this in mind. Use, as a process of learning, is a prerequisite to design. Through use, new needs arise, either as a result of changing conditions of work or as a recognition of problems with the present artifacts. To design with the future use activity in mind also means to start out from the present praxis of the group(s) of people that are the projected future users. It is through their experiences that the need for design has arisen, either directly through use of the artifact or through conflicts between the current use and demands from external forces (e.g., management), and it is their praxis that is to be applied and changed in the future use activity. Recognizing this, the UTO-PIA project based its design strategy on the idea that computer support should be designed to be a collection of tools for the skilled worker to use.

A computer application is seen as providing the user with a tool-kit containing tools which under complete and continuous control of the user can be applied to fashion materials into more refined products. The user is seen as a person who possesses skills relevant within the domain. The development of computer-based tools is based on this; that tools are used by skilled users to create high-quality products. (Bødker, Ehn, Kammersgaard, Kyng, & Sundblad, 1987)

To start out from the skilled workers' present practice, in this case, meant a learning process for both workers and designers. Mutual workplace visits, simulation of present work processes on mock-up equipment, and mutual analyses of the history of typographical tools were just some of the ways in which this was accomplished.

Design of computer-based artifacts is a meeting place for many different practices, where sharing experiences is something which requires a deliberate effort. Design is a process of learning, when viewed both as a collective process and as an individual process for the participants. The different groups involved learn about the praxis of the other participating groups. For all groups the confrontation with practices of other groups contributes to learning about their own praxis. This, at the same time, brings to design an innovative character: The confrontation with different practices, and thus, with one's own, is opening possibilities for new ways of doing things, and transcending the traditional praxis of the users.

Design is trying to predict the future, without ever being able to fully predict it. We should note the never-ending "wheel of design" here (see Henderson, this volume), as design will change the activity and introduce new contradictions (which may in turn lead to new design, etc.). In particular, in relation to HCI, the human activity approach focuses on the character of the operations and their material conditions: Operations and their conditions for a specific activity will change, and for that reason it is necessary to focus on both actual operations and conditions, and future changed ones. However, we cannot, by asking people to predict their future operations in a future action, get the full truth about these actions and operations; they are triggered by the material conditions, by the meeting with the specific sociocultural situation, not by any quantifiable set of conditions: "For a user to recognize a good tool from a bad one it must be tried out in the work process. . . . This means that in the design process we need experiments" (Bødker et al., 1987).

(By "experiments" here we mean experimental design where users try out proto-types and mock-ups, a different meaning to the traditional psychological idea of "experiments.") We agree with Engeström (1987) that when we, based on our investigations of the domain (the artifacts used, the use setting, the use of proto-types), design a new artifact, we theoretically predict how the new use process will be. But we will never be able to find the full truth – there is always a difference between the predicted new and how the situation actually is changed by the artifact – which in turn creates conflicts that lead to further design activities.

To design an artifact means not only to design the "thing" or device that can be used by human beings as an artifact in a specific kind of activity. As the use of artifacts is part of social activity, we design new conditions for collective activity (e.g., a new division of labor), and new ways of coordination, control, and commu-nication. Design of educational support is thus also important, because the artifact is to be integrated into an existing praxis. The introduction of the artifact changes not only the operational aspects of the artifact, but also the other aspects of praxis. A good educational process can facilitate this change.

Summarizing these discussions, it seems that we have to take the use process, and not the artifact, as the central object for our study. The way cognition is viewed in human activity theory is socially and historically situated, and it is tied to the physical conditions in which it takes place. Whatever action a human being makes in the world, this action is mediated by artifacts. In this view, the study of mediation becomes essential for HCI.

Differing Perspectives: Some Lessons from Software Engineering

To a large extent we find that the traditions we have presented in this chapter constitute different, complementary, and at times contradictory perspectives on HCI. In her paper on software engineering, Floyd (1987) talks about parallel experi-ences, comparing two "paradigms" in software engineering, the traditional perspec-tive, which she calls *product*-oriented, and an emerging new perspective, called *process*-oriented. In this discussion she identifies a number of issues that the two perspectives deal with differently. We have found these issues useful in our attempt to discuss the different perspectives in and around HCI, because the focus in both areas is to build more useful and usable computer applications for people. It is neither Floyd's idea, nor is it ours, to claim that one perspective is always better than the other. Instead we aim to recognize the limitations as well as the utility in each of the perspectives. In many ways, though, her attitude is similar to ours:

Taking the product-oriented perspective as the ruling paradigm, however, these problems (user acceptance, etc.) must be considered as additional aspects outside the realm of systematic treatment. They may influence how we proceed in actual projects, while the product-oriented perspective models are what we supposedly should aim for, ideally. . . . I hold this situation is inherently unsatisfactory and can only be remedied if we adopt – in research, teaching and professional practice – the richer process-oriented perspective as our primary point of view. (Floyd, 1987)

Floyd first discusses differing views on computer applications (which she calls *programs*). The distinction can be made between the traditional view, which holds that computer applications are self-contained objects that are derived by formalized procedures, the correctness being provable by formalized methods or models, and the alternative process-oriented view, which holds that computer applications are tools for people, designed in a learning process, adequacy being established in a process of controlled use and subsequent revision. The traditional view that Floyd presents in software engineering fits closely to that of traditional cognitive science approaches to HCI, as we have discussed in here. The kinds of formalized procedures are somewhat different, aiming not at mathematically provable programs, but at mathematically tractable user models and measurable, statistically significant experimental results. A more process-oriented view is represented not only in the human activity approach but also for example in the work of Whiteside and Wixon (1988).

Floyd makes a distinction between the traditional view, which sees the user organization as static, with the interaction between the person and the computer as something fixed and predefined, and the designer appearing as an outside observer. Again, this comes close to traditional cognitive science frameworks. The alternative perspective notes that organizations are under continuous change, that human–computer interaction changes accordingly, and that the designer cannot avoid being involved in these changes. This alternative perspective is partially represented from within a cognitive science tradition by, for example, Campbell, Carroll, & DiBello, (1989), and by Engeström as a representative of the human activity tradition.

A static view of the user organization is behind the assumption that a task analysis is a sufficient basis for design – that is, once uncovered, the tasks are assumed to remain the same throughout the design process. The idea of the designer (pyschologist) as an outside observer is also inherent in many of the cognitive science positions we have seen (Whiteside & Wixon excluded). In opposition to this stands again the human activity approach where it is a fundamental belief that we cannot design the future totally, and that design is a learning and change process for *all* the involved parties, both designers and users.

Concerning the concept of quality, two points are important: In the product-oriented view quality is associated with features of the product, and moves, in a sense, from the computer application toward the user (e.g., user friendliness). From the process-oriented view, quality has to do with the *process of use,* and is defined in terms of relevance and adequacy for the user when dealing with the computer application. Notice the language we use in HCI: people as "users" of a piece of technology, rather than people who are doing real work. Our view of "users" may have progressed and expanded since the days when we discussed "idiot-proof" systems, but many current interfaces to systems have a very rigid underlying model of the human being who is expected to use the device. Our emphasis in many cases is still on "easy to use" systems – the lowest common denominator approach we could call it, which assumes most people are relatively dumb and need an interface to suit.

Floyd talks about competence in the product-oriented view in terms of operating the application, and errors as improper operation and incompetence. In the process-oriented view competence has to do with the work task being conducted with the help of the application, and errors are viewed as a precondition for acquiring new competence. Errors are thus inherently connected with learning. In many cognitive science studies the examples deal only with novices conducting very specific tasks, detached from any real work situation. The lack of concern with learning over time (weeks, months, years) is a serious neglect in many studies to date. What happens to the skills of the users as they master the new artifact? Do the traditional skills atrophy, or remain stagnant, or are there new avenues for growth? From the human activity theory the continuous encounters with "errors" (breakdowns) are the driving force, both in understanding how a certain artifact works in real use, and in understanding how the artifact eventually gets changed. Even though human activity theory stresses that we cannot fully predict the future, designers (and activity theorists as well) are of course trying to predict the future all the time, and it is recommended to build into the computer application flexibility as to how objects can be treated through the application, depending on the repertoire of operations of the user.

Paradoxically most of the researchers mentioned under the "reframing from within" section in this chapter wish to include many of the aspects covered by the process-oriented side, at the same time, though, as they maintain an ideal of being able to do design based principally on analysis rather than interaction with real people conducting work. We find it necessary to take a more radical step out to where the users are, at the same time as we share Carroll's concern, namely to find a theory to explain what we are doing. What we have to show in this chapter is that such theories exist, but that currently they are not nearly as instrumental for detailed studies of HCI. In other words, there is still work to be done both theoretically and empirically before we can give an adequate account of the HCI field within an alternative framework. We see this as a gap to be bridged in the future.

Conclusion

We have raised questions concerning the status of the HCI field, and the status of supposed underlying disciplines, such as cognitive science, and even cognitive psychology, as currently constituted, but our emphasis is on design issues. If our quest is to design more usable computer artifacts, then a better knowledge of the "users" is required as a part of our analysis – one that sees people acting in a situation, with motives, and intentions, in interaction with others and the environment. We subscribe to the idea that good design comes from an empathy with the work process itself, with possibilities for individual and societal growth. As scientists and researchers we are not removed from, but are ourselves a part of the process. We argue for more design to be done in conjunction with those using the technology, but that does not mean that psychological methods have no role. We are concerned that the separation of a field of activity such as HCI may not be the best way to proceed, as it tends to emphasize aspects of the interface per se rather than how people can be supported in their work practice. Domain knowledge is crucial as we have noted. A framework such as activity theory – which looks at ongoing human interaction with the world, and encompasses relations with others, and the sociohistorical mediation of learning and development – seems to provide an interesting alternative framework if we wish to develop a more comprehensive unit of analysis for our studies. Perhaps the real challenge we face is how to combine aspects of these different perspectives so that the end result, or more correctly, the continually evolving applications we develop, can utilize the knowledge gained from differing approaches.

Acknowledgments

We would like to thank Klaus Bærensten, Arne Raeithel, Preben Mogensen, and Steen Folke Larsen for comments on earlier drafts of this paper, and John M. Carroll for editorial comments.

References

Bannon, L. (1985). *Extending the design boundaries of human–computer interaction* (ICS report 8505). San Diego: University of California, Institute for Cognitive Science.

Bannon, L. (1986). Issues in design: Some notes. In D. A. Norman & S. W. Draper (Eds.), *User centered system design: New perspectives on human–computer interaction* (pp. 25–30). Hillsdale, NJ: Lawrence Erlbaum Associates.

Bernsen, N.O. (1988, October). *Cognitive science – A European perspective.* Report to the FAST program of the Commission of the European Communities.

Bødker, S. (1990). *Through the interface – A human activity approach to user interface design.* Hillsdale, NJ: Lawrence Erlbaum Associates.

Bødker, S. (1989). A human activity approach to user interfaces. *Human–Computer Interaction, 4*(3), 171–195.

Bødker, S., Ehn, P., Kammersgaard, J., Kyng, M., & Sundblad, Y. (1987). A Utopian experience. In G. Bjerknes, P. Ehn, & M. Kyng (Eds.), *Computers and democracy – A Scandinavian challenge* (pp. 251–278). Aldershot, UK: Avebury.

Bødker, S., Ehn, P., Romberger, S., & Sjögren, D. (Eds.). (1985). *Graffiti 7. The UTOPIA project. An alternative in text and images.* Stockholm: Arbetslivscentrum.

Buxton, W. (1986). There's more to interaction than meets the eye: Some issues in manual input. In D. A. Norman & S. W. Draper (Eds.), *User centered system design: New perspectives on human–computer interaction* (pp. 319–337). Hillsdale NJ: Lawrence Erlbaum Associates.

Bærensten, K. (1989). Mennesker og maskiner [People and machines]. In M. Hedegaard, V. R. Hansen, & S. Thyssen (Eds.), *Et Virksomt Liv [An active life]* (pp. 142–187). Aarhus: Aarhus Universitets Forlag.

Campbell, R., Carroll, J., & DiBello, L. (1989, June). *Human–computer interaction: The case for a developmental approach to expertise.* Paper presented at the Jean Piaget Society meeting, Philadelphia.

Card, S., Moran T., & Newell, A. (1983). *The psychology of human–computer interaction.* Hillsdale, NJ: Lawrence Erlbaum Associates.

Carroll, J. (1989a). Evaluation, description and invention: Paradigms for human–computer interaction. In M. C. Yovits (Ed.), *Advances in Computers* (Vol. 29, pp. 44–77). London: Academic Press.

Carroll, J. (1989b). Taking artifacts seriously. In S. Maass & H. Oberquelle (Eds.), *Software-Ergonomie '89* (pp. 36–50). Stuttgart: Tentner.

Carroll, J. (Ed.). (1987). *Interfacing thought: Cognitive aspects of human–computer interaction.* Cambridge, MA: MIT Press.

Carroll, J. M., & Campbell, R. L. (1986). Softening up hard science: Reply to Newell and Card. *Human–Computer Interaction, 2,* 227–249.

Carroll, J., & Campbell, R. (1989). *Artifacts as psychological theories: The case of human–computer interaction* (IBM RC 13454, No. 60225). Yorktown Heights, NY: IBM.

Carroll, J., & Kellogg, W. (1989). Artifact as theory-nexus: Hermeneutics meets theory-based design. In K. Bice & C. Lewis (Eds.), *Proceedings of CHI '89: Human Factors in Computing Systems* (pp. 7–14). New York: ACM.

Cole, M., John-Steiner, V., Scribner, S., & Souberman, E. (Eds.). (1978). *Mind in society: The development of higher mental processes* (by L. S. Vygotsky). Cambridge, MA: Harvard University Press.

Cole, M., & Maltzman, I. (Eds.). (1969). *A handbook of contemporary Soviet psychology.* New York: Basic Books.

Draper, S., & Norman, D. (1984). Software engineering for user interfaces. In *Proceedings of the 7th International Conference on Software Engineering* (pp. 214–220). Silver Spring, MD: IEEE Computer Society Press.

Ehn, P. (1988). *Work-oriented design of computer artifacts.* Falköping, Sweden: Arbetslivscentrum/Almqvist & Wiksell International.

Ehn, P., & Kyng, M. (1984). A tool perspective on design of interactive computers for skilled workers. In M. Sääksjärvi (Ed.), *Proceedings from the Seventh Scandinavian Research Seminar of Systemeering* (pp. 211–242). Helsinki: Helsinki Business School.

Ehn, P., & Kyng, M. (1987). The collective resource approach to systems design. In G. Bjerknes, P. Ehn, & M. Kyng (Eds.), *Computers and democracy – A Scandinavian challenge* (pp. 17–58). Aldershot, UK: Avebury.

Engeström, Y. (1987). *Learning by expanding.* Helsinki: Orienta-Konsultit.

Floyd, C. (1987). Outline of a paradigm change in software engineering. In G. Bjerknes, P. Ehn, & M. Kyng (Eds.), *Computers and democracy – A Scandinavian challenge* (pp. 191–212). Aldershot, UK: Avebury.

Frese, M., & Sabini, J. (Eds.) (1985). *Goal-directed behavior: The concept of action in psychology.* London: Lawrence Erlbaum Associates.

Gould, J. (1988). How to design usable systems. In M. Helander (Ed.), *Handbook of human–computer interaction* (pp. 757–790). Amsterdam: North-Holland.

Gould, J., & Lewis, C. (1985). Designing for usability: Key principles and what designers think. *Communications of the ACM 28*(3), 300–311.

Gray, W. D., & Atwood, M. E. (1988, October). Review of J. M. Carroll (Ed.), *Interfacing thought.* In *SIGCHI Bulletin,* 88–91.

Helander, M. (Ed.) (1988). *Handbook of human–computer interaction.* Amsterdam: North-Holland.

Hydén, L.-C. (1981). *Psykologi och Materialism. Introduktion till den materialistiska psykologin (Psychology and materialism: An introduction to materialistic psychology).* Stockholm: Prisma.

Ilyenkov, E. V. (1977). *Dialectical logic: Essays on its history and theory.* Moscow: Progress Publishers.

Karpatschof, B. (1984). Grænsen for automatisering (The limit of automation). *Psyke og Logos 2,* 201–20.

Kozulin, A. (1986). The concept of activity in Soviet psychology. *American Psychologist, 41*(3) 264–274.

Landauer, T. (1987a). Psychology as a mother of invention. In J. Carroll & P. Tanner (Eds.), *Proceedings of CHI + GI '87: Human Factors in Computing Systems and Graphics Interface (Toronto, April 4–6)* (pp. 333–335). New York: ACM.

Landauer, T. (1987b). Relations between Cognitive Psychology and Computer Systems Design. In J. Carroll (Ed.), *Interfacing thought: Cognitive aspects of human–computer interaction* (pp. 1–25). Cambridge, MA: MIT Press.

Larsen, S.F. (1987). Remembering the archaeology metaphor. *Metaphor and Symbolic Activity, 2*(3) 187–199.

Lave, J. (1988). *Cognition in practice.* Cambridge: Cambridge University Press.

Leontiev, A. N. (1978). *Activity, consciousness, and personality.* Englewood Cliffs, NJ: Prentice-Hall.

Leontiev, A. N. (1981). The Problem of Activity in Psychology. In J. V. Wertsch (Ed.), *The concept of activity in Soviet psychology.* Armonk, NY: Sharpe.

Newell, A., & Card, S. K. (1985). The prospects for psychological science in human–computer interaction. *Human–Computer Interaction, 1,* 209–242.

Newell, A., & Card, S. K. (1986). Straightening out softening up: Response to Carroll and Campbell. *Human–Computer Interaction, 2,* 251–267.

Newell, A., & Simon, H. (1972). *Human problem solving.* Englewood Cliffs, NJ: Prentice-Hall.

Norman, D. (1980). Twelve issues for cognitive science. *Cognitive Science, 4,* 1–32.

Norman, D. A. (1986). Cognitive engineering. In D. A. Norman & S. W. Draper (Eds.), *User centered system design: New perspectives on human–computer interaction* (pp. 31–62). Hillsdale, NJ: Lawrence Erlbaum Associates.

Norman, D. A., & Draper, S. W. (Eds.). (1986). *User centered system design: New perspectives on human–computer interaction.* Hillsdale, NJ: Lawrence Erlbaum Associates.

Polanyi, M. (1967). *Personal knowledge.* London: Rutledge & Kegan Paul.

Pylyshyn, Z. (1984) *Computation and cognition: Towards a foundation for cognitive science.* Cambridge, MA: MIT Press

Raeithel, A. (in press). Semiotic self-regulation and work: An activity-theoretical foundation for design. In R. Budde, C. Floyd, R. Keil-Slawik, & H. Züllighoven (Eds.), *Software development and reality construction.* Berlin: Springer Verlag.

Reisner, P. (1987). Discussion: HCI, What it is and what research is needed. In J. Carroll (Ed.), *Interfacing thought: Cognitive aspects of human–computer interaction* (pp. 337–352). Cambridge, MA: MIT Press.

Rosson, M., Maass, S., & Kellogg, W. (1988). The designer as user: Building requirements for design tools from design practice. *Communications of the ACM 31*(11), 1288–1298.

Rubinstein, R., & Hersh, H. (1984). *The human factor: Designing computer systems for people.* Burlington, MA: Digital Press.

Shneiderman, B. (1987). *Designing the user interface: Strategies for effective human–computer interaction.* Reading, MA: Addison-Wesley.

Smith, D. C., Irby, C., Kimball, R., Verplank, B., & Harslem, E. (1982, April). Designing the Star User Interface. *Byte, 7*(4), 242–282.

Suchman, L. (1987). *Plans and situated actions: The problem of human–machine communication.* Cambridge: Cambridge University Press.

Tanner, P., & Buxton, W. (1985). Some issues in future user interface management system (UIMS) development. In G. Pfaff (Ed.), *User Interface Management Systems* (pp. 67–80). Berlin and Heidelberg: Springer Verlag.

Thomas, J., & Kellogg, W. (1989, January). Minimizing ecological gaps in user interface design. *IEEE Software,* 78–86.

Vygotsky, L. (1978). *Mind in society: The development of higher mental processes.* (M. Cole, V. John-Steiner, S. Scribner, & E. Sauberman, Eds.). Cambridge, MA: Harvard University Press.

Wasserman, A. I. (1981). Software tools in the user engineering environment. In A. I. Wasserman (Ed.), *Tutorial: Software development environments* (pp. 181–194). Washington, DC: IEEE Computer Society Press.

Wertsch, J. V. (1985). *Vygotsky and the social formation of mind.* Cambridge, MA: Harvard University Press.

Wertsch, J. V. (Ed.). (1981). *The concept of activity in Soviet psychology.* Armonk, NY: Sharpe.

Whiteside, J., Bennett, J., & Holtzblatt, K. (1988). Usability engineering: Our experience and evolution. In M. Helander (Ed.), *Handbook of human–computer interaction* (pp. 791–818). Amsterdam: North-Holland.

Whiteside, J., & Wixon, D. (1987). Discussion: Improving Human–Computer Interaction – A Quest for Cognitive Science. In J. Carroll (Ed.), *Interfacing thought: cognitive aspects of human–computer interaction* (pp. 353–365). Cambridge, MA: MIT press.

Whiteside, J., & Wixon, D. (1988). Contextualism as a world view for the reformation of meetings. In D. Tatar (Ed.), *Proceedings of the Conference on Computer Supported Cooperative Work (CSCW '88)* (pp. 369–375). New York: ACM.

Winograd, T., & Flores, C. F. (1986). *Understanding computers and cognition: A new foundation for design.* Norwood, NJ: Ablex.

Young, R.M., & Barnard, P. (1987). The use of scenarios in human–computer interaction research. In J. Carroll & P. Tanner (Eds.), *Proceedings of CHI + GI '87: Human Factors in Computing Systems and Graphics Interface (Toronto, April 4–7).* New York: ACM.

Young, R. M., Barnard, P., Simon, T., & Whittington, J. (1989). How would your favorite user model cope with these scenarios? *SIGCHI Bulletin, 20*(4), 51–55.

Young, R. M., Green, T. P., & Simon, T. (1989). Programmable user models for predictive evaluation of user interface designs. In K. Bice & C. Lewis (Eds.), *Proceedings of CHI '89: Human Factors in Computing Systems.* New York: ACM Press.

13
A Development Perspective on Interface, Design, and Theory
Austin Henderson

This book is concerned with the role of theory in human–computer interaction, a key concern of which is the creation of human–computer interfaces. As a designer, and as a researcher who is interested in the processes of design, I see this as a question about the role of theory in a particular human activity – the designing of human–computer interfaces. In order to understand the role of theory, one must first understand the activity. Consequently this chapter will primarily explore the nature of the activity of designing interfaces. At the end it will address the consequent role of theory in that activity.

It has been said that design is a process of making things right (Caplan, 1982, p. 9). Even this plain (but not simple) view captures the fact that design is an interplay between two entities: the "things" being made right and the "process" of the making. Consequently, to understand the design of human–computer interfaces it will be useful to look at three components: the interfaces, the process of making them, and the interplay between these two. I argue that each of these three components must be understood more broadly than is traditionally done: Interfaces must be understood to include not only the technology, but also the work applications in which it is used, and the practices of that work. To make interfaces right requires not an isolated act of creation but rather a continuing process of development incorporating many acts of inventing, embodying, experiencing, observing, and analyzing carried out by many people in many roles. And not only must the interface be the focus of the processes of development, but, with tailorable technology, development must be included in the subject matter of the interface.

This chapter first addresses these three shifts in viewpoint, resulting in an argument that the development process is central to the reality of human–computer interfaces in use and that their design is best understood from that perspective. A model of the development process follows, and a metaphor to support it is presented. Finally, from this "design in development" perspective, it is argued that theory's role in user interface design is to serve the processes of development, including the need to provide domain theories for the subject matter of the interfaces, including folk development.

From Interface to Work

In exploring the design of human–computer interfaces, the first component that must be addressed is the issue of what is included in the human–computer interface. What is the subject matter of human–computer interaction? Consider an office copier. Although it is ostensibly much less complex in user interface than a computer workstation, or even than most single applications, it is nonetheless a rich source of interface design problems (Suchman, 1987). It is also an example of a wide collection of devices that have computers central to their interface mechanisms, and whose interfaces can therefore be regarded as essentially interfaces to computers. In what does the interface, the interaction between human and machine, consist?

Technology

First, there is the technology. From the perspective of someone from facilities, the copier's interface might be characterized as follows:

The machine requires 120 square feet of floor space in the shape of an "L" (details are shown in the "Site preparation manual"), floor loading of 10 lb/sq ft, and 30 amps at 220 v. not more than 20 feet from the back left corner of the machine. . . .

To the copy's operator, the technology includes grey boxes with paper feeders, buttons, and displays:

There is a panel of buttons on the front edge of the machine (so people in wheelchairs can reach them) that control the machine. I use the buttons to construct a description of the job that I want the machine to do. I do this by selecting choices of some dimensions, sometimes directly, and sometimes through typing numbers. When I'm finished the description, I put my "originals" in the paper feeder and push the big green button labeled "Start" which will cause the machine to make copies. The panel also includes a display that gives status reports on what I've just done and instructions on what I should do next. The control panel is arranged. . . .

But these paper feeders, buttons, and displays are only there in service of providing access to, and control over, the functionality:

The copier will be able to take one- or two-sided originals and copy them as a single job into one- or two-sided copies. To aid handling of cut-sheet originals, it will have a recirculating document handler for the original. It is going to be sold worldwide, so it will handle all paper sizes between A5 and A3. It will copy from and onto any 20 to 110 lb stock, with and without tabs. . . .

Work Applications

All these aspects are similar for all copiers of the same class. However, there is much more that needs thinking about in order for a copier to be put to use. Some of these issues will be the same for many copiers. Others will be pertinent only to particular situations.

There is the question of what you can do with the technology – the work applications:

You can copy a single sheet, copy a document that is a set of loose sheets (we don't get many of these on this floor), copy a book chapter. Our expense report form is a special instance of the single-sheet copying job. Project reports are examples of collated jobs, unless they get over 50 pages, in which case they require using a big table and a large stapler (which usually jams).

Applications and the technology come together with mappings[1] that capture how you get those jobs done using this machine:

The expense report is pink and requires messing around with the settings for contrast and darkness if you want to be able to read the copy, or – which is tougher – copy it. The best bet is to set the contrast on "4" and darkness on "darker," and copy. If you want to clean that up even more, try copying the resulting copy using regular darkness but a contrast still set on "4.". . .

To copy a book chapter, you make single sheet copies of each page, gather those together into a one-sided document, and make two-sided copies of that. You can use the top of the machine as a place to stack the single originals as they come out, or you can copy them in reverse order letting them gather in the output tray. Hand stacking allows you to check that you are getting good copies of the pages as you go along, while if you use the trick with the paper tray you will have to check them all as a separate operation when you are done. Checking as you go along has the advantage that you are still in the right place in the book for trying again if the first crack failed. Checking only at the end has the advantage that you can set up a smoother pattern of hand motions in flipping pages and pushing buttons than if you have to stop and wait for the machine to dump out the copy so you can check it before doing the next page. . . .

Work Practices

Organizing all of this for the person using the copier is the practice – all the (local) arrangements that they would come to know (and add to) as part of becoming competent in using this machine in this situation:

There are three copiers in this area of Fitch RichardsonSmith. Only the large one in the hall upstairs – right beside Jerry's office, I think – has an automatic document handler for originals; so use that one to copy book chapters. That machine is kind of the property of the product design people; so if they come along, particularly Joe who seems a little sensitive about "outsiders" using it, let them break in. If it is a really long job, you probably want to see if you can get one of the "co-op" students to do it for you; ask Annette to make the arrangements. In fact if you are not pushed for time, you can just stick a Post-it in the pages marking where to start and stop copying and leave it on Annette's desk – in the pile beside her "in" basket – and she'll make it happen. Better indicate which project you are doing it for, so Annette or the co-op student knows how to charge her time. We copy a lot of books, which is probably illegal, but nobody worries about it when it is only a single for our own use (after all, we bought the book); making

---

1. A significant component of the work of operating a copier, particularly if you are new to the machine, is figuring out these mappings. See Moran, 1983.

a single copy for a client is sort of OK if you're in a hurry, but we prefer to buy the client a copy of the book and send it. . . .

And finally, but centrally, there are the details of *this* particular instance of use:

I am making 7 copies of the 17-page first-phase "design themes" study, which I just got finished pasting the photos into, for use at tomorrow morning's workshop with the client. It is late, so I am hoping this copying does not take too long, and is not too problematic. I remember that there is a particular trick to copying documents with photographs. . . .

So the interface that is being designed includes technology, work applications, and work practices including aspects of the particular situation. All of these enter into determining the interaction that people will have with the machine. That is, starting with a focus on interface, the subject matter inevitably expands to encompass the complete working circumstances that occasion and motivate the human interaction with the machine.

From Design to Development

What is the process by which the situation of copier use just described comes about? The situation is the outcome of an extended set of human activities that have anticipated various aspects of this moment, planning for and making decisions affecting how it will be.

Many Designers, Continuing Design

Given this expanded view of the interface, it is clear that the design is not something that can be completed by the manufacturer of the machine. Much of the application and practice is specific to the particular circumstances of the particular machine. These designs are carried out by those planning for the particular situation, the particular use, the particular practice. So, far from being able to complete the design, the manufacturer is confronted with the difficulty of providing an incomplete design, which will be completed by others as part of installation and use. This requires that the manufacturer design the technology so that it will fit into all sorts of use situations, only a few of which are available to the manufacturer at the time the design is being done. Although the manufacturer can use the applications and practices of particular available situations to drive the design, the product will be instantiated technology (including manuals), but only imagined generic applications and work practices.

Thus, there are many other people who must carry out the rest of the design, and who must share credit for the particulars of any specific setting. Very few of these people would think of themselves as designers. There are salespeople who, in talking to customers, develop stories about how the technology can be used. There are service and repair folk who add to this body of knowledge from knowing the applications and the work practices of the particular user site. There are trainers and "applications specialists" working for either the manufacturer or the customer. There are "indigenous experts" provided by the pressures of the local social situation and individual motivations to help. All of these "designers" help set up machines for particular classes of work and specific situations.

The most important designer of all is the "end" user. The details of the application at hand and the work practices are both, in the end, individual ones. They are informed by, indeed heavily shaped by, the design that has already been carried out, bit by bit until it reaches the moment when the machine is used to get a particular job done.

Under this view, the task of learning to use a technology can be seen as a problem in design coordination. The user is seen as continuing the design started by others. The learning needs can be seen as stemming from the fact that the user has had no involvement in the preceding design and has either to be taught it, or must somehow infer it. These designs and learning needs address the full range of the interface:

The technology – If I'd designed this thing, then I'd understand what this thing does, and how the user interface delivers those capabilities to me.

The work application – What jobs will this thing do? How do I make it copy a book?

The work practice – Am I really supposed to be able to go away and leave this thing running? For how long? What if there's trouble and someone else walks in? How will they know what's going on?

Of course, users will often find that *they themselves* are the designers who have set up this situation and from whom they are receiving the design, because they have available the patterns established in prior interactions. These patterns are both *with* the machine, in learning and using it, and *about* the machine, in discussions over lunch and reading memos giving policies and procedures for applications and work practices.

But in that final act of use, for which all the design has been prologue, it is the user alone who *makes use* of the machine to fill some need in his or her work. Indeed, the phrase "making use" focuses attention on the fact that use is something to be *made,* that it takes work to bring it off. Use is, indeed, the culmination of design.

Thus, the view is of a collection of designers contributing to the situation as it develops, and continues developing, over time. This design continues to develop all the way up to and through use.

Iteration

In this view, use is seen as the end of design, and the user as the final designer. However, it is also the act of use – with all the effort or lack thereof required to make it – that drives the need for change in the first place. Difficulties with accomplishing the work occasion the thinking about what is wrong with its definition or the way it is being accomplished. Understanding these needs leads to thinking about what will improve the situation. Thus use is also the beginning of design, and design is clearly iterative.

This iteration can involve any of the designers. It might be the user deciding to make only one-sided copies to save time at the expense of paper, or to use a nearby table to gather the intermediate output. It might be a service person, fixing a jamming hinge. Or a corporate designer studying use during the design of a new product. They are different people with different interests working to different time scales having different impacts. But they are all involved, at best, in using prior use as a basis for designing a better situation of subsequent use.

This iteration is also unending. The technology may continue to develop, with repairs, upgrades, and new products. There will be new applications and new practices. So long as work goes on, design goes on. That is, design is *continued* not only for manufacturer through user, but also from cycle to cycle of use and change.

A Development Perspective

This expanded view of design thus provides a number of significant shifts in perspective. It draws attention:

from technology to technology being used by people;

from technology being used by people to people using technology;

from people using technology to people working;

from generic people working to particular people working in particular situations;

from a process done by a corporate design team to a process carried out by many people in many capacities;

from a process that happens once for a product to a process that continues happening over the lifetime of the product's use;

from a process that ends in use to a process that repeatedly moves from use through understanding to new designs and better use.

from a process pertaining to a single product to a process that addresses the applications and practices that will continue, appropriately adjusted to accommodate it, when a product is replaced with another one.

Furthermore, this process involves more than just design. In order for the use situation to be part of the design process, the design must be implemented, the product sold, and the situation of use created by all the rest of the designers including the user. In order to discuss all the sources of design that this viewpoint considers, it is necessary to comprehend the whole process of development, including the observation and analysis processes that drive further design. It is only from such a development perspective that one can address the full range of objects and processes that need designing, and the full range of human activities that occasion and encompass that design.

From Development of Interfaces to Interfaces for Development

The processes involved in developing interfaces must clearly address those interfaces. The copier interface described previously is developed through a series of human activities that focus on the copier. However, under the expanded view of what is being developed in which the interface includes the applications and practices of use, the processes of development must also focus on those applications and practices. Further, because the users are involved in the development process, that practice includes development itself. That is, the development processes, at least insofar as they are carried out by users, are part of the interface which the development processes must address.

That these processes of development are not addressed in the normal product development work is one of the sources of difficulty in achieving the potential for products being more readily integrated with work situations. Instead of designing for the continuation of design, that further development is left to the creativity of the "downstream" designers. There are exceptions: Facilities people are provided with documentation for the physical requirements when new copiers are ordered. These planning sheets anticipate the continuing design for transporting, locating, and powering the machine. Training courses are provided for customer staff who will maintain the machine locally, and for those who will use the machine in their work. However, development of support for the development of practice within a user community, including the flow of information about the machine, is important (Blomberg, 1986) and is not usually designed for.

The preceding discussion of development as part of the user's interface for copiers focuses on the development of work applications and practices. This is due to the fact that the technology of most copiers, and indeed of most products, is essentially fixed once they have been "configured" and "installed" in their situation of use. Thus the only things that will continue to be developed by the user will be work applications and work practice.

However, so-called tailorable technology is changing all that. Unlike traditional copiers, modern computer-based products change after they leave the manufacturer, as indeed do some modern copiers. As technology alone, they can be quite malleable in the hands of even minimally skilled users. The word processor that I am using at this moment has an elaborate "style" mechanism that I may use (if I can) to make it easy to shape the looks of my document. The operating system of the supporting computer provides a hierarchical filing system that I can use to group my files in any way that suits me. A desk top of windows gives access to documents and software applications, and these can be arranged by me to meet my needs. The spreadsheet I use for handling expenses is essentially unusable without adding information that the manufacturer did not choose to provide in the basic package: I craft my own spreadsheets, or buy and modify ones that are near to what I need.

In short, unlike most of the older more fixed technologies, computer-based technologies are intended to be modified to meet local circumstances, specialized in the light of those circumstances to behave in a way that eases the user's burden. This means that the role of continuing design in the use situation is even more evident for these products than it has been for less malleable products. Provided one adopts a perspective that considers only the technology, it has been possible to see the copier as something that the user does not change very much. From this perspective, the user's involvement in continuing design is limited. However, adopting the same technocentric perspective, it is not so easy to overlook the user's role as designer where this new malleable technology is concerned.

As a result of this heightened awareness of the presence of continuing design as part of normal practice, the need for supporting those design processes is also becoming evident. Editing tools for interdependent text styles in word processors simply do not reflect the rich structuring of styles that it is possible to create and is needed for common documents. Although editing tools for spreadsheets are becoming marginally acceptable, debugging tools are far from adequate.

Thus, the expanded view of interface and the expanded view of the processes of development entail an expanded view of what it means for the processes of development adequately to address the interface. In particular, because development processes themselves are part of the interface, the processes of development must address the processes of development – at least as they involve the users. That is, the development of development, and "folk" development in particular, must have an important place in our understanding of modern user interfaces.

Views of the Development Process

This perspective on design of user interfaces is thus centered on the development process. Therefore, the role of theory will be argued in terms of supporting this process. To aid in both understanding design and presenting the role of theory in design, this section will present a simple model of the development process and a metaphor based on that model. Much of this has already been alluded to in the preceding discussion, but this will provide some notions and terminology.

A Model of the Development Process

A simple model of development is that it is composed of five activities: use, observation, analysis, design, and implementation (see Figure 13.1). Each of these activities is a long story in itself and will not be greatly expanded here. However, let us consider a few thoughts germane to our purpose.

Use is the carrying out of work, supported by the product. Use is the start and end of development, and the essential grounding of the development process. Depending on who is carrying it out, use may be experienced personally, observed

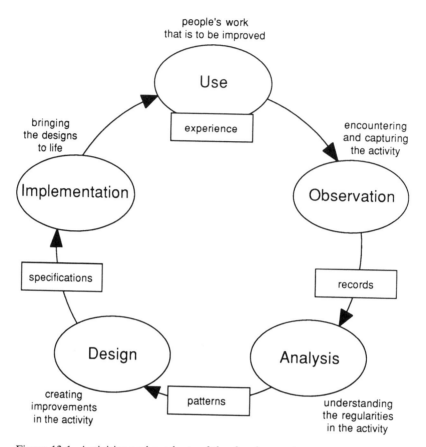

Figure 13.1. Activities and products of the development process.

from outside, imagined when described, or even fantasized about. The product of use is experience.

Observation is the interaction with use for the purpose of recording what happens. The product of observation is records. Observation requires access to the activity of use, and will inevitably reflect a methodological viewpoint informed by the nature of the use activity and the kind of analysis anticipated. The records may take the form of videotapes, written notes, or even mere memories of what happens.

Analysis is the seeing of regularities in the observational records. The product of analysis is patterns capturing those regularities, of which theory is just one kind. Analysis rests on a methodology that addresses how regularity is seen in the record, what terms are used in describing those regularities, how the regularity is generalized, and how the generalization is justified. Analyzing may also challenge the perspectival and methodological basis of the observation and the analysis, yielding changes in method and perspective. That is, analysis may produce new views both by looking at new things using existing methods and perspectives, and by looking at old (and new) things using new methods and perspectives.

Design is the identification and choice of what needs should and will be addressed, and the creation of solutions that meet those needs. Design produces specifications for how things will be if and when they are changed. Specifications can be abstract or concrete, and can be expressed in many forms (words, drawings, models). The needs and solutions can concern anything in the interface: technology, work applications, or work practice. Design is required because the results provided by the analysis do not, except on rare occasions, completely determine what should be done to improve the situation. Indeed, answering the question of whether improvement is even desirable is itself an act of design.

Implementation is the realizing of the new use situation specified in design. The realization can take the form of an envisionment as scenarios of use, or storyboards, or videotapes, or foam-core mockups. It can be a prototype that "works" to varying degrees of completion and reality. It can be full-scale implementation. Implementations of technological solutions will take technological skills; implementations of work applications or work practice will take social and managerial skills.

These five activities are presented as though they were phases (in time) of development. Sometimes, with hard and often unnatural effort, development methodologies may enforce such a temporal constraint on those involved in the development. However, the usual, and I think more productive, arrangement has all the development activities interwoven in time and mutually informing. Also, since development is continuing, these activities may be carried out by many different people. As development is iterative, these activities are repeated. As development can address any scale of change, these activities can stretch out for a long time, or can be completed in just a few seconds. The creation of a new version of a piece of software can take a year; the repositioning of a stapler so that it can be more easily reached may take a second.

It is noteworthy that the five activities presented here seem to leave out certain phases of the traditional model of the development process. Consider testing, installation, and maintenance, for example. From the development perspective, these appear as particular configurations of the five activities: Testing is smaller-scale iterations of the five activities, with a focus on observation and analysis, undertaken as part of a larger activity of implementation. Physical installation is part of implementation. The human part of installation is simply development of work applications and work practice. Maintenance is development after delivery. The separate identification of these phases may be seen to reflect a technocentric view of the traditional model: Technology is tested, technology is installed, technology is maintained. In particular, seeing the human part of installation as a "phase" of the development (of technology) is an indication of how little is thought of the importance or difficulty of continuing the design, and how little it is understood that the same activities that are so important in the development of technology are equally – indeed, more – important to the development of applications and practice.

A Metaphor for the Development Process

This model of the development process suggests a common development metaphor, that of a "cycle." The cycle of development is depicted as a circle with the activities ("phases") laid out around the circumference, and with a development focus moving along that circumference from one to the next. The problem with this metaphor is that it does not suggest that the activities of development can take place concurrently and be interwoven.

It is preferable to see the development circle as a wheel that rotates, with all activities advancing together, inextricably hooked together by a rim and spokes of interaction. The wheel, unlike the cycle, suggests that the whole development process is going somewhere: The wheel rolls. Alternative directions of the design are captured as alternative rollings of the wheel; sometimes we have to roll the wheel back, and then head off in a different direction.

To address the many scales at which development happens, the single wheel becomes a set of interacting wheels. Some are small, others big. Some are stopped, others rolling fast. These wheels often interact: Should the metaphor be gears, or clockworks?

People, advancing the various processes, make the wheel roll. Small wheels may be rolled by one person alone, carrying out all activities of a developmental change. Big wheels take many people, each attending to only one of the activities. The spokes of their interaction are interpersonal, or interdepartmental, or inter-company. However, even in big wheels, it is attractive to engage in more than one of the development activities: I find it difficult when observing not to be doing some simple-minded analysis on the fly, and when analyzing not to be thinking about what would make things better. I love to dive into a lightweight or incomplete implementation and then to try it out to see if things get better, or to see how my designs are right, or wrong, or – better yet – reveal an inappropriate way of observing or analyzing.

The Role of Theory in Development

What then does this enlarged development perspective of the design of human–computer interfaces suggest that the role of theory should be?

Theory of the Work

Recognizing that more is being designed than just technology dictates the need for an understanding of the work being supported. Because this work includes not only technology but applications and practice as well, the theories required will necessarily be from many disciplines. The technical disciplines will address the machines; the social sciences will address the applications and the practices. Theories in human–computer interaction crosscut this distinction, focusing as they do on the interaction between the technical and the human.

Such a theory of the work plays a role in the activities of development.

Observation

A theory of the work provides a basis for deciding what things to be looking for in observing that work. For example, a theory of office work might encompass the operating of machines (including copiers). This theory might alert one to the fact that, unlike classical problem solving, the job you are using the machine for may change while using the machine. For example, if the job as originally conceived turns out to be too hard to complete in the allotted time, it may get redefined in the midst of the work. This would suggest trying to observe the constraints under which the operator is working.

Analysis

As with observation, a theory of work provides a starting point for analysis. The analysis modifies the theory, resulting in a better description of the activity. An analysis might, for example, add detail to the description of how copier operators change the description of their jobs (e.g., operators change the number of copies, and the sidedness; the change is made after the job has started to run).

Design

A theory of work provides the basis for design. It will on rare occasion completely determine how a choice must be made in design, but most often will simply constrain the possible choices. More powerfully, the theory of work can, by its analytical categories, suggest dimensions of the design and choices that must be made. Thus, for example, knowing how people change the copying job while they are in the midst of doing it suggests providing mechanisms in the interface to support such midcourse reroutings.

Implementation

A theory of work provides constraints to the embodiment of the design in implementation. So, the messages that indicate an operator's choices while the machine is running should include mention of adjusting the job's definition – for example, altering the number of copies being made.

Theory of Development

Recognizing that the design of an interface is a continuing development process dictates the need for a theory to provide the underpinnings for the methods and practices of the activities of development. On the analytical portion of the development wheel (observation and analysis), these are the theories of science (e.g., the sociology of science, the theory of statistical analysis). On the synthetic portion (design and implementation), these are the theories of design, engineering, and construction. These theories of development interact with the theory of the work for which development is being done. An account of this interaction would also be useful.

Observation

A theory of observing provides the basis for the methods that are used for seeing what is going on in the human activity (supported by technology) under consideration. These would include theories underlying the use of questionnaires or videotape.

Analysis

A theory of analysis addresses the production, from the observational records, of descriptions of patterns in the work. These descriptions embody claims about the activity, claims on analytical concepts, and regularities. The theory also accounts for the nature of the warrants that can be advanced to support these claims.

Design

A theory of design is not very far advanced yet. Studies of the "design process" are quite recent. Theories of "need finding" and creativity will probably play an important role here.

Implementation

Theories of implementation cover the much broader range of human activity constituting the building of things and the putting of them in place. They would include theories addressing, for example, manufacturing, change in organizations, finance, and sociology.

Theory of Multiperson, Multirole Development

Recognizing that development is carried out by lots of people (there are lots of development wheels running and interacting concurrently) dictates the need for accounts of the way these multiperson, multirole interactions work. This would be a theory of communication and organization, of the management of change, of rationale and history.

   Such a development theory will also have to account for the transitions between the processes of development. When does a user stop using and start developing? What drives users over the edge to stop and improve their circumstances? Of course, breakdown is one clear driver of the shift to development. What are others? An observer, watching and making a record, may well see an activity quite differently than will the user in the midst of using. But when development is contemplated from the midst of use by the user, what access to the circumstances of use does the user then have? How does development proceed, and use resume?

A theory of multiperson, multirole development would have to account for the different-sized development wheels. An interesting advantage that such a theory has over a single-scale theory is that it can use its own structure to account for activity at finer grains. This can have a reductionist feel to it. For example, certain use experiences (errors, trouble, repair) can be accounted for by a development process at a smaller scale. As a result, accounts of use may become much simpler, relying on accounts of how particular instances are brought out of the generic case.[2]

Theory of Folk Development

Recognizing that development is an important component of using modern technology – tailoring the technology and creating work applications and work practices – dictates the need for a theory of work for the particular work that is development. I have already argued that a theory of development to help with the development process is needed anyway. However, this is the special subcase in which the developers are not professionals, but rather are those forced into development by the circumstances of their work. That is, we need a theory of how ordinary people do development – a theory of "folk development."

As development, folk development has some distinct special properties. First, development by the user can be focused on the particular situation in which the need arises. Over time, as other situations occur, the user may perceive patterns and may generalize the design to cover these patterns. In any given situation, even when more general patterns are perceived, the solution taken may nevertheless be specific. A specific solution is all that the situation taken by itself demands. User development thus differs from professional product development in that it is not aimed at general situations. Furthermore, rather than being removed from the situation of intended use, the development is done within it and therefore can make full use of the resources of that situation for immediate observation, analysis, design, and implementation.

Second, the intended user is also at hand, so that the determination of success can also be immediate. Beyond this, the whole process can be tacit, without the need for articulation. This significantly lightens the development task. However, it also renders some of the support of the multiperson, multirole aspects of development considerably harder. Understanding how folk development solves these problems would be one of the interesting results from such a theory.

Third, folk development takes place in interaction with all the other (professional) development that goes on in creating the situation of use. Therefore its processes must coordinate with those of all the other developers. For example, participatory design can be seen as a central part of these interactions. Here again, these interactions are an important subject matter for a theory of development.

Fourth, nonprofessional developers will have to learn a great deal about develop-

2. Not that this is simple. One view of anthropology is that the central task of that discipline is to account for how people see the circumstances of a situation as indicating an instance of a regularity. That is, how do people wrest regularity from the world? Related is the concern as to how people act so as to produce situations that will be understood by others as being instances of intended regularities.

ment, particularly when they start to modify technology. This will include, for example, all the skills of needs finding, and creativity; of generalization, special-case and end-point design, and debugging; of backup, and testing in safe environments; and the skills of trying it out on users other than oneself. So a theory of folk development will have to address the inevitable learning aspects of the situation.

Finally, it should be noted that this theory of folk development applies to professional developers too, when they are in the role of user. That is, even professional developers may well act in distinctly nonprofessional ways when they are developing in the midst of use.

Conclusion

Interfaces must be viewed as including not only technology but also work applications and work practice. Design is an integral part of the development process and is inextricably entwined with it; development is an integral part of the use of technology. Consequently, any theory of use, including any theory supporting human–computer interaction, must encompass a theory of development. In particular, it must include a theory of folk, rather than professional, development. Thus, a theory of development will provide a rich basis for the design of human–computer interaction, and hence the design of interfaces.

Acknowledgments

My thinking on this issue and its exposition have been greatly clarified by the comments on earlier drafts of this chapter by Linda Tetzlaff, John Tang, Sara Bly, and Jack Carroll. I wish to acknowledge their contributions and indicate my appreciation for their help.

References

Blomberg, J. L. (1986). Social interaction and office communication: Effects on user evaluation of new technologies. In Kraut (Ed.), *Technology and the transformation of white collar work*. Hillsdale, NJ: Lawrence Erlbaum Associates.

Caplan, R. (1982). *By design: Why there are no locks on the bathroom doors in the Hotel Louis XIV and other object lessons*. New York: McGraw-Hill.

Moran, T. P. (1983). Getting into a system: External-internal task mapping analysis. *Proceedings of CHI '83: Human Factors in Computing*. New York: ACM.

Suchman, L. A. (1987). *Plans and situated actions: The problem of human/machine communication*. New York: Cambridge University Press.

14
Working within the Design Process: Supporting Effective and Efficient Design
John Karat and John L. Bennett

We are articulating a user-centered design framework for supporting the design of systems that meet user requirements. Conducting this work in a research environment has prompted us to ask how theories developed in various fields (e.g., the study of design, cognitive psychology, or computer science) can be used effectively in development. Answering this question is not easy. We start with the notion that maintaining a user-centered perspective during design is necessary, and then we examine the role of various techniques within the system design environment. Our purpose is to understand how we might improve the quality of human–computer interaction (HCI) made possible in the system resulting from the design process. In this chapter we focus on two key questions in our exploration:

1. From the perspective of those working within the design and development process, what factors are critical to success?
2. Can the design of interactive systems benefit from application of techniques derived, for example, from cognitive science?

As we model the design process in-the-large (i.e., we distinguish components of successful HCI design processes), we observe a variety of activities. Different representations of the design problem being addressed seem to facilitate "constructive probing" by those involved in the design. The alternation between representations can bring into focus distinctions that will be important to users and can help designers provide system solutions that will lead to resolution of potential user problems. Through group discussion, the participants in the design process can build a shared understanding of user-sensitive issues and can develop a common vision of how to meet requirements for ease of learning, ease of use, and user satisfaction.

The design of systems to support productive HCI clearly includes consideration of both humans carrying out tasks and computer systems to support those tasks. The human information-processing focus in cognitive science is typically on cause-and-effect relationships that make prediction of human performance possible. Those working in cognitive science, including those represented in this volume, may have a variety of goals in carrying out their work. Advancement of our knowledge of human cognition does not necessarily have close ties to advancing our ability to produce useful systems. If we consider HCI as a scientific "field" with focused activities, it makes sense to think of development of useful and usable systems as a primary goal. With this in mind, application of cognitive theory becomes just one possible means of achieving this goal.

People trained in behavioral science disciplines have provided useful evaluation of system designs and have made contributions to development methodologies

(most notably behaviorally oriented iterative testing and prototyping) that are com
ing into acceptance. Behavioral data are now collected at many points in the design
of a system rather than just in the final stages. Although such evaluations are
valuable, the body of knowledge accumulated through such testing has not led to
generally useful "design rules" for the critical early stages of design.

By working within the design process and focusing our attention on activities
carried out during the process, we see an opportunity to have a stronger constructive influence on the system design. Design begins well before the first prototype
can be built and before the first test of a user interacting with a prototype. Although
we recognize that design and development of a system is a lengthy and complex
process, we focus here on the activity that takes place at the earliest stages of
design.

As part of our development of a user-centered design framework, we are exploring the use of various techniques within a design setting. In this chapter we describe
briefly some aspects of this framework and present a summary of our experiences
with one technique. We start with an assumption that maintaining a user-centered
perspective during design must be done in concert with engineering realities of
function to be provided, schedules to be met, and development costs to be managed. By user-centered we mean that the total system function is crafted to meet
requirements for effective user learning and efficient user access to that function.
That is, the eventual users must see the system as useful and usable in their ongoing
environment in addition to the system being affordable, logically complete, and
technically sound. In the longer run, from a research perspective, we seek to
distinguish components of successful HCI design processes in order to improve the
quality of design, especially with respect to HCI. We take seriously the challenge of
Simon (1969) to discover a science of design that is:

intellectually tough (as contrasted with soft),

analytic (as contrasted with totally intuitive),

at least partly formalizable (as contrasted with empirical, totally informal), and

including teachable skills (as contrasted with rote learning).

Our purpose has been to gain a better understanding of where support might be
useful in the design of systems and where it might help bring focus to, and help
resolve, the user-centered design issues that arise. Our work has aspects of theory,
modeling, science, and engineering, and it cannot be fruitfully labeled as limited to
any one.

Bringing User-centered Views into Design

An essential aspect of the HCI design process is a search for workable answers (in
contrast with searching for the single "right" answer). Our general theme is that
design is a complex activity involving problem-solving trade-offs among multiple
perspectives, and that though we hope to increase understanding of "good" design
we are not likely to find or develop a cookbook receipe for it. Design of any

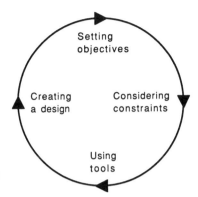

Figure 14.1. Generic system design
iterative activities.

complex system requires consideration of many points of view, of which the usability of the system is only one. Managing design in such an environment is so difficult that issues that are not clearly represented as a part of the design activity simply become lost in the sea of those issues that are in focus.

From the point of view of user-centered design, we have detected an unspoken, perhaps unconscious, general background perception on the part of many working within the software development process – usability topics have "very little technical content." That is, the evaluation of HCI quality is considered to be an ultimately "arbitrary, idiosyncratic, subjective opinion." Against such a background, representations successfully used in the process must relate to system qualities that are seen as important, measurable, and subject to management – technical function, cost-effective allocation of resources, and development schedules. The issue is how to get user considerations reliably inserted into the search for workable designs.

Although user requirements may be explicitly considered at some points in the design process (e.g., in developing objectives or in behavioral testing), the continued focus needed to achieve systems that support high-quality HCI is difficult to maintain. We find it helpful to consider design as an iterative spiral or wheel rather than a set of linear steps (see Figure 14.1). For example, the initial step of choosing system objectives from a universe of perceived user requirements often results in a loosely stated goal for the system (e.g., build a system to facilitate software development). As design proceeds, focus turns to considerations of constraints (e.g., cost and schedule), the techniques to be used by the designers (e.g., prototyping tools, problem-analysis techniques), and then the specifics of the design-in-progress. As as result of a drift encouraged by circumstances, we have seen cases where the focus of the behavioral testing that takes place later in system development bears little resemblance to the broader initial design objectives. Here the original intent of the objectives relating to HCI quality gets lost or translated into function-centered rather than user-centered goals. We do not see a single cause for this problem, but in this chapter we will point to some difficulties in providing representations of usability issues and also will discuss some factors associated with the group design process which may contribute to it.

Although there are some very detailed descriptions for many of the activities involved in designing a system, those that touch on user interactions are often only loosely specified. Software development methodologies vary widely in the attention given to user interactions in design, with some calling for user focus through consideration of general issues (e.g., Rubenstein & Hersh, 1984; Shneiderman, 1987), but most failing to provide specific guidance (for a discussion, see Boehm, 1988). For example, in "waterfall" models user interactions may be considered as part of the gathering of requirements, but there is practically no mention of the nature or form of user requirements necessary. None of the formal techniques that we have examined offers much guidance for maintaining or defining "appropriate" user focus during the early steps in the process.

A central question is how to bring topics of system use into focus so that they remain vital throughout the design process. We see a variety of candidate techniques that can contribute to developing and maintaining an effective perspective on the user. Examples we have found useful in design settings are:

1. Tabular formats for representing system objectives, including those relating to usability (Whiteside, Bennett, & Holtzblatt, 1988); provide specific indicators for knowing when the objectives are met;
2. Abstract statements of guiding visions for design, including the qualities to be observed by users as they carry out tasks (e.g., interface style guidelines such as IBM Corporation, 1991a);
3. Early design prototypes to provide a sense of sequence dynamics and to serve as a basis for design iteration (Gould, Boies, Levy, & Richards, 1987);
4. A focus on the (abstract) objects important to users and the actions that users can take on those objects (Wegner, 1987); and
5. Scenarios of use illustrating a flow of (specific) user actions needed to achieve a result, concentrating on what the user will see, what the user must know in order to interpret what is displayed, and what the user can (or in some cases must) do to achieve the needed task results (Karat & Bennett, 1991a).

We will not repeat here the detail found in the references.

It is clear to us that whatever we suggest must be as robust as – and be seen as useful as – the many "partial-solution" tools accepted by designers and currently used in the design process. We see it as important from the outset to consider how any suggested innovation will fit into existing design activities and how it will be recognized by designers to demonstrate "obvious value" during the process of use in the design and development process. Additionally, while we emphasize a framework for early design activities, we believe that the results of the activities should be viewed as useful throughouut the design process. We believe that this is largely achieved through techniques that support group collaboration through development of a shared vision of the goals of the design project. That members of the group do not know what is going on is a complaint nearly everyone working with design teams has an experience with.

Again we emphasize that the design process is a search for workable answers, the art of "satisficing" (Simon, 1969). We are confident that we can collect, compile, adapt, and try out in practice a variety of representations and ways for using them during actual design sessions. We expect that the result will be a description of techniques useful in raising the probability of acceptable answers through adequate consideration of important factors rather than a prescription for how to get the "right" answer to design. Our criteria for success in this endeavor are to be perceived as providing "useful" and "usable" tools and representations for designers.

While some design tasks may be carried out by individuals or small teams in close contact, most commercial system development involves a fairly large group of people. Even those creative design breakthroughs created by individuals are explained and worked out in groups. In these cases, and in the case of work in large teams, it is particularly important to achieve a shared understanding both of the objectives and of the suggested design. Critical for this is use of representations that make important design distinctions explicit. The need is to construct a shared understanding of the evolving design solution and to develop effective techniques for supporting group processes in design.

Constructing a Shared Understanding of an Evolving Design

Team design can take place in many ways. An individual can develop and maintain a "vision" of what is to be designed and can distribute subproblems to members of the team. To the extent that the leader understands the system to be developed (i.e., has a vision for the system that matches user needs) and is successful in decomposing design problems, such a design approach can succeed. In fact, one way to understand good HCI design could be to observe what designers acknowledged as successful do. This can be reported at the level of work in development groups (e.g., Kidder, 1982), through individual accounts of design practices (e.g., Lammers, 1986), and through studies of designers (e.g., Rosson, Maass, & Kellogg, 1988).

The common practice for systems developed in an industry environment is to describe the design in a product specification document. This enables opening the design vision for inspection and modification by diverse members of a design team and for review by marketing and management personnel outside the team. Although such documents are intended to capture the product vision, they often concentrate on details of the implementation technology and fail to present user-centered content effectively (a comment that has been echoed by several of our colleagues). Participants in current design reviews must study the specification, deduce implications for the user interface from clues distributed over a (typically) 300-page document, and synthesize the results into an effective analysis of the evolving system.

In addition, Conklin (1989) points out that what is missing in current design process products (such as product specifications) is a way to capture the rationale (the "why") of a given design. Because the rationale for design decisions is frequently unavailable when system maintainers alter a design, we are also interested in how representation might be used to "capture" the reasoning for later access.

Advocates of usability engineering (Gould & Lewis, 1985; Gould et al., 1987; Whiteside, Bennett, & Holtzblatt, 1988) strongly recommend iterative design and

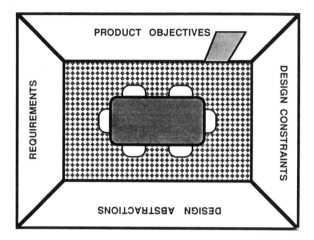

Figure 14.2. Room layout for four-walls design environment.

testing as an important factor in successful user interfaces. Quite aside from user-interface considerations, the cognitive capacities of designers are already taxed by the design challenges faced when using computer-based technology to meet demands for software performance and integration (Guindon, Krasner, & Curtis, 1987). Trying to maintain a cumulative user perspective (i.e., design a system that meets user needs) simultaneously with a technology perspective (i.e., design a system that can be built within resource constraints) is very difficult. Thus, shifts in focus and repeated iteration are essential to keep user and computer aspects evolving in parallel. Techniques that support a group "memory" for important discussions leading to prototype development and iteration seem not to be in common use.

In our evolving user-centered design framework we have concentrated on ways to bring a user perspective to design reviews and to maintain it throughout the design process. We address here the description of a process we have found useful in a variety of meetings. To facilitate a user-oriented overview, we have brought together on the walls of a room (large enough for two to eight people, small enough so that the walls are nearby) an organized and high-level view of the entire context within which the development process takes place (see Figure 14.2). The use of walls provides a large space with distinct regions (different walls) to help with the separation of complex issues within the array of problems typically encountered in design. As a general guideline, each of our walls contains representations for an aspect of the design environment.

Using walls to post various design representations is not entirely new to design. We have heard reports that "war rooms" containing various diagrams arrayed on walls have been used during development. Individual experiences and guidelines for use seem quite varied, but typically these rooms are used to help interpret a large quantity of information. Walls seem particularly useful as providing a surface for easy manipulation of content readily visible to the group. We organize content through the use of the four walls to present descriptions of the emerging system objectives, constraints, resources, and design-in-progress. The material on some of the walls (e.g., constraints and resources) might be seen as remote from being user-centered. But by bringing these concerns within the broader context of objectives and design-in-progress, we find that discussions that balance such concerns are facilitated.

On one wall we outline the product objectives in a tabular format, identifying the factors and features thought to be critical to success (Whiteside, Bennett, & Holtzblatt, 1988). Such objectives, typically developed by the team using input from people familiar with marketplace requirements, can serve as a basis for making design trade-offs in the ongoing allocation of development resources (design skill, feature optimization, manpower, scheduled attention). For example, in reviewing the design for one system we collected text describing the high-level goals (in this case, to "meet the information needs of business professionals"). Below this we placed text describing what some of those needs were perceived to be (e.g., provide a tool for easy data access, provide tools for data analysis and presentation). Placing these objectives on the wall led to a variety of discussions (What are the information needs of business professionals? What would constitute "easy access" to data?) that helped us form an understanding of the objectives. We do not claim that placing the descriptions on the wall "caused" the questions to be asked or that they were answered clearly or correctly, but we do suggest that such representation can help trigger a fruitful exchange.

On a second wall (spatial separation emphasizes the different dimensions under consideration), we outline constraints such as evolution from previous systems, guideline compliance, and likely user and management expectations (e.g., must code in C++) not covered under objectives. In continuing our analysis of the system mentioned earlier, we gathered information concerning guidelines that were intended to influence the design. These guidelines (in the form of user interface design principles) were placed on the wall and discussed. The wall included items such as "make rigorous use of a small set of common commands," and "use see and point rather than remember and type." Discussion of such distinctions can lead to a better understanding of the range of possibilities for the design of the system.

On a third wall we outline resources and tools available for constructing the system (e.g., data base support, data interchange architectures, libraries of existing programs). For example, these might include tools for software engineering, rapid prototyping, or user-interface screen design, which are in common use within the organization. Although the general objective of providing such tools is to facilitate system design and development (compatible with project schedule and resource demands on the project), invariably they will also place constraints on what can be designed. By explicitly including the tool capabilities in this environment, discussion of possible impact on user-centered objectives represented on other walls is encouraged.

On a fourth wall we extract from the functional specifications and from any available prototypes some representative images of the interface that will be seen by users. Rather than show these on a display screen, we provide an overview of the entire system on a wall with screen images arrayed horizontally and in a menu-accessed hierarchy, if that faithfully reflects the design approach. In this way observers can see at a glance how the entire system fits together (from a user perspective). In addition, this array facilitates walk-throughs of typical scenarios reflecting user learning and productive user work to bring out the dynamics of system operation. The size of the area required can itself give some sense of how much the user will have to learn.

This fourth wall is an arena for analysis and action at a variety of design levels and perspectives.

Questions can be asked about the infrastructure in the organizations that will use the system: How much resource will be required for training and who will provide it, how will the data needed by users be supplied, and how will the system fit with existing systems?

Questions can be asked about the system design itself: What are the aspects of intrasystem consistency and on what dimensions is consistency to be measured? What is a static description of system objects (such as files and directories), and what are actions that the user can take on those objects? How do the parts of the system fit together, and what conceptual and path-length distance between parts is traversed in typical scenarios?

Those providing the underlying utility services (communications, the database) can debate the likely response time and data access requirements of users.

We have outlined the use of spatially separated surfaces (i.e., the walls of a room) as a way of representing multidimensional areas of concern that arise in the course of design. Each wall serves as a focus for particular design questions, and the whole room provides an arena for holding questions open while the team searches for solutions. We do not hold the particular wall content or the use of the walls in the design review as fixed (i.e., many different distinctions might be used in laying out content on the walls). The spatial separation of walls containing particular content does assist in orienting discussions within the meeting. These and other techniques serve to provide a group working on a problem with a basis for forming a shared understanding of system technology and user-centered opportunities and for delving into aspects that do not seem clear. The power of spatial separation also relates to observations of Simon (1969, p. 78): "The representation of space and of things in space will necessarily be a central topic in a science of design."

Supporting Group Processes in Design

The social context in which the design activity takes place is an important factor in the quality of the resulting design (Bennett, 1986, 1987). As a result of our experiences we became particularly interested in the role of meeting facilitators (i.e., the formal or informal "leader" of the meeting).

Generally it is considered good practice for the design team to include participants from different backgrounds so that the team may benefit from a variety of experiences, insights, and opinions. Moving from potential benefit to realization in practice depends on the ability of these individuals with differing personalities and viewpoints to work as team members.

In addition, many researchers have grappled with the problem of bringing user concerns effectively into the design arena (Bødker, Knudsen, Kyng, Ehn, & Madsen, 1988). The teams we have worked with have been charged to build systems that are sound from an engineering perspective and at the same time support effective HCI. However, direct participation in the meetings by eventual end users has, so far, not been practical. Given this lack of direct user input, it has been particularly important for the facilitator to use the representations on the walls to help build a group perspective on the overall system that is emerging (including HCI quality).

The process of laying out the representations on any of the walls has invariably led to questions and discussions that explore the reasons for the content of that wall. Any explicit representation will include a background of assumptions that may not initially be shared by all in the design group. Some of the discussion may simply lead to clarification (e.g., "Yes, that seems an appropriate objective"), but often we find that it points to areas in which something overlooked is recognized or disagreement surfaces. Although no facilitator or no technique can promise to catch all oversights or resolve all disagreements, we feel that a variety of representations can support design by encouraging comprehensive discussion.

Because our framework is still evolving, we cannot yet offer a case study that clearly illustrates the full range of issues involved. We have had some early productive experiences that lead us to believe the direction is useful. We have taken part in a number of design reviews for products under development and have been able to assist the design teams in "discovering" design issues. In some cases, the discoveries have related to items such as "holes" in the design (e.g., differences in the actions that could be taken on similar objects with no known motivation for the differences). In other cases the discoveries have been in the nature of clarifications of what different members of the team thought was contained in the existing design specification (e.g., typically characterized by the "Oh, so that's what you meant" response). The environment has been useful in helping design teams focus on "real" objectives (such as making a system easy to use), in contrast to translations of such objectives (such as use menus for all interactions because that will – is assumed to – make a system easy to use). We can not directly attribute such insights to any particular aspect of our process, but we do note that such discoveries are important and that they had not occurred within the existing design activities.

Not all of our positive responses to the four-walls approach have come from what might be termed "design activities in trouble." We have used the same framework in some of our work to understand exsisting systems. In order to develop an understanding of one commercial system, we prepared a four-walls description of the system from publicly available documentation about the system and its design. Although this may not have accurately portrayed the design process for the system, it did serve as an effective introduction, and it aided in design discussions for related products. Specifically, it helped us to understand the relationship between some aspects of the product that had seemed "strange," and the high-level design principles stated for the product (in this case the Metaphor system, which uses a different convention for copying objects than Macintosh systems).

Some Detailed Examples

Our experiences in design reviews have covered a number of topics including the use of measurable behavioral objectives, the nature of team building in design, and the use of system prototypes to name a few. We have become particularly interested in two topics, which we would like to briefly expand on here: techniques for developing and representing scenarios of use in designing a system, and the role of the facilitator in design review meetings.

Developing and Using Scenario Representations

One process we have used in the four-walls environment is the use of scenario-driven walk-throughs for focusing design discussion. By scenarios we refer to descriptions of user work to be carried out with the system. In doing this we have attempted to consider different ways of representing the scenarios, and asked questions about the value of each for design. One source of representation techniques that we have explored is the use of analytic models of human–computer interactions, many of which have roots in cognitive science. Examples of analytic approaches are the goals, operators, methods, and selection rules of Card, Moran, and Newell (1983), the extension of Kieras and Polson (1985), the formal grammar of Reisner (1984), and the task–action grammar of Payne and Green (1986). Central to all of these techniques is a rather loosely defined task analysis (which includes hypothesized user mental operations as well as physical actions) and some level of language for modeling the distinctions presented by the theory.

For several years we have been exploring whether approximate models of human–computer interaction could become useful in the design of computer systems (Bennett, Lorch, Kieras, & Polson, 1987; Karat, Fowler, & Gravelle, 1987). This theory-based methodology might help designers to "understand the user" and to "analyze the users' tasks." We found the prospects for quantitative predictions (which would be quite valuable if available to designers) of particular interest in the NGOMSL modeling framework of Kieras and Polson (Kieras, 1988; Kieras & Polson, 1985). We view this as one possible process in the user-centered design framework, applied when considering what users see, what they must know, and what they must do to carry out typical tasks. The value could be realized through considering the impact of alternative designs on the amount, content, and transfer of user knowledge (Polson, 1987).

We investigated the role of GOMS-like models in design by selecting a "design scenario" focused on user support for managing files. We began by modeling user actions on files in two existing systems, and we established "use scenarios" for important tasks to be performed with the system. We assumed that the analysis would have value for understanding how to design a future system.

The details of this design exercise are presented elsewhere (Karat & Bennett, 1991b); we offer here a brief summary of our experience. In an initial exercise we looked at the low-level operations for "move," "copy," and "delete" as elements in file maintenance. This led to initial quantitative estimates for comparative "ease of use" and much discussion about the relative merits of the two systems. In an iteration on our initial view of the function provided by the system, we developed models at a higher "file-maintenance" level. The quantitative results comparing "ease of use" then "reversed" from those estimated in the initial exercise. At the heart of this reversal was a reinterpretation of what function would be most useful in "managing files." Design decisions made in one of the systems that did not show up earlier (level of granularity) came into play. Defaults (system assumptions about whether a user action was interpreted as a "move" or a "copy") reduced the number of required user actions.

We learned that while current models might produce quantitative estimates of human behavior of value for engineering low-level interactions with the system, of greater importance for design is clear articulation of distinctions important to users. The modeling activity provided us with a valuable way to review systematically the trade-offs available in design. Thus, the discussion ranged productively far beyond the current limits of cognitive theory. For us the power resided in forming qualitative questions rather than in offering quantitative answers (of doubtful accuracy). We strongly suspect that forming questions is an important level of activity that HCI research needs to address.

Important Distinctions in Scenario Development

Rather than focusing on the development of quantitative measures of usability to aid in user-centered discussions, we have turned to more general use of scenarios in design meetings. In recent projects we have found it quite useful to articulate the design-in-progress by iterating through descriptions of tasks that the system is to support at increasing levels of detail.

We currently describe scenarios using the following elements. First, a *situation description* provides a high-level account of the task to be carried out. Next we expand the description to include *logical essentials* required for completing the task. For example, if two items are to be linked, it is logically necessary to identify the objects to the system and to specify the kind of connection to be made – note that there are many possible designs for accomplishing this. The description of the scenario continues by adding *generic steps* (which are relatively implementation independent), and finally *specific steps* (to complete the task given the design-in-progress).

We have used this framework for scenario description in several design projects, and found that it is not only useful in focusing discussions, but also provides a good outline for capturing the scenario description in text. For one project (developing a general-purpose linking architecture), we iterated through the elaboration of several scenarios (covering different types of "links" between objects) before the design group indicated "comfort" with the problem at hand. The benefits of reaching such a level of shared understanding in a design group are difficult to quantify, but we maintain that both the individual and group design work that follows is facilitated by such discussion.

Again, this is not a cookbook process. All of the description is captured on the walls of the design room, and it is subject to discussion as it develops. Once a design-in-progress begins to unfold, focus can be developed through questions related to the specific steps. Questions that we have found useful in this process concern how the user might know what to do next in a sequence of steps, what happens if an error is made, what is the recovery path from errors, and where does the sequence fit in the expected use of the system (frequency of use). This shares some of the direction provided in the description of "cognitive-walkthrough" (Lewis, Polson, Wharton, & Rieman, 1990).

Support for Design Meeting Facilitation

Large-scale computer support for the group as a whole and for the review process in the large (e.g., display walls that allow both sketching by team members and display of computer-generated data from a data base) appear both technically demanding and expensive. Rather than speculating about (or trying to design) a high-technology room for design meetings, we have been focusing on "practical" ways to support the activities we have observed so far. Low-technology walls and charts are readily available.

When we consider the kinds of activities carried out by a facilitator, we see value in (and have used) computer-based function. We will carry out the discussion of this topic utilizing a mixture of descriptions and examples.

The first step is *preparing for meetings*. The facilitator can bring a valuable, fresh perspective to the meeting by reviewing existing artifacts (functional specifications, requirements documents, paper or running prototypes) to find potential representations for placing on a wall. As most of these artifacts are computer-based, use of an editor that can handle text, image, and graphics is valuable. Thus, facilitator insight on what representations are likely to stimulate needed discussion and skill in organizing the walls is supported by tools that make production easy.

Keeping track of the flow of the meeting is a second aspect. Facilitator listening skills are already taxed by the need to sense what is going on in the room at all levels of communication. As practiced note takers, we have used the rapid and silent technology of paper and pen effectively. Use of a text editor must support equal flexibility (flipping rapidly between pages) and unobtrusiveness (silent keys) so as not to get in the way. Whiteside and Wixon (1988) are making progress on managing the quantity of data by concentrating on speech acts – recording in a way that highlights requests and promises.

Responding to needs in the moment is another task of the facilitator. During the course of the meeting, discussion will range over a variety of topics. The facilitator (and team members) can populate the walls with initial representations. If the facilitator has done the requisite homework, he or she will have an idea of what background material is available in a data base to support an in-depth decision. It would be handy to compile a catalog of specific techniques (e.g., King, 1987) and to index data specific to the project under review. We can see potential value in being able to match data to representation technique on the fly (or during a break) to produce support of discussion. Because scenarios illustrating possible user action sequences can be particularly helpful for bringing some sense of user-interaction dynamics into the discussion, we can see that access to an indexed collection of sample tasks could be valuable.

Developing a summary of results is important during and after the meeting. The facilitator can advance the progress of the meeting by looking for appropriate moments to illustrate a resolution, highlight a result through rearranging the content of a wall, and labeling the result for future reference. This important activity seems likely to remain a "low-tech" process pending the advent of practical electronic wall displays. However, pointing to the results of the meeting, representing the actions that need to be completed before the next meeting, and displaying open questions can be supported even by a simple text editor and local printer. We have observed the power of team members making explicit commitments during and at the close of the meeting for action to be taken subsequent to a meeting. After the meeting has concluded, support might be usefully provided to assist the team to track promises made during the meeting (J. Whiteside, informal communication, 1989).

Communicating results is also the job of the facilitator. We have often been in meetings where one or more members of the team could not be present. One way both to preserve some of the context of the meeting and to inform missing team members is to videotape a member of the team providing a narration of the representations present on the walls at the end of a meeting. The process of creating this review can itself be revealing (which aspects are featured as results; the comments added by other team members as they hear the summary). However, we echo Simon (1969, p. 76) as we "attach value to the search as well as the outcome," regarding "the design process as itself a valued activity for those who participate in it."

Maintaining team continuity and momentum between meetings is also essential. To counter an inevitable "out of sight, out of mind" phenomena – especially with an increasing frequency of geographically dispersed team members – we see effective use of express-mail communications to maintain a "presence." Fafchamps, Reynolds, and Kuchinsky (1989) report an interesting study of express-mail flow in the activities of a design group. We suspect that assisting continuity will be an important facilitation role supported by technology.

No one of these activities requires a particularly challenging technical innovation, but the synthesis into a coherent process carried out by skilled facilitators does require innovation and could be quite effective.

Observations

We have characterized design as a complex problem-solving situation in which multiple views of the problem (e.g., users' need for function and effective access to that function, development-time constraints, cost of development resources, hardware capabilities) must be considered. A primary problem in existing design is that it is difficult to present a total design environment to the design team in a way that effective discussion of user-related issues can take place.

Our experiences in developing our user-centered design framework have led us to the following conclusions in considering future work.

First, a variety of representations (or models) can be used to describe system objectives, static features of a system (tables of system objects and actions), dynamic uses of a system (descriptions of scenarios), and other important system constraints (such as hardware capabilities). Central to this work are representations that enable participants in the design process to understand an important aspect of the design context and that serve as a basis for insightful discussion and fruitful revision.

Second, we have found that the quantitative estimates available from our modeling based on cognitive science theory did not address the range of design issues we see as essential. In general we have found it more beneficial to represent human–computer interaction scenarios in natural language than in formal notations. The distinctions that seem useful to make (and thus those that we suggest to be considered by designers) are those between logical essentials of a task and the steps specified in various designs. The costs in terms of time required to learn and use various formal techniques have not seemed justified so far in our experiences. While approximate modeling techniques may prove useful for evaluating low-level interactions, we did not find it wise to rely on the quantitative estimates in our design scenarios. However, the discussions that arose in the course of developing explicit expressions of various aspects of systems were valuable.

Summary

Should we conclude that "adequate" theories (those with quantitative–predictive power) are beyond what we can reasonably expect from current behavioral science? Although it may be hard to see what it would mean to do "science" in this domain, we may be giving up an opportunity for a real contribution to building a user perspective if we decide that it is just too complicated to address systems issues. Some of our experience suggests that a number of techniques for representing parts of a large design problem might be useful in user-centered design even though they are not well established as accepted cognitive theory. MacLean has suggested (Butler, Bennett, Polson, & Karat, 1989) that though the science base lags far behind the needs of designers, cognitive science can contribute to design by making the concepts behind developing theories known to the HCI design community. This will require some "tuning" of cognitive theory, and such an activity may not be of interest to all in the field, but we do believe that useful "field tests" would result from such interactions.

Some of the aspects of user-centered design that could most benefit from theory-based distinctions are in the area of task analysis. For example, once a system is released and put into use, users do not wish to change their arduously learned patterns of effective interaction. However, they may welcome no longer having to carry out system-required utility functions (e.g., backing up files as a precaution against lost data). What analytic techniques could aid developers in bringing out such distinctions as they consider design changes?

Theories (or models) need to be evaluated by different criteria within cognitive science than within a human–computer interaction design process. The development of accurate cognitive models is a goal for cognitive science, and the scientific methods for determining success or failure are well established. The value of such theory in the design process, even if it is scientifically accurate, remains unclear. Our approach contrasts with one that starts from cognitive science as an activity, develops it from that perspective, and then looks for possible value in design. We start from design and seek ways to enhance the process, including use of techniques adapted from cognitive science.

Evaluating the role of theory in HCI – taking design seriously – means evaluating the usefulness and usability of applying the theory to artifact design. Much of what we have said in this chapter suggests that this may require consideration of design as a group problem-solving activity. One suggestion here is that theories that might assist us in HCI design need to consider the social context. This may mean that we need to broaden the science base from which we have been attempting to draw useful theory, or it may simply mean that we have not adequately looked at fields that do focus on group activities.

Throughout our work we have been interested in providing an appropriate focus on HCI considerations during design review meetings. We have emphasized the power of representations, taking a cue from Simon (1969, p. 78): "A deeper understanding of how representations are created and how they contribute to the solution of problems will become an essential component in the future theory of design." For this reason we have been challenged to construct representations that make user-centered issues real for all the members of the design team.

Our experience to date suggests that the use of large surfaces (walls) in a design review encourages both breadth of view on issues and an in-depth focus on details for those taking part in a meeting. The large space provided by the walls provides room to capture design representations, and it provides for appropriate shifts in attention during the meeting (often a shift from one wall to another), while developing a sense of the overall relationship between the issues. We expect that as we continue our work in this area, we will be able to develop the kind of organized knowledge about design necessary to advance it.

References

Bennett, J. L. (1986). Observations on meeting usability goals for software products. *Behaviour and Information Technology, 5,* 183–193.

Bennett, J. L. (1987). Collaboration of UIMS designers and human factors specialists. *Computer Graphics, 21,* 102–105.

Bennett, J. L., Lorch, D. J., Kieras, D. E., & Polson, P. G. (1987). Developing a user interface technology for industry. In H. Bullinger & B. Shackel (Eds.), *Human–Computer Interaction: Interact '87,* participants edition (pp. 21–26). Amsterdam: North-Holland.

Bødker, S., Knudsen, J., Kyng, M., Ehn, P., & Madsen, K. (1988). Computer support for cooperative design. In *CSCW'88 Proceedings of the Conference on Computer-Supported Cooperative Work* (pp. 377–394). New York: ACM.

Boehm, B. W. (1988). A spiral model of software development and enhancement. *IEEE Computer, 5,* 61–72.

Butler, K., Bennett, J. L., Polson, P., & Karat, J. (1989). Predicting the complexity of human–computer interaction. *SIGCHI Bulletin, 20*(4), 63–79. New York: ACM.

Card, S. K., Moran, T. P., & Newell, A. (1983). *The psychology of human–computer interaction.* Hillsdale, NJ: Lawrence Erlbaum Associates.

Conklin, J. (1989). Design rationale and maintainability. *Proceedings of the 22nd HICCS* (pp. 1–12). New York: IEEE Computer Society Press.

Fafchamps, D., Reynolds, D., Kuchinsky, A. (1989, September). The dynamics of small group decision making over the e-mail channel (Hewlett-Packard, Palo Alto, STL-89-21). Paper presented at the first Euorpean Conference on CSCW, Gatwick, UK.

Gould, J. D., Boies, S. J., Levy, S., & Richards, J. T. (1987). The Olympic message system: A case study in system design. *Communications of the Association for Computing Machinery, 30,* 758–769.

Gould, J. D., & Lewis, C. (1985). Designing for usability: Key principles and what designers think. *Communications of the ACM, 29,* 300–311.

Guindon, R., Krasner, H., & Curtis, B. (1987). Cognitive processes in software design. In *Human–Computer Interaction: Interface '87* (pp. 383–388). Amsterdam: North-Holland.

IBM Corporation. (1989). *Common user access, advanced interface design guide, systems application architecture (SC26-4582).* Boca Raton, FL: IBM.

Karat, J., & Bennett, J. (1991a). *Using scenarios in design meetings – A case study example.* In J. Karat (ed.), *Taking software design seriously: Practical techniques for human–computer interaction design.* Boston: Academic Press.

Karat, J., & Bennett, J. (1991b). *Modelling the user interaction methods imposed by designs.* In M. Tauber & D. Ackermann (Eds.), *Mental models and Human–Computer Interaction 2.* Amsterdam: Elsevier.

Karat, J., Fowler, R., & Gravelle, M. (1987). Evaluating user interface complexity. H. Bullinger & B. Shackel (Eds.). In *Human–Computer Interaction: Interact '87,* participants edition (pp. 489–498). Amsterdam: North-Holland.

Kidder, T. (1982). *Soul of a new machine.* New York: Avon.

Kieras, D. E. (1988). Towards a practical GOMS model methodology for user interface design. In M. Helander (Ed.), *Handbook of human–computer interaction.* Amsterdam: Elsevier.

Kieras, D. E., & Polson, P. G. (1985). An approach to the formal analysis of user complexity. *International Journal of Man–Machine Studies, 22,* 365–394.

King, R. (1987). Better designs in half the time; implementing QFD quality function deployment in America. Bob King, GOAL/QPC, 13 Branch Street, Methuen, MA 01844.

Lammers, S. (1986). *Programmers at work.* Redmond, WA: Microsoft Press.

Lewis, C. H., Polson, P. G., Wharton, C., & Rieman, J. (1990). Testing a walkthrough methodology for theory-based design of walk-up-and-use interfaces. In J. Chew & J. Whiteside (Eds.), *Proceedings of CHI '90: Human Factors in Computing Systems* (pp. 235–242). New York: ACM.

Payne, S. J., & Green, T. G. R. (1986). Task–action grammars: A model of the mental representation of task languages. *Human–Computer Interaction, 2,* 93–133.

Polson, P. G. (1987). A quantitative model of human–computer interaction. In J. M. Carroll

(Ed.), *Interfacing thought: Cognitive aspects of human–computer interaction*. Cambridge, MA: Bradford Books/MIT Press.

Reisner, P. (1984). Formal grammar as a tool for analyzing ease of use. In J. C. Thomas & M. L. Schneider (Eds.), *Human factors in computing systems*. Norwood, NJ: Ablex.

Rosson, M. B., Maass, S., & Kellogg, W. A. (1988). The designer as user: Building requirements for design tools from design practice. *Communications of the Association for Computing Machinery, 31,* 1288–1299.

Rubenstein, R., & Hersh, H. (1984). *The human factor: Designing computer systems for people*. Maynard, MA: Digital Press.

Shneiderman, B. (1987). *Designing the user interface*. Reading, MA: Addison-Wesley.

Simon, H. A. (1969). *Sciences of the artificial*. Cambridge, MA: MIT Press.

Wegner, P. (1987). Dimensions of object-based language in design. In N. Meyrowitz (Ed.), *Object-oriented Programming Systems, Languages, and Applications (OOPSLA) Conference Proceedings* (pp. 168–182). New York: ACM.

Whiteside, J., Bennett, J., & Holtzblatt, K. (1988). Usability engineering: Our experience and evolution. In M. Helander (Ed.), *Handbook of human–computer interaction*. Amsterdam: Elsevier Science Publishers.

15
Discussion: Perspectives on Methodology in HCI Research and Practice
Linda Tetzlaff and Robert L. Mack

Introduction

The Kittle House Workshop focused on the role of cognitive theory – past and future – as a driving force in human–computer interaction (HCI) research and practice. The question was whether psychological principles and theories and the empirical data associated with them could provide substantive direction for the design of usable software systems, and ultimately provide a science foundation for HCI. However, the upshot of the workshop was a generally pessimistic view of the power of such theory to effect timely change in this rapidly evolving technology. While the participants might differ in the degree to which they endorse this conclusion, they generally appeared to find progress in the field coming from elsewhere. These alternatives to cognitive theory were themselves a major topic of the workshop.

One important source of progress is the methodology that researchers apply to their domain of study. While theory gives substance to methodology, the methods can also be considered on their own. Indeed, a methodology can service a broad range of theories. Our perspective is this: Regardless of whether HCI has adequate theoretical foundation, or qualifies as a science, those working in the field have goals, and can evolve a set of methods to achieve them. Although this was not a workshop on methodology, running throughout the wide-ranging discussions of the workshop papers were concrete methodological case studies and proposals that we believe can advance the practical goals of HCI, and which could become an explicit program for researchers and practitioners in the years to come. We will assemble these proposals and explore some of the questions to which they, in turn, give rise.

Achieving Relevance and Managing Complexity

The commitment of HCI as a discipline is to create useful and usable computer artifacts to support and enhance people's work. Classical psychological theory has provided too little guidance in real design or has been available too late to influence practical results in the marketplace. As Carroll puts it in his introduction, cognitive theories have failed to provide adequately *specific* or *applicable* information to guide effective action.

This commitment to useful and usable artifacts inevitably immerses HCI practitioners in the real world complexity of people's work, as it relates to their use of computer technology. At the same time, despite limitations in knowledge, methods, and theories, there are frameworks for action in what has variously been called empirical design (Gould, 1988; Landauer, this volume), user-centered design (e.g.,

286

Norman & Draper, 1986), or usability engineering (e.g., Whiteside, Bennett, & Holtzblatt, 1988), the term we will use here. Usability engineering is a loose collection of methods to help developers deal with complexity by articulating objectives and specifying operational measures of success. Objectives help frame direct methods of empirical evaluation and exploration, and guide the analysis and iterative improvement of design.

However, the state of the practice in usability engineering is not sufficient, retaining, as it does, a large element of intuition, empiricism, and even guesswork. No sooner have basic principles of usability engineering been articulated than the framework has been revised. There has been a progressive shift from observation in the laboratory to understanding people's tasks in their actual context of work. The methodological consequences of such shifts were a key topic at the workshop.

Creating and Cumulating Knowledge

A commitment to practical effectiveness in solving real world problems, and an acceptance of their complexity leads to the questions: How can we abstract general principles that can guide future development? How can we learn to manage the complexity and accumulate experience?

Usability engineers have proposed a variety of means for archiving and propagating experience, such as guidelines, application, and interface architectures, toolkits, case studies, architectures and "technology catalogs" (e.g., Bennett, 1984). In many cases, these proposals are not well developed, and they have been subject to criticism (e.g., the limitations of guidelines, Barnard, this volume). It remains to be understood how well these possibilities support cumulation and application of expertise. The need to provide reliable means and mechanisms is all the more urgent as usability engineering practice becomes increasingly immersed in the contextual complexity of technology in use.

In this chapter, we take a critical look at the methodologies discussed at the workshop. Following roughly the order in which the methodologies might be applied in practice, we will discuss the utility of general principles to guide design, representations employed to describe and analyze the design space, the empirical process used to evaluate the resulting artifact, techniques proposed for assembling and transmitting the collective knowledge, and finally work on the design process within which these other methodologies take place. Our objective is to extract the concrete proposals that might guide future research and practice in the design of usable systems.

Methodology

Because this was a conference not on methodology but on the role of theory in HCI, some aspects of methodology seemed to be taken for granted. For example, iterative design was pervasively accepted, as was the methodological repertoire of empirical methods and measurement schemes characteristic of usability engineering. Everyone expects to begin with a design and work with it to inform the next. No one felt the need to talk about objectives – either defining them, or converging on them. The meaning of *usable* was taken to be self-evident in context.

If the participants had been asked directly about the role of methodology in HCI, perhaps a different picture would have emerged from the one to be presented here. Nonetheless, methodology, the more context-situated, pragmatic partner of theory, was an active presence both in the papers and in the discussion. It is to these strategies for research and practice in HCI that we now turn.

HCI researchers want to contribute substantively to the design of real systems. At the same time, they want to extract more general lessons that cumulate expertise and principles for the future. To begin, we will consider the discussions of general guidelines and principles, as a way to capture generalizations on the one hand, and as starting points for the development of specific computer artifacts on the other. Throughout we will be concerned with the interplay of the general and specific: We are concerned with representations and processes that enable general principles and past experience to be applied in the context of new users and tasks, technological opportunities and constraints. At the same time we need to look at the abstractions that enable designers to assess and ensure design coherence and consistency across the system, whether at the interface or within the underlying system.

Principled Design

It is in the way of science or engineering or even ordinary life to develop guiding principles to organize and direct activity. The world of HCI abounds with detailed guidelines and recommendations for design of usable systems (e.g., Rubenstein & Hersh, 1984; Shneiderman, 1987). Unfortunately, the granularity of the advice and magnitude of the detail make much of this material difficult to assimilate. Part of what workshop participants seemed to be grappling with was the level at which useful abstractions or generalizations might be made. The following gives a flavor for this search for usable generality:

Develop abstract statements of guiding principles (diSessa).

Extract and evaluate the psychological claims implicit in extant artifacts (Carroll, Kellogg, & Rosson).

Build "theories" from "empirically based modeling of user behavior" (Landauer).

Construct representations that integrate critical phenomena in the real world for representation to the science base and application representations for their dissemination into design (Barnard).

Collect "small-scale generalizations, minimodels, and sets of related principles of limited scope" (Pylyshyn).

Continue the search for pivotal mechanisms underlying mental processes from which implications for design can be productively inferred (Lewis).

The source of the principles varies. Lewis, Barnard, and diSessa look for context independent mental models (inner theory, as Lewis calls it) to help assess and guide work in HCI. For Carroll et al., Landauer, and Pylyshyn, general principles are extracted from concrete design experiences and cast into a form that is intended to provide guidance for future design efforts and possibly a basis for theory. Carroll et al. work heuristically within the context of an artifact to extract bounded claims that can be used to reason about the redesign of the next artifact. Landauer similarly derives what he refers to as "mundane theories" from empirical study, statistical characterization, and numerical modeling.

Procedurally, Carroll et al. begin with the artifact and the tasks it is intended to support, analytically extract principles, and inform design of the next artifact. DiSessa begins with guiding principles, homes in on a tractable problem, and then moves to artifact design and analysis. However, as Carroll et al. point out, ontologically, the artifact is always there, the principles always derivative.

As practical guidelines, these principles, theories, or claims are important to the extent that they effect a successful design. As theory, these principles are of a different order from classical psychological theory. Rather than stimulated by a search for *how things are,* they are driven by the pragmatic concern for *how things might be* (Simon, 1969). Thus, a corollary concern, more explicit for some than for others, was how to incorporate these principles into the design process. Some approaches seem to favor the eclectic assemblage of potentially useful principles and techniques (e.g., Pylyshyn); others more aggressively single out a modest number of principles as a conceptual framework for design (e.g., diSessa). It is the latter approach to which we now turn.

The following discussion samples different efforts to provide guiding principles for design. To facilitate comparison, the principles cited have been rephrased, when necessary, as assertions about the interface. All make psychological claims about the user, whether or not they have explicitly referenced the literature in doing so. No matter what their original formulation, all constitute "theories" about the user and entail corollary exhortations to the designer.

In his chapter, diSessa applies "principled design" to the acquisition of advanced computer literacy, his principles in support of a theoretical model of the learning of high-level programming (Figure 15.1). DiSessa cites mental models as his illustration of a guiding principle. However, we believe that the design principle, included here though seemingly secondary to his discussion, was every bit as fundamental to the course of his design.

DiSessa's set of principles only incompletely anticipated the needs of his system, which he then expanded through the use of "functional wedge-ins." Functional wedge-ins were heralded as a valuable "generic pattern" uncovered in the process of doing "local science." These "modest corruptions" of Boxer's structural design might conceivably be viewed as errors of omission or fundamental design flaws. However, diSessa viewed the wedge-ins as a necessary and even desirable feature of the development process. Perhaps it is the case that this "feature" is a corollary of principled design. Principles may narrow the designer's vision and hence the scope of the design.

1.	*Interface isomorphs of mental models*
	facilitate comprehension of complex problems.
2.	*Spatial / visual representation*
	is isomorphic with the structural modeling component of program comprehension, and hence will facilitate development of the learner's model.
3.	*System simplicity and structural integrity*
	are an important aspect of system learnability.

Figure 15.1. DiSessa's design principles, derived from his chapter.

1.	*Appropriately constructed menu item names and organization*
	facilitate goal identification and suggest analogical subgoal mappings.
2.	*Prominent positioning of core functionality*
	makes appropriate subgoals more salient.
3.	*Menus and prompt sequences construct an action path*
	that is self-evident.

Figure 15.2. Carroll et al.'s design principles, derived from their chapter, but decontextualized from the original user-interaction scenario.

Carroll et al., working backward from an existing artifact, make assertions about the psychological effects of the interface structure. Although their observations are derived from particular artifacts, they are of a kind and at a level that would appear to generalize readily to other artifacts (Figure 15.2). The claims are embedded in trade-offs that are a key element in positioning the claims in context. For example, "Menu item names and organization facilitate goal identification (but can also suggest many inappropriate goals)." The *general* principle (relating to menus) starts a designer down a path, but the *specifics* of the larger context (e.g., the set of menu options required by function, history, or whatever) beget new considerations that cannot be represented in general principles, beyond noting the possible trade-off.

---

1. *Real world metaphors*

    give users "a set of expectations to apply to computer environments."

2. *Direct manipulation with immediate feedback*

    gives users valuable and timely information about their activities

    that helps them to feel that they are in control of a real world object.

3. *See-and-point (instead of remember-and-type)*

    supports users' reliance on recognition over recall.

Figure 15.3. Apple's first three general design principles: a sample from their *Human Interface Guidelines* (Apple, 1987). The design principle is highlighted; the psychological "claim" follows.

It is worth comparing this research in principled design with published commercial guidelines. The example (Figure 15.3) is taken from Apple's *Human Interface Guidelines* (Apple, 1987a). Apple claims that ten fundamental principles guided the design of the Apple Desktop Interface. The principles are quite general, although they are elaborated with examples and discussed informally. It seems significant that there are relatively few of them (and indeed that the entire book of guidelines is a tidy 121 pages). Apple applications are often cited as the paragon of user interface consistency and have been manifestly successful, at least in part because of their efforts at principled interface development (Tognazzini, 1989).

Apple's first principle is to use real world metaphors. The "desktop," the little trash can, and assorted other representational icons are among the hallmarks of the Apple interface style. They are intended to enable the user to build on prior experience. But as Apple itself hastens to add in its discussion of this principle, "many of the elements of the Apple Desktop Interface don't have a clear physical counterpart. . . . Once immersed in the desktop metaphor, users can adapt readily to loose connections with physical situations." In other words, users' expectations based on real world experience may mislead them (see Carroll & Mack, 1984; Mack, 1990, for examples of empirical consequences for novices), but in the long run *it doesn't matter:* The principle captures something crucial to the character of the interface, even if imperfect in detail. The injunction may be powerful, but at the same time, it is not to be taken too literally. The truth of the principle is subsidiary to its effect on design. Greif puts it another way: Artifact design can be "interpreted as a theory-*oriented* problem solving process" (emphasis added). In invoking principle as pretext, he reveals the approximate and essentially atheoretic nature of the process.

Discussion

Each set of principles gives rise to a complementary set of caveats. For diSessa, principled design necessarily entrained functional wedge-ins. For Carroll et al., each claim embodied a counterclaim. For Apple, concrete metaphors paved the way for acceptance of abstract technological inventions. These caveats do not undermine the value of principled design, but point to the complex dynamics of application to actual design.

These independently developed sets of principles are strikingly similar in their degree of domain independence. The invitation to consider design from a principled point of view, as opposed to or in addition to an eclectic or empirical one, is attractive and would seem to have as a natural outcome simplicity, elegance, and guiding vision. Guiding vision, cited as much of Alan Kay's successful contribution to Apple development (see, e.g., Kay, 1984), or Doug Engelbart's vision to reach further back (Engelbart & English, 1968), are not to be dismissed lightly.

But there is a fundamental tension between simplicity and elegance on the one hand, and functional and contextual completeness on the other. Parsimony, generally valued by designers, entrains computational power and conciseness of expression. DiSessa's call for principled design, and Carroll et al.'s search for psychological claims support this way of thinking. In contrast, eclectic and empirical approaches incur a plethora of detail that may obscure abstractions important to coherent design. Henderson's elaborated descriptions of copier usage (although in service of a different argument) give a flavor for a kind of almost distressing, if nonetheless relevant, detail that may emerge from contextual inquiry. A comprehensively elaborated, context-situated task description, a fully permuted set of scenarios, or a comprehensive set of guidelines may work against the production of parsimonious and elegant design. It is imperative that the striving for completeness and the desire for elegance form a dialectic. From the integration of coherent, general principles to drive design with comprehensively described, concrete systems in contexts of use emerges a key methodological challenge for the field of HCI.

Representation

Representation techniques are among the more popular recommendations for the analysis and encapsulation of design. However, no single technique completely covers the problem space, and some combinations are essentially redundant. At minimum, to represent and evaluate a design adequately, we believe that it would be necessary to include one method to express the temporal experience of the artifact in use (e.g., scenarios, GOMS-style descriptions), a second to depict the concrete representation of the interface (screen images, menus, commands, dialogs), and a third to represent the conceptual abstractions that are critical to design and user understanding [e.g., taxonomies (Brooks), task description languages (Payne), claims analysis (Carroll et al.)]. Concrete representations of the interface are quite common, and no one at the workshop explicitly addressed them. The discussion that follows addresses the temporal experience of the artifact and the conceptual, interface abstractions.

There are two fundamental objectives that these representations address. The first is to model the procedural richness of the environment, task, or artifact, to make sure that the proffered solution meets the users' needs. The second is to abstract the distinctions and similarities pertinent to the development of an effective, conceptually coherent, and usable interface. The first looks out toward the users' experience, the second in toward the designer's or user's structural model.

Experiential Representations

Scenarios

Scenarios are already highly valued and widely used in design. They are a device for making contact with an artifact in use and for thinking concretely about the details of design. Designers often work in the abstract, and scenarios force their attention to the procedural consequences of their decisions (diSessa, Karat & Bennett). But often their use is informal, with designers carrying about in their heads small, limited-purpose scenarios that capture various aspects of design rationale. Documented scenarios, as a shared vision of design, can be powerful indeed. As Carroll et al. note, their use is growing more formal, as they find their way even into commercial design specifications.

Carroll et al.'s abstraction of canonical scenarios (e.g., identification of core scenarios as a key component of a well-constructed suite) is an interesting approach. Could this be extended to provide a framework for the development of scenario suites? Because a fully permuted set of scenarios is not even feasible, let alone practical, how should the scenario space be sampled to exercise the design-in-use most effectively and focus attention on critical usability issues?

At minimum, one needs to systematically compare designed elements against the set of scenarios to ensure coverage, both of the design with respect to user needs, and the scenario suite with respect to designed function. In addition, the sampling could follow well-established rules-of-thumb for software testing: Test main path code; test all uniquely processed inputs; test at and beyond boundary conditions, and so forth. However, well beyond the scope of such traditional scenarios are the context sensitive examples provided by Henderson: Given that your expense report is pink and the system is set to the default darkness setting, produce a readable copy. In contrast to traditional testing, which is oriented toward the exercise of implemented functionality, independently developed, contextualized scenarios can reveal new concerns with the artifact in use.

Scenarios, however, should not be used as the *sole* representation of design, as they need to be coupled with the more abstract representations that capture the regularities and structure in the interface. Scenarios of use express functional possibilities that are both selective and open-ended, whereas system functional capabilities are finite and can be completely described. Scenarios are necessarily redun-

dant, and if they completely specified an interface would be prohibitively voluminous. They would likely obscure the regularities in the interface that are essential to
effective design. The sort of analysis that would highlight commonalities (identification of common terms, objects, and actions) creates precisely the sort of distinctions captured by taxonomic exercises or even traditional design specifications.
Once such analysis has been performed, it is important to situate these well-formed
elements appropriately in contextualized scenarios, but the more concise representation cannot be discarded.

We offer a final, somewhat parenthetical, caution on the use of scenarios. There
are times, such as in the development of partial prototypes, when using scenarios
developed to guide design to evaluate the implementation is an attractive, indeed
almost an essential, conservation measure (Carroll et al.). To the extent that prototypes are a representation of a design, rather than a complete instantiation, they
will have been built to perform particular representative tasks. They are necessarily
exercised with a constrained suite of scenarios, and must be built to support them.
The danger in using the design scenarios to drive evaluation of a fully instantiated
design is that the design may have been tuned to scenario execution. That is, it may
support the designed scenarios and *little else*. It is critical for effective software
testing to distinguish scenarios that drive design, and which may validate what a
designer was trying to achieve, from more broadly based scenarios that stretch the
system in ways unanticipated by design.

Prototypes

Prototyping was mentioned as an important design tool by nearly all the participants, but its value was so pervasively accepted that it was mentioned only in
passing. In some sense it is the representation of the interface par excellence,
reflecting both its appearance and behavior. Coupled with a suite of scenarios, it
becomes an opportunity for exploring the proposed interface behaviorally and, to
at least some reasonable approximation, in the context of use (Bannon & Bødker).

Prototypes emulate the intended design as faithfully as the implementation resources and technology permit. Interface design can be very difficult to picture and
evaluate in the abstract or from stimulus and behaviorally impoverished representations such as static drawings or verbal description. Prototypes make explicit and
concrete visual details and make interactive behavior of the interface available to
both analysis and testing. As with any programming representation, they mandate
rigorous specification of the problem and force interface designers to grapple with
issues otherwise readily lost to abstract thinking and unarticulated assumptions.

However, prototypes engender problems of their own. In the first place, a high-
fidelity prototype, one that faithfully renders the design, can be expensive to
build, containing, as it must, nearly the same functionality of the intended product. Second, many decisions must be made that, while germane to application at
hand, are only incidentally related to the systematic or principled aspects of the
interface design. When, during the course of evaluation, it becomes clear that
something does not work, it may be a nontrivial exercise to determine the root

cause of the error. In evaluating the effectiveness of guiding principles, care must be taken to discriminate between the *essential* and the *incidental* aspects of the interface.

Finally, software prototyping significantly shifts the personal task of the interface designer (Norman) from that of interface design. The task concerns of programming are substantially different from those of interface design, and they turn the designer's attention away from interface considerations. The tasks become ones of *internal* design, run-time stability, acceptable performance, and so on. (It is precisely this effect that motivates Karat and Bennett to look at techniques to regain the designers' focus on the user – see below "Group process.") Programming environments that permit visual, or at least rapid, construction of new interfaces, such as HyperCard, mitigate some of this difficulty and are attractive for those interfaces whose characteristics conform to the constraints of the design tool.

Abstract Representations

Scenarios and prototypes concretely lay out and articulate design possibilities. Another set of representations is needed to recover, if not create, abstractions that allow designers to see and evaluate the underlying coherence of an emerging design. For example, Karat and Bennett, working with conventional functional specifications, derive tables relating the basic application and interface objects to the actions performed on them. These are intended to enable designers to compare and contrast the essential semantics of the interface, abstracted from the surface details of terminology or interface presentation. Out of such a representation might evolve a smaller set of generic actions and the potential for a simpler interface. Claims analysis (Carroll et al.) also forms abstractions about the interface primarily in the form of assertions about the psychological characteristics of the interface. However, the technique is still representationally informal and is not included in this discussion. The most formal proposals for abstract representations at the workshop were taxonomies (Brooks, Pylyshyn) and task-description languages (Payne).

Taxonomies

An analysis often begins with identification of its component parts. Taxonomic analysis, particularly in service of design and evaluation, implies an articulate decomposition of the relevant problem space. A problem central to all solution strategies predicated on problem-space decomposition is the character of the decomposed nodes. Pylyshyn recommends that regularities be summarized "at a level appropriate for the design task," and that task demands be characterized "in a way that is as independent as possible of the way that the tasks are currently being carried out." Pylyshyn, and Brooks, in a more elaborated discussion, recommend task and interface taxonomies as a technique for extracting useful abstractions to facilitate analysis and foster innovation in HCI. The purpose is to guide design and to elicit the similarities and differences among designs.

Tasks, which are analyzed with respect to:

    Conceptual schema

        Temporal phases – major sequential events

            Activities

                Concurrency – temporal overlap with other activities

                Memory load – cognitive resources needed

    Work content

        Input

            Information type

            Constraining parameters

        Processing

        Output

            Information type

Applications, which instantiate a particular task, with:

    Implementation

    History / experience

Implementations (tools), which integrate:

    Presentation considerations

    Information type

Figure 15.4. Components of the taxonomic world: analysis of Brooks's scenario, derived from his abstract narrative. Primary component elements are
in bold; linking elements are italicized.

Brooks proposes taxonomizing the tasks, on the one hand, and the interface or
device characteristics of the implementing artifact, on the other. The introductory,
abstract application narrative in his chapter sketches the components of this taxonomic world. Constructing the implicit taxonomic hierarchy from his narrative, we
find that the components group together under the broad classifications of *tasks,
applications,* and *tools* (Figure 15.4). The mapping between tasks and tools (or

Table 1. *HCI taxonomic decomposition strategies: ordered from task concerns to device operations*

Decomposition strategy	Example	Reference
Generic task types	Core scenario	Carroll
Generic task features	Memory load, information type	Brooks
Domain-independent goals	Edit object, move target	See text
Domain-dependent goals	Edit text, move line	Moran, 1983
	Modify text, create polygon	Payne
Problem-solving techniques	Data-based iteration, simulation	Brooks
Interface features	Window management techniques, icons	Myers, 1988
Operations in device space	Mark string, copy buffer	Payne
Primitive interface operators	Get, change, destroy menu	Petzold, 1988
Physical operators	Keystrokes	Card et al., 1983

artifacts) is evidently performed at the level of "information type," though it is not obvious how this would be done in practice.

As Brooks points out, a key question for all representational schemes is finding a useful set of primitive elements and constructs to decompose a domain and express distinctions of interest. Representation primitives can significantly affect the kinds of comparisons that can be drawn. Brooks provides a process control example involving the design of nuclear power plant operations. He observes that the conventional task–analysis approach, which yielded the node "start recirculation pumps" precluded comparisons of operational procedures (Is the pump started with a switch or by adjusting a control?). However, so would a decomposition based on general problem-solving techniques, as he proposes. Furthermore, the original decomposition actually *facilitates* comparisons of ways to start operations and comparisons of things having to do with circulation pumps. One could imagine that it would be advantageous for *all* starts (or at any rate all stops) in a nuclear power plant to be implemented using the same physical technique (e.g., the flip of a switch). Calling out "starts" as a taxonomic element might in fact be useful.

Brooks is attracted to the taxonomies being developed for knowledge work, which are based on the "methods required to solve problems," although this would seem to lack useful task relevance. What would this taxonomy look like? Would it include trial and error, tree search, arithmetic computation, and visual scan? The problem with such an approach is that the task *interacts* with the problem-solving technique (Norman, Payne): A problem that once had to be solved by, say, serial search, with appropriate reorganization of the underlying data, can be solved by menu traversal. The user's goal is the same but the interface task has changed.

Table 15.1 compares a number of different decomposition strategies. The first two categories are organized by conceptual attributes of the task and interface.

These are interesting decompositions, in part, because they focus on considerations not normally addressed in interface analysis. However, it is difficult to see in Brooks's analysis how problem-solving techniques would integrate with the task description. Should they be included as part of the conceptual schema or be considered as part of the work content?

Myers (1988) provides an example of a taxonomy that classifies artifact presentation features. Window management schemes, for example, are decomposed into tiled or overlapped arrangements; icons are described with respect to their referent, their conditions of presentation, their content dynamics, their mobility and size. He uses his taxonomy to compare a variety of window management systems. It could be used as readily to recombine or extend features, informing the design of a new artifact. It does not, however, relate usefully to task-oriented decompositions.

The next three decompositions, which come from the GOMS tradition, span the problem space more coherently, if also more narrowly. Although Brooks objects to the GOMS style "locate-line" because it obscures comparison with other tasks, it strikes us that for much context-situated work, this may be an appropriate decomposition. Furthermore, with minor revisions, it can be generalized in such a way (e.g., locate-target) that would facilitate cross-artifact comparisons. Such generalizations should evolve naturally from the well-structured, domain-specific beginnings.

We agree with Brooks, however, that decomposition to the level of physical operators is inappropriate for most purposes and that current toolkits (e.g., Windows, Petzold, 1988; MacApp, Apple, 1987b) are at too low a level. Most toolkits are still deeply rooted in system internals, a fact that interferes both with conceptual comparisons as well as with the ability of the designer–programmer to develop a coherent model of the interface under construction.

Semantic Manipulation of Conceptual Elements

Having built a vocabulary with which to talk about tasks and artifacts, you then want to have something to say, to manipulate the elements in a way that enables comparison, evaluation, and exploration of the interaction dynamics among the parts. Brooks proposes constructing hierarchical representations of taxonomic elements, from which, presumably, similarities will become manifest by congruences within the tree structure. As with all such techniques, but perhaps most obviously here, the utility of the method hinges critically on the decomposition strategy. Despite his concern for a rich and effective task analysis, the approach remains static and does not address the dynamics of the interface.

Payne's representations, on the other hand, focus primarily on the dynamics of the interface interactions. Payne, like Brooks, begins with a semantic representation of components. However, the content of his taxonomy is more tightly focused on operations available in the device space, and his representations of the dynamics of the interface are much better elaborated. The task–action grammar (TAG), described in his chapter, relates artifact-oriented goals with actions in the device space and characteristics of the device display. The TAG provides a formal and regular description of the relevant interface components. Interaction trees, still a preliminary representation, attempt to capture the interaction characteristics of the interface of a conversational model.

There is much to be learned about an interface from such explicit formulation of its dynamics. More than any other technique described in the workshop, this bridges the conceptual gap between temporal representations, such as scenarios, and abstract representations, such as taxonomies, incorporating, as it does, elements from each. As Payne observes, there is much to be gained simply from the intellectual exercise of rigorous description. With an appropriate taxonomic decomposition, even a relatively superficial examination of the description should reveal inconsistencies, awkward interactions, and conceptual inelegance.

However, many of the insights obtained in Payne's examples are only incidental to the formalism. The user's confusions about how to fill polygons stem from particular strategies chosen in the original polygon construction. The confusions about text creation and editing – the inadvertent creation of new text – seem to hinge on the order in which the user has made discoveries about the system. Nothing in the representation addresses how a user arrives at a given strategy. Nor does it address issues related to learning sequence. Surely these are also a function of the interface design – in the salience of the particular methods, whether inherent in the interface itself or its supporting tutorial or help mechanisms. Symmetry or simplicity in the rule representation may not correspond to salience in the interface. Although there may be a number of rules that a user may exercise to achieve a particular goal, nothing addresses the weighting of the usage of the rules. It may be that the rule which corresponds to the most *frequent* goal is the one the user remembers, not the "simplest" rule, as is suggested here. Once again, we note the importance of the sampling strategies for the goal or scenario space.

The limitations notwithstanding, this work is a concrete, precise, and integrated effort at interface description. It is not likely to afford insight into the greater contextualized domain of work, but this type of analysis may well help to evaluate artifacts in their own terms.

Discussion

The workshop provided several examples of representational schemes that claim to analytically represent user tasks, interface structure and function, and possibly elucidate the psychological implications of user interaction with the interface. We must, however, be concerned with trading off the "cost" or effort of building and applying such models with effectiveness of what the models reveal about design. The growing discomfort (e.g., Karat, 1989) with formal modeling stems in part from just this limitation, namely the scope of the problems that they can tractably and economically address.

In addition, these representations entail unique perspectives that may highlight some aspects of design, but obscure others. Representations need to make important design distinctions explicit (Brooks, Karat & Bennett, Pylyshyn). In some sense, each of these techniques contributes to that goal. But there are also ways in which they tend to obscure it. Scenarios, for example, follow a time course. Unless they are properly chosen and "diagrammed," the commonalities present (i.e., the abstractions necessary for a tractable design) may be lost. Similarly, while prototypes require the same ruthless precision as all implementations, they are still an inarticulate vehicle for the specification of the abstractions in the design, because far more may be required to implement code than was intended by its architecture. Thus the limitations of any single technique underscore the necessity for adopting multiple perspectives, and for understanding the analytical scope and utility of each.

What we may need, as Norman suggests, is a comparative analysis of representations with respect to their congruence with the represented domain, and/or their ability to express useful distinctions with respect to design goals. Scenarios, for example, seem well suited to a description of user activities, mirroring as they do the procedural character of the interaction. However, scenarios as artifact representation are most congruent with novice approaches to program construction, with serially considered paths through the problem space, and with subsequent amendment to accommodate new scenarios of use and error conditions. They resemble unstructured programs – what in the early days of programming was known as "spaghetti code." In contrast, the temporal dimension of scenarios is only indirectly represented in contemporary, well-structured designs, whether implemented by procedural, structured programming advocates, or object-oriented designers. On the other hand, although taxonomic hierarchies and task description languages are structurally more congruent with the hierarchic and parameterized constructs used in software engineering, they make only minimal contact with the broader context of use.

Empirical Discovery

With the exception of Landauer's discussion, empirical methods characteristic of usability engineering were not discussed in any depth at the workshop. Conventional, evaluative methods were taken for granted as established HCI practice. Empirical evaluation was regarded as important to enable designers to assess their work but insufficient. The discussions of theory at the workshop can be seen as attempts to transcend the limits of empirical data in order to influence design effectively and to go beyond the issues that can be tested or tied directly to empirical data. Workshop participants seemed drawn to the possibility of innovation in empirical methods, especially those aimed at uncovering phenomena that may lead to discovery and innovation in design (see especially Landauer, Barnard, Lewis).

Exploratory Research in Artifact Construction

Landauer and his colleagues' development of more effective information retrieval technology (Egan, Remde, Landauer, Lochbaum, & Gomez, 1989) represents a prime example of artifact construction in HCI. They developed both from basic principles of usability engineering, as well as from a style of research which Landauer characterized as *exploratory* (see also Landauer, 1987b).

Exploratory research can be distinguished from theoretically motivated research strategies in cognitive psychology by its commitment to real world tasks and from conventional evaluative methods in the HCI domain. Although Landauer and his colleagues used ideas about semantic memory to analyze naming and retrieval tasks, they were interested in those real world tasks, and not necessarily in advancing those theories (Furnas, Landauer, Gomez, & Dumais, 1984). In contrast to evaluative empirical evaluation, exploratory research is aimed largely at *discovery* and systematic exploration, in the context of solving a problem that lies in the interaction of technology and human performance (construed broadly to include cognition).

For example, in the case of information retrieval, the problem is that people are not especially consistent or specific in how they describe and name things. Existing technology, from document indexes to computer query systems, does not provide adequate alternatives or compensation. As exemplified in the development of SuperBook, exploratory research is directed toward finding behavioral and technical factors that account for large differences in behavior, whether the differences pertain to problems that hinder task performance, or strategies and factors that produce markedly successful results. Exploratory research uses psychological theory where available and useful, and quantitative and approximate modeling to extrapolate effects and to simulate and explore factors that might account for variations in performance.

We see in this work the essence of HCI research in its commitment to real world relevance, the creation of useful artifacts, and the exploitation of both technology and psychological concepts and methods. It tackles problems, not by abstraction into constrained laboratory tasks, but by psychological reasoning, modeling, and empirical methods closely tied to real world phenomena and data. Exploratory research is, however, distinguished more by its intent than by its specific methodology. In Landauer's example, the research exploited conventional prototyping, iterative evaluation, and even controlled experimentation where appropriate. It was the broader objectives that created a focus and unique synergy among methods.

Finally, it is worth noting that the goal of solving practical problems may not only lead to practical results, it may also stimulate interesting psychology. As Landauer has argued, psychologically motivated artifact construction could be a model for basic psychology at large (Landauer, 1987b; see also Anderson, 1987).

Research on Artifacts in Their Context of Use

There are many kinds of data that might be derived from the study of artifacts in their context of use. Prominent among those discussed at the workshop was contextual inquiry, an empirical and interpretive method for understanding and analyzing people and work. The papers by Grief and by Bannon and Bødker talked in part about how such inquiry might be conducted, but the reader will have to look elsewhere to find specifics (e.g., Bennett, Holtzblatt, Jones, & Wixon, 1990; Bødker, 1989; Whiteside et al., 1988; Wixon, Holtzblatt, & Knox, 1990). Much work remains to be done to understand what these methods can accomplish in designing more useful and usable computer systems. Case studies of how these methods were used in developing artifacts and improving work flow would be valuable, especially with focus on how these methods take us beyond conventional usability engineering. Many of the methods described seem to have much in common with field and ethnographic techniques.

For example, Bannon and Bødker use strategic questioning to guide the process of coming to understand the context of use. They try to determine:

What is the object of the activity in which the artifact is used?

What is the outcome produced to be used for?

Where do the breakdowns occur?

What is the praxis of use? What is the "specific material, social, and historical setting of that use"?

What is the social role of the artifact? Does it divide work? Is it used as an instrument or tool of production?

Questions here are used in a context of open-ended and opportunistic inquiry. Some seem to follow from conventional methods of field inquiry: They try to describe what people do and why and, in particular, where people are having problems with existing tools and practice. Other questions seem to come from a commitment to specific values, and could stimulate more profound assessment of how to improve people's work practices. In the practice of HCI, these values may influence the interpretation of people's work and the proposals to support it.

Discussion

Moving from contextual inquiry toward artifact development, informed by holistic and contextual involvement with users, we need to explore the possibility that there are differences in tasks that have some predictable relationship to interface differences. Can we determine the contexts in which direct manipulation is appropriate? Are there classifiably regular differences in vocabulary, content, format, and organization? Is there a useful set of canonical tasks that can be used to benchmark interfaces? Task decompositions that enable matching of task features to interface features (Brooks) may facilitate such analysis. They may enable evaluation of designs, not only across levels of experience, but also across tasks that tap broadly different cognitive resources, such as document creation, complex problem solving, information search, and high-pressure–real-time control tasks.

The shift from laboratory evaluation to working with artifacts in their context of use raises the question of whether HCI professionals can find more effective ways to deal with the volume and multivariate diversity of real world, user feedback. Can we capture, and treat as data, the broader experience with artifacts, as products competing in the marketplace? Can we make better use of automatic logging (Tetzlaff & Cleveland, 1990; Yoder, McCracken, & Akscyn, 1984)? Such data exist but are voluminous and are not the sort that analytic models can readily handle (Barnard, in workshop discussion). What can we learn from such feedback?

At the same time, the notion of what constitutes "context" must continue to broaden. Although a particular context integrates otherwise discrete applications, the personal computer integrates previously disparate *contexts* into a common environment. As a result, at the same time we are honing applications to the context of use, users are developing *task-independent* expectations for their use. Thus, there is enormous boundary instability as contexts of use become more and more permeable: Computers are widely available for personal use, at the same time that work enters the home. How long will users tolerate a change in in rface style simply because they have changed context of use? Still, in the long run the problem may become simpler as the contexts of use become anchored in, and consequently leveled by, computer technology.

Encapsulation Techniques

We began with a discussion of how general principles can start the design process, followed by discussion of representations that enable design to be carried out concretely in a specific artifact or product. We want to work back out to capture what was learned and what might be more generally applicable. The focus of techniques here is not the formation of abstract principles, so much as how to make design and user experience more accessible to future designers.

Traditionally the collective wisdom has been encapsulated in books (e.g., Rubenstein & Hersh, 1984; Shneiderman, 1987), technical reports (e.g., Engle & Granda, 1975), and style guides (Apple, 1987; International Business Machines, 1989). Certainly written materials have many desirable characteristics for supporting encapsulation. The skills and resources for processing printed text are universally available to the designing public. Text can be readily encoded in machine-readable form, and hence is amenable to mass storage, sophisticated indexing, and facile dissemination. It is easily generated, and is still perhaps the most effective technique for the capture of information, history, argument, considered thought, and theory. Multimedia presentations emphasizing video are becoming attractive extensions, but effective multimedia presentations are not easy to create, and to date are not much more interactive than documentation.

Although it is a matter of common knowledge that end users are fundamentally doers, with little use for exhaustive documentation, it still seems to be implicitly assumed that programmers, designers, and scientists are readers, of necessity, if not by preference. Documentation is a pivotal feature of the canonical software development process (Aron, 1974), despite the fact that programmers are notoriously aversive to generating documentation and are, perhaps correspondingly, skeptical as to its value. When people have difficulty making effective use of hard-copy documentation, it is assumed to be an anomaly of "information overload" (Krasner, Curtis, & Iscoe, 1987).

A second, probably more important, vehicle for significant change is the development of interesting and successful artifacts. Their tractable components are analyzed by human–computer interaction specialists and their salient characteristics incorporated into new artifacts by designers. Apple's Macintosh, based on many of the ideas developed in the Xerox Star, is the best current example of this. Most contemporary graphical user interfaces share the Star world view (Myers, 1988; see also Johnson et al., 1989; Smith, Irby, Kimball, Verplank, & Harslem, 1982; Williams, 1983), and menus, windows, and direct manipulation techniques are the grist of much current HCI research.

Artifact Construction

Although Carroll, Kellogg, and Rosson make the argument most pointedly with their task–artifact framework, artifact construction as the ultimate experiment and as the vehicle for theoretic advance was generally accepted by workshop participants. Landauer's theoretic explorations culminated in the production of Superbook, diSessa's in Boxer, Carroll's in Displaywriter and ViewMatcher, Grief's in Genetic Growing Systems, Bødker's in UTOPIA (Bødker, Ehn, Romberger, & Sjogren 1985), Henderson's in Trillium (Henderson, 1986), Lewis's in NoPumpG (Lewis, 1990). Pylyshyn, more broadly even, recommends the collection of paradigm cases to represent the generalizations, empirical demonstrations, experimental methods, and apparatus.

Artifacts are undeniably compelling. They are rich, concrete, engaging manifestations of "theory." Laboratory artifacts effectively support iterative experimentation and behavioral observation. Commercial artifacts enlist an enormous, if uncontrolled, subject population that runs a hearty, longitudinal, context-situated experiment, providing abundant feedback to the "experimenters."

Of course, artifacts are a good deal more than theory, whatever implicit or explicit principles have gone into their design. As a result, it may not be clear where theory leaves off and the artifacts of the artifact take over. These atheoretic components of the artifact may nonetheless be essential aspects of their success or failure. Landauer (also Gould, 1988) notes the extent to which the success of a design may hinge on seemingly mundane detail, quite peripheral to the principled technique under consideration. It may be a considerable challenge to understand the regularities among the anomalies to bring them within the domain of theory.

So to the extent that research can work directly and effectively in the medium that it aspires to change, to the extent that it can minimize the transformations of understanding and representation that must be endured to absorb fully the implications of its findings, then to that extent close coupling with the artifact will be an important domain of investigation. Further, as researchers share concerns, methodology, and objects of study with designers, their work should become increasingly and reciprocally accessible.

Expert Systems

Of all the participants, Barnard was the most optimistic about the strength and utility of the science base. Barnard would like to abstract the regularities (generalizations, theory, or science) from contextualized HCI activity, absorb the perceived regularities into the science base, and then codify and operationalize this knowledge in an expert system for use by designers. Although an expert system is more indirect than the incorporation of collective knowledge into artifacts, it might supplement it in interesting ways. In principle, such an approach has at least three inherent advantages over artifact construction. One is that it offers a clean and independently manipulable model of the human processor. The second is that it might be able to represent aspects of the collective wisdom that cannot be effectively embodied in the artifact per se. Guidelines that address the set of circumstances under which a technique should be applied might be captured here. Third, such a system could permit flexible evaluation of alternatives prior to labor intensive, expensive empirical evaluation.

The vision is an appealing one, particularly for those reluctant to abandon the belief that basic cognition constrains human–computer interaction in important and interesting ways. However, it depends to a great extent on the condition of the science base, and Barnard, too, acknowledges that the science base is spotty. Coherent interpolation would require the kinds of engineering approximations utilized by Card, Moran, and Newell (1983). If it were feasible to construct a reasonably comprehensive set of such approximations, this might be of service to the design community, even if the notion of the system as an encapsulation of the "science base" had to be relinquished. However, it seems likely that such a system would of necessity be of extremely limited scope for well into the foreseeable future. The requirement to describe fully the environmental and task considerations, because of its inherent impossibility, will cause the system to suffer from the very lack of contextualization that it purports to overcome. An appropriately comprehensive extension would be at best expensive, and at worst inherently intractable (Winograd & Flores, 1986).

Moreover, expert systems are best adapted to well-understood domains with well-organized structure. HCI is still young, with a highly dynamic and idiosyncratic empirical base. Expert systems support elaboration of a knowledge base within a defined framework; they are less well suited to the restructuring that must follow as the gradually accumulated knowledge is subjected to reformulation.

Discussion

Encapsulation methods must balance the extraction of generalities that take us beyond a particular artifact with preservation of the richness of the concrete artifact. Explicit documentation can capture underlying rationale or principles; the artifact is needed to elaborate these abstract ideas concretely and dynamically.

An enhancement to the expository accumulation of knowledge might be the development of more effective, integrated frameworks for providing access to artifacts, and their larger context of understanding and experience. This larger context of understanding could include interpretations of design experience, design rationale, the user's experience with the systems, and the results of systematic research carried out with the artifact (Carroll et al.; diSessa; MacLean, Young, & Moran,

1989). Current research in this area exploits the same information technology being applied more generally to the support of cooperative work in groups (e.g., project NICK, Cook, Ellis, Graf, Rein, & Smith, 1987; the gIBIS prototype, Conklin & Begeman, 1988; see also Neches, 1988), and may exploit hypermedia to develop large multimedia information systems.

Artifacts as an encapsulation mechanism could be advanced by the development of systems specifically architected for the exploration of interface issues. Current toolkits, which support application development (e.g., MacApp, Apple, 1987; Microsoft's Windows, Petzold, 1988), are generally constrained to enable application development within a well-defined style. While they facilitate the development of new applications, and while they are critical to the development of consistent interaction techniques across applications, they are basically conservative in orientation, fostering the preservation of an interface standard, rather than an innovative exploration of the interface itself.

Abstracting the toolkit methodology one level further could produce a prototyping tool that incorporates what is already "known" about usability and interface design but that allows experimentation programmatically or opportunistically to elaborate both a theoretical model of effective interaction as well as the construction of successful applications. Such a tool or environment could enable vigorous and flexible examination of interface techniques, styles, and semantics, while at the same time providing the facility to snapshot and preserve those discoveries that prove felicitously supportive of user interactions. The emphasis would be on the usability of the end product on the one hand, and the flexibility and usability of the tool itself (its representational character) on the other. In addition to providing normal facilities for application development, the system would enable *style-independent,* experimental flexibility on issues germane to human–computer interaction. For example, a current-style toolkit might enable undo of the most recent user action, supported by a single-level store. In contrast, the architecture of the proposed system might support infinite undo and then provide facilities for its pragmatic constraint, arbitrarily by time or size, semantically in terms of meaningful user events or interactively by user tailoring. The salient parameters of undo would be defined and externalized in such a way that they could be manipulated to explore a variety of design solutions. Figure 15.5 provides a sampling of other kinds of capability such a system might include. In some areas considerable research has already been performed; others are much more exploratory. The objective is to integrate results into a single platform and to explore them holistically and cumulatively.

Design Process

Process methodologies are basically tactical, providing ways to approach a problem that have solutions only as an emergent feature, not by providing a well-structured framework for their representation. Two of the chapters in this collection focus primarily on the design process: Henderson calls for a fresh and comprehensive look not merely at the traditional design process, but also the range of activities that should be absorbed into the inquiry; Karat and Bennett, working within traditional

Data semantics, enabling exploration of:

> Structural navigation (by word, sentence, paragraph, header, file. . .)
>
> Organizational navigation (e.g., fisheye (Furnas, 1986))
>
> Content navigation (e.g., by critical fields, indexing (Landauer))
>
> Content organization (e.g., filtering – Malone et al., 1986)
>
> Structured, content sensitive and generic editors

State semantics enabling exploration of

> Temporal navigation (e.g., marking, tracking, escape, return, interface maps)
>
> Undo
>
> Context sensitive help

Interface semantics enabling exploration of

> Redundant cues
>
> Consistency specification
>
> Object relations

Function layering (for help, tutorials, and application, context or user driven tailoring)

Object libraries

> Interface "templates" (Windows style, Mac style. . .)
>
> Icons

Design rationale support

Figure 15.5. Partial function list for an exploratory interface environment.

scope of design, are looking for a set of techniques whose usage will improve the likelihood of building usable systems.

Henderson broadens the purview of design to include the creative accommodations made by the many people who create artifacts and interact with them throughout their life cycle. His notion of design includes not only the explicit development of technology, but also all the adaptations and creative extensions made to and around technology in its context of use. He draws attention to the design process as it reveals itself over time and across the variegated population of designers, each with their different roles and perspectives.

Karat and Bennett believe that important leverage will come from influencing early stages of design. They characterize design as "a complex activity involving problem-solving trade-offs among multiple perspectives," and discuss a number of techniques for managing the necessary shifts in perspective, with particular attention to considerations of group process. Many of the techniques that they recommend, particularly the representational schemes for portraying aspects of the design, necessarily deal with the artifact per se. But their objective is to focus design group interaction on usability. They believe that usable designs are much more likely if designers constructively and self-consciously attend to the problems of usability on a technical footing comparable with other technical development concerns such as schedule and function.

Group Process

Design is often a group activity, in part because a project may be larger than a single individual can handle and because of the range of skills that may come into play for its successful execution. Programmers, interface design experts, user domain experts, and users themselves may be brought into the process (Bannon & Bødker; Wiecha, Bennett, Boies, & Gould, 1989).

When in the throes of their trade, even well-intentioned designers become absorbed by the technical demands of the design and programming process. Explicit interventions may be required to maintain focus on usability concerns. Karat and Bennett have developed a technique they label "four walls," in which the design proceeds with the key design considerations in view on the walls of the design room. The walls display product objectives, constraints, resources, and representative images of the interface, providing a system overview. They also accumulate the issues and critical elements of the design itself. The intent is for the omnipresence of these representations to facilitate discussion based on the issues germane to user-centered design. The four-walls technique attempts to organize and institutionalize the time-honored pedagogical technique of making dynamic, visual instantiations of verbally presented material.

Implicit in the methodology is the claim that in design people lose track of considerations relevant to their task, in particular the task of creating usable systems: If the relevant considerations can remain salient during the design process, they will more likely be appropriately incorporated into the design product. This is a joint claim about the cognitive capacities of the designers and the complexity of their task. It assumes that the resolution of a problem can be facilitated by the coresidence of the disparate elements in the same visual space. How successful is this likely to be in practice? Karat and Bennett did not present a detailed case study, but several observations are worth making.

First, the group dynamics are important. Enlisting commitment, reinforcing active and constructive involvement, and managing the overall dynamics need explication and study in their own right. One problem in evaluating this aspect of the four-walls technique is disentangling the personal skills of Bennett and Karat from the methodology they propose. How can we be sure that the effectiveness of the

discussions they witnessed within their four walls was due to the inherent characteristics of their technique and not due to their substantial interpersonal skills relentlessly applied to the preservation of a user-centered perspective?

Second, the framework makes use of specific, concrete techniques such as the use
of 4- by 6-inch cards to lay out design issues, and pictures on walls to facilitate group
review and discussion. Here again, we would like to understand the relative role of
these representational and material techniques, compared with that of conversation
and facilitation. So, for example, it is possible that the desirability of being able to
read the materials on the walls leads to a large print–abbreviated content abstraction of what has been said, with a resulting loss of detail. The cards may operate
primarily as individual cues to recall rather than representing a shared vision. Their
spontaneous and telegraphic quality means that there is a secondary task to translate the generally brief notes into fully elaborated design. If the cards have been
freely generated by more than one participant, this may not be an easy task.
Futhermore, participants may become habituated to the presence of the cards, and
the original objective lost.

Discussion

One subjective, but highly potent process for coming to understand a task domain is
to experience it personally – become a task expert, understand the task from the
inside (Pylyshyn). Although this could be a way to understand how a user thinks
about a task, it can also be conceived of as a process for achieving an understanding
of the task itself. As a technique, it is quite different from an analytic, necessity
analysis (Payne, Pylyshyn), which attempts to discover by inspection only those
procedural and functional elements essential to completion of the task. However,
not much was made of personal process in design, although to some extent, the
spectrum of representational techniques presented here constitutes tools for individual assessment of the design problem.

As personal computing becomes more prevalent, individual process may become
a more important matter of concern. Furthermore, it is likely that the issues will be
colored by this change in the demographics of the designer (diSessa), and the tools
available for design. In the early days of computers, programming was essentially
an individual effort. With the advent of operating systems and large applications,
design became a massive group effort, which is still only barely understood. While
group design continues to be important, individual design can be expected to take
on a new significance.

In this context, it would be interesting to follow up a suggestion by Barnard:
Although much of the thought in the workshop was directed toward design, and by
extension toward designers, little is known specifically about their decision heuris-
tics, or more generally about designers as users of tools. How do designers make
decisions about questions of usability? What kind of evidence weighs most heavily
with them – personal experience, empirical evidence, logical exposition? How
much evidence do they entertain before making a decision? In research on real
world reasoning (e.g., Voss & Post, 1988), we find that physicians reviewing appli-

cants for house officer seem to rely on a rather eclectic search of loosely integrated information, whereas judges deciding a case systematically reason across a well-integrated body of laws and procedures that structure the evidence. The solution process of the two experts differs in part because the magistrates must justify their decision, whereas the physicians need not. Preliminary research on psychology of programming and design (Rosson, Maass, & Kellogg, 1988) has just begun to characterize qualitatively how designers think about usability issues in the broader context of programming and design.

Conclusions

Although this book is the result of a workshop convened to discuss theory, and although its contributors are primarily researchers in this world of HCI, they have outlined a plan for future activity that seems directed more toward designers than toward researchers. In fact, what we have is a corollary of "artifact as theory" (Carroll & Kellogg, 1989); we have design as research. With only a few exceptions, the methodologies espoused live within a design cycle (or wheel), broadly conceived. Design has become the ultimate experiment. Of course, much remains to be worked out in the domain of both theory and the methodologies associated with them, and many of the workshop proposals are programmatic. We would expect HCI research and its contribution to design practice to make progress on at least three fronts.

First, we would hope to see more case studies to explore the usefulness and validity of the research programs outlined here. We would expect these case studies to center around the concrete experience of applying the research strategies to design problems of practical interest and consequence. Landauer and colleagues' work on information retrieval is a good example of what we might hope for. Developing cogent and informative case studies may be a challenge in itself, resulting in its own artifacts and techniques (Carroll et al. and Pylyshyn). Creating effective case studies would seem to contribute to achieving the goal of creating a sciencelike cumulation of knowledge and expertise in the HCI domain.

The second challenge for HCI research is to understand the contribution of specific methodologies to successful design, and the ways in which methods can work together. It seems clear from the workshop that there are many useful methodologies that can contribute to design. The diversity in conceptual and methodological focus reflects, in our view, the inevitable multifaceted and multidisciplinary character of design. We believe complementary methods are needed to mediate, for example, the dialectic between the richness and complexity of people's experience in the context of work, and general principles and abstractions needed to effect coherent, consistent, elegant, and ultimately usable design. This can be supported only by diversity in research as advocated by Lewis and exemplified by Landauer's pragmatic approach to HCI research and design.

From a practical perspective, this diversity of methods poses the third and final challenge, which is to turn these methodological approaches into practical tools within usability engineering practice. It will not be a trivial step to turn theory or methodology into practical, usable, and cost-effective techniques (e.g., Kieras, 1988).

At an earlier conference on research directions in HCI (Carroll, 1987), Whiteside and Wixon (1987), and Landauer (1987a) challenged the researchers convened to move beyond the prevailing cognitive science approaches to research (e.g., narrowly construed applications of information-processing psychology) and ground their research in solving real world problems. They urged the participants to be open to the possibility that new roles and methodologies might be needed to tackle these problems. They suggested that HCI research would be enriched by this focus on design. The HCI researchers at this workshop have made this shift by grounding their research in design. At the same time they are directing ideas and methods toward the enrichment of usability engineering practice.

Acknowledgments

We thank Robert Campbell, Steve Payne, and Phil Barnard for comments on earlier drafts, and Jack Carroll, John Bennett, and Wendy Kellogg for extensive reviews of this chapter.

References

Anderson, J. (1987). Methodologies for studying human knowledge. *Behavioral and Brain Sciences, 10*(3), 467–505.

Apple. (1987a). *Human interface guidelines: The Apple desktop interface.* Reading, MA: Addison-Wesley.

Apple. (1987b). *Inside Macintosh.* Reading, MA: Addison-Wesley.

Aron, J. D. (1974). *The program development process: The individual programmer.* Reading, MA: Addison-Wesley.

Bennett, J. (1984). Managing to meet usability requirements: Establishing and meeting software development goals. In J. Bennett, D. Case, J. Sandelin, & M. Smith (Eds.), *Visual display terminals: Usability issues and health concerns.* Englewood Cliffs, NJ: Prentice-Hall.

Bennett, J., Holtzblatt, K., Jones, S., & Wixon, D. (1990). Usability engineering: Using contextual inquiry. In J. C. Chew & J. Whiteside (Eds.), *Proceedings of CHI '90: Human Factors in Computing Systems.* New York: ACM.

Bødker, S. (1989). A human activity approach to user interfaces. *Human–Computer Interaction, 4*(2), 171–195.

Bødker, S., Ehn, P., Romberger, S., & Sjogren, D. (Eds.). (1985). *Graffiti 7. The UTOPIA project. An alternative in text and images.* Stockholm: Arbetslivscentrum.

Card, S., Moran, T., & Newell, A. (1983). *The psychology of human–computer interaction.* Hillsdale, NJ: Lawrence Erlbaum Associates.

Carroll, J. M. (Ed.). (1987). *Interfacing thought: Cognitive aspects of human–computer interaction.* Cambridge, MA: Bradford Books/MIT Press.

Carroll, J., & Kellogg, W. (1989). Artifact as theory-nexus: Hermeneutics meets theory-based design. In K. Bice & C. S. Lewis (Eds.), *Proceedings of CHI '89: Human Factors in Computing Systems* (pp. 7–14). New York: ACM.

Carroll, J., & Mack, R. (1984). Learning to use a word processor: By doing, by thinking and by knowing. In J. Thomas & M. Schneider (Eds.), *Human factors in computer systems* (pp. 13–51). Norwood, NJ: Ablex.

Conklin, J., & Begeman, M. (1988). gIBIS: A hypertext tool for exploratory policy discussion. *ACM Transactions on Office Information Systems, 6*(4), 303–331.

Cook, P., Ellis, C., Graf, M., Rein, G., & Smith, T. (1987). Project Nick: Meeting augmentation and analysis. *ACM Transactions of Office Information Systems, 5*(2), 132–146.

Egan, D., Remde, J., Landauer, T., Lochbaum, C., & Gomez, L. (1989). Behavioral evaluation and analysis of a hypertext browser. In K. Bice & C. H. Lewis (Eds.), *Proceedings of CHI '89: Human Factors in Computing Systems* (pp. 205–210). New York: ACM.

Engel, S., & Granda, R. (1975, December). *Guidelines for man/display interfaces* (Laboratory Technical Report, TR00.2720). Poughkeepsie, NY: IBM.

Engelbart, D., & English, W. (1968). A research center for augmenting human intellect. *Proceedings of Fall Joint Conference on Computing 33*(1), 395–410. Montvale, NJ: AFIPS Press.

Furnas, G. W. (1986). Generalized fisheye views. In M. Mantei & P. Orbeton (Eds.), *Proceedings of CHI '86: Human Factors in Computing Systems* (pp. 13–23). New York: ACM.

Furnas, G., Landauer, T., Gomez, L., & Dumais, S. (1984). Statistical semantics: Analysis of the potential performance of keyword information systems. In J. Thomas & M. Schneider (Eds.), *Human factors in computer systems*. Norwood, NJ: Ablex.

Gould, J. (1988). How to design usable systems. In M. Helander (Ed.), *Handbook of human–computer interaction* (pp. 757–790). Amsterdam: Elsevier Science Publishers.

Henderson, A. (1986). The Trillium user interface design environment. In M. Mantei & P. Orbeton (Eds.), *Proceedings of CHI'86: Human Factors in Computing Systems* (pp. 1–10). New York: ACM.

International Business Machines (1989). *IBM common user access advanced interface design guide*. Boca Raton, FL: IBM Corporation.

Johnson, J., Roberts, T., Verplank, W., Smith, D., Irby, C., Beard, M., & Mackey, K. (1989). The Xerox Star: A retrospective. *Computer 22*(1), 11–29.

Karat, J. (1989). Approximate modeling as an aid to software design. *Bulletin of the Human Factors Society, 31*(9), 1–3.

Kay, A. (1984). Computer software. *Scientific American, 251*(3), 52–59.

Kieras, D. (1988). Towards a practical GOMS model methodology for user interface design. In M. Helander (Ed.), *Handbook of human–computer interaction* (pp. 135–158). Amsterdam: Elsevier Science Publishers.

Krasner, H., Curtis, B., & Iscoe, N. (1987). Communication breakdowns and boundary spanning activities on large programming projects. In G. M. Olson, S. Sheppard, & E. Soloway (Eds.), *Empirical studies of programmers: Second workshop*. Norwood, NJ: Ablex.

Landauer, T. (1987a). Psychology as a mother of invention. In J. Carroll & P. Tanner (Eds.), *Proceedings of CHI + GI'87: Human Factors in Computing Systems and Graphics Interface (Toronto, April 5–9)* (pp. 333–336). New York: ACM.

Landauer, T. (1987b). Relations between cognitive psychology and computer systems design. In J. M. Carroll (Ed.), *Interfacing thought: Cognitive aspects of human–computer interaction*. Cambridge, MA: Bradford Books/MIT Press.

Lewis, C. (1990). NoPumpG: Creating interactive graphics with spreadsheet machinery. In E. Glinert (Ed.), *Visual programming environments*. Los Angeles: IEEE Computer Society Press.

Mack, R. (1990). Understanding and learning text-editing skills: Observations on the role of new user expectations. In S. Robertson, W. Zachery, & J. Black (Eds.), *Cognition, computing and cooperation* (pp. 304–337). Norwood, NJ: Ablex.

MacLean, A., Young, R., & Moran, T. (1989). Design rationale: The argument behind the artifact. In K. Bice & C. S. Lewis (Eds.), *Proceedings of CHI '89: Human Factors in Computing Systems* (pp. 247–252). New York: ACM.

Malone, T. W., Grant, K. R., & Turbak, F. A. The information lens: An intelligent system for information sharing in organizations. In M. Mantei & P. Orbeton (Eds.), *Proceedings of CHI '86: Human Factors in Computing Systems* (pp. 1–8). New York: ACM.

Myers, B. A. (1988). A taxonomy of window manager user interfaces. *IEEE Computer Graphics & Applications, 8*(5), 65–84.

Neches, R. (1988). Knowledge-based tools to promote shared goals and terminology between interface designers. *ACM Transactions on Office Information Systems, 6*(3), 215–231.

Norman, D., & Draper, S. (Eds.). (1986). *User-centered system design: New perspectives on human–computer interaction.* Hillsdale, NJ: Lawrence Erlbaum Associates.

Petzold, C. (1988). *Programming windows.* Redmond, WA: Microsoft Press.

Rosson, M. B., Maass, S., & Kellogg, W. (1988). The designer as user: Building requirements for design tools from design practice. *Communications of the ACM, 31*(11), 1288–1298.

Rubinstein, R., & Hersh, H. (1984). *The human factor: Designing computer systems for people.* Bedford, MA: Digital Press.

Simon, H. (1969). *The sciences of the artificial.* Cambridge, MA: MIT Press.

Shneiderman, B. (1987). *Designing the user interface.* Reading, MA: Addison-Wesley.

Smith, D., Irby, C., Kimball, R., Verplank, B., & Harslem, E. (1982, April). Designing the STAR interface. *Byte, 17,* 242–282.

Tetzlaff, L., & Cleveland, L. (1990). *Application logging for usability analysis of graphical user interfaces* (IBM Research Report, RC15602). Yorktown Heights, NY: IBM T. J. Watson Reseach Center.

Tognazzini, B. (1989). Achieving consistency for the Macintosh. In J. Nielsen (Ed.), *Coordinating user interfaces for consistency.* Boston: Academic Press.

Voss, J. F., & Post, T. A. (1989). On the solving of ill-structured problems. In M. T. H. Chi, R. Glaser, & M. J. Farr (Eds.), *The nature of expertise.* Hillsdale, NJ: Lawrence Erlbaum Associates.

Whiteside, J., Bennett, J., & Holtzblatt, K. (1988). Usability engineering: Our experience and evolution. In M. Helander (Ed.), *Handbook of human–computer interaction* (pp. 791–818). Amsterdam: Elsevier Science Publishers.

Whiteside, J., & Wixon, D. (1987). Discussion: Improving human–computer interaction – a quest for cognitive science. In J. M. Carroll (Ed.), *Interfacing thought: cognitive aspects of human–computer interaction.* Cambridge, MA: Bradford Books/MIT Press.

Wiecha, C., Bennett, W., Boies, S., & Gould, J. (1989). Tools for generating consistent user interfaces. In J. Nielsen (Ed.), *Coordinating user interfaces for consistency.* Boston: Academic Press.

Williams, G. (1983). The LISA computer systems: Apple designs a new kind of machine. *Byte, 18,* 33–50.

Winograd, T., & Flores, F. (1986). *Understanding computers and cognition.* Norwood, NJ: Ablex.

Wixon, D., Holtzblatt, K., & Knox, S. (1990). Contextual design: An emergent view of system design. In J. Chew & J. Whiteside (Eds.), *Proceedings of CHI '90: Human Factors in Computing Systems* (pp. 329–336). New York: ACM.

Yoder, E., McCracken, D., & Akscyn, R. (1985). Instrumenting a human–computer interface for development and evaluation. In B. Shackel (Ed.), *Proceedings of the First IFIP Conference on Human–Computer Interaction: Interact '84* (pp. 907–912). Amsterdam: North-Holland.

Index

Abrams, 154
abstract representations, 295–8, 299
abstract thinking, in action theory 207
abstraction(s), 52, 89, 99, 201, 288, 292, 300; conceptual, 292, 293–300; design rationale and, 81; in development of technical theory, 53; of mental processes, 156; in psychology of tasks, 96, 97, 98; of scenarios, 97; theoretical, in models of cognitive activity, 119–21
acceptances, in interaction trees 140–1, 148
Ackermann, D., 209, 220
acoustics (example), 2–3, 4, 13
ACT, 128, 165, 184
action, 1, 17; defined, 207; feedback mechanism in, 23; and interactivity, 139–41
action cycle, 23, 23f
action regulation theory; *see* action theory
action theory, 7, 14, 18, 83, 204, 206–21, 266; basic concepts and regulatory models of, 207–8; related concepts and models, 209–11; work design guidelines, 222
activity (concept), 8, 99, 209–10
activity flow, 23–4
activity theory, 7, 14, 18, 83, 204, 210, 216; *see also* human activity theory
ACTS, 109
additive dimensions (scales), 28, 28f, 30, 32, 35; inappropriate use of, 35f
aesthetic design, 218
aesthetic(s), 166–7
Akscyn, R., 302
Allinson, L., 103
Alpert, S. R., 99
Amabile, T. M., 215
analogical reasoning: and task psychology, 91, 92
analysis, 10, 11, 51, 104, 105, 129, 294; in assessment of programming knowledge, 186, 187; in design process, 46, 47, 259; in development process, 261, 262–3, 267; in task–artifact cycle, 79–80, 107, 108; taxonomic, 295–8; and theory, 265, 266; *see also* artifact analysis
analytic models, 9, 10; in group design process, 278; techniques, 283; tools, 59, 132
Anderson, J. R., 74, 103, 128, 129, 166, 184, 301
anthropology, 1, 45, 228, 239, 267n2
anthropomorphism, 185, 189
apparent motion illusion, 159
Apperley, M. D., 57
Apple Desktop Interface, 291
applicability requirement, (of theory), 1–2, 3–4, 9, 10, 13, 14, 104, 150, 203

application(s), 1–2, 175; basic science and, 104–5; bridging to/from theory, 118–22; and context, 2–4; design as part of, 10, 168; problem of separating user interface from, 233–5; of psychological theory, 6–8; role of, 203; science and, 11, 13–14, 79–80; of science base, 108–10; in taxonomic analysis, 296–7; and theory, 65–6, 155–6, 206, 212
application development, 306
application domains, 114, 116
application representation(s), 107, 108, 110, 112, 114, 123, 150, 206, 214; enhancing, 115–22; novel forms of, 111
application strategy, 148
applications specialists, 258
applied science, 2; cognitive research, 231; cognitive science, 229n1; psychology of HCI, 4, 9, 13–14; research, 105; science paradigm, 104–5, 105f, 120f, 123
appropriateness principle, 29, 35
architecture(s), 46–7; application and interface, 287; in principled design, 167, 168, 169, 170; *see also* cognitive architectures
Argyris, C., 213
artifact analysis, 148–51, 244–5; ecological approach and, 131; level of generality, 132; YSS in, 135–6
artifact construction, 300–1, 303–4; artifact design, 166, 204, 210, 222–3, 231, 236n6; in action theory, 208–9; articulate and tacit knowledge in, 214–15; bridging from science base to, 106–8; criteria for, 209; for human growth, 210–12; role of German work psychology in, 203–26; as theory-oriented problem-solving process, 215–21, 222, 291;
artifacts, 5–6, 14, 17, 97, 160; abstracting descriptions and principles for, 79; active/passive, 8; aspects of, 35–6; bounded claims extracted from, 289; bridging between basic theories and, 103–27; descriptive study of, 44–5, 53; in design, 74, 280; development over time, 238; as encapsulation mechanism, 306; enhancing human abilities, 17–19; evolution of, 78–84, 287; human ability to create, 17, 18, 36; interface between person and, 26; mediating human activity, 22, 83, 132–4, 241–2; in modeling cognition, 116–22; psychological theory embedded in, 237–8, 288; research on, in context of use, 301–3; representation and, 25–35; role of, 36; study of, 8–9; and tasks, 46, 82, 99, 131–4, 139, 148–51; and taxonomies, 298; temporal

artifacts (*cont.*)
    experience of, 292, 293–300; theories as, 212–13; as theory, 131–4, 139, 148–51, 237–8, 310; as things vs. in use, 242–3; typology of, 8; in use settings, 228; useful/usable, 296; views of, 19–22
artifacts in use, 227–53; functionality and simplicity of, 218–19
artificial intelligence (AI), 61, 108, 116, 132, 228; (AI)-oriented models, 115; (AI) research: critiques of, 239
assessment, 209; Boxer, 187–90; technology, 183–7
assimilation, 106, 108
attention, 17, 18
Atwood, M. E., 236
auditory perception: laws of, 60, 65
auditory warning systems, 109
Ausubel, D. P., 3
automatic indexing, 71
automatic logging, 302
automatization of effort, 24

Backus Nauf Form (BNF), 150
Baerensten, K., 244
Bannon, L. J., 6, 7, 10, 12, 19, 74, 81, 83, 107, 111, 132, 155, 160, 172, 204, 206, 209, 210, 212, 227–53, 231, 237, 237n7, 294, 301, 302, 308
Barnard, P. J., 3, 5, 6, 11, 12, 65, 79, 103–27, 105, 106, 107, 111, 112, 113, 114, 115, 116, 117, 118, 119, 121, 123, 130, 132, 138, 144, 150, 154, 160, 203, 206, 212, 213, 214, 236, 237, 287, 288, 289, 303, 304, 305, 309
Bartlett, F. C., 112
Basalla, G., 74, 75, 76, 77, 78
basic science, 5, 13; and application, 1–2, 104–5; principles, 41–2, 44, 163, 184; research, 40, 105; technical theory derived from, 52–3; theories: bridging between artifacts and, 103–27
Bateson, G., 42
Beard, M., 304
Begeman, M. L., 80, 306
behavior modification, 42, 43
behavioral engineering research, 111
behavioral psychology, 18
behavioral sciences, 5, 269–70
behaviorism, 99, 240
Bellamy, R. K. E., 90, 91, 97, 99
Bellcore Cognitive Science group, 12, 62–3, 66, 69; schematic history of work on textual information, 70f
Bennett, J. L., 10, 74, 107, 132, 155, 158, 160, 167, 206, 212, 237, 238n9, 269–85, 272, 273,

275, 276, 278, 282, 287, 289, 293, 295, 301, 306, 308
Bentham, J., 211
Berkeley Boxer Group, 170
Berlyne, D. E., 218, 219, 221
Bernsen, N. O., 228
Bever, T. G., 5
Bibby, P. A., 149
Biggerstaff, T. J., 80
Bittitalk browser, 97
blame (assessment), 183–4; partitioning, 184–7, 188, 190
Blättner, F., 210
Bloomberg, J. L., 260
BNF grammar, 115; *see also* Backus Nauf Form
Bødker, S., 6, 7, 10, 12, 19, 22, 24, 74, 81, 83, 107, 111, 132, 155, 160, 172, 204, 206, 209, 210, 212, 227–53, 232, 234, 237, 245, 246, 277, 294, 301, 302, 304, 308
Boehm, B. W., 272
Boies, S. J., 272, 273, 308
Bonar, J., 185
bounded-rationality theory, 157, 158–9
Bovair, S., 149
Boxer programming language, 6, 221, 289, 304; design practice, 181–3; as a principled design, 170–83; review of learnability of scoping in, 187–200
Boxer project group, 162; *see also* Berkeley Boxer Group
Boxer system, 7, 13; *see also* Boxer programming language
Bram, M., 13
bridge building (example), 2, 4
bridging: analogy with interface design practice, 110–11; between basic theories and artifacts, 103–27
bridging representations, 104–6, 108, 109, 110, 111, 122–3
Broadbent, D. E., 108, 150
Brocke, B., 203
Brodbeck, F., 216
Brooks, R., 3, 7, 8, 11, 44, 50–9, 74, 83, 105, 107, 132, 155, 160, 206, 212, 237, 292, 295, 296, 297, 298, 299, 302
Bruner, J. S., 131
Burr, B. J., 154
Butler, K., 282
Buttigeig, M. A., 158
Buxton, W., 234, 237n7

calculational models, 235
Campbell, R. L., 74, 79, 106, 107, 220, 231, 237, 248

Cannata, P. E., 71

Caplan, R., 254

Card, S. K., 1, 7, 11, 29, 51, 52, 53, 55, 62, 66, 74, 103, 106, 110, 112, 115, 116, 130, 154, 156, 157, 203, 204, 205, 210, 211, 212, 214, 235, 278, 305

Cardwell, D. S., L., 76, 77, 78

Carrithers, C., 84, 87, 92, 99

Carroll, J. M., 1–16, 8, 10, 12, 47, 61, 64, 68, 74–102, 75, 79, 80, 81, 82, 84, 86, 87, 90, 92, 97, 98, 99, 103, 104, 106, 107. 108, 109, 111, 112, 123, 131, 132, 150, 155, 160, 166, 183n3, 203, 206, 209, 212, 214, 215, 216, 217, 218, 219, 220, 222, 231, 235, 236, 237, 238, 248, 249, 286, 288, 289, 290, 291, 292, 294, 295, 304, 305, 310, 311

case studies, 287, 310

Casey, E. J., 158

Catrambone, R., 84

Cattell, J. C., 205

causal principles, 41–2, 44

Chase, W. G., 159

checklist ("to-do" list), 20–2, 24, 231–2

Chen, D., 185

Chomsky, N., 112

Church, K., 67

Chuen-Tsai Sun, 187

circuit theory, 11, 52, 53–4

civil engineering, 3–4, 52–3, 54

claims analysis, 150, 292, 295; from Displaywriter (Training Wheels), 84–8, 85t, 90; from Training Wheels interface, 91–6

Clancey, M. J., 175

Clark, H. H., 140

Clark, I. A., 105

Clark, N. A., 156

Clegg, C., 210

Cleveland, L., 302

Clevenger, W. A., 54

cognition, 228, 239, 247, 269; artifacts in, 18, 19, 20f, 36; distributed, 22; modeling, 61–2, 116–22; as type of computation, 229

cognitive activity: approximate models of, 118–22

cognitive architectures, 114, 118, 128, 165, 169; arguments for, 130; in AI, 116–17; decomposable, 158; research driven by, 128–9, 130; tools based on, 12

cognitive artifacts, 8, 17–38; defined, 17, 25; development of, 19; in human performance, 35–6; interface, 27

cognitive behavior modification, 217

cognitive benchmark: for comprehensibility of procedural languages, 183–4, 197, 201

cognitive complexity theory, 115, 116, 130

cognitive description approach, 75, 237

cognitive development, 5, 221

cognitive engineering paradigm, 111

cognitive models, 123, 157–8

cognitive objects, 163–4, 165

cognitive phenomenology: diversity as, 164–5

cognitive psychology, 5, 18, 132, 203, 211, 249; critiques of, 239; inner theory in, 156

cognitive schemas, 220

cognitive science, 18, 103, 248, 249, 269, 311; current framework of, 228–35; and design, 235–7, 282–3; emic/etic properties in, 45–6; in HCI, 162–202, 231–5

cognitive system, 156, 157

cognitive theory, 227; applicability and impact of, 104; application to design of technology, 108–10; in applications representations, 116–22; current state of, 228–31; in design of human–computer systems, 60–73; in HCI research, 122–3, 286; representations in, 104

coherence, 174, 288

Cole, M., 17, 18, 19, 36, 83, 230, 240

color, 60, 65

command-language designs, 136

command names, 66

comparative task analysis, 50–9

comparison, 58; cross-artifact, 298; cross-task, 55, 56, 57–8; of user interfaces, 57

competence, 248–9

complete task cycle, 209

complex systems, 174; organization types in, 164f

complexity, 107, 115, 209, 211, 218; of cognitive system, 156, 170; in HCI, 68–9, 79, 104, 156, 286–7; and impossibility of useful theory, 60, 61, 62–3; and learning environment, 219–20; reduction of, 213, 216, 220, 221; stepwise enlargement of, 219, 220

comprehensibility: in Boxer, 179, 181; causes of, 184–5; of procedural languages, 183–4; programming, 173–8; of programming languages, 172–3, 184–5, 187, 201

compromises: in design process, 169

computational artifacts, 131

computational devices, 25

computational medium, 171, 172

computational metaphor, 7

computational power, 128

computational theory, 129; of task-action mapping, 137–9; YSS as, 134–5

computer applications, 243, 245, 246, 247; views of, 248–9

computer-based products, 260–1

computer equipment: design of usable, 99

computer interfaces, 18; *see also* user interface

computer literacy, 171, 289
computer models: of human thought process, 229
computer simulation, 61
computer support: for design meeting facilitation, 280–1
computer systems, 9, 14; description of, 55; design of, 10, 67, 209
computer technology, 1, 303
computer tools, 74
computer training, 216–17; *see also* learning; training
concepts: related to action theory, 209–10
conceptual elements: semantic manipulation of, 298–9
conceptual level, 207
concrete representations, 292–3
Conklin, J., 80, 273, 306
connectionism, 229n1
connectivity, 173
consistency, 136, 145, 186, 288
constraints: in cognitive architectures, 116, 117; in design, 271, 275, 282; general cognitive, 130–1; implementation, 158
content appropriateness, 2, 9
context(s), 81, 82–3, 96, 243, 303; effect on behavior, 159; importance of, in invention, 78; learning, 186, 187, 188; research on artifacts in, 301–3; science in, 2–4; of technical development, 98–9
context-guided search, 71, 72
contextual inquiry, 301
contextualized scenarios, 294
contextualizing phenomena, 106, 110
contrast, dichotomous (experimental logic), 4–5
control, 209, 211
control operation: and system state, 26–7
conversation (model), 140
Cook, P., 306
cooperative work in groups, 306
copy and execute model (Boxer), 189, 190, 197, 198f, 199f, 200
Corlett, E. N., 55
Cosgrove, P., 109
counting, representations for, 32–3
craft, 43, 107, 109; in invention, 75, 77
Cranach, V., 206
creation, 10, 215; MacDraw, 144, 145, 148, 149f
creativity, 182, 221, 266, 268, 307
crystallized knowledge: artifacts as, 243
cultural psychology, 18
culture, 18, 223, 240; workplace, 239
cumulation: in psychology of tasks, 96, 97
cumulative assessment technology, 183–4
Curtis, B., 4, 10, 274, 303

cut-and-paste editor, 134, 136, 143
cycle of development, 264

Dark, J., 46
Darwin, C. R., 42
data base: Boxer, 179
data base query expressions, 71
data-based simulations, 12, 60, 66
data boxes, 180, 181
debugging, 6, 176, 177, 186, 187, 268; tools, 261
decomposition, 7, 9–10, 302; strategies for, 297–8, 297t; taxonomic, 296–8, 299
deduction, in applying science, 75–6, 78, 79; application paradigm, 107, 203–4, 206, 212, 214; bridging, 107, 111; science, 7; *see also* applied science; theory-based design
Deerwester, S., 71
Degani, A., 24
"degree-of-interest" function, 70
density, graphical 30–2
Dertouzos, M., 67
description(s), 7, 84, 299; abstracted from artifacts, 79; design rationale and, 81; in HCI, 57–9; as means of communicating design experience, 53–4; of patterns, 266; as prerequisite to technical theory, 52–3, 58, 59; scenario, 279–80; status of, in HCI science, 54–7; in task analysis, 232–3; of tasks, 8; terms for, 29
description system(s), 54, 58–9
descriptive science(s), 44–5, 83
design, 1–2, 12, 14, 249, 257–60; activity theory and, 7; applied psychology in, 74; cognitive issues in problems of, 60–1; cognitive modeling in support of, 116–22; as cognitive science, 162–202, 235–7; cognitive theory in, 60–73, 108–10, 162, 286; as complex problem-solving situation, 281–2; of computer-based artifacts, 245–7; of computer interfaces, 18; continuing, 257–8, 261; development perspective in, 254–68; in development process, 261, 263, 267, 268; early stages of, 270, 272, 308; by emulation, 82, 84, 150; failure in, 169; general principles guiding, 287; HCI work in, 238–9; ill-structured, 10; impact of psychology on, 148–50; individualization of, 221; and interface problems, 132, 141; as intuition pump, 168–9; as iterative spiral, 271, 271f; levels of, 171; participatory, 267; in principled design, 168–9, 178–83, 201; principles as conceptual framework for, 289–91; psychological studies of, 46–8; psychological theory in, 7, 154–61, 310; as representation, 34; as research, 12–13, 310–11; scenario-based, 80, 81–2, 84; science and, 75, 96–8, 108, 109, 168, 200–1, 270; shared under-

standing of evolving, 273–6; supporting, 11–12, 269–85; technical theory as basis for, 52; theory and, 103–4, 111, 123, 131, 160, 206, 223, 265, 266; understanding of application in, 233–4; unexpected properties in, 68–9; usefulness/usability-oriented, 67–8, 288; user-centered views in, 270–8; *see also* group design process; principled design; theory-based design
design choice/decisions, 43, 51, 110, 111, 150
design concepts: and human development, 216–17
design cycle, 310
design experience: description as means of, 53–4; general principles extracted from, 289
design guidelines, 9, 130, 222, 231
design meeting facilitator, 280–1
design practice, 98–9, 155–6; codification of, 2; local scientific, 181–3
design principles, 233, 289, 290, 290f, 292, 291, 291f, 303
design process, 74, 170, 214, 261, 266, 287, 306–10; study of, 46–8; trade-offs and compromises in, 169; understanding, 10–11; working within, 9–10, 269–85
design rationale, 80–1, 82, 84, 89, 91, 96, 99, 108, 123, 273; defined, 80
design review, 278, 280, 283; facilitator role in, 280–1
design rules, 213, 214–15, 270
design solution, 215, 222
design space, 10, 287
design strategies, 96, 97–8
design teams, 10, 223; *see also* group design process
design wheel, 10, 271, 271f; *see also* "wheel of design"
designer(s), 215, 274, 295, 307, 309; in group process, 308–9; and HCI science, 50–1; methods of, 209; multiple, 257–8, 259; as outside observer, 248; prediction by, 249; role of, 203; and theories, 213–14; and usability issues, 309–10; view of HCI, 231
detail(s), 75–6, 78, 98, 292; of application and work practice, 258; in principled design, 182–3; in psychology of tasks, 89; of situation in use, 206; in success of design, 304; user–action scenarios, 82
development: cycle of, 264; theory in, 264–8, 269; theory of multiperson, multirole, 266–7
development perspective, 259–60; in interface, design, theory, 254–68
development process, 254, 259–60, 267, 289; interfaces in, 260–1; metaphor for, 264; model of, 261–3, 262f; views of, 261–4

development wheels, 264, 265, 266, 267
developmental psychology, 6–7, 56, 209, 211, 220
device(s), 131, 173, 298; coordination of task with, 139–41
device model, 117, 134–6, 143, 149–50; for MacDraw, 141–4, 144f, 149
device space, 134, 136, 298; MacDraw, 141–4, 145; and task-action grammar, 145
device use, 130, 132
Devlin, S. J., 71
dialectical materialism, 240
Di Bello, L. A., 220, 248
differential and dynamic work design, 209
Dillon, A., 69
direct engagement (concept), 22
direct manipulation interfaces, 78–9, 83; techniques, 304
directness level, 17, 22–4
discovery, 301
discovery representation(s), 6, 105–6, 107, 110, 111, 119; enhancing, 111–15
Di Sessa, A. A., 6, 7, 12, 74, 107, 132, 155, 160, 162–202, 165n1, 166, 172, 173, 174, 178, 190, 206, 212, 220, 237, 288, 289, 292, 293, 304, 305, 309
display, 138–9; design, 132, 156, 158
Displaywriter, 84–96, 304
distributed, cognition, 22
distributed models, 6, 176–7, 178, 186, 190, 193, 200
distribution across time/people, 22, 132
Dix, A. J., 123
Doane, S., 160
documentation, 260, 303, 305
documented scenarios, 293
do-it boxes, 180, 181
domain knowledge, 5, 250
Donders, F. C., 205
Dowell, J., 104
Draper, S. W., 26n1, 138, 139, 233, 235, 287
drawing: MacDraw, 141–4, 142f
Drury, C. G., 55
Dumais, S. T., 63, 66, 71, 301
Dunbar, K., 158
dynamic scoping, 189, 190, 193
Dzida, W., 83

ease of use, 172, 248
Eberhardt, J., 64, 69
ecological (problem/resource-oriented) approach, 129–31, 132, 150–1; task-action grammars in, 137–8
ecologically valid data, 40, 41
editing tools, 261

education: Boxer in, 171; humanistic reform of, 210

Edworthy, J., 109

Egan, D. E., 64, 65, 69, 300

Ehn, P., 232, 234, 246, 277, 304

Ehrlich, K., 185

Ellis, C., 306

Ellis, J., 115

emic properties, 45–6

empirical analysis, 4–5

empirical demonstrations: paradigm, 42

empirical design, 286

empirical discovery, 300–3

empirical evaluation, 108, 203, 300, 301

empirical generalizations, 12, 60, 66

empirical methods, 60, 103, 182, 287–8; in design, 64–5; design information discovered by, 62–3

empirical modeling, 60, 66–7, 107; adequacy of, 67–72

empirical process, 287, 289

empirical work: in principled design, 178, 179; and theory, 159–60

emulation: in design, 82, 84, 150; in evolution of technology, 75–6, 78, 79, 82, 98; invention as, 77, 131

encapsulation techniques, 303–6

engagement level, 17, 22–4, 36

Engelbart, D., 1, 78, 292

Engels, F., 231

Engeström, Y., 240, 244, 247, 248

engineering, 54, 68; model, 11; principles, 12; representations, 108; science/theory, 41–2, 52–3, 59

Engle, S., 303

English, W., 1, 78, 154, 292

environment, 13–14, 17, 18; task, 83

ergonomic design criteria, 208

Ericsson, K. A., 114, 159

error blocking: Training Wheels interface, 91, 93t, 94–5, 96, 97, 98

errors, 105, 115, 116, 185, 186; error rate, 4, 9; error recovery, 5, 7; freedom from, 172; inappropriate generalizations and, 148; and learning, 217, 220, 249; risk of, 216, 219

ethnographic techniques, 302

etic properties, 45–6

evaluation, 9, 271, 300, 302; in design, 183, 206; early, 149; gulf of, 23–4; iS, 217; predicting, 118; psychology in, 68; research, 203; scenarios in, 82, 294; of theory, 283

examples, methodological importance of, 99

execution: artifacts as mediators in, 22; gulf of, 23–4

experience (human), 1, 41, 99, 291; accumulating, 287, 288; as product of use, 262; structures determinants of, 8

experiential representations, 293–5

experimental manipulations: critique of, 236–7

experimental paradigm(s), 42, 106

experimental psychology, 203, 205

experiments: assimilating design to, 168; controlled, 301; in design, 246–7; function of, 212–13; in principled design, 170

expert systems, 11, 41, 56, 58, 304–5; in approximate models of cognitive acitivity, 119–22

expertise, 5, 164, 172; cumulating, 287, 288; programming, 175, 176

experts, 6; indigenous, 258; and mapping terms, 29; task demands vs. action of, 46–8

exploration: time and self-regulation of, 221

exploration theory, 220

exploratory environment, 216, 217, 219

exploratory learning, 216–17, 218

"Exploratory Learning by Errors," 217

exploratory research: in artifact construction, 300–1

exploratory styles, 218

exploratory tasks, 219–20

expressiveness principle, 29n2

facilitation: design meeting, 280–1

facilitators, 276–7, 280–1

factorial experimental designs, 4, 112

Fafchamps, D., 281

failure, 3, 182, 216

falsifiability doctrine, 162

Farr, J., 221

feedback, 207, 210; in design decisions, 170; user, 302–3

Feyerabend, P., 162

field techniques, 282, 302

files, 134, 181

Fischer, G., 160

fisheye views, 63

Fitts, P. M., 154

Fitts's Law, 12, 60, 65, 154, 205, 214; in SuperBook design, 70

Flach, J. M., 158

Flores, C. F., 232, 239, 242

Floyd, C., 204, 209, 228, 247, 248

Fodor, J. A., 4, 5

folk development, 254, 261; theory of, 267–8

forcing functions, 24, 34

formalisms, 53, 57, 58, 150

formative evaluation, 60, 67–72, 107

four-walls design environment, 274–6, 277–8, 283, 308–9; scenario use in, 278–80

Fowler, R., 278
Frankish, C., 110
Frederiksen, C., 173
Frese, M., 83, 206, 207, 216, 219, 240n10
Freud, S., 42
full-text indexing, 62–3, 70
function, in scenario-based design, 81; vs. structure, in Boxer, 179–81, 182, 183
function list, 307f
functional attributes, 173
functional context, 185
functional levels, 207
functional models, 6, 175–6, 177, 185, 186, 190; strengths/weaknesses of, 176
functional specification documents, 81
functional wedge-in, 181–2, 289, 291
functionality: of artifacts, 132; of artifacts in use, 218–19; hidden, 90–1, 97, 98; partitioning, 51
Furnas, G. W., 63, 66, 69, 71, 301

Gablenz-Kolakovic, 207
Galanter, E., 65, 206, 207
Gale, W., 67
Galilei, Galileo, 40, 76
Galotti, K. M., 66
Garner, W. R., 158
Garrett, M. F., 5
Gediga, G., 204, 205, 208, 209, 211, 214, 216, 218, 220
general principles, 287, 288, 290, 292, 303
generalities, 162, 177, 305
generalizability, 203, 206, 217, 236
generalization(s), 168, 268, 290, 304; in demonstrator system, 121; in MacDraw, 141, 142, 145; small-scale, 8, 42, 288
generic functionalities, 175
"Genetic Growing System," 215'b221. 304; theoretical bases and design of, 217–18
Gentner, D., 173
German work psychology; *see* work psychology
Gestalt theory, 210
Gibson, J. J., 14, 99, 129, 221
Gizienski, S. F., 54
goal(s), 74, 210, 272; goal-directed behavior, 132, 207–8; goal-setting theory, 213; space, 134, 136, 142–4
Gomez, L. M., 63, 64, 66, 69, 71, 72, 300, 301
Gomory, R. E., 78
GOMS model, 45, 55–6, 103, 115, 130, 204–6, 210, 235, 278–9, 292, 298; rejection of, 211
Good, M. D., 66, 69
Gould, J. D., 235, 238n9, 272, 273, 286, 304, 308
Graf, M., 306
grammatical techniques, 115

Granda, R., 303
graphic design, 218
graphs, 34, 35
Gravelle, M., 278
Gray, W. D., 236
Green, T. G. R., 57, 112, 115, 116, 117, 123, 130, 136, 137, 144, 145, 235, 278
Greene, S. L., 71
Greeno, J. G., 134
Greenspan, J., 185
Greif, S., 6, 7, 11, 12, 83, 97, 107, 108, 132, 155, 160, 203–26, 204, 206, 208, 209, 211, 212, 213, 216, 217, 218, 220, 235, 237, 240n10, 291, 301, 304
Grey, S. M., 55
Griffin, P., 19
grounding: of development process, 261; in principled design, 168, 169, 170, 173, 174, 177–8, 182–3, 200, 201
group design process, 167, 269, 271, 273–6, 281, 283, 308–9; shared understanding in, 280; supporting, 276–8
groups, 18, 306
Grudin, J. T., 67, 107, 119
Guha, R. V., 61, 67
guidelines, 10, 106, 287, 288, 292; commercial, 291; for design, 9, 130, 222, 231
guiding vision (design), 272, 273, 292
Guindon, R., 10, 274

Hacker, W., 206, 207, 209, 214, 222, 240n10
Halasz, F. G., 149
Hamborg, K-C., 208, 216, 218
Hammond, N. V., 103, 105, 106, 119
Handschy, M. A., 156
Hanson, W., 111
hardware, 107, 234, 245
Harrison, M. D., 123
Harshman, R., 71
Harslem, E., 80, 232, 304
HCI: *see* human–computer interaction
hearing (human): psychoacoustic models of, 109
Hegel, G., 240
Heidegger, M. 242
Heinbokel, T., 216
Helander, M., 238n9
Henderson, D. A., 10, 74, 103, 107, 111, 132, 155, 160, 206, 212, 237, 240n12, 244, 246, 254–68, 292, 293, 304, 306, 307
Herman, J. F., 221
Hersh, H., 235, 272, 288, 303
Herzberg, F., 211
heterarchic task analysis, 208, 209
heuristic evaluation methods, 64

heuristic guidelines, 214, 215
heuristic orientation models, 216
Hick's Law, 12, 60, 65, 205
hierarchical system, 164–5
hierarchy: in description systems, 58; information
  display methods, 62–3; menus, 65; taxonomic
  elements, 298
Hindle, B., 1, 74, 76
Hollan, J., 23, 24, 78
Hilling, H., 211, 213
Holtzblatt, K., 64, 158, 238n9, 272, 273, 275,
  287, 301
Hoppe, H. U., 138
Howes, A., 134, 136, 138, 144, 145
hue, 28, 31, 65
human activity theory, 239–40, 248, 249, 250; artifacts in, 242–3; central tenets of, 240–2; cognition in, 247; *see also* activity level
human behavior: difficulties of modeling, 61–2
human beings: distinctive characteristics of, 17
human–computer interaction (HCI), 5, 18–19,
  212; applied psychology of, 1; cognitive science
  tradition in, 231–5; current framework of, 228–
  35; defined, 1; description in, 57–9; as descriptive, engineering science, 51–7; design of systems to support, 269–85; emergent properties
  in, 61–2; evolution of tasks and artifacts in,
  78–84; inner/outer theory in, 154–61; kinds of,
  130–1; ontologically minimized, 74–5, 82, 99,
  155; perspectives on, 247–9; perspectives on
  methodology in, 286–314; and practical design,
  238–9; as practical science/science of practice,
  84; psychology and, 1–2, 13–14; reanalyses of,
  74–5; reframing issues of, from within, 235–9;
  reframing issues of, from without, 239–47; status of, 249–50; subject matter of, 254–7; usability, 98–100
human–computer interaction science: cognitive
  theory in, 60–73; comparative task analysis in,
  50–9; designers and, 50–1; status of description
  in, 54–7
human–computer interaction systems: design of,
  as cognitive science, 162–202
human consciousness, 240
human criteria, 212
human development: design concepts and, 216–
  17; materialistic theories of, 229–30; praxis as
  basis for, 231
human factors, 231; approach, 166; engineering,
  55; evaluation paradigm, 9; paradigm, 237; research, 111, 238
human information processor, 229, 267; *see also*
  information processing (human)
human operation: of computer application, 245

human personality development, 207, 223, 240;
  artifact design for, 210–12; goal of work design, 208–9, 214
human thought processes: computer models of,
  229
humanism, 210–11; humanistic management
  theory, 213; humanistic organization psychology, 211
humanistic values, 204, 206, 209, 210–12; in artifact design process, 212
"Humanization of Working Life" (renamed
  "Work and Technology"), 212
Humboldt, W., 210
Hutchins, C. M., 3, 13
Hutchins, E., 21, 23, 24, 26, 78
Hyden, L. C., 240
hydrocarbon-well-log interpretation, 58
HyperCard, 107, 237, 295
hypertext systems, 69; Boxer, 179
hypothesis testing, 111, 112, 114

icons, 179, 298
identifiability, 156
"idiot-proof" systems, 237n7, 248
Ifrah, G., 33
Ilyenkov, E. V., 242
impartiality: in review of principled design, 184
implementation: in development process, 261,
  263, 267; and theory, 265, 266
indexicals, 45–6
indexing: automatic, 71; full-text, 62–3, 70; rich,
  12, 66, 69
individual differences, 12, 121, 159, 186, 208,
  217, 238; in action theory, 209; training and,
  218
individual System (iS), 212, 214, 216–22
individualized system design solutions, 209
industrial organization, 211, 223
information flow, 79–80, 107–8, 118, 130, 209,
  260
information overload, 303
information processing (human), 17, 117, 232,
  267; description, 5; mechanisms, 36; models,
  115; psychology, 5, 9, 82–3, 107, 108 (better
  utilization of, 5–6; cognition in, 228, 229; critiques of, 239; and design process, 10; extending scope of, 8–9; science base of, 6); role of
  artifact, 17, 18; theory, 7, 13, 118; workload,
  29
information retrieval, 65, 71, 301; research, 66–7,
  310; technology, 300
inner theory, 6, 204, 206, 213, 289; arguments
  con/responses pro, 155–9; in HCI, 154–61;
  principled design as, 170; risks in, 159

innovation(s), 75–6; in design, 300; in empirical methods, 300; in HCI, 79

installation, 263

instruction: in programming languages, 185, 186, 187, 188, 190, 197, 200

instruction languages, 117, 118

instructional mental models, 149–50

intellectual level, 207

integration, 107, 206

integrative organization theory, 213

intentionality, 45

Interacting Cognitive Subsystems, 116, 118–19, 130

interaction: levels of directness and engagement in, 22–4; with MacDraw, 147–8; unpredictable, 156

interaction effects, 66

interaction language: MacDraw, 145

interaction scenarios, 6, 108

interaction tree(s), 140–1, 150, 298–9; MacDraw, 147f; for selecting multiple objects, 147–8, 148f notation, 147–8

interactivity: action and, 139–41

interface, 26, 34, 107, 248, 295; concrete representations of, 292–3; content of, 254–7, 260; development perspectives in, 254–68; in development process, 260–1; between internal and surface representations, 25; prototype as representation of, 294; as work applications/ practices, 268

interface characteristics, 115

interface description, 299

interface design, 26

interface design experts, 308

interface design practice, 110–11; *see also* practice

interface development, 291

interface interactions: dynamics of, 298–9

interface issues: analysis of space of, 132

interface language, 136–9; notations for, 136

interface options, 114

interface problems: and interface resources, 128–53

interface structure, 290

interface taxonomies, 11, 295–7

interface techniques, 11; as instantiations of design strategies, 97–8

intermediary representations, 104

internal representations, 25, 26, 178

intuition, 64, 287

intuition pump: design as, 168–9

invention, 60, 109, 171, 178, 182; as emulation, 131; evaluation of, 68; process of, 75–8; radical, 6, 176, 177, 186; routine, 177, 186

Irby, C., 80, 232, 304

Iscoe, N., 303

interation, 75–6, 258–9, 263, 274; in basic theory, 109; in design-in-progress, 279

iterative design, 273–4, 287–8

iterative evaluation, 301

iterative experimentation, 304

iterative process, 81, 82; in evolution of technology, 98–9

Janikowski, A., 216, 217

Jensen, A. R., 158

job-enrichment concept, 211

John-Steiner, V., 230

Johnson, J., 304

Jones, J. C., 4

Jones, S. J., 66, 69, 301

Jung, C. G., 42

Kammersgaard, J., 246

Karat, J., 10, 74, 107, 132, 155, 160, 167, 206, 212, 237, 269–85, 272, 278, 282, 293, 295, 299, 306, 308

Karpatchof, B., 240

Kay, A., 292

Kay, D. S., 82

Keil-Slawik, R., 209

Keller, H., 216, 217, 218

Kellogg, W. A., 8, 12, 74–102, 80, 97, 107, 108, 109, 131, 132, 150, 155, 160, 166, 203, 206, 212, 234n5, 237, 238, 239, 273, 288, 304, 310

Kernighan, M., 67

keystroke-level models, 62, 116, 204–6, 210; rejection of, 211

keyword query, 62–3; indexing terms, 66

Kidder, T., 273

Kieras, D. E., 1, 55, 116, 130, 149, 212, 278, 311

Kimball, R., 80, 232, 304

King, R., 281

"Kings Way" (work design), 209

Kintsch, W., 157, 160

Kirchoff's Law, 40

KISS design philosophy, 237n7

Kittle House Manifesto, 1–16

knowledge, 74, 114–15, 116, 178, 287; transmission of accumulated, 17, 18, 36

knowledge acquisition, 218, 219–20, 221

knowledge architectures, 165–7, 173, 201

knowledge assessment: programming languages, 186

knowledge engineering, 56, 58

knowledge requirements, 115, 116

knowledge systems, 172, 174, 201; communal, 167; diversity of, 164–7; modest architectures of, 167, 168

knowledge work: taxonomies for, 297
Knox, S., 64, 301
Knudsen, J., 277
Kornblum, 154
Kozulin, A., 240
Krasner, H., 10, 274, 303
Krogoll, T., 207
Kuark, J., 206
Kuchensky, A., 281
Kuhn, T. S., 167
Kyng, M., 232, 234, 246, 277

laboratory artifacts, 304
laboratory experiments, 13, 206
laboratory tasks, 109
Laird, J. E., 117, 130
Landauer, T. K., 7, 8, 12, 60–73, 63, 64, 65, 66, 69, 71, 72, 74, 83, 103, 104, 106, 107, 110, 112, 132, 155, 160, 184, 206, 212, 222, 236, 237, 286, 288, 289, 300, 301, 304, 310 311
language(s), 18, 61, 71, 241; for description, 8, 54–5, 57; information processing descriptions, 5; transmission of knowledge through, 17
language constructs, 176–7
Larsen, S. F., 238n8
Latent Semantic Indexing (LSI), 71
Laudan, R., 1, 74, 76
Laurel, B. K., 22
Lave, J., 230, 239
Lawson, B. R., 46
learnability, 130, 135–6; assessment of, 183–4; of Boxer scoping, 187–200; of computer systems, 172, 173; consistency in, 136; interface language as problem in, 136; programming languages, 175, 185–7; of structural/functional models, 176; TAGS in indexing of, 139
learner characteristics, 186–7
learning: context of, 185, 186, 187, 188; in design, 10, 246; in development, 268; early, 177; errors in, 249; by exploration, 7; knowledge requirements of, 115; mediation of, 250; psychological analysis of, 3, 4; to use technology, 258
learning environments: minimalist and maximalist design of, 219–20
learning modes, 165, 175; in aesthetics, 166–7
learning-regeneration, 186
learning theory, 3, 4
legends (map, graph), 32
Leibniz, G. W. von, 40
Lemke, A., 160
Lenat, D. B., 61, 67
length of description, 29
Leont'ev, A. N., 18, 83, 210, 231, 240

level of generalizations, 288–9
Levy, S., 272, 273
Lewis, C. H., 64, 86, 106, 107, 112, 122, 132, 154–61, 155, 160, 170, 204, 206, 212, 213, 235, 237, 238n9, 273, 280, 288, 289, 300, 304, 310
linguistics, 44, 45, 71, 115, 228
Linn, M. C., 175
Lisp programming, 166
literacy, 171, 173
local sciences, 162–202, 289; design practice, 181–3
Lochbaum, C. D., 63, 64, 66, 69, 72, 300
Locke, E. A., 213
log-file analysis, 208
Logo, 174, 189
Lohmann, I., 216, 217
Long, J. B., 104, 105
Lorch, D. J., 278
Love, T., 4
Lower, M. C., 109
Luria, A. R., 18

Maass, S., 234n5, 273, 310
McCracken, D., 302
McDermott, J., 56
MacDraw, 133–4, 150; analysis of, 141–51; conceptual difficulties with, 136, 141–2, 149; interaction tree, 140–1, 140f, 147f; task–action grammar (TAG), 137f, 138–9, 139f; yoked state space model of, 134, 135f
MacDraw screen, 133f
McGregor, D., 213
McGregor, M. A., 138, 139
Macintosh, 133, 171, 304l; menu dimming, 97–8
Mack, R. L., 86, 106, 107, 112, 132, 155, 160, 206, 208, 212, 216, 217, 218, 237, 286–314, 291
McKendree, J. E., 82
Mackey, K., 304
Mackinlay, J. D., 29, 35
McKnight, C., 69
MacLean, A., 80, 81, 106, 110, 111, 112, 114, 115, 119, 121, 123, 282, 305
MacLeod, C. M., 158
Madsen, K., 277
main effects, 156
maintenance, 263
Malhotra, A., 8, 10
Maltzman, I., 240
management theories, 1, 213
Mangel, I., 216, 217
Mann, L., 176
Mannes, S. M., 157
manuscript editing task, 11, 56
mapping, 5, 54, 104; device space to goal space,

142–4; between mental processes and their realizations, 156; naturalness of, 28–9, 30–1, 31f; operations into actions, 136–9; between representing world and represented world, 26; between technology and applications, 256; unnatural, 30f

mapping rules, 32, 33–4

mapping terms, 29

Marcus, S., 56, 110

market analysis, 222–3

Marr, D., 129

Marx, K., 231, 240

Maslow, A. H., 211

mass production, 211

materialistic theories, 229–30, 231

materials science, 183

maximalist design, 219–20

Maxwell's Laws, 11, 52

Mayes, J. T., 138, 139

measurement schemes, 287–8

mechanical engineering, 52, 54

mechanisms, 129, 169, 288; defects in, 159; of mental processes, 154, 155

mediation, 240–2, 245, 247; artifact, 22, 83, 132–4, 241–2; of learning, 250

medicine, 54; as model, 155, 156, 159–60

memory: artifacts and, 17, 18, 19, 20–1

memory aids, 21–2, 25

memory research, 129

mental mechanisms, 230

mental model interfaces, 166

mental models, 6, 11, 45, 165, 178, 182, 183, 201, 216, 217, 289; context independent, 289; instructional, 149–50; for programming comprehensibility, 173–8

mental processes: abstraction of, 156; associative models of, 157–8; inner theories of, 157; mechanisms of, and user-interface technology, 154

mental regulatory processes: hierarchical network of, 207–8, 209, 210

mental representations: mappings between, 118

mentalism, 99, 240

menus, 131, 133, 158, 292; dimming, 97–8; functions: blocked, 216; graphs, 71; menu-driven systems, 136; menu-selection format, 219; structure: notation for, 8, 57

message-passing paradigm, 181

metacognition, 162

metaphors, 291, 292

methodological issues, 99, 203

methodological techniques, 111–12; discovery representations, 111–15

methodology(ies), 42–3, 52, 287–8; in analysis,

262, 263; in cognitive science, 230; in design process, 306–10; development, 269; in observation, 262, 266; perspectives on, 286–314; software development, 272

Mill, J. S., 211

Meyer, 154

Miller, G. A., 206, 207, 228

Millman, P., 4

Milroy, R., 109

Miner, J. G. 213

minimalist design, 218, 219–20

mini-models, 42

Mioduser, D., 185

model human information processor, 116, 130, 210, 214, 229

modeling, 5, 111, 282; approximate description, 121; in exploratory research, 301; user, 55–6, 235–6

models, 52, 53, 59, 115–16, 156, 203; action theory, 207–8, 209–10; analytic, 10; approximate quantitative, 154; cognitive, 123; of control processes, 128; cost-effectiveness trade-offs in, 299; distributed, 176–7, 178; enhanced application and representations, 116–22; rejection of scientific, 204; *see also* functional models; structural models

modes: in knowledge system, 165; in principled design, 167, 168, 169, 170; of learning/use, 165, 166–7, 174, 175, 177; of operation, 177

Molich, R., 62, 64

Monecke, U., 208, 216, 218

Mooser, C., 216

Moran, T. P., 1, 7, 9, 11, 55, 56n1, 62, 80, 81, 82, 103, 106, 110, 116, 123, 130, 149, 154, 203, 204, 210, 211, 212, 214, 235, 256, 278, 305

Morrison, E., 1, 74, 76

Morton, J., 105, 106, 110

motivation, 1, 7, 238; theory, 211

mouse pointers, 78

movement: control of, 154–5

multimedia information systems, 306; presentations, 303

Müller, M. 216, 221

Munsterberg, H., 203

Myers, B. A., 298, 304

Nachbar, D. W., 65

Nachmias, R., 185

names: "shadowed" (Boxer), 188–9

naming, 301

natural domains, 8

natural language, 29, 180, 282

natural-language processing, 65, 71

naturalistic observations, 67

necessity analysis, 11, 47, 309
Neches, R., 306
"need finding," 266, 268
Neisser, U., 129
Newcomen, T., 76, 77, 78
Newell, A., 1, 5, 7, 11, 25, 45, 51, 52, 53, 55, 61,
    62, 66, 74, 103, 106, 110, 112, 116, 117, 128,
    129, 130, 132, 154, 157, 203, 204, 210, 211,
    212, 214, 230, 235, 278, 305
Newman, S., 166
NGOMSL, 278
Nicholson, N., 211, 213
Nickerson, R., 33
Nielsen, J., 62, 64, 69
NoPumpG, 304
Norman, D. A., 5, 8, 17–38, 23, 24, 26, 34, 42,
    74, 78, 83, 97, 107, 108, 110, 111, 114, 131,
    136, 157, 158, 160, 178, 180, 212, 229, 233,
    235, 287, 295, 297, 300
notation, 56–7, 150; for description, 54–5; for in-
    terface languages, 136; for menu structures, 57;
    text string, 57
novelty, 218, 219–20
numerical quantity: representations for, 32–3,
    32f, 35
numerical value: density to represent, 30–2

Oatly, K., 138, 139
object displays, 158
objectives, 287, 288; in design, 271, 273, 275, 277
object-oriented programming systems, 79, 220
object symbol, 26–7, 27f, 180
objects, 81, 134, 173; in Boxer, 179–80, 188;
    graphical, 181; interaction tree for selection of
    multiple, 147–8, 148f; MacDraw, 141–4, 145
observation, 10, 114, 259, 287, 304; in develop-
    ment process, 261, 262, 267; naturalistic, 67;
    and theory, 265, 266
observational paradigm, 105–6
Oesterreich, R., 206, 207, 209, 222
office copier, 254–7, 260, 261, 265, 292
Olson, D. R., 131
Olson, G. M., 103
Olson, J. R., 103
"one best way" models, 83, 209, 211
ontological issues, 99
ontologically minimized HCI science, 74–5, 82,
    99, 155
operant conditioning, 42, 43
operational tests, 58, 287
operations, 245, 246; in human activity, 242
ordinary language, basis for criticism of task
    analysis, 232n2
organizational structures, 211, 213

"Orientation Posters," 217
Orr, J., 158
outer theory, 6, 204; in HCI, 154–61

Palme, J., 220
Palmer, S., 33
Papin, D., 76, 77
paradigm cases, 42, 98, 304; development of
    steam engine as, 75–8
paradigms, 104, 105–6; of basic psychological re-
    search, 109; empirical, 112; in psychological re-
    search, 128–30
parameter loop scenario (Training Wheels), 87–
    8, 89, 90, 91, 94–5, 97, 98
Paramore, B., 55
parsimony, 292
partial decomposability, 9–10
partial prototypes, 294
"partial-solution" tools, 272
Pascal, B., 76
pattern prediction, 110
patterns, 262, 266, 267; recurring, 44
Patterson, R. D., 109
Payne, S. J., 8, 11, 57, 83, 107, 115, 128–53, 132,
    134, 136, 137, 138, 139, 140, 144, 145, 149,
    155, 160, 206, 212, 237, 278, 292, 295, 297,
    298, 299, 309
Pea, R. D., 173, 185
perception, 17, 18, 22, 129; inner theory of, 157
perceptual primitives, 29
perceptual process: computer simulation of, 61;
    inner theories of, 156
performance: artifacts and, 19, 20, 21; irratio-
    nally good, 158, 159; unusually poor, 159; ver-
    bal protocols and, 112, 114–15
Perlman, G., 158
personal views of artifacts, 8, 17, 19, 20f, 21–2
personality theories, 209, 211
perspectives: in design, 308
Petzold, C., 298, 306
phenomena, 41; contextualizing, 106, 110; re-
    search driven by, 128–9, 130
phenomenological background theory: idealized,
    208
physical principles, 163
physical sciences, 11, 40, 41
physics, 2, 52, 168, 175
Pike, K. L., 45
plan repertoire, 184
planning framework, 239
point-of-sales (POS) system, 244
Polanyi, M., 242
Polson, P. G., 1, 55, 64, 103, 116, 130, 160, 212,
    278, 280, 282

polygons: filling, 299
Popper, K. R., 162
Post, T. A., 309
power-generality trade-off, 44–5
"Power Law" of practice, 60, 65, 128, 205
practice, 94, 100, 230; perspectives on methodology in, 286–314; relevance of scientific research to, 42–3; scientific research vs. scientific theory applied to, 43–6; theory of, 39–42, 48, 235
Pratt, H., 47
praxis, 231, 239, 240–1, 243; artifacts in, 242; in design, 245–7; in groups, 245, 246; of use, 243–5; of users, 243, 246; *see also* practice
precomputation, 21, 22
prediction, 53, 116; in design, 246, 247, 249; in PUMs, 118; testable, 208
predictive user models, 167
presentations, in interaction trees, 140–1, 148
Pribram, K. H., 206, 207
Priestley, J. B., 160
principled design, 12, 167–70, 288–92; Boxer as, 170–83; focus for, 172–3; review of, 183–200
principles, 295; abstract statements of, 288; abstracted from artifacts, 79; basic, 41–2, 44, 163, 184; as conceptual framework for design, 289–90; efforts to provide, 289–92; general, 287, 288, 290, 292, 303; in principled design, 167, 168, 169, 170, 172, 173, 174, 178–9, 180, 183, 200–1, 287, 291; for programming comprehensibility, 173–8; source of, 289
problem/resource artifact analysis, 129, 148–51
problem solving, 45, 51, 182, 301; artifact design as, 215, 222; in cognitive science, 230; ecological approach to, 129–30; information processing descriptions, 5; as learning mode, 175; self-organized, 216–17; theories in, 213–14; YSS in, 136
problem-solving methods, 58; weak, 167
problem-solving process, 10, 291; theory-oriented, 215–21
problem-solving systems: taxonomy of, 56
problem-solving techniques: taxonomies in, 297–8
problem space (hypothesis), 129, 132, 134, 292; conceptual entities in, 134; decomposition of, 295–8
problems: in cognitive science research, 230; description of, 175; in design, 281–2; research driven by understanding, 128, 129, 131; and resources, 131–2
procedural languages: cognitive benchmark for comprehensibility of, 183–4, 201
process (design); *see* design process; group design process

process appropriateness, 2, 9
process-oriented paradigm, 247–9
product(s), 74, 222
product development, 260
product-oriented paradigm, 247–9
product specification document, 273
programmable user models, (PUMs), 11, 12, 116–18, 121–2, 130, 235–6
programmers, 67, 308
programming, 171, 175, 295, 309; Boxer, 7, 179; learning high-level, 289; psychology of, 4, 310; scale of complexity in, in principled design, 172–3; structural/functional models and, 176
programming comprehensibility: principles for, 173–8
programming languages, 172–3; decomposition, 185–6; executing inputs, 181–2; initial structural understanding of, 184, 186–7; structural core, 184; and structural models, 174–5
programming systems, 175, 177–8
propose-and-revise method, 56
protocol techniques, 112
prototypes, 67, 263, 274, 294–5, 300; in design process, 272
prototyping, 12, 301; tools, 306
psychoacoustic models: of human hearing, 109
psycholinguistics, 65, 112
psychological research in HCI, 130–1
psychological research method: design work as, 12–13
psychological-theoretical approaches, 211
psychological theory, 5, 286; broadening range of, 6–8; in design, 154–61; design representations and tools grounded in, 11–12; in exploratory research;, 301
psychology, 1–2, 45, 61, 100; applied, 5, 74; and basic principles, 40–1; descriptive, 7–8; in evaluation, 68; in HCI design process, 9–10; impact on design, 148–50; kinds of, 128–30; research paradigms, 112; as science of the artificial, 14; subdisciplines of, 211; task-artifact cycle and, 99; *see also* information processing psychology
psychology of tasks, 80, 82–4, 88–9, 91–2, 97, 98, 108, 208, 209, 222
psychometrics, 56
puzzle-solving tasks, 132
Pylyshyn, Z. W., 7, 8, 10, 11, 39–49, 46, 74, 83, 107, 229, 288, 289, 295, 299, 304, 309, 310

qualitative task models, 12
quality, 248
Quality Circles, 217
quality control, 214, 216
query expression, 71–2

Raeithel, A., 240
rapid prototyping, 12
rationalists, 40
reaction-time models, 204–5
real world, 5–6, 40–1, 301, 311; briding to, 106–
    8, 109; representation of, 104–6; relation of
    theoretical representations to, 122–3
reasoning, 103, 185, 229, 309–10; models of, 239
redesign, 149, 180, 187, 200, 209, 289
reduction, 52, 163
reductionism, 156, 267
Rein, G., 306
Reisner, P., 9, 115, 138, 236, 278
Reitman, W. R., 9
relevance, 71, 174, 286–7
Remde, J. R., 64, 69, 300
representation(s), 5–6, 10, 287, 288, 292–300,
    303; and artifacts, 22–3, 25–35; in cognition,
    228; in design, 10, 81, 280, 282, 283; in design
    process, 269, 271, 272–3, 275–6, 277; in group
    process, 308; hypotheses regarding form of, in
    cognitive artifacts, 28–9, 30–5; intrinsic proper-
    ties of, 33–5, 34f; layers of, 23; for numerical
    quantity, 32–3, 32f; primitive elements in, 297;
    scenario, 278–80; supporting design with, 11–
    12; *see also* application representation(s); bridg-
    ing representations; discovery representations
representational dimensions/scales: additive/
    substitutive, 28, 30–5
representational format, 23, 34, 36
representational naturalness, 28–33
representational properties, 17
representational schemes, 299–300
representational systems, 25–6
represented world, 23, 25, 26, 29
representing world, 23, 25, 26
Resch, M., 207
research, 39–40, 123; on artifacts in context of
    use, 301–3; design as, 310–11; perspectives on
    methodology in, 286–314; theory-based, 103–
    27; training in, 43
research life cycle, 103–4, 107, 110, 111; enhanc-
    ing application representations in, 115–22;
    modification of discovery representations in,
    111–27
research methods, 208
research paradigms: psychology, 112
resources: artifacts and, 131; design, 275; and
    problems, 131–2
Restle, F., 28
review: of learnability of Boxer scoping, 187–
    200; in principled design, 169–70, 183–200,
    201; *see also* design review
Reynolds, D., 281

rich indexing, 12, 66, 69
Richards, J. T., 272, 273
Richardson, J., 69
Rieman, J., 64, 160, 280
Rittel, H. W. J., 10
Roast, C. R., 123
Roberts, T. L., 82, 304
Robertson, G. G. 29
Rohwer, W. D., 158
Romberger, S., 234, 304
Rosenbloom, P. S., 117, 128, 130
Rosson, M. B., 12, 74,–102, 81, 90, 97, 98, 99,
    107, 131, 132, 155, 160, 166, 183n3, 203, 206,
    212, 234n5, 237, 273, 288, 304, 310
RPN calculators, 174
Rubenstein, S. L., 210
Rubinstein, R., 235, 272, 288, 303
rule schemata: higher-level, 137, 139f
rules of thumb, 60; for software testing, 293
Rumelhart, D. E., 25
Runciman, C., 123

Sabini, J., 83, 206, 240n10
Sanderson, P. M., 158
satisficing, 272
Saunders, F. A., 3
Saussure, Ferdinand de, 8, 44
Savery, T., 76
Scandinavia, 18
Scapin, D. L., 106
scenario-based design, 80, 81–2, 84, 90, 96, 99;
    task psychology in, 97, 98
scenario development: important distinctions in,
    279–80, 282, 283
scenario schemes, 89
scenario set, 12
scenario suites, 293, 294
scenario techniques, 64
scenario work, 236
scenarios, 112, 263, 292, 293–4, 295, 299–300;
    canonical, 293; contextualized, 294; design,
    166, 282; in design process, 272, 276; elements
    in, 279; generalization of, 96, 97; in group de-
    sign process, 278–80, 281; test-driving theories
    in, 113–14; for Training Wheels interface, 89–
    91; of use, 293
Schaefer, E. F., 140
Schiele, F., 144
Schilling, A., 206
Schleiffenbaum, E., 216
Schölmerich, A., 217
Schüpbach, H., 206
science(s): and application, 11, 13–14, 74, 79–80;
    descriptive, 44–5; in context, 2–4; and design,

74, 75, 108, 109, 168, 200–1; HCI as descriptive, engineering, 51–7; paradigm for doing, 163–70; and practice, 99; role of, 203; technology and, 9
science base, 6, 106, 283, 304–5; bridging to/from, 106–8, 111; cognitive architecture in, 117, 118, 119; contextualized, 82–3; and design, 89, 282; and its application, 6, 108–10; psychological, 9; representations in, 104; research incorporated into, 112, 115; specializing, 4–5; *see also* applied science; basic science
science-based design, 96–8
scientific analysis, 3–4, 87
scientific management, 211
scientific method, 4, 5
scientific principle, 12, 106
scientific progress, 162
scientific research: relevance of, to practice, 42–3; vs. scientific theory applied to practice, 43–6
scientific theory(ies): and practical improvements, 40–1; scientific research vs. 43–6
scoping, 13, 128, 129; Boxer, 187–200; dynamic, 189, 190, 193
Scribner, S., 83, 230
self-actualization, 211
self-consciousness, 210
self-regulation, 7, 83; cognitive system, 156, 159; of exploration, 221
semantic manipulation: of conceptual elements, 298–9
semantic mapping, 134, 136, 142–3
semantic memory, 301
Semmer, N., 207
sensitivity, 43, 48
sensorimotor level, 207
Shailer, M. J., 109
Sheppard, S. B., 4
Sherard, J. L., 54
Shneiderman, B., 4, 69, 78, 206, 272, 288, 303
short-term memory, 118, 159 research, 110
Siegel, A. W., 221
signature phenomena, 128
Simon, H. A., 5, 9, 14, 45, 99, 112, 114, 115, 117, 129, 131, 132, 138, 210, 230, 270, 276, 281, 283, 289
Simon, T., 113, 116, 123, 130, 235, 236
simplicity, 292; of artifacts in use, 218–19
simplification, 6, 9–10, 213
simulation(s), 67, 82; data-based, 12, 60, 66
simulation methodology, 116–17
Singer, J. A., 99
situated action, 18
situated cognition school, 158–9
situated semantics, 46

situated trial and error, 12
Sjögren, D., 234, 304
skill development, 7; *see also* developmental psychology
Skwarecki, E., 103
Slater, S. C., 156
Sloane, K. D., 175
Smeaton, J., 78
Smith, D. C., 80, 154, 232, 304
Smith, T., 306
SOAR, 117, 128, 130, 165
social context, 283
social/cultural level: design at, 171–2, 173
social factors: effect on behavior, 159
social sciences, 5, 264; data analysis in, 58; descriptive, 45; research in, 40–1. 42–3
social support: in training, 217
society, 229–30; division of labor, in, 241; individual development and, 240
sociocultural (sociohistorical) school, 240
software, 123, 234, 245, 274; specification languages, 57
software design: guidelines for, 222; iS, 217; participative, 209
software development, 272, 303
software engineering, 104, 150, 228, 247–9
software systems, 216, 286; perceptual control of, 218–19; prototype genetic-growing, 220
software testing, 294; rules-of-thumb for, 293
software tools, 51
Soloway, E., 173, 174, 184, 185
solutions, 10, 310; applied, 79; description of, 175; research driven by, 129
Souberman, E., 230
Soviet Union, 18
spatial arrangements, 173
spatial cues, 71
spatial separation, 276
spatial–visual capabilities, 1278–9, 200
special-case/end-point design, 268
specifications, 263, 294; redesign of, 149
specificity requirement, 2–3, 4, 5, 13; approaches to, 9
Spence, R., 57
Spohrer, J. C., 173
spreadsheets, 67, 79, 260–1
Squibb, H., 134, 136, 144
stability, 174
stack model (RPN calculators), 174
state spaces, 134, 136, 174
statistical semantics, 70, 71, 72
steam engine, 98, 155–6, 160; development of, 75, 76–8
Stevens, A., 173

Stevens, S. S., 28, 65
stimulus–response conpatibility, 130
stimulus structure, 158
storyboards, 82, 263
strategic questions, 302
Strauss, L., 42
"Stress Inoculation Training," 7, 217
string(s), 136, 141
Stroop, J.R., 158
Stroop effect, 158–9
structural models, 6, 174–5, 176, 178, 185, 186, 187–8, 200; Boxer, 182; spatial vocabulary, 178; spontaneous versions of, 177
structure(s), 8, 44; vs. function, in Boxer, 179–81, 182, 183
subjective task analysis, 208; *see also* task analysis
substitutive dimensions, 28, 28f, 30
Suchman, L. A., 82, 123, 158, 239, 255
Sundblad, Y., 246
SuperBook, 12, 64, 66, 69–72, 301, 304; text browser, 63, 63f
sufficiency analysis, 11, 47
surface representations, 25, 26, 29, 178; in Boxer, 179
Sutherland, I. E., 1, 78
symbols, 25
synonym problem, 71
syntax: in Boxer, 181–2
synthesis, 46, 78, 98, 106; in assessment of programming knowledge, 186, 187
system design, 67, 232; goals of, 211–12
system functional capabilities, 293
system state: control operation and, 26–7
system techniques: generalization of, 96, 97–8
system view of artifacts, 8, 17, 19, 20–1, 208
systematic frameworks, 212

tacit knowledge, 220, 232, 233; in artifact design, 214–15
TAG; *see* task–action grammar
Tanner, P. 234
task–action grammar (TAG), 57, 115, 137–9, 141, 150, 278, 298; display-oriented (D-TAG), 138, 145, 146f, 147; MacDraw, 137f, 144–6; organization of, 148
task–action mapping: computational theory of, 137–9
task–action theory, 209, 222
task analysis, 11–12, 45, 51, 55–6, 58, 115, 130, 209, 214, 231, 297, 298; of complex tasks, 112; critique of, 232–3; in design, 248; in group design process, 278; hetararchic, 208, 209; in iS, 216; objective, 47–8; in operationalization of

degree of functionality, 218, 222; in user-centered design, 282–3
task–artifact cycle, 9, 74–102, 107, 109, 206, 209, 222, 237; analysis of, 97, 212; illustration of, 84–96; information flow around, 107–8
task–artifact framework, 83f, 84, 304
task comparison, 44, 57–8
task demands: vs. what experts do, 46–8
task-dependent theories, 130
task description(s), 208, 292
task description languages, 292, 295, 300
task design, 222; criteria for, 209
task differences: and interface differences, 302
task domain(s), 233, 234, 309
task-oriented menus, 208
task performance factors: qualitative understanding of, 60, 66
task taxonomies, 7, 11, 51, 56, 58–9, 105, 130, 295–7
tasks, 9, 46, 67, 74, 114, 116, 130; canonical, 302; changed by tools, 131, 134; complex, 112, 220; descriptive study of, 8, 14, 44–5, 54–6, 58–9; design, 168; discovering, defining, 98–9; effect of artifacts on, 19, 20f, 22; evolution of, 78–84; psychology of, 80, 82–4, 88–9, 91–2, 97, 98, 108, 208, 209, 222; real world, 301; restructured by artifacts, 131–4, 139, 148–51; structure and, 8; in taxonomic analysis, 105, 296–7; and tool complexity, 219
Tauber, M., 138
taxonomic elements: hierarchical representations of, 298, 300
taxonomy(ies), 42, 52, 292, 294, 295–8, 299; components of, 296–7, 296f; decomposition strategies, 297t; derivation of abstractions from, 53; inner vs. outer, 45–6; interface techniques, 11; of problem-solving methods/systems, 56; of task–artifact domains, 83; *see also* task taxonomies
Taylor, F. W., 209, 211
Taylorism, 211, 244
team design, 273–6
Teasdale, J., 118
technical theory, 7, 51; adequate description as prerequisite to, 52–3, 54, 58, 59
techniques: in design process, 271, 272, 273
technocentric view, 261, 263
technology, 11, 19, 160, 301; adaptations of, 307; application of cognitive theory to design of, 108–10; catalogs, 287; context of, 98, 99; contextual complexity of, 287; and development, 267, 268; development of, 243, 259; evolution of, 9, 74, 75–8; evolution of, in HCI, 78–84; implementation of, 263; of interface, 254, 255,

257, 260, 263, 268; learning to use, 258; tailorable, 260–1; transfer, 74; transformative, 48;
in use, 227–8
Tesler, L., 69
test-cycle approach, 68
test-driving theories, 113–14
testing, 263
text, 303; Boxer, 180
text creation, 144, 145, 148, 149f, 299
text design, 64–5
text editing, 141, 142, 145, 148, 149f, 150, 299;
Boxer, 179; command naming in, 119;
MacDraw, 143–4
text editor, 131, 280, 281
text objects: MacDraw, 143, 145, 148, 149f
text retrieval and browsing systems, 70f
text systems: computer-based, 69
Tetzlaff, L., 107, 132, 155, 160, 206, 212, 237,
286–314, 302
theoretical knowledge: articulate and tacit, 214–
15
theoretical representations, 110
theory(ies): abstracted from artifacts, 79; applicability of, 203; and application, 11, 65–6, 155–6,
206, 212; and artifact construction, 304; in artifact design, 222; as artifacts, 212–13; artifacts
in, 237–8; as artificial tools for thought, 213–
14; bridging to/from application, 118–22; and
design, 111, 123, 131, 160, 206, 282, 283; and
development, 264–8, 269; development of,
113–14, 128, 288; development perspectives in,
254–68; in development process, 261; empirical
work and, 159–60; empirically based, 66–7;
function of, 212–13; in interface design, 254;
and methodology, 286; ontologically minimized, 74–5, 82, 99; and practice, 235; relation
with artifact, 107; and situation of use, 227; as
tools for thought, 212–15; use of, in HCI, 62–5
theory, useful, 60; impossibility of, 60–2; kinds,
impact of, 65–7
theory-based design, 74, 108, 203, 214; applicability dilemma of, 205–6; experimental problems
of, 204–6
"theory-based walkthrough" method, 64
theory of practice, 39–42, 48
theory practice gap, 39–49
Thiemann, P., 216
Thimbleby, H. W., 123
thinking-aloud technique, 208
Thomas, J. C., 8, 10, 47, 158; 238, 239
thought, 17, 18, 19; shaped by tools, 131; theories as artifical tools for, 213–14; theories as
tools for, 212–16
three-dimensional arrays, 180–1

Thurmes, W. N., 156
time: in development process, 263; and exploration, 218, 221
time-and-motion studies, 210, 211
Tognazzini, B., 291
tool making/usage, 17
tool-rich learning cultures, 172
tool sets, 78
toolkits, 287, 298, 306
tools, 12, 19, 42–3, 122, 175, 241, 242, 309; complexity of, 219; design of, 275; supporting design with, 11–12; in taxonomic analysis, 296–7;
theories as, for thought, 212–16; thought
shaped by, 131
Torricelli, E., 76
TOTE-units, 207
trade-offs, 6, 8, 110–11, 290; in design process,
81, 169, 270–1, 275
trainers, 257–8
training, 221; and individual differences, 218; social support in, 217
training principles, 216–17
Training Wheels, 75, 97, 216, 219, 237; interface,
12, 84–96; 107 (developing scenarios for, 89–
91; error blocking technique, 91, 93t, 94–5, 96,
97, 98; psychological claims in, 92–6, 93t); psychological claims of Displaywriter, 84–8, 85t,
89, 90–6, 99
transfer: in Boxer scoping, 193, 197, 200
transfer of knowledge, 106
transfer of learning: Training Wheels, 91, 95–6
transferability, 177
transformation rules, 203
transformational grammars, 112
transformed actions, 242
Trillium, 304
Tullis, T. S., 65
type-print task (Training Wheels), 86–7, 90, 92–
4, 96, 98

Ulich, E., 83, 206, 209, 210, 220
uncertainty of effects phenomenon, 139–40
universal principles, 162, 170
University of Osnabrück, Work and Organizational Psychology Unit, 215–16
unlimited aliasing (principle), 70
usability, 134, 151, 270–1, 273, 293, 306; assessment of, 7, 9; assumptions about, 107; cognitive theory and, 60–73; constraints on, 1; HCI
theory, 98–100; MacDraw, 141, 142–4, 145,
149, 150; of theory in artifact design, 283
usability engineering, 273–4, 287–8, 300, 310–11;
defined, 287
usability evaluation, 66, 82

usability phenomena, 130
usability specifications, 183n3
use, 10; as beginning and end of design, 258–9; in
    development process, 261–2; prerequisite to de-
    sign, 246; theory of, 268
use process, 247, 248
use scenarios, 84, 278–9
use setting, 228, 237, 244
use situation, 257, 259; continuing design in, 261;
    development in, 267
usefulness, 273, 283
user action: monitoring, 114
user activities: representation of, 300
user-centered design, 269, 270–8, 282–3, 286–7
user concerns, 96, 97, 98
user domain experts, 308
user feedback, 302–3
user interaction scenarios, 12, 81–2, 88–9, 107
user interface(s), 1, 11, 57, 178, 231–2, 243; de-
    scription of, 55, 56–7; design of, 209; graphical,
    304; MacDraw, 133–4; problems in separating
    from application, 233–5; psychological implica-
    tions of, 148; *see also* interface
User Interface Institute, 74–5
user–interface management system model, 57
User Interface Management Systems (UIMSs),
    234
user interface techniques, 8, 12
user–interface technology, 154
user knowledge, 110–11, 249; model of, 136–7
user modeling, 55–6, 235–6
user organizations, 248
user questions, 81
user-system exchanges, 113, 116
user tasks, 6; taxonomies of, 7; *see also* tasks
users, 248; and design, 231–2, 258, 269, 261, 295;
    in design process, 10, 308; in development pro-
    cess, 260, 267–8; in group design process, 277;
    and partitioning blame, 184, 185; praxis of,
    243, 246; psychological claims about, 289; stud-
    ies of, 46
UTOPIA project, 233, 246, 304

validity: problem of, 203
values, 204, 212, 223
Van Cott, H. P., 55
variables, 62
VERA, 207
verbal protocols: and performance, 112, 114–15
Verplank, B., 80, 232, 304
Vertelney, L., 82
video confrontation interview, 208
videotapes, 263, 264
View Matcher, 304

violin as acoustic system (example), 2–3, 4
virtual objects, 22–3
vision, 61, 129
visual analogs, 179
visual models, 197
visual perception: laws of, 60, 65
visual reasoning, 178–9
visuomotor control, 45
Volpert, W., 83, 97, 206, 207, 209, 212, 214, 222,
    240n10
von Guericke, O., 76
Voss, J. F., 309
Vygotsky, L. S., 14, 18, 83, 131, 231, 241

Waern, Y., 216
wagon wheels, 215
Walba, D. M., 156
Wasserman, A. I., 233
"waterfall" models, 272
Watt, J., 76, 77, 160
Webber, M. M., 10
Wegner, P., 272
Wertheimer, M., 222
Wertsch, J. V., 18, 230, 240
West, M., 221
West German Research and Technology Ministry,
    212
Weyer, S. A., 69
Wharton, C., 64, 160, 280
"wheel of design," 246; *see also* design wheel
Wheeler, P. D., 109
White, 173
Whiteside, J. A., 66, 69, 82, 106, 107, 158, 159,
    236, 238n9, 248, 272, 273, 275, 280, 281, 287,
    301, 311
Whittington, J., 112, 113, 117, 138, 236
Wiecha, C., 308
Wiener, E. L., 24
Williams, G., 304
Wilson, M., 111, 112, 114, 115, 121, 123
window management schemes, 298
windows, 304
Winograd, T., 232, 239, 242, 305
Wixon, D. R., 64, 66, 69, 82, 106, 107, 159, 236,
    248, 280, 301, 311
Wolff, P., 205
Woodward, R. J., 54
word meanings, 71
word processors, 79, 139, 260, 261
work, 240–1; theory of, 264–5, 266, 267
work analysis, 209, 214, 244
work application, 258, 259; in interface, 254,
    255–6, 257, 260, 263, 268; implementation of,
    263

work behavior sequence, 207–8
work design, 208, 210; in action theory, 208–9;
    goal criteria of, 210; guidelines for, 222; human
    personality development as goal of, 208–9,
    214; humanistic values in, 212
work organization, 228
work practice, 258, 259; implementation of, 263;
    in interface, 256–7, 260, 263, 268
work process, 23n6; and design, 249
work psychology, 7, 83, 206–21; in design of arti-
    facts, 203–26; *see also* action theory
Wright, A. L., 65, 71, 154
Wright, P., 79

Wright, P. C., 123
Wundt, W. M., 18, 203
WYSIWYG, 233

X Window tool kits, 57
Xerox PARC, 78
Xerox Star, 231–2, 304

Yoder, E., 302
yoked state space (YSS) hypothesis, 11, 134–6,
    135f, 139, 141, 149, 150
Young, R. M., 80, 81, 110, 112, 113, 114, 116,
    123, 130, 138, 174, 175, 235, 236, 305